Fund Monitor 2000

Fund Monitor 2000

Prentice Hall Canada Inc.
Scarborough, Ontario

Canadian Cataloguing in Publication Data

Main entry under title:
Fund monitor

Annual.
Began with 1998 issue.
"An expert's guide to selecting outstanding mutual funds" — Spine.
By Duff Young
Description based on: 1999
ISSN 1482-7492
ISBN 0-13-015995-6 (2000)

1. Mutual funds - Canada – Periodicals. I. Young, Duff, 1967- .
II. Title: Duff Young's fund monitor. III. Title: Duff Young's fundmonitor.
IV. Title: FundMonitor

HG5154.5.F86 332.63'27 C97-900994-4

Prentice Hall Canada Inc., Scarborough, Ontario

Prentice-Hall, Inc., Upper Saddle River, New Jersey
Prentice-Hall International (UK) Limited, London
Prentice-Hall of Australia, Pty. Limited, Sydney
Prentice-Hall Hispanoamericana, S.A., Mexico City
Prentice-Hall of India Private Limited, New Delhi
Prentice-Hall of Japan, Inc., Tokyo
Simon & Schuster Southeast Asia Private Limited, Singapore
Editora Prentice-Hall do Brasil, Ltda., Rio de Janeiro

ISBN 0-13-015995-6 (2000)

Editorial Director, Trade Group: Andrea Crozier
Copy Editor: Martha Wilson
Production Editor: Jodi Lewchuk
Art Direction: Mary Opper
Cover and Interior Design: Alex Li
Cover Photograph: Kirk McGregor
Illustrations: Dave Klug
Production Coordinator: Kathrine Pummell
Page Layout: Heather Brunton/ArtPlus Limited

1 2 3 4 5 TCP 03 02 01 00 99

Printed and bound in Canada

Visit the Prentice Hall Canada Web site! Send us your comments, browse our catalogues, and more. **www.phcanada.com**.

Dedication

I dedicate this special new book to my wife, Jennifer, and our kids, Courtney and Austin, for their enduring patience and endless support.

Table of Contents

Foreword

We're all monkeys when it comes to investing in mutual funds. We all pick the wrong funds at the wrong times and we all lose faith in their active managers just when they're about to impress. We all get fooled into paying too much in fees. Once wise to that, we often fall for cheap stuff that just doesn't deliver.

It's silly but it's true. Mutual funds do fine. People don't.

So I think these tired old stale-dated fund guidebooks are missing the mark. That's because they all focus on fund details instead of dealing with the stuff that derails investors. Stuff like unrealistic expectations, misleading advertising, the discipline of knowing when to sell. And the mystery of measuring our own individual past performance.

That's where we'll find the greatest clues, the greatest lessons: By studying our own blunders. So this book is designed to teach you how to interpret the source of your own returns – and how to use resources on the web to monitor, track and stay on top of your entire portfolio easily.

Knowing where your success has come from is good. Knowing how to repeat that success is better. Knowing how you've done versus other investors is now possible with a little technology and a generous free service being made available to buyers of this book. It's an online account monitor from my firm, FundMonitor.com Corp. I hope you'll take advantage of the service and use it in conjunction with the book, because they're really designed to go together. (If you don't have access to the Web, we can offer the same service offline for just $50. Just call our toll-free number on the back cover).This book covers the ground my FundMonitor series always has, as indicated in the title. But there's a fresh new tilt this year that makes my argument about the importance of our own personal behavior more vivid. It's really not in the details of what you do, but in your overall approach.

The purpose in my career — as I'm learning it — is really about how to identify new, common-sense approaches to evaluating mutual funds and then convey them without all the nonsense, in a way that's easy to understand, even for the average investor.

I hope that this book will be — of all of the mutual fund books — the easiest to understand and use. Furthermore, I hope it's the one that uses the most rigorous fund research, the most legitimate evaluation criteria, and the most credible top picks.

I've been learning over time that financial advisors play an important role in successful mutual fund investing, at least for most Canadians. But the research I've done lately really brought it home: People simply do better when they work with a pro.

So it's time to look carefully at how much you pay for advice and to make an informed decision about the benefits of that advice. In this area I'll think you'll find that this 2000 version of my book presents the most advanced thinking on the concept of value.

Use the book as a reference. Or feel free to just browse. Respond to a quiz, or look up a fund. This book really isn't intended to be read from cover to cover so much as it's meant to be used as a reference guide on your shelf. I hope it will be an important addition to the work that you're already doing with your financial advisor or on your own.

I'm sensitive to the timeliness factor in preparing a book like this. After all, mutual fund guides don't really sell until February, but use data ending the previous June. That's why I designed this book as a kind of living volume — one that can be updated monthly and personalized for you. By using a special password (printed on page 98) you can log into my Web site, **www.fundmonitor.com**, to make this book a handy, personal Fund Monitor.

In the mutual fund industry, nothing is static. Fund mandates change; mergers happen. (And need I mention the notorious difficulty of predicting which way the market is headed?) In preparing our data, my team has developed a strenuous audit and reconciliation process which we apply to every statistic included here.

Most people buy this book because they want opinions from an independent thinker. Since I don't work for any mutual fund companies, I can give you my insights without having to measure my words.

From time to time I hear from readers who have complaints about something I've said. By all means, if you think my arguments are unsupported and you have a different opinion, don't be shy. I welcome the controversy that my books create. Drop me a line any time at the following e-mail address: **duffyoung@fundmonitor.com**.

And keep in mind that, ultimately, it's not picking the perfect fund that's important. Focus on investing steadily and staying in it for the long haul. That's what it's all about.

The road to financial independence is one filled with both opportunity and risk. You've probably already recognized that mutual funds can play an integral role in that journey.

This book — I hope — will become your guide.

Duff Young, CFA
September, 1999

Acknowledgments

Writing a book is fun — but only if you get support like I get from some of the most promising talent in the business. Like my top analysts, Norm Rothery, Kathleen Pabla, Dan Hallett, and David MacDonald. Or the younger analysts, like James Gauthier and Marc Marzotto. The book would not read as well without Martha Wilson, a wonderful editor. I would also like to acknowledge the contributions made by countless editors, readers, proofreaders, artists, and designers — including Jodi Lewchuk, Dave Klug, and Alex Li. Their support and guidance continue to make this annual project a win for investors everywhere.

1 A New Take on Mutual Funds

HEY, JUST BECAUSE THIS IS A BOOK ABOUT how to pick mutual funds, don't think I'm gonna tell you that picking mutual funds is important. It's not. Such trivial details are, in fact, the least important consideration in the building of a plan that leads to financial security.

That's right. The process of actually choosing particular investments is one of the last steps in getting your financial house in order.

Before you even begin to fall in love with a particular fund or before you become a fund expert (too many people are), you must get the foundation of your financial security in place. Now.

In fact, if we think about that metaphor of a financial "house," we could say that your mutual fund purchases are somewhere up near the roofline. To begin, you need a solid foundation and sturdy walls. The various components of your financial plan depend on one another; but together, they provide you with a solid and secure financial future.

Risk Management — The Foundations of Your Financial Security

The focus of this book is mutual fund analysis — which funds are good at the moment, which ones are reliably good, and which ones aren't worth your attention. But nothing I tell you in the FundMonitor Profiles is as important as the basic principles described in this chapter. If after reading this chapter you discover that you don't have the foundation of your financial plan in place, go and look after the basics right away. In fact, do it before you read Chapter 2.

The first cornerstone of your financial plan is insurance. If you have other people who depend on you — family members, for example — you need insurance. In terms of life insurance, basic term insurance will probably suffice. I say purchase it at the lowest price you can find, but make sure that you get adequate coverage. And don't forget long-term disability coverage. After all, you are considerably less likely to die between now and age 65 than you are to develop a disability. And if you become permanently disabled, it could be more expensive for your family than if you had died.

The second cornerstone of your financial foundation is your emergency fund. This fund is a nice chunk of money that you have tucked away for any little surprises that could wreak havoc on your household cash flow. Few people make this emergency fund a priority. But if you're faced with a huge dental bill, a flooded basement, or if you lose your job, you'll need an emergency fund. Without one, you're faced with some unappealing options, such as borrowing money at a high rate of interest on a credit card or borrowing from a family member. How large should your fund be? Some people suggest as much as three months' salary should be available to you in an emergency fund.

for more information

Nice Work!

Estimated average fund manager salary (with bonus): $300,000 – $450,000. In later chapters you'll see why some of them really are worth it.

Third, and related to the point above, get a line of credit — even if you don't need it right now. Lines of credit come in two varieties: secured and unsecured. Secured lines of credit offer larger credit limits and better interest rates. The way I accomplished this was through a "collateral mortgage" against my house. Some paperwork and expense are involved in setting this up, but it allows me a large line of credit at attractive interest rates if I ever need it. It's also good if you ever lose your job; you'll find that you have access to low-rate cash that is repayable on attractive terms. When you need the money, you don't have to apply for it — you just write a cheque. If you're not carrying a balance, there's no cost to having a line of credit. That's another reason to consider a line of credit as a third cornerstone in the foundation of your financial security.

Where Mutual Funds Fit in Your Financial Security Structure

Mutual funds offer you access to professional money management, which, over time, can extend the margin and possibilities of your financial security. Your mutual fund strategy rests on more fundamental aspects of financial security that include various forms of risk management and the disciplines of retirement savings and debt reduction.

The final cornerstone involves having a will. Honestly, no one in Canada would want to die without one. Things can become very messy very quickly. If you're like me — with a spouse and kids — you won't believe what could happen upon your death. For example, in my case, the Province of Ontario children's guardian would be responsible for administering the money that would go to my children, which would be half of everything over $200,000. Clearly, that's not my wish. No one I know would want the government looking after his or her money. But in the absence of a valid, up-to-date will, your wishes aren't even relevant in determining how to divide your money and how to manage your family's affairs in your absence. And that's a scary thought.

Taken together, these four cornerstones provide a basic level of security — by managing the major financial risks. Most working families can afford them. Few can afford to be without them.

Discipline: Retirement Savings and Reducing Debt — The Building Blocks of Financial Security

If the foundation of financial security calls for putting risk management tools and decisions in place, the building blocks of financial security call for a regular discipline of saving for retirement and reducing debt.

Most working Canadians need to tackle these two tasks at the same time because our tax and registered retirement savings plan (RRSP) rules make it sensible to begin saving for retirement long before mortgages and other debts are cleared off. Handling both tasks at the same time can feel like a tough slog. But the time-honoured wisdom on this subject says that a regular approach — such as making RRSP contributions from each pay cheque and shortening the amortization on your mortgage by paying more than the minimum each month — can help you achieve financial security.

Registered Retirement Savings Plans

Canada's RRSP program is one of the most generous plans of its kind anywhere in the world. That's why it's so disappointing that only a minority of working Canadians make their maximum allowable contributions every year.

If you have any RRSP room available from prior years, find a way to backfill those contributions. Some people become stalled by deciding how they will actually invest that money once it's in an RRSP. The key move, however, is making the contribution. You could just open an RRSP account at a bank and invest the money in a 30-day term deposit while you do some homework and talk to a professional about how to get the money invested properly for the long term.

Pay Down Your Mortgage or Buy Funds?

Outside of your RRSP, the surest investment you can make is reducing debt.

Think About It | Would you buy a mutual fund with a guaranteed double-digit rate of return? One that you could get cash out of (if you needed it later) without any penalty? Well, that's exactly what you get when you make lump-sum mortgage payments.

Action!

Are You Too Deep in Debt?

If you make only minimum monthly payments on your credit cards, or if your credit card and loan payments are more than 20 percent of your after-tax pay (excluding mortgages and car loans), you've probably got a debt problem, but you are not alone.

I recommend that you tackle this immediately. I know because I've been there.

Here's my tip list for helping you to get the information you need to help you get out of debt faster.

- When you've got some money available, pay off your highest rate debt first.
- If you're having trouble paying down your debts and believe that it has become a problem, contact a non-profit credit counselling service.
- Request a copy of your credit report. Call Equifax at 1-800-937-4093.
- Consolidate. For instance, if you own your home, a home equity loan with a flexible repayment schedule could consolidate all of your bills at high interest rates into one low monthly bill at a lower rate of interest.

Assuming that you've already | maximized your RRSP contributions and you've still got some extra cash to invest (in a bank account or an investment account earning taxable income), one of the smartest decisions is to take that cash and, if there is no penalty for doing so, make a lump-sum payment against your mortgage.

That way you'll save the interest costs on the debt. The interest savings, of course, are equivalent to the interest rate on your mortgage, but since your mortgage isn't tax deductible, paying off your mortgage with a rate of seven percent is like earning seven percent after tax — guaranteed. No mutual fund in Canada can guarantee a return anything like seven percent after tax. In fact, let me repeat that. As a mutual fund analyst, I can attest that no mutual fund in Canada can offer anything like seven percent after tax guaranteed.

The second benefit to paying down that mortgage — in addition to making a great investment — is that you'll boost your home equity.

When you're just getting started as an investor, it's your rate of savings that really drives your success, more so than your rate of return. So don't swing for the fences right away by trying to earn big returns. Instead, try socking a bit more money away every month by just diving in with discipline.

That equity is a resource you could tap in the future if you're ever strapped for cash due to an emergency. Some mortgages will allow for lump-sum repayments that allow you to skip payments later. This could be a nice little security blanket during some tough times down the road.

Why Leverage Is the Rage

Here's the seductive pitch: Borrow against your house and invest the cash in mutual funds. The funds will probably earn about 15 percent a year, the sales rep says, and the interest on the loan will only be about 6.5 percent. So the difference is like earning something for nothing, by putting someone else's money to work for you.

The interest paid on the loan is tax deductible, so the net cost of the borrowed money is actually only three percent or so. What knucklehead couldn't earn at least that much in mutual funds over the long term?

It sounds so appealing, and some financial advisors hype the concept so vigorously, that it's really tough to know whether it's the right strategy for you. The fact is that too many people have been leveraging lately, egged on by advisors with the wrong motive.

That said, here's my checklist for borrowing to buy funds:

1. Recognize that the financial advisor stands to make more money, since this is a sale that's not possible unless you borrow.
2. Don't do it unless you really understand the risks, can handle the loan payments without encroaching on your capital, and have some experience with investing during tough times.
3. Always "average in" any lump sum.
4. Remember that leverage will exaggerate any market decline — and potential loss.

5. Look beyond the five- and ten-year returns, and be aware that even great funds have suffered declines of 20 or 30 percent — more than once. To make money by leveraging, you'll have to keep your drawers dry when markets tank.

Eliminating "Consumer" Debt

Consumer debt is generally connected with credit cards. It may be obvious that credit cards are an expensive way to borrow money. Still, in the United States, 70 percent of credit-card holders carry a balance from month to month, at rates of interest that average 18 percent. For those who maintain a practice of paying the minimum monthly payment, big-ticket items such as a $1500 television or stereo system will take 13 years to pay off — and cost twice as much as the initial cost of the item!

While data isn't available for Canada, consider that two out of five Americans under age 35 have such bad credit that they have been turned down for more. The discipline of getting

Action!

Three Things You Can Do Right Now!

This is a test — a big test — of your resolve. Think of three things that you could do now to improve your financial situation.

For some people, a simple move would be to pay down their credit cards by spending the cash in their bank account. For others it would be a consolidation of high-rate credit-card debt with a low-rate line of credit. Other people will have cash sitting around that they should move into an RRSP right now — even if it's not February. Some people might say that they could improve their situation right now by putting their will in order or getting some quotes on cheap term insurance.

No matter what, writing out an action plan with three basic moves that you can make right now to improve your situation is a key way of becoming more psychologically committed to those actions. So write them out now and make a commitment to act on these things soon.

1. ______________________________

____

____

____

2. ______________________________

____

____

____

3. ______________________________

____

____

____

Action!

What Have You Done for Me Lately?

My prediction is that financial advisors will become more like their clients' quarterbacks, helping them with all sorts of areas — not just investment. In last year's edition of this book, I discussed the new trend toward total financial planning. This new holistic approach is a big deal because one person can help with so many inter-related concepts. Estate planning, tax planning, and mortgage shopping. Advice on whether to lease or buy a car. Capital funding. Even corporate finance advice.

I don't know vendors who are yet offering all these services, but my feeling is that the market is looking for them. So let your advisor know what you need.

out of credit-card debt, and other high-cost consumer debt vehicles, should be another building block in your financial security program.

Getting your financial house in order is the first step in achieving financial independence.

Later we'll talk about mutual funds — and the role they can play in helping you to achieve that independence.

A Crash Course in Mutual Funds

THE ONLY REASON I HAVE A JOB IS BECAUSE the mutual fund industry keeps cranking out more a more funds every day, leaving lots of people hopelessly confused about which ones are right for them. With a mind-numbing 2500 or so different funds now available in Canada, it's easy to get overwhelmed with the choice. But the fact is that mutual funds are (or ought to be) the picture of simplicity. After all, they let you hand over your investment work to a pro.

What accounts for the spectacular growth of the mutual fund industry in the past decade? Two trends, really: a recognition by average Canadians that they will need to take their retirement planning into their own hands, coupled with an increasingly complex and globalized marketplace, which has experienced the longest bull run in history. Faced with the need to invest, and the complexity of the task, Canadians have turned to "managed money" — and especially to mutual funds.

Demographers remind us that baby boomers are moving from their spending years (on the house and the kids) into their savings years (the house is paid and the kids are gone). Retirement looms ahead, and boomers are saving their money.

This demographic group is educated and confident, and they like what they see in mutual funds. Most recognize that they are no longer restricted to their parents' traditional investment choices — whole-life insurance policies, Guaranteed Investment Certificates (GICs), Canada Savings Bonds (CSBs), treasury bills, or term deposits. On the other hand, they clearly welcome an alternative to direct stock market investment.

The growth of the mutual fund industry has also been fuelled by the recognition that even an extra single-percentage-point return, when compounded over the long term, can yield significantly more accumulated wealth — and a full-time professional will almost always achieve better investment results than a part-time amateur will.

All of these events have contributed to phenomenal growth in the mutual fund industry in Canada, as shown below.

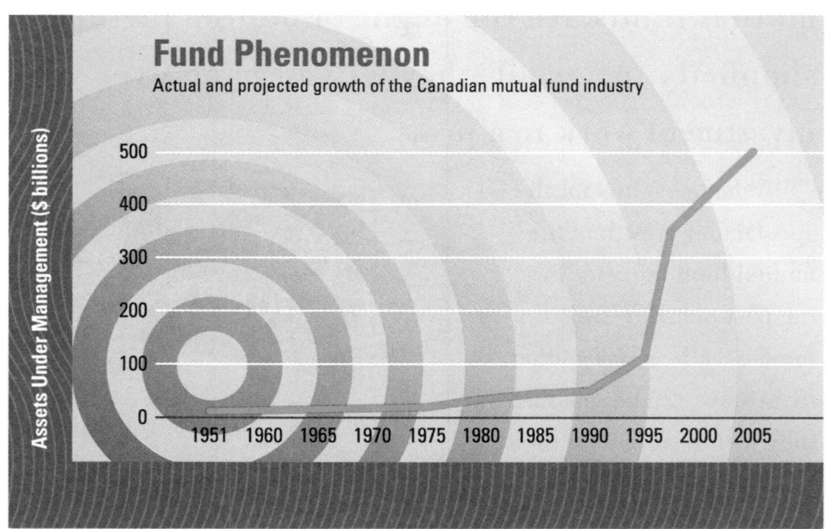

In this sea of choices — and opportunities — my FundMonitor mutual fund research can help you make sense of your options.

If you've been around the block a few times as a mutual fund investor, you may want to skip ahead to my fund reviews — the research analysis that is the main purpose of this book. But if you're new to mutual funds, or you'd like a recap, let's first look at the basics.

Harnessing the Power of Professional Money Management

A mutual fund is a "pool" of money composed of the investments of many individuals — sometimes thousands or even hundreds of thousands of people. A professional money manager invests the pool of money in a selected, predetermined range of investments. A mutual fund must be sold by prospectus, and this document provides the basic information about the fund: its investment objective, the investment style of its manager, and the types of investments that the fund is mandated to participate in.

Stripped to the bare asset classes, there are only three types of investments: cash (generally in the form of treasury bills), bonds (usually very secure government or corporate bonds), and equities (the shares of Canadian or international corporations).

Face it. If you're like most working Canadians, you probably don't have the time or tools to oversee your investments effectively. And you're probably not trained to be an expert money manager. But with an investment in mutual funds, you can benefit from the experience and skills of some of the world's best money managers.

Your fund manager works full time to capture the best opportunities for the fund. A manager's tasks include scrutinizing national and international news, and staying abreast of any economic, political or demographic trends. In the case of an international fund, you can expect your manager to be closely connected with the markets in which the fund invests. Many even take up a home base in their international market.

Ultimately, the goal of a fund manager is to produce superior, long-term growth for the fund. Your most important job is to choose

A Mutual Fund Does Not Equal a Stock Market Investment

I've heard people exclaim that they'd never buy a mutual fund because they don't want to "play the stock market." Obviously there's a misconception that a mutual fund equals a stock market investment. This is not necessarily the case.

Many mutual funds are based on equities — that is, stocks in publicly traded companies. But not all mutual funds are equity funds. As you can see by the way I've categorized my fund research, many mutual funds are based on bonds or are "money market" funds, based on treasury bills, or very liquid investments. Others are based on mortgages, or gold, or real estate, to name a few.

your mutual funds carefully. I recommend that you use a financial advisor for this task — and then let the money manager do the best work possible over the long term.

Diversifying with Mutual Funds

When you were growing up, your mother probably warned you not to put all your eggs in one basket. That sage advice also applies to investing. The problem is that the average investor isn't wealthy enough to diversify his or her investments effectively. If you wanted a well-diversified portfolio of stocks, you would need to buy many shares in several different companies — both in Canada and abroad.

Thanks to the economies of scale provided by the mutual fund "pool" (which often totals millions or even billions of dollars), even a small investment is well diversified. Your mutual fund holding represents a vast array of stocks, bonds, and/or other investments. In fact, I don't know of any better way to diversify your investments than through carefully selected mutual funds.

A World of Investment Choice with Mutual Funds

The good news is that, no matter what your investment needs or your financial situation, there really is a mutual fund for everyone. In fact, there are many mutual funds that suit your unique needs.

Maybe RRSP savings are your key investment priority, and a portfolio of mutual funds is a way to achieve your retirement goals. Perhaps you're a very aggressive investor looking for maximum growth, and willing to weather some dramatic ups and downs to get there. Or maybe the ups and downs make you seasick, and you'd prefer a slower, steadier path to growth.

You may want to invest in equities, or real estate funds, or mortgage funds. Or you may have an interest in a specialty fund, such as gold, or a particular market, like Japan or Europe.

A wealth of choices is open to you. You can use this book to explore some of the best funds in every category. And, as always, you should discuss your preferences with your financial advisor.

Types of Mutual Funds

The vast array of mutual fund choices can leave investors paralyzed. With over 2500 mutual funds to choose from, it's hard to find the right one for your needs and preferences.

A terrific first step is to identify the type of fund you would like to invest in. I've described each major type of fund and then offered some subgroupings that you may find helpful. Equity funds, in particular, can be extremely varied. You'll see here that, for example, I've categorized Canadian equity funds by the size of the companies they usually in-vest in.

For simplicity, I've grouped the major fund types into four categories: money market, fixed income, equity, and balanced.

1. Money Market Funds: Canadian and U.S. Funds

While a money market fund should provide you with a return that beats the average savings account, it is not designed for superior returns, and is not a particularly attractive long-term investment.

A money market fund can provide an important cash component in a balanced portfolio, but it is most often viewed as a place to park investment money temporarily.

Money market funds generally invest in very safe, short-term debt securities. They invest in government treasury bills, or bank-guaranteed deposits, with the purpose of providing current income without taking any risks with the capital.

As a category, money market funds have the lowest level of risk among mutual funds. Not surprisingly, money market funds are very popular when interest rates are high, and investors lose interest as interest rates drop.

Canadian money market funds | are fully RRSP-eligible, since they are invested in a range of Canadian short-term investments: federal or provincial government guaranteed treasury bills (T-bills), for example.

You might ask, why not just buy T-bills on your own? Besides the advantages of convenience and simplicty, the fund buys enormous quantities (that "strength-in-numbers" feature again) of T-bills, so they can be purchased at a significantly lower price than average investors could purchase them. The cheaper price improves your chances of a better return. And besides, you don't have to roll over your maturing T-bill every few months, because the manager does it for you.

Money market funds also invest in GICs, short-term promissory notes issued by major corporations (called "corporate paper"), and bankers' acceptances, which are promissory notes issued by corporations and guaranteed by a bank that the amount of the note will be paid in full on the date specified.

As with T-bills, all of these are short-term and highly liquid investments that are usually issued in amounts of several hundred thousand dollars, so most individual investors only have access to these vehicles through a mutual fund.

Many fund companies also offer U.S. money market funds. These funds work the same way as their Canadian counterparts, but offer a better return when U.S. rates are higher than those in Canada (as they are at the moment). An investment in a U.S. money market fund is a good choice for investors who are looking for a hedge in the event that the Canadian dollar falls. They're also good for investors who frequently need access to U.S. currency.

If you spend a lot of time or money in the U.S. on a regular basis, keeping some of your funds denominated in U.S. dollars is a good idea.

2. Fixed-Income Funds: Bond, Mortgage, and Dividend Funds

Many types of fixed-income funds are available. The term generally refers to mutual funds based on any asset that pays a fixed rate of return: bonds and mortgages, or preferred stocks that pay dividends. These are all relatively secure investments, and they provide a steady source of income. This feature makes them especially popular with conservative investors and retirees alike.

If long-term interest rates decline, you may earn a capital gain — a bonus on top of your interest. Still, the main objective of these funds is generally to achieve maximum income while preserving invested capital and minimizing risk.

Fixed-income funds are an especially good choice during times of declining interest rates, but may actually lose value when rates rise. As a result, these funds are riskier than money market funds. On the other hand, they have the potential to provide higher returns than money market funds.

Bond Funds

Bond funds generally invest in very secure government (federal, provincial or municipal) or corporate bonds. The focus of a bond fund is typically to maximize income. If

When Interest Rates Rise: Winners and Losers

When Dan Richards, president of Marketing Solutions, surveyed investors and asked them whether they believed that the value of their investments would increase with rising interest rates, the answers were surprising. Thirty percent of respondents believed that yes, their investments would increase in value. Sorry, folks — guess again.

In fact, higher interest rates have a negative impact on all fixed-income investments except cash (that is, money market funds).

Stocks, too, often fall in value when interest rates rise. This occurs because companies that are big borrowers will face higher interest rate charges (and less profits) when rates rise.

Guaranteed investment certificates can also fall in value, but their prices are generally not listed daily, so you don't notice the change. In fact, there would be little point in tracking the value of a GIC, since you probably couldn't sell it anyway. Your money is generally locked in. Do GICs offer a higher return to compensate for this lack of liquidity and lack of pricing? Not usually. Government bonds often yield higher rates of return, are liquid, and have higher credit quality, generally speaking, than bank GICs, which offer only limited deposit insurance.

the fund also manages to make a capital gain, it's considered a very nice bonus.

If you're looking for an international bond market, seek out an economy that's recovering from a recession. If interest rates are declining, bond prices should rise — and that will translate into returns for your fund.

Think about your diversification strategy; a fixed-income component is important to any well-balanced portfolio, and an international bond fund can diversify your portfolio two ways.

International bond funds with a European tilt continue to offer the best opportunities today.

Mortgage Funds

Mortgage funds are just what you might expect them to be: They invest in residential first mortgages, like the one I've got in my filing cabinet at home.

If you've ever applied for a mortgage, you'll know this is a fairly secure investment for the lenders. Generally, mortgage funds are based on "conventional" mortgages, where the loan does not exceed 75 percent of the appraised value of the home. However, they may also include "insured" mortgages, in which the loan may exceed 75 percent of the appraised value, but is insured against default by Canada Mortgage and Housing Corporation (CMHC). Some mortgage funds also hold commercial mortgages. A prospectus can provide such details.

These funds are generally very conservative and offer comparatively little risk. Returns are mostly in the form of interest income.

Dividend Funds

Scan the list of investments for a dividend fund and you'll often find a list of familiar names: the big, steady "blue-chip" companies, as they're called. Dividend funds invest in high-quality, common and preferred shares (which pay fixed dividends) of taxable Canadian corporations. They also invest in the common shares of banks and utilities, which also pay regular dividends.

A dividend fund has an important tax advantage: dividend income is taxed at a much lower rate than interest income. If you must claim income, this is the best kind. Dividends represent the lowest-taxed form of income.

Because of this, of course, it makes sense to hold your dividend fund in a non-registered account. A dividend fund in an RRSP is a lost tax-savings opportunity. (It can still provide steady growth, though.)

3. Equity Funds

Growth is the main reason to own an equity fund; you're looking for the best possible gains in the value of your investment over a period of time. That gain, incidentally, is a capital gain.

Equity funds are the riskiest category of investment in the short term. But if you have several years to invest, you should remember that — over the longer term — equity funds have left the other fund categories in the dust.

Think of it this way: whereas money market and fixed-income investors are "loaners," equity investors are "owners." Equity funds have one thing in common: they all hold stocks. The type and nationality of those stocks will depend on the fund's objective and investment mandate. A huge variety of equity funds is available to Canadians.

Let's look at some of the main equity fund categories:

Canadian Equity Funds

Canadian equity funds invest in the common shares of Canadian corporations. Most are eligible for RRSP investments.

But not all of these funds are alike. Look for other clues about investment styles. Is the fund a *large-cap* fund? If so, it specializes in big, blue-chip corporations, and you'll recognize many of the names. They call these large-cap because the companies they focus on have very large market capitalization, which is the total value of all a company's outstanding shares. If the fund specializes in small caps, it will be more aggressive in its investment style — seeking out the best small Canadian companies.

Sometimes a fund will have a *top-down* sector approach. It presumes, for example, that medical technology will be hot, and invests in a range of companies in that sector. These are called *sector funds*.

Some funds take a *value* approach to choosing stocks. They look for companies that are cheap; that is, they represent a bargain stock price, considering their assets and sales. The fund buys at a bargain price, then waits for the stock price to rise.

A *growth* fund, on the other hand, doesn't look for bargains, but seeks out stocks of companies that are growing. Some of the most aggressive growth funds are invested in stocks that already appear overvalued, but are continuing to soar.

Recently, there's been a proliferation of *ethical funds* — those funds that invest only in companies that meet certain moral or ethical standards. These funds would typically avoid manufacturers of armaments, tobacco, or alcohol, or those companies that (directly or indirectly) carry on business in countries with oppressive or discriminatory political regimes.

U.S. Equity Funds

These funds are similarly varied in their styles and objectives, but invest almost exclusively in the United States — the world's largest market. As a caution, though, I'll observe that — after 15 years of extraordinary growth — these funds seem unlikely to maintain their current pace for much longer.

International Equity Funds

International equity funds invest in the stocks of companies in several countries, and many roam the world looking for the "best of the best." Some limit themselves to investing in certain geographic areas (the Pacific Rim, Latin America, Europe), while others restrict themselves to investing in a specific country. Latin America has been one of this year's international success stories.

Precious Metals Funds

You'll find lots of gold in most precious metals funds. The fund invests either by purchasing bullion directly or by investing in the shares of gold mining companies. Some funds also hold other precious metals such as platinum and silver, and can invest worldwide. If you think we'll see a jump in inflation, a precious metals fund is a good way to hedge your savings from that risk.

Real Estate Funds/Real Estate Investment Trusts (REITs)

These funds invest in income-generating commercial and industrial property. They make their money three ways: through the income generated by the property, through the capital gains earned when the property is sold, and through the interest on short-term deposits, which the fund holds in preparation for upcoming opportunities.

If you've been around for a few years, you'll remember that real estate — especially commercial real estate — took a serious punch in the last recession. As a result, these funds have been largely redesigned; most real estate funds are closed-end funds that now trade on stock exchanges. This allows investors improved liquidity — even in a tough market environment.

4. Balanced Funds

These funds spread your assets between equities and cash or fixed-income investments. The result is a single fund with a smoother ride in overall returns from year to year, and a hedge against a sudden drop in either equities or bonds.

Managers of a balanced fund will generally hold different weightings of asset types, depending on current or anticipated economic developments. A balanced fund will often work within some constraints: no more than 60 percent, or less than 40 percent, in equities or fixed income at any given time, for example.

Counting the Cost

Since there's a lot of anxious talk about the cost of owning a mutual fund, it makes sense to clarify this issue.

First, two costs are involved in your mutual fund purchase: the sales charge (or load) and the ongoing annual management fees. Both of these costs can affect your final return.

It's ironic that many investors believe that they are beating the system by buying a no-load fund, yet fail to realize that the management expenses to hold that fund year after year may actually be higher than those for the "load" fund they were considering.

Let's take a look.

The Big Panic: Sales Charges, or "Loads"

If the fund has a sales charge (many do), you have two choices. You can either pay a front-end load — in which the fund company claims a small percentage of your investment right away — or you can choose a back-end load, in which you might have to pay later if you remove your money from the fund within the first five or six years.

These rear-load funds' redemption charges decline each year you hold the fund — eventually reaching zero after about six years. If you're not sure what type of fund you own, look at your statement. If it says "DSC" (Deferred Sales Charge) beside the fund name, then it's a rear-load fund.

Front-End Loads

In the earlier years of mutual fund investing, sales charges of up to nine percent were levied on investments. Today, you shouldn't pay more than five percent on even a small investment. (If, for example, your sales charge was four percent on a $10,000 purchase, the actual amount invested will be [$10,000 – 4%=] $9600.) If you are investing a large amount, most advisors will negotiate a lower rate.

If, however, you are purchasing through a discount broker, you will be restricted in your negotiating; loads are pretty well fixed. One popular discount broker advertises a rate of 2.5 percent on mutual fund investments under $5000, two percent on orders from $5000 to $25,000, and one percent on orders larger than $25,000.

A final caution on front-end loads. Since you will lose some of your investment potential right off the top, you will have less money going to work for you.

Back-End Loads

With back-end loads all of your money goes to work for you right away. This option was first offered in 1987, and has become very popular. People are very resistant to upfront costs. More than 90 percent of load-fund sales in recent years have been of the back-end load variety.

Here's how it works. If you redeem these units before a certain period (usually about six years or so) has elapsed, you'll be required to pay a fee based on the value of your investment. This percentage declines over time.

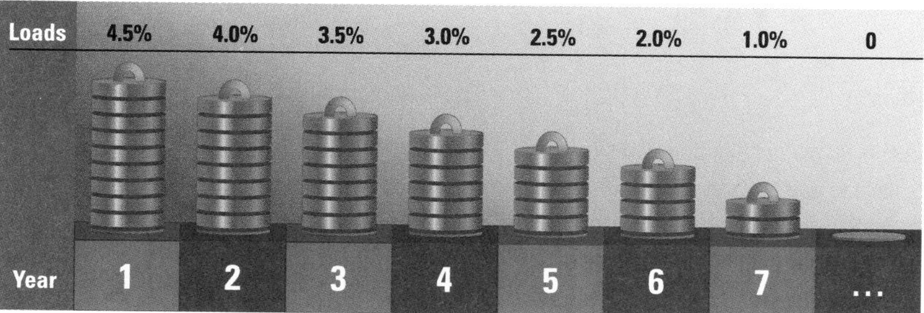

Some companies charge the redemption fee on the original amount invested; a few, however, charge on the market value of funds when you cash them. In most cases, the first option is preferable.

Redemption Charges

Here's the way several of the larger fund companies currently handle their redemption charges:

Redemption Policy	Acquisition Cost	Redemption Value	Redemption Policy	Acquisition Cost	Redemption Value
AGF	●		Investors		●
Canadian International	●		Mackenzie		●
Dynamic		●	Templeton	●	
Fidelity		●	Trimark	●	
Global Strategy	●		Spectrum United	●	
Guardian	●		United	●	

Due to the popularity of back-end load funds, many funds that used to charge only a front-end load can now be purchased either way. In fact, Trimark set up the Select group of DSC funds to mirror their successful front-load funds, such as the **Trimark Fund** (the DSC clone is **Trimark Select Growth**) and the **Trimark Canadian Fund** (the DSC clone is **Trimark Select Canadian Growth Fund**).

Before I completely sell you on the back-end load approach, you must also factor some additional fees into your decision.

Management Fees | If you manage to avoid the front-end sales charges, fund companies will get you anyway with management fees

— which can sometimes be higher for funds purchased on a back-end load basis. Trimark, for example, charges as much as 0.8 percent more annually for their back-end load funds. Therefore, if you're buying a Trimark fund, I'd advise you to choose the front-load option.

Do your homework on your fund costs. They directly affect the bottom line, and the differences between the options can be significant over time. Based on how long you will be invested in the fund, ask how much it is going to cost you. Put your advisor on the spot before you put your money on the table.

A Word on Taxes

Common sense tells us that mutual fund taxes reek of unfairness. We have to pay taxes every year on distributions we don't even receive in cash. And new investors have to pony up for the gains other people made before the new folks even came on board. Looks pretty bleak, right?

Those things are true, no question. But mutual funds still do a great job of sheltering us from tax.

I've calculated the after-tax return on every fund in Canada over the past decade and a half (assuming then-prevailing tax rates for an Ontario investor at the top bracket). And guess what: The rate of returns (after tax) has been just two percentage points lower than the pre-tax returns you see hyped in the funds' advertising.

Over the 10 years ended Dec. 31, 1998, for instance, our even-weighted composite of every available fund showed a net return of 7.1 percent annually, after tax. Which compares pretty favourably with the 9.1 percent return you would have gotten if you had held this same basket of funds inside your RRSP. (The after-tax research isn't relevant for you if you've got all of your money stashed in an RRSP or RRIF.)

Here's why it works out so well: Stock turnover for, say, a domestic fund is typically around 40 percent, which means that every year about four stocks out of 10 in the fund get traded. So figure the average stock is in a fund for about two and a half years — long enough to defer any gain on it by three tax years. Second, capital gains are taxed at a lower rate than interest income (from a GIC, for example). Both these factors work in your favour with the taxman.

How Come Mutual Funds Cost So Much in Canada?

Only a couple of hundred miles from the Sky Dome in Toronto there's a little town called Valley Forge, Pennsylvania. It's home to Vanguard Group — a terrific fund company for the thrifty investor. Their fees are so low that their most popular fund, the Vanguard S&P 500 Index Trust, charges total expenses of just 0.19 percent annually.

Yup. Zero point one nine.

Now, that's cheap. It's not, say, half the cost, or even one-third the cost, of what you or I might have to pay to buy a fund in Canada. It's around one-fifteenth of what we'd typically pay. But you can't buy it. Some group in our government thinks you should be protected from American mutual funds. "They're not regulated by our authorities," they say.

But neither are the shares of Disney, for example, which trade on the New York Stock Exchange and are regulated only by U.S. authorities.

How Main Street Canada got hooped on the final version of NAFTA

Despite the obvious contradiction, Canadians can buy and sell shares of U.S. stocks — but not U.S. funds. The North American Free Trade Agreement set out to establish free trade in mutual fund services, among other things. But somewhere along the line, Canadian special interest groups seem to have intervened, quashing the the idea of reciprocal access.

It's not fair. We should be allowed to buy U.S. funds. There are 9000 available, totaling more than $5 trillion in assets. It's a mature, well regulated, hotly competitive marketplace.

True, there wouldn't be many Canadian funds for our RRSPs, and there's almost no pricing of units in Canadian dollars. But the benefits of choice and huge cost savings would make up for it. And with my idea, we'd still deal with Canadian advisors — as we do to buy U.S. stocks — we'd just get access to more and better funds.

Our regulators should accept the Securities & Exchange Commission's regulation of mutual funds, the way they do for stocks.

The irony, of course, about our protected mutual fund industry is that the cats getting fattest are the ones who most vocally support free trade in general. That's right: the politically conservative folks on Bay Street. The suspender crowd is right about the concept of free trade; it's a win/win idea because it allows different nations to specialize in what they do best and export their excess. With the proceeds they can import what they need. Freer trade has created the low inflation and higher stock prices we currently enjoy.

What's funny is that we let Bay Street talk us into free trade, then exempt their mutual fund services from it.

The fund companies are the ones that benefit from this protection — they get to charge higher fees. On average our fees are 110 percent higher than those in the United States. Accordingly, fund companies here earn margins that are twice those of U.S. firms.

And so it's Main Street Canadian savers who are being punished for this unfair protection of the investment industry.

So I say we talk it up. Even if it takes a while to change the rules, we'll at least accomplish one goal: We'll let the fund company executives know that we won't stand for goofy fees of nearly three percent on domestic stock and balanced funds.

Average Total Management Expense Ratios	
Canadian funds	2.13%
U.S.-based funds	1.04%

For more ideas on how to cut costs, see Chapter 6. It's got loads of ideas to help the thrifty, the rich, the busy and the beginner save money year after year.

The No-Load Option

No-load funds have been popular with the banks and trust companies — and of course with Altamira, the best-known no-load seller.

When you deal with a direct seller, however, remember that typically you will not be discussing your financial plans with an independent financial advisor. The salaried employees who manage the phones can only provide information about the funds offered by their company.

Still, Canadians are warming to the idea of no-load funds. Nothing is deducted on purchase, and there are no redemption charges. No-loads are very popular in the United States, and Canadian fund companies are now waking up to the message.

A New Twist: Zero Commission

This is where things can get a little confusing. Some discount brokerage firms are now offering zero commission on all mutual funds, which is quite a deal for the do-it-yourself investor.

But you'll have to be picky with these programs; almost all of them exclude the better no-load funds — you know, the ones with low annual expenses. So let's examine the importance of these ongoing charges.

What You Don't See: Management Expenses

Investors must recognize that all mutual funds — even no-load funds — charge these fees. After all, this is how money is generated to pay the fund managers, and to support the advertising and education efforts for the fund. You've gone looking for the best manager in the country; someone has to pay her.

Management expenses generally range between 1 and 2.5 percent of the total assets in the fund. Not surprisingly, some of the biggest funds have the lowest management fees, since the cost of the management team, the research facilities, and all the other necessities are spread over more unitholders. Although the percentage of management fees may decline as a fund grows in size, this is not always the case.

Fees are determined by the type of assets managed by the fund. Obviously, more infrastructure is needed to support an equity fund (which requires lots of company and industry research) than to manage a cash fund, which really just rolls T-bills. Look for expenses of about two percent for equity-based funds, and about one percent for cash management funds.

You don't see management fees. Since they're charged directly to the fund, you never see a statement of the amount. That doesn't mean they're invisible, however; you'll see the impact on your final returns. For example, if a fund charges two percent in management expenses and earns a 20 percent return in a given year, your net return is 18 percent. The law, by the way, states that mutual fund ads must always show returns after expenses have been deducted.

My advice is to disregard management fees, and focus instead on the management expense ratio. That's the total of all management fees plus other expenses, divided by the number of fund units. It includes legal, accounting, custodial, and safekeeping costs, as well as the costs of producing prospectuses and other reporting materials. Annual reports

Once More: Taxes

Tax-managed mutual funds are easy to understand, but tough to nail down. (Their goal is to buy great stocks for the long term and hold them, basically, forever.) As I've mentioned before, there's a downside (if not several): Newcomers to the funds get hit disproportionately hard; selling is difficult, even when it would be wise.

When Gerry Coleman left the big Ivy Canadian Fund to run the C.I. Harbour Fund, he steered clear of many of the stocks from his old portfolio. In other words, he started fresh — something the investor who's stuck in the old Ivy fund doesn't have the luxury of doing. So be careful with the buy-and-hold-forever tack.

But we're probably going to get more of such offerings in the near future. U.S. firms like Vanguard have really pushed up the popularity of these funds. Over at Mackenzie Financial Corp., John Rohr employs a similar strategy with the Universal Future Fund and Universal Science and Technology Fund. Other tax-managed funds in Canada include those from AIC.

from Guardian and Maxxum, as well as the big Fund Choices chart from Royal Mutual Funds, have all used "management fees" to describe their costs, or left out a discussion of fees entirely. How the Investment Funds Institute of Canada (IFIC) can allow fund companies never to mention the management expense ratio (in, for example, a 72-page annual report) is beyond me.

All else being equal, the higher the management expense ratio, the more money being spent by the manager and the lower the return to the investor. As a result, examine these factors when considering any fund purchase.

Nickels and Dimes

A few other charges may apply to the fund you are considering. These include:

- **Set-Up Fees**
  This one-time fee is often charged by no-load companies. Set-up fees usually fall in the range of $40.

- **Close-Out or Transfer Fees**
  You may be charged a modest fee for closing out your account with a particular fund company. Many fund companies charge $20 on the termination or transfer out of a tax plan for an RRSP or a Registered Retirement Income Fund (RRIF). Growing numbers of financial institutions are also charging this fee.

- **Trustee Fees for RRSPs, RRIFs, or Registered Education Savings Plans (RESPs)**
  For these types of accounts, an annual trustee fee may be charged, usually about $50. Some fund companies reduce or eliminate such fees from time to time as a promotional strategy. If your mutual fund units are held in your RRSP at a brokerage or financial planning firm, you'll be charged between $100 and $200 per year.

- **Systematic Withdrawal Fees/Charges**
  A systematic withdrawal plan (SWP) allows investors to receive regular income from their fund. A few companies charge an annual fee, while others charge a fee for each withdrawal.

- **Pre-Authorized Chequing Fees**
  If you set up a regular investment program and invest monthly by pre-authorized cheque, you may have to pay a service charge. If your bank account has insufficient funds to make this monthly investment, expect to pay a fee of about $15.

- **Switching Fees**
  Almost all companies allow funds to be switched within the same family. Often the prospectus will allow for a negotiable charge of between zero and two percent. When your advisor works hard to rebuild your portfolio in a way that improves your overall investment without leaving a fund family (and triggering a big fee), then he or she deserves that small (two percent or less) switching fee.

The Bigness Debate: Big Is Beautiful in Choosing the Best Funds

Investors prefer large funds. In fact, two-thirds of fund industry assets are clustered in about 120 of the 2000+ funds sold in Canada.

And my research suggests that Canadians are on the right track. Indeed, the big funds are better performers. These giants consistently beat the smaller funds — sometimes by a little, sometimes by a lot.

In a study a few years ago I found that global equity funds are the most striking example. Just 11 funds, which comprised a staggering 75 percent of the assets in this group, trounced the pack of 100 smaller ones with which they compete. These large funds earned 13.9 percent annually over the five years ending June 30, 1996, dwarfing the nine percent earned by the rest of the group.

You also see this pattern in Canadian bond funds. Of 129 bond funds, the 13 largest comprise 60 percent of the assets. Over the prior five years, these few big funds earned 11 percent annually, versus 10.5 percent for the small funds. An annual difference of half a percent point may not sound like much, but in the world of bonds, it's a big deal.

Jumbo U.S. equity funds enjoy a similar performance advantage. Their annual return is half a percentage point higher than the little guys in their group. The fact that monster funds perform better might shock investors who are fearful about bigness when it comes to equity funds. Many believe big funds won't be nimble enough to trade in and out of stocks at the best prices.

People also believe that large funds miss out on the sizzle from small-cap stocks — an area proven to offer higher returns — because their size makes a tiny small-cap position meaningless. The net asset value of a $2-billion fund won't even budge if a $1-million stock holding doubles in value. But these fears are unfounded. Lipper Analytical Services, a U.S. firm that monitors fund returns, says big-fund superiority has held stable every year since it has been breaking out performance by size.

My calculations went beyond taking a simple look at how today's biggest funds did over the last five years. Naturally, today's giants would have better track records — after all, that's why they became big.

Instead, each month I looked at how the biggest funds were doing that month. By rejigging the list monthly, I crafted a composite of what the returns of the biggest funds really were at various moments in time. Why the performance gap between big and small funds? There are three key reasons, all of which relate to success breeding success.

The first is simply great fund management. Not every big fund is superbly managed, or triumphs in every market climate. But consistency wins investor loyalty and builds a fund over time. While some funds balloon because of great marketing, lasting size is usually the result of investment success.

The second reason is lower expenses. For example, consider bond funds, where expenses are so important. The average management expense ratio for the 13 largest bond funds is 1.5 percent — low, but still not low enough in my opinion — versus 1.7 percent for the rest of the pack. The economies created by size allow for a wider base across which to spread the fixed costs of managing a fund.

Mutual funds are a curious product: The highest quality is often found at the lowest price. Successful and established funds usually have lower expenses, while unproven upstarts often charge a bundle.

The third reason is trading and research economies. Bigger funds can afford more talent, whether in the form of more attention from brokerage analysts or more money for in-house analysts, and they pay even lower commissions on some trades than the already slim institutional rates.

You'd do well to stick to the big names, as the majority of Canadians do, for most of your portfolio. But don't get me wrong. Lots of great small funds exist. Setting aside up to 20 percent of your mutual fund dollars for an undiscovered gem, especially a small-cap player, could be very rewarding.

3 Good Performance: What It Is; What It Isn't

What the Advertising Says

When a mutual fund advertisement provides numbers for a fund's performance, the company is using what are known as standard performance figures. The mutual fund company doesn't have a choice in how they present them; it's the law (although you'll find that many companies are very opportunistic about when they advertise performance).

Standard performance figures are both the bait and the bane of mutual fund companies. They're designed to show a fund's results over time, based on the belief that the longer the performance period, the more reliable the guide.

Look at any mutual fund advertisement and you are likely to find a lot of impressive numbers that attest to the fund's performance over the past six months, one year, three years, or five years — all of which make the fund appear to be a fairly attractive investment. But in the worst cases, the numbers are simply statistical hocus-pocus that's ideal for marketing funds.

Since provincial securities regulators recognize that performance figures can be deceiving, they've added their own fine print to mutual fund advertisements. At the bottom of each advertisement, a snippet of copy appears that usually reads something like this: "Past performance is not necessarily indicative of future returns...."

Granted, this is fairly obvious to most investors. No one can be certain that a fund will keep performing the way it has in the past. But that's only part of the problem. The disclaimer should actually read something like this: "This is a really dumb way to calculate past performance, but we couldn't think of anything better at the time. Buyer beware."

I think that past performance data is an extremely valuable tool in predicting future returns — but only if the performance is measured properly. The problem is that it's still very difficult to find the right kind of performance data in conventional sources.

What the Newspaper Says

You may think that the performance figures reported in most of the daily newspaper listings are likely to be more accurate and unbiased than the advertising numbers. Think again. They're the same standard performance figures, reported exactly the same way.

For the clearest picture of a fund's performance history, you will have to look beyond the advertising and beyond the usual daily listings. Why? Because they're biased. Ending-date biased, that is.

The Fatal Flaw: Ending-Date Bias

A while back I wrote a newspaper column explaining how long-term performance figures can mislead investors. In it, I described how a fund with a fairly mediocre track record became an overnight star; in a mere four months, the fund's 10-year performance leaped from a lacklustre seven percent annually to a handsome 11.8 percent annually for the 10-year period.

Can a 10-year performance figure make that kind of jump in four months? You bet.

Let's just say that column generated some heated response — with most of the heat blowing in the direction of the fund companies' marketing departments.

We've been led to believe that long-term return figures are fairly reliable. So what's the issue? Well, while the standard performance figures don't actually lie, they seldom tell the whole truth. In the case of the fund I wrote about in my column, the portfolio earned a cool 60.8 percent in the three months. Because all of the calculations for the one-, three-, five-, and 10-year rates of return are always tied to a single ending day, we could be looking at distorted returns for years to come.

Beware of Performance-Claim Ads

You're getting the gist of why the ads can be problematic. They only advertise when the numbers are good. And the numbers look good when the fund's been hot lately. Et cetera, et cetera.

So really, advertising contributes to the almost chronic investor problem of buying high. Luring unwitting investors in at the top is exactly what mutual fund performance-claim ads do.

By a margin that is stunning, performance is doomed to fall after the ad appears — and in most cases it falls by a mile. I did an exhaustive study of each and every ad that has appeared in the *Globe and Mail*'s *Report on Mutual Funds* since the supplement was launched at the beginning of this decade. In it I analyzed how each fund did after the ad ran and compared that actual performance to the historic returns cited in the ad. Among those eligible, fully 92 percent of the funds advertised did worse over the subsequent three years after the ad appeared than the three year return quoted in the ad. This is across all asset classes and in an environment of generally increasing returns.

Allowing a fund to rewrite its own history on the basis of very recent returns (as the ending-date sensitivity does) is surely an advertising executive's idea. The system allows for a terrible bias: to show the numbers only when they look great, which is after the fund has been on a tear.

Performance After the Ad Appeared

Declined By	In
More than 10 percentage points	45% of the cases
More than 15 percentage points	36% of the cases
More than 25 percentage points	24% of the cases

The table here shows how severe the performance declines were in the one-year periods following the appearances of the ads. In fully one quarter of the performance-claim ads that have appeared, the subsequent one-year performance fell off a cliff, declining by more than 25 percentage points. Almost half of the 436 ads that qualified for this part of the study had actual returns that were more than 10 percentage points lower.

Separately, the study concluded that resource funds were the worst offenders. The average one-year return cited in every resource fund ad since 1991 was 51 percent. But the average of all the subsequent one-year results was a mere one percent.

Overcoming the obstacle of buying high is easy. Just pay special attention to the one-year performance number cited in any ad. If it seems high, be aware of the unseen impact that hot year has had on the fund's history. Then check out my ultimate tables at the back of the book to see how the fund compared, on a year-by-year basis, with its peers.

The Best Solution: Average Monthly Rankings

To get a clear look at a fund's ability to perform over time, we need to eliminate the end-date bias that gives us those funhouse mirror figures.

I've developed a simple, mathematical model based on the average monthly ranking of a fund's performance since inception — or to a maximum of 20 years. Each month, I measure how a fund stacks up against its peers. With this method, a mediocre fund that's been hot for only a few months has no place to hide.

By measuring each fund against others in their same category, I can get a good sense of how each fund manager weathers the ups and downs of the markets.

Rookie fund ratings

Many funds on the Canadian scene are relative newcomers, so they don't have that much track record to study. I've always maintained a three-year minimum for any funds that get a full-page profile in this book, and that remains. But newer funds are rated in the Ultimate Tables at the back of the book, where each gets a 40-word essay.

For example, each Canadian equity fund is ranked against other Canadian equity funds for as many months as the fund has been in existence. Then I average the various rankings to find the cream of the fund crop.

The funds that emerge as winners in this system are the ones that perform consistently well in most periods. Funds that do spectacularly well in some periods but spectacularly poorly in others are unlikely to make the grade. Consistency generally wins — especially in the mutual fund game.

Standard performance figures are everywhere — at least for now. Use them to identify the funds you'd like to know more about. Develop your shortlist. Then look at real performance numbers.

Ask your advisor to help you find calendar-year returns for the fund (or watch for this special edition in the *Globe and Mail*). Look for your fund in my Ultimate Fund Tables to see what my performance analysis has turned up.

Good Performance or Good Performers?

Beyond all this number stuff, there is a softer side. We say that picking funds is all science, but deep down you and I both know that finding the right fund manager is very personal. And therein lies the danger. Personal decisions are often excessively influenced by personality, which isn't that relevant. In fact, there are a few common traps we all fall into when we approach the softer side of fund research. Sure, we've got the right intentions — we're looking for someone who's smart, experienced, and successful. But when we get down to the core, we come up with just one thing. We want someone who's trustworthy.

Here's where things get dangerous. Most people only get exposure to money managers through the fund's marketing bumph and through the media. Neither is a perfect indicator of trustworthiness, because both are highly subjective forms of communication that purport to report on very cold, hard facts. So herewith, some of the traps and how to avoid them.

1. Don't fall in love with the great communicator. It's easy to be swayed by a polished presenter who has got a good story, good looks, and great jokes. But while these qualities are okay in an advisor, they're neither common nor ideal in a portfolio manager.

   Most of the world's best money managers are geeks. No kidding. Securities analysis is very — you know — analytical.

   And most managers don't even begin to do much in the way of presentations until well into their career. So you have to be careful not to discount a real gem just because his or her speech fails to inspire a crowd. Trust is very cosmetic, so it's important to try to look beneath the surface.

   Don't get me wrong. Being shy socially isn't the same as lacking confidence professionally. You do need a confident fund manager pulling the trigger for you, taking a stance and riding out storms. It's possible to find managers who've really got a unique and viable approach, as long as you're listening for content, not style.

2. Look out for cover stories. Media exposure can poison a manager in a number of ways. With his mug on a magazine cover, a manager is certain to be dragged into commando duty, running all over the country hustling more exposure and more assets. Besides the drag on time and focus, there's the issue of ego and believing one's own press.

   That can sometimes alienate the analysts who work with and contribute to the famous manager's success. Plus, media exposure creates marketing allure that breeds job offers from other firms. Turnover and discord are common in these situations.

3. Don't take recent performance too seriously. Hot fund managers are everywhere. Brokers hype them, ads tout them, and lucky unitholders chat about them. After you hear the name a few times from sources that seem credible, you tend to get attracted to these

successful people. And they tend to get confirmation that their approach works. Imagine a fund manager who has been making a big, bold call on the United States for the past few years. She looks like a hero and reaffirms her own ideas about how the only thing that matters is getting the country decision right. She starts to spend lots of time worrying about big, macro factors like each nation's gross domestic product growth rate and M-2 money supply — instead of following whether her companies are doing all the right things to boost business.

That inattention to the core job of fundamental company research can have bad results, even if mitigated by decent country picks. Yes, managers can take their own recent success too seriously.

But so can we.

With so many funds available, pure random luck suggests that some will have a hot streak at any given moment. But common sense and empirical evidence suggest that any fund on, say, a three-year hot streak is probably just lucky — and, worse, is probably about to fade out.

In the end, what we're all really looking for is a manager who's still fresh and passionate, but has lots of experience. Experience is a hard teacher because it gives the test first and the lesson afterward.

Star-Chasing Can Be a Losing Game

In the past few years, some star managers have left behind the funds they made famous. If this happens to your fund, should you bail, too?

Probably not. There's compelling evidence that investors should stay put, rather than chasing the star.

A couple of years ago I decided to examine the impact of major manager changes in Canadian equity funds over the past decade. I looked at the performance record of high-profile managers who defected to run or start a competing fund, and then I directly compared their performance in their new role with the performance of the fund they left behind. In almost every case, the "fund faithful" are rewarded for sitting tight. And where new managers outperformed the departed star, they did so by margins that ranged from modest to mammoth.

Why do departing stars so consistently underperform the funds they left behind? I believe that they are constrained by a combination of market environment and the marketing process. Combine a hot market with a hot new star (heavily promoted) and assets soar. It's tough to buy and maintain a good portfolio with tens of millions of dollars coming in every day.

So, it's not that these managers are falling stars; it's just that the very marketing machine that builds them up can also poison their performance. For the investor, the evidence is clear. Star-chasing is almost always a losing game.

4 The Scoop on Diversification

BY FAR, THE BIGGEST BLUNDER MOST PEOPLE make in investing is that they fail to take advantage of the easy things, the free lunches, so to speak. Diversification is the last free lunch in investing. It promises a way to both increase returns and lower risk. The only people who don't need diversification are gamblers and clairvoyants.

Since you're neither, let's dig in and understand risk. I've devoted much of this book to describing the losses and loss potential of different funds. That's because I think it's good to know up front that even a great fund like ABC Fundamental Value has once dropped 31 percent during a bear market and spent 16 months just recovering to break even. And that's a great fund.

How can you avoid that kind of risk? You can't exactly. But you can reduce the impact of event-driven risk with these simple rules:

1. Invest for the long term.
2. Develop a balanced portfolio composed of different asset classes.
3. Diversify within each asset class.

Let's look at each of these.

Invest for the Long Term

You've likely heard this advice before. However, the mathematical support for this truism is powerful.

We all know that stocks are risky. The shaky summer we experienced in 1998 saw the TSE lose more than a quarter of its value. It was the third decline of 20 percent or more in just over 10 years. The crash of 1987 saw values plummet by 25 percent in one day! But the reality of equity investing is that occasionally you are going to be hit with such an event. The past is always a prologue to the future. Crashes will recur, and, ultimately, stock prices will continue to grow at a rate faster than other assets such as bonds.

If all of these statements are true, then risk measures from the past will undoubtedly provide some forecasting for the future. Keep in mind, though, that the stock market is a machine driven by crowd psychology. As such, its machinations are often exaggerated — for better or worse. Bull markets generally run too high. Crashes cut too deep. Over time, equity growth rates are fairly steady at around 10 percent. But on any given day, anything can happen.

Even though stocks have the potential to lose 25 percent of their value suddenly, the best way to hedge against that occurrence is to extend your holding period.

If stocks can fall 25 percent in a day, how much can they fall in a five-year period?

Not much. Strangely, the math works as follows. Over a one-year period, stocks have fairly high variability. There can be terrible years, like 1973 and 1974 — one of the worst bear markets ever. But

AIC Concerns

Turnover, taxes and liquidity

I reiterated my negative opinion on the domestic funds from AIC this summer in a report to my clients. Essentially, I'm concerned that the funds could suffer a real meltdown on top of (or in some ways because of) the drubbing they had already taken at the time of the report. (AIC Advantage was down 28 percent.)

I'm worried about management changes (Jonathan Wellum seems to be on the way out) and I'm worried about turnover. Dig this: Of the 23 stocks the fund held the summer before, fully 21 of them were way off their highs. I mean way off, like Newcourt and Fairfax, which had previously been the fund's biggest holdings. They had fallen by 73 percent and 52 percent, respectively. AIC insist that they buy and hold forever. But when 21 of 23 stocks are getting creamed in a bull market, that's taking the Warren Buffett approach a bit too far, no?

What's scary is that the managers have probably been doing a little selling of such long-held winners, realizing massive capital gains. Now believe me, you don't want to be the last one stuck in these funds when the taxable distribution gets paid (maybe December 31). That's because you'll have to pay tax on a fund that's way underwater and you'll have to pay more because most people will have sold out before you.

Worse, if everybody starts selling AIC's domestic funds (which total more than $9 billion) the way they have in previous redemption riots at Altamira and Trimark, then we think the investors could create a liquidity crisis in the funds. The big funds held almost no cash at last reporting, so the $3 billion in redemptions my firm is forecasting will have to be met by selling stocks. Stocks that have accrued big taxable gains. In the rush to avoid the tax bill, we think investors may speed up their selling, exacerbating the problem and forcing the managers to sell more of their stocks, including all those massive, illiquid positions in Canada's public fund companies. Recall that AIC owns minority stakes of about 20 percent (the legal limit) in most of Canada's public fund companies. That's as much as 200-plus days of normal market trading in the shares. We fear that the mere possibility of AIC's selling could wreck the market price of the shares.

It gets even scarier. We think the public is about to learn of the protectionism these Canadian fund companies have benefited from because we believe U.S. fund companies are going to tear down the trade barriers and start selling really cheap funds to Canadians really soon. That's gotta hurt Canadian providers—and their shares. So the AIC funds' NAVs will fall further, sparking more redemptions, more turnover, more taxable gains, and more pressure to sell stocks.

interestingly, as the chart on page 43 shows, the longer the time horizon, the more likely that subsequent equity growth will over-come even the scariest losses. Over time, the riskiness of stocks will diminish.

Hold for any five-year period and history tells us that you simply would not have ever lost more than about three percent of your money annually. Hold for 20 years and the same detailed analysis of history in the Canadian market shows that the worst that any investor could have done by holding stocks was about plus 15 percent annually.

Get a Balanced Portfolio Composed of Different Asset Classes

It's humbling for me to recommend that you diversify broadly. Humbling, that is, because it's an admission that I can't tell you what'll do best in the year ahead.

Diversification involves owning different kinds of investments, so that at any given time, you'll own some investments that are doing quite well and others that are doing poorly. The idea here is simple: over time, good investments will rise in value. Along the way, the ups and downs can cancel out each other to some degree.

Diversification out of conservative investments (such as bonds, for example) may involve a tough sell for some folks because they believe that bonds are safe. But stocks sometimes perform well when bonds are having a rough time, and so they can be an ideal match (in some proportion) with bonds, even for conservative investors.

Historically, in fact, as the chart on the following page shows, investors combining stocks with their bond portfolio (in a mix of about half and half) have actually improved returns quite a bit without adding any risk at all. That's the power of diversification by asset class.

You've no doubt heard that asset allocation — your mix between stocks, bonds, cash, and even other types of securities — is by far the greatest contributor to your return. This means that it doesn't matter whether you own Ford Motor or Apple Computer. What matters is whether you bought any stocks at all. Or cash. Or bonds. And how you balanced your holdings of each asset type.

Since market returns in the future aren't predictable, but risk definitely is, asset allocation approaches that are strategic in nature (which simply means that they are focused on the investor's risk level, not the manager's forecasting abilities) are legitimate ways to structure portfolios that meet a particular investor's need for growth, liquidity, or whatever special circumstances may be necessary.

In Chapter 7, I'll walk you through an example of using strategic asset allocations to structure portfolios to meet the individual needs of the investor. In going through this exercise, we'll show how you can predict fairly accurately the future risk levels and ensure that they are in a range that is tolerable for any individual.

Diversify Within Each Asset Class

I'll admit it. I have made a big deal about the investment style of each mutual fund shown in my FundMonitor Profiles.

Style is very important. That's because understanding the approach of each fund helps us to choose and pair funds for our own needs. After all, funds of one style will likely perform very well when that style is in vogue. For example, in the 1980s, there was a frenzy of leveraged buy-outs, and most acquisitions were targeted at companies with fairly low prices in terms of their book value. These so-called "value" stocks, as they are known, enjoyed a great run at the time, whereas growth stocks faded.

The following chart shows that the difference between growth and value isn't generally predictable but it is sizeable. I can tell you that growth and value funds (and, for that matter, a third unusual stock group called "sector rotation funds") will perform differently from one another in the future. Combining them may reduce your risk without any sacrifice in terms of your return. That's one way to diversify within asset classes.

Let's see if we can diversify in the traditional bond category. Sure, you could only buy Canadian bonds, but history shows us (in a way similar to the growth/value disparity) that global bonds — or for that matter corporate high-yield bonds — all move to the beat of different drummers. So, within the bond or fixed income asset class, diversifying

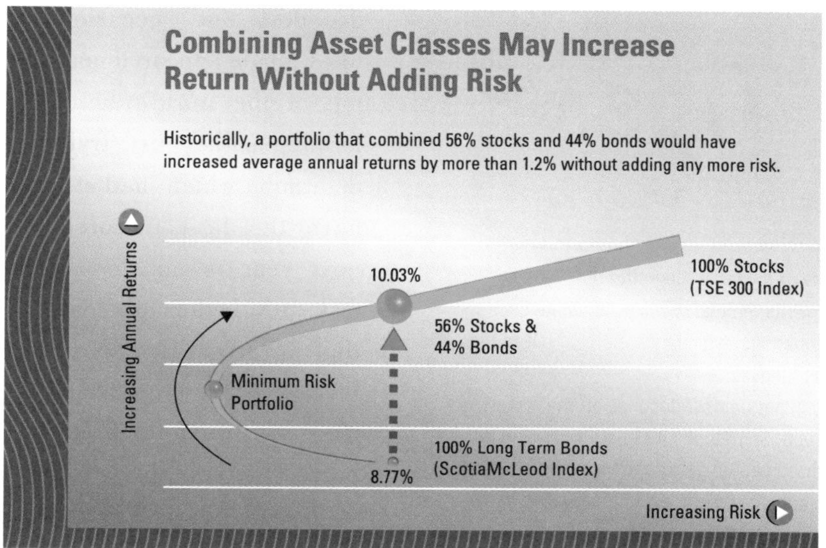

into funds of these three distinct asset types (Canadian government, global, and corporate high-yield) can reduce risk by reducing your exposure to the likelihood of one type of bond going down the tubes.

Diversification is inherently conservative. Diversification means never shooting the lights out. Never having a blockbuster year. For that, you have to be "un-diversified." You'd have to be concentrated in one particular "hot" area of whatever market. Diversification's humble nature suggests that none of us try for hot years. Unless you can reliably predict what will be hot next year, diversification is your best strategy.

Diversify Internationally

The argument for international diversification is very powerful. Canada represents a mere three percent of the world's investment opportunities, so investing strictly within Canada means eliminating 97 percent of your options. That would be like walking into a bountifully stocked grocery store, and limiting yourself to one section, of one shelf, of one aisle. You're unlikely to find great bargains with such a narrow approach.

International investing also has merits because often Canada simply isn't the best single place to invest. In fact, in the past couple of

The December Tax Whack on Mutual Funds

Over the course of a year, through the buying and selling of their investments, mutual funds accumulate capital gains and distributions, which must be paid out to the investors in the fund.

When do you get paid? It depends on the reporting period of the fund. Sometimes it's quarterly, but more often, any realized capital gains and income distributions are divided up among any current unitholders over the Christmas holidays — when you're not watching. However, if you're holding your fund in a non-registered portfolio, you might want to pay attention.

In a big year — where the markets are very, very strong (as they have been for U.S. stock funds in the past couple of years), large profits will be realized. And here's what happened in the case of those hot U.S. funds. New sales of the U.S. stock funds have been quite weak — even in such a hot market — because people seemed afraid of a sudden cold snap. So what we've got is a recipe for high distributions: strong returns and a small number of unitholders to share the tax bill.

This is the reason behind a phenomenon I call the December chill: holding off new purchases until the new year. If you're planning an unregistered investment in a fund where the market has been hot and the assets are stalled, you may want to wait, and let those who have enjoyed the gains foot the bill for the coming distribution.

Even investors with registered plans might feel a December chill this year as they hold off on new contributions because of Y2K concerns.

decades, only occasionally has Canada appeared near the top of the world's best-performing markets list. Trying to determine which markets will have the best performance next year is an impossible task. It's better to recognize that a diversified portfolio investing in different countries will benefit from the highs and lows experienced by each nation's own economic environment. International diversification is not only a great safety blanket, it can be a good strategy for growth. Historically, investors have been able to improve upon returns dramatically without any increase in risk simply by holding one-third of their stock portfolio in Canada and two-thirds internationally.

The European Story

For the same reasons that Canada and the United States experienced a "liquidity-induced" bull market during the 1990s, Europe may be beginning to experience the same thing. Until recently, Europe was (like Canada seven years ago) suffering from a very slow economy, very high unemployment, and unconscionably high interest rates (designed to defend each local currency's value).

Source: Ibbotson

Gradually, and thanks to a series of events, European interest rates have begun to fall. The European situation has mirrored Canada's in other ways. New legislation to support corporate restructuring was effective in kicking the Canadian economy out of recession. European corporate restructuring has provided the economic engine there, as well.

Also, while European currencies have been weakening (just like the Canadian dollar has been since 1991), interest rates have been falling and, not surprisingly, company profits and stock prices have been on the move. Today, because of the lag in their economic cycle, Europe looks like an excellent diversification candidate.

A Word on Asset Allocation Programs

Recognizing the powerful benefit to be had by simply diversifying client accounts properly, the brokerage industry has developed lots of services to do it for you. That's good.

But sometimes you have to watch out, because the good and necessary services are bundled with very expensive in-house product. That's bad.

Here's how it works. Your advisor suggests a simple way for you to achieve instant diversification and professional management on your entire portfolio. You'll also get automatic rebalancing — which, your broker adds, will improve your returns.

Then he churns you out of all your current funds and into his house funds, which

a. cost a lot more;

b. pay a much fatter commission; and

c. are proprietary — so you lose the independent monitor you had.

That said, it's important to recognize that diversification is easy to achieve, and working with an advisor is almost always very rewarding.

My real issue with these in-house managed account programs is that they're just a slick way of selling you new funds that don't have a track record. In-house funds are a great deal for the broker, who gets to keep both the manufacturing profit and the distribution profit. But your needs get squeezed, because you went to an independent broker for independent advice. More and more, advisors' incentives are geared toward selling the house funds, which is all these fancy new vehicles are — pooled, prospectused mutual funds.

So to get the best of both worlds (good funds and good services), simply ask for the best services. You can use the asset allocation suggestions from any profiling questionnaire without buying the funds they're tied to. Then tweak your mix of currently held funds to meet the asset mix that was suggested for you. Or choose new funds from the universe of available choices.

Smoke and Mirrors

When is a four percent annual management expense ratio on a fund considered a bargain? When it only costs investors two percent after tax.

That's the claim being made by some of today's mutual fund substitutes, which go by the more exclusive-sounding "wrap account" or "managed account" monikers. The hot new products have an unusual way of collecting their management fees: They charge investor accounts directly.

It sounds simple. But it can be misleading. The controversial billing method is widely touted as being a real positive, because investors actually get a tax receipt for the fees paid (which is certainly not the case with normal mutual funds). But the advantage of tax-deductible fees is a myth. The nature of the billing doesn't result in any advantage when compared with mutual fund fees. Charging fees directly is fine in and of itself; chopping the fee in half to disguise its real after-tax cost is just a game of smoke and mirrors.

There are other problems that can arise from this direct-billing scheme, too — particularly in the area of calculating performance. Let me start with the basic rules for mutual funds. A fund takes its fee right off the top, from the pool of assets. So the returns quoted on funds are always calculated after the deduction of those fees. It's the law.

Let's consider a simplified example. Imagine that a fund and a wrap account both gross 12 percent in a year. Let's further pretend that both programs charge two percent annually in management fees and expenses. The fund earns 12 percent but takes its fee off the top, so investors only see the net return of 10 percent. Even funds with a capital appreciation mandate get this deduction "at source," as it were. They simply deduct the amount of fees from their year-end distribution.

(Mutual funds and wrap accounts must distribute any net realized gains earned in the year, as well as all dividends and interest earned. For mutual funds, the deduction of management fees "at source" simply diminishes the size of the taxable distribution.)

The managed account, by comparison, gives you the full 12 percent. You see the gross return. But then you get billed separately for the two percent. Since you pay for it separately, you get a tax receipt for it (all of this assumes that yours is a taxable account). Your tax receipt is hyped as some big advantage, when it isn't. That's because investors in the managed account have more gain to declare. The tax deduction merely takes them back to the net position of the mutual fund investor.

It's a serious issue, because some of the most successful of these wrap accounts are using the mythical mechanics of this tax-deductibility advantage to help justify fees that are out of this world. All charge way more than you'd pay for a comparable mutual fund — some charge twice as much.

Don't get me wrong. Lots of great wrap accounts exist. My beef is with the confusion created by a wrap account that's technically a mutual fund. Some of these aren't that bad, and lots of good financial advisors sell these products without hyping this tax angle. Still, confusion over the fees and tax benefits is rampant. The attached table shows how a few of these programs bill their fees.

Let me point out that many mutual fund substitutes represent a good deal over the real thing. Some income trusts, closed end funds, and segregated wrap accounts are examples of areas where investors are better off bypassing mutual funds.

But the pooled, prospectused products that call themselves managed accounts do skirt the reporting and disclosure rules that all mutual funds are supposed to abide by — which is a problem for the average investor.

My advice: Compare fees on an apples-to-apples basis before deciding to plonk down $100,000 in a managed account program. If the fee seems high, then it probably is.

While technically mutual funds, these managed accounts don't report fees and performance in the standard fashion:

Program	Fees Off the Top	Charged Directly to Client	Total
Nesbitt Burns	0	2.50%	2.50%
Harmony	0.60%	2.25%	2.85%
Optima Strategy	0.41%	3.30%	3.71%
Sovereign	0	2.50%	2.50%

Source: Prospectus filings and company material. All fees are for a balanced investment mix.

Diversify by Management Style

Management styles can vary dramatically — especially in equity fund investing. I have provided a style matrix for each of my FundMonitor picks, which are profiled in Chapter 9.

So to achieve extra diversification within a particular category, select funds with different — and thus complementary — styles.

"Value" and "growth" styles are excellent complements, for example. The chart on page 42 shows the complementary performances of value and growth stocks in an unmanaged index. Managers of the growth and value disciplines will perform well at different times.

Getting More Foreign Content Inside Your RRSP

Bay Street lawyers have been in a panic to finalize prospectuses for novel new funds that have found a better way to skirt the foreign content limits on registered savings plans. At least ten major fund companies are rolling out new, fully RSP-eligible clones of their most popular foreign funds.

How do they do it? With a new twist on derivatives. I call it an "RSP wrapper," but it's really just a special kind of derivative contract written between the fund company and an investment bank. It's very cool because it's the first derivative-based structure that actually lets us own our favorite foreign funds — instead of indexes.

The strategy is an aggressive new interpretation of an old Revenue Canada rule that says we're not supposed to hold more than 20 percent of our RSP in foreign securities. The Street has lobbied for years that the 20 percent limit should be eliminated over time. But until the rules change, the lawyers are making a bundle coming up with creative new ways to get around it.

The new structure's different from the older breed of fully foreign but fully RSP-eligible funds that skirt the rules by buying options or futures on foreign stock exchange indexes. Different and better. The new approach allows for active management, reasonable fees and fewer surprises.

The older breed of foreign/RSP equity funds have had some trouble matching their index returns. Take the Canada Trust AmeriGrowth RSP Fund. It's supposed to track the S&P 500, but has lagged the index every year since inception, sometimes by more than 4 percent. That's because the manager of this and other funds of the same ilk has to stickhandle the portfolio's foreign currency exposure decision actively. That left this fund long the loonie at times when its investors would have preferred U.S. market exposure and U.S. currency exposure.

But the new cloned funds coming from AGF, C.I., Global Strategy, Mackenzie, Templeton, and others operate differently. Unitholders own a contract with rights to a basket of securities that exactly matches the securities in the underlying fund. Since the unitholders only own a contract with a domestic bank, it's deemed Canadian property. Voilà, full foreign content that's fully RSP eligible.

It seems convoluted because it is. But the upside is that you and I can now get the majority of our long-term savings invested in popular foreign funds. Getting your money outside of Canada is critical for growth, since only two per cent of the world's investment opportunities exist within our border. Some managers argue that Canada's market is cheap right now — that we're on a roll. And I agree. But over time, it's silly to think that the TSE will beat the global market.

There is a cost to all this, of course. So far, the MERs and other implicit costs on these new cloned funds are likely to be about 0.50 per cent higher than the regular foreign fund they copy. To me, that's pricey. So I say do what you can to lower the rest of your costs to make up for the hefty fees you'll pay on these foreign clones. That way, your overall MER will be reasonable — and you'll get more foreign diversification. Which is ideal for anyone, but remarkable for someone who's got the majority of their savings tied up in a registered plan.

Obviously you shouldn't buy these funds outside your RSP. You'd be paying higher costs and you'd get whacked with a worse tax bill than the regular fund, since these puppies earn their gains as interest income.

Even though these new vehicles share some similarities with index-linked GICs, don't confuse the two. Index-linked GICs are for ultra-conservative people because they severely limit gains in exchange for protecting capital.

Why Mutual Fund Investors are Turning to Stocks

It's more fun and it's cheaper too.

"I could do better than that" is something I'm hearing more and more today from investors frustrated with the performance of their mutual funds. Their motivation is predicated mostly on the negative attributes of funds, but in part they just think buying stocks seems like more fun.

On the negative side, they cite mutual funds' high costs and unfair taxes, and the dubious value of active management. But while these feelings have long been common at the fringe, the difference today is the speed with which the trend is spreading into the mainstream.

Mutual fund sales are way down — more than 40 percent — compared with a year ago, while the TSE is up in the same period. The U.S. market has been even stronger, but sales of U.S. equity funds were a measly $2 billion in the first half of 1999. Not that Canadian retail investors aren't buying U.S. stocks — they are. But they're buying them individually, not through funds.

The reasons behind the trend away from mutual funds are obvious. Funds can be dull. And awareness of performance problems is now widespread. Fund investors, you see, haven't done all that well in the past four years, despite the surging index levels. That's because most fund money went in either at the wrong time or in the wrong funds. If you're like most, you probably feel the frustration. It isn't so much that your funds have bombed — they haven't. It's just that, well, you figured they'd do better. You buy funds to beat the market. Period. And these days, most don't.

This expectations gap is exacerbated by today's unusual bi-polar market action. At one extreme there are the few huge, hot stocks — the half-dozen or so big-cap names whose explosive performance has alone accounted for an amazing 80 per cent of the market's return since 1998. But at the other extreme are the 290-odd names that are in something of a bear market.

Hey, high flyers like BCE and Nortel make up a whopping 22 percent of the TSE 100 Index. So very, very few active managers have even a market weight in the darlings of the day. It's no wonder, then, that people are losing faith in active management. In many ways, I see their point. Maybe we should own a core set of big, blue-chip stocks just like the index — something to buy and hold forever.

So why buy funds? They cost too much compared with management fee-free alternatives like TIPs, which are exchange-traded units of the 35 companies that make up the TSE 35 Index. Holding some of these will reduce your overall management fee burden when averaged over your whole portfolio — a concept that's gaining more and more attention.

You only need mutual funds for two reasons: Diversification and professional management. So in areas where you need neither, lots of people are now choosing individual securities. Beyond index baskets (like TIPs and their foreign equivalents) that trade like stocks, there are other ways to augment a mutual fund portfolio with individual securities. Domestic government bonds, for example, are fairly easy to pick and manage. Ditto for a portfolio of blue-chip preferred shares.

Or perhaps you work in, say, the medical device business. Why not research a few of your suppliers and competitors? You probably already know more about their business prospects than the Street — so you can make good money while you learn and have fun.

Brokerage firms are catering to this crowd by offering defined portfolios of individual stocks, sold and tracked as though they're a single bundle. It's a hybrid way of giving people the benefits of individual stock ownership without the headaches of trading. And by packaging the stocks together, they're trying to be sure to sell stocks that aren't just good, they're good together.

If I'm right about these trends, then mutual funds may find themselves relegated to the role of running only specialty, small-cap, or global funds — the areas where we need diversification and professional management. In fact, those are the areas where active management still reigns — even in a tough environment like the one we're in now.

5 Investor Behaviour and Why It Matters

WRONG QUESTION: WHICH FUND SHOULD I buy? Right question: Can I hold onto this mix of funds for a long time?

Everyone screws up the sell decision. Instead of selling for logical reasons, they tend to sell for irrational, emotional reasons. It's good to punt a bad fund, but it's bad to sell just because a fund went down, or because it finally returned to your original purchase price.

Yet these are precisely the motivations behind most people's exit moves. To see how big a problem investor behaviour really is, just consider the difference between our index of investor performance versus fund performance: 90 percent of precious metals funds investors, for example, have underperformed their funds.

The research shows that in the aggregate, people simply don't do as well as their funds, having underperformed by more than three percentage points annually for the last decade.

Over time, the funds do fine; the people don't. Here's why.

First, people systematically buy high. Remember that the only way to actually earn, say, the ten-year rate of return posted for a fund is to have bought it ten years ago and held it until today. That's very rare.

But the ten-year rate of return and the other compound average rates of return are used to sell funds, and they're used only when their funds' performance is peaking (as we saw in Chapter 3). So, really, investors buy in because of a systematic problem. They buy when optimism is high and the fund is hyped — when things look as if they've always been rosy.

The trouble is that's often at the top.

And the first part of the age-old axiom on investment wisdom is to buy low. So investors have already violated the first half of that rule when they get sucked into a hot fund.

The second reason that investors underperform their own good funds is that, at the margin, at least, they tend to sell low. Often because of a panic (though few see it as such at the time). Because expectations have been set so high through advertising, optimistic journalism, and an overexcited sales force, lots of people just have no idea that the fund they own could go down by so much. When it does, they're horrified. It's one thing to tell new investors that mutual funds are a long-term investment, and quite another to tell them up front that there's a distinct possibility this fund may occasionally lose a third of its value.

People buy funds on the basis of seeing only average returns, which generally show double-digit performance over every conceivable time frame (short-term, long-term, you name it). So they expect the fund to continue like this in the future. Why shouldn't they?

After all, they've had no exposure to some of the basic truths you'll find in this book: this fund lost, say, 24 percent of its value during its biggest drop; it's been a dog in bear markets; it spent three years recovering to break even after its biggest drop; and it has underperformed GICs over half of its history.

In a Better World

Knowing such messy details might scare some investors away from buying a fund, but at least those who did buy would be pre-qualified. They'd understand that even great funds suffer frequent temporary setbacks, and they'd understand that the only way to get positive double-digit rates of return over time is simply to buy and hold. And hold. If things go down, you hold — or buy more. Selling after a fall thus violates the second part of the "buy low, sell high" axiom.

Enough people are guilty of failing at least one of these tests to drag down aggregate investor returns considerably. Investors' underperformance is most profound in the riskiest categories, like resources and precious metals, and other sector funds. Interestingly, the worst culprits for this "buying high, selling low" syndrome are investors in no-load funds, including those in some terrific ones now available in Canada. It seems that the marketing machine that uses advertising exclusively to push its funds is the very same machine that poisons the performance of the individual investor. I see big problems with not disclosing this downside risk; my fear is that the industry will be shooting itself in the foot if it just keeps selling funds instead of truly educating people about the importance of riding through downturns.

6 New Strategies for the Thrifty Investor

FUND FEES ARE CHANGING RIGHT BEFORE our eyes. Not so much to make things cheaper (the approach I would have preferred), just to make them more visible and more honest. Brokers and planners are starting to sell dirt-cheap funds and add in a modest fee for all their advice and planning work. It's called "unbundling" the MER to strip out the cost of advice — which typically accounts for about half the annual levy of every load fund in Canada.

It used to be that "no-load" meant "no help." Brokers wouldn't even accept orders for no-load funds, let alone recommend them.

But now a shift is migrating north from the United States, where an independent advisor is actually, well, an independent advisor. Soon you'll be buying cheap no-load funds from your favorite pro, without the six-year commitment. There is a catch, of course, but the shift is a big plus for consumers.

First, a little background. Five or ten years ago it was easy for advisors to sell load funds and earn a five percent upfront commission. Most people were in GICs. So a guy with savings of $50,000 was a potential $2,500 commission. Why sell no-loads?

But now, as accounts have swelled, the compensation gap between load and no-load is narrowing. Now many no-load funds even pay a modest trailer of 0.25 percent annually — which is pretty decent when you figure that the five percent upfront commission is now very tough to earn.

The problem is saturation. Let's say you've got $200,000. Odds are that you already own a bunch of funds. So nobody's gonna talk you into new funds — because that would require selling everything you've got. Selling everything is a bad move because it often triggers nasty tax bills and deferred sales charge penalties. So the current system of big upfront compensation is flawed in today's saturated marketplace. Under the current system, brokers have a big incentive to try to churn you out of decent fund families and into something brand new — where they can earn that five percent up front. Since few people go for this, brokers end up only holding the assets — which pays far less than churning them.

Your Advocate

A better system would simply reward the advisor for helping you manage what you've already got — even if it means no transactions are necessary. Such a system would ideally make your planner your advocate, your shopper. If the planner were really working for you, then it would be in his or her interest to find you the very best funds — which are sometimes the cheapest funds. That's why this new flat-fee concept is so popular in the States. There, advisors charge something like one percent a year to offer advice on the account and to do reporting, tax planning and hand holding. That's the catch.

For that price, the advisor hunts aggressively for the best funds at the lowest possible MER. It's a highly sophisticated marketplace (like ours in some ways), so shopping really pays dividends. And who better to shop for you than an insider? The net result is that clients end up with unbundled fees: cheap MER funds and a separate fee for advice. Since it's easy to build a bare-bones, no-load portfolio for an average MER of about one percent annually, the sum of the advice fee and the fund fees is two percent. Two percent annually is a fifth cheaper than a typical balanced fund today. But with these unbundled advice fees, there are no DSC commitments to make, no bias in fund selection, and no incentive to churn.

Better still, the shift to asset-based advice fees will force advisors to be more sensitive about total costs and their impact on returns over time. Plus, to justify any new fees, advisors will have to somehow get the average MER down without triggering penalties. That's no small feat, but the benefits can be enormous.

One way load fund companies will retain market share through this new shift is by launching new "stripped" versions of their funds: clones that pay no trailer and no upfront commission. Since those two items constitute about half of the MER now, the new lean funds' MERs will probably fall by half — making them look great against the current field of no-loads.

In the end, this new pricing won't save people a bundle — as you can see from that typical total cost of two percent. But it will improve accountability while offering more flexibility than we currently have.

The rest of this chapter lays out a couple of ideas that you can use to help cut costs irrespective of how your advisor's fees change. The key is to use your knowledge to help you get a good deal and make a sound decision about what you need and what's available.

Doing It Yourself

I should point out a bias. Most of my firm's revenue comes from selling software to financial advisors. I'm therefore biased towards the advice channel. Of course, the reason I sell them my stuff is that I just don't think investors ought to be doing this stuff themselves. It's complicated and ever-changing. Besides, the cost of the advice isn't that high — especially if you're savvy about it.

So I'm not the best one to see if you want to do it yourself. I appreciate that picking funds doesn't have to be complicated. And I recognize that some advisors are awful and don't add value. But wow, can you tell me that you're sure you've taken advantage of every tax-planning opportunity available to you? I doubt it. Having someone around that does this stuff for a few hundred people is a good idea. If you do want to do it yourself, there's only one rule. Do it as cheaply as possible while getting the best research possible. Try not to get so sucked into it you spend all your time reading, researching, and trying to eke out that extra nickel. Go play golf. Have fun. If investing is fun for you, then that's okay too. Maybe you should get into the business.

Unbundling to Go Passive

You do the math: Half the assets in a typical balanced fund are sitting around in bonds yielding 5.5 percent, tops. The average management expense ratio for the group is 2.2 percent. Thus, half the portfolio has a net yield of just 3.3 percent. Forget about big capital gains rescuing these funds — it won't happen. Even the long Canada bond that matures in the summer of 2029 only yields 5.8 percent at the time of writing. Will it fall dramatically? Don't hold your breath.

So the best-selling category of funds this year is doomed. Investors bought in — as they always do — because the historic returns have been fabulous. And why not? Interest rates have been falling for 17 years.

Times have been so good for balanced funds for so long that until the past few months, I couldn't even calculate and assign what I call down market grades for any fund in the group — because there hadn't been any down markets. In fact, until last summer, there hadn't been a double-digit decline in nearly two decades — since the bull market for bonds began.

If you remember only one thing about balanced funds, make it this: Balanced funds are stock funds in disguise. They carry all the risk of stocks, but mask it by hiding under a coat of interest rate sensitivity that makes them dangerous in certain markets. Like when rates are rising. But guess what: That's just when bonds run out of steam, so the diversification inherent in balanced funds is a bit of a myth.

Of course, the premium pricing of balanced funds is also problematic. Dig this: Great-West Life has a stock fund and a bond fund with management expense ratios of 2.83 and 2.26 percent, respectively. They also offer a balanced fund whose assets are split about evenly between stocks and bonds. But instead of the MER for the balanced fund being an average of the MERs for the two funds from which it derives, it charges more. More, in fact, than either of the other two.

The larger pricing problem for funds in this category, however, is more structural. You'll hear me say it again and again: It's silly to pay for the active management of bonds. Canada's $300-billion mutual fund industry was premised on the notion that you need diversification and professional management. A mutual fund pool provides just that. And for stock funds, it works. You really wouldn't want to own just one or two stocks — the risk would be too high. And picking stocks yourself is tricky because most people simply can't match the time and resources of a pro.

But with domestic government bonds, those arguments in favour of pooling go right out the window. Do you really need the diversification that comes from owning the Canada bond of 2003 and the issue maturing in 2006? Not really. And do you really need some Bay Street crackerjack bond trader picking your bonds for you? Again, not really.

In fact, actively managed fixed income portfolios are seldom very actively managed. You can't blame the managers. Most of their assets are run for big pension clients paying just one quarter of a percentage point in annual fees. So there's much, much more room to add value. If they can shift into bonds maturing, say, just one year later, then a little rate drop can be a comparatively big win.

But in the bond portion of balanced funds, there's no way for even the best manager to add enough value to make up for expenses of 2.2 percent. No way at all, especially in this low-yield environment. The message for investors is clear. After an incredible run in the bond market, there's simply no choice. It's time to unbundle your expensive balanced funds by switching half the money into an equity fund and the other half into bonds directly.

Get a Grip on Your Bonds

Yup, just buy a bond or two. A midterm maturity of five years or so is fine. Buy it and hold it. You'll earn a respectable 5.8 percent, guaranteed. I know, it doesn't look like much compared with the 10.6 percent 15-year return shown for a typical bond fund — but returns like that are history. Almost any firm can sell you a bond, not just big full-service stock brokers. So it pays to ask. But remember that I'm not calling for a shift in anyone's asset mix, just a change in what you pay for fixed income management. Get help if you need it to figure out how you can switch your funds around without triggering redemption fees or taxable gains.

Buying Individual Stocks

This section is for you if you are interested in trying your own hand at picking stocks but don't know where to start. I'll discuss some of the details you should consider before going it alone. And keep in mind that the whole process is definitely worth a second thought. For those who remain undaunted, there's a simple stock-picking strategy (based on a value-oriented large-company approach) that has performed well over the last decade. The strategy generates two mechanical, disciplined portfolios (called Sensible Starters and Super Starters), which are geared to those who are just starting out.

There are two main points that you need to consider before trying to pick your own stocks. First, you should acknowledge that even the professionals find it a difficult area. Don't underrate this point. The pros spend all day trying to figure out which stocks are the best; most individual investors have busy schedules that preclude similar efforts. But, if you think you can beat the pros (or at least want to try), continue on. The second point is a crucial one and has to do with the expenses related to stock-picking. To pick your own stocks you'll have to pay a commission when buying or selling; you'll end up paying for materials such as books and newspapers; and you'll spend time researching and selecting your stocks. So sit down and figure out if picking your own stocks is likely to be cost effective. Equity mutual funds typically charge about two percent per year for the managers' expertise. On the other hand, managing your own stock portfolio can easily cost more than $1,000 per year (we'll say $300 on newspapers and books, $300 in time spent, and $400 on commissions).

Mutual funds, then, represent great value for those with small amounts of money (say, less than $25,000); but for those with larger portfolios stock-picking *may* be worth it. In any event, try to be realistic about the costs and difficulties associated with picking your own stocks before giving it a try.

Rein In

When just starting out you should use "risk capital" to finance your endeavors. Your initial forays will be a learning experience. Don't even remotely endanger your retirement while learning the ropes. The amount to be allocated is something to discuss with your financial planner, but it ought to be limited to about 10 percent of your savings.

Two Variations on the Model

There are two variations of our stock-picking method. The Sensible Starters portfolio is designed for the more conservative investor with at least $25,000. The Super Starters portfolio is designed for the aggressive investor and requires a more modest $5,000.

When it comes to a stock selection method for beginners, it's ideal to stick to large, well-known Canadian companies. These companies should also have large profits and large dividends, and should happen to be selling at low prices. Other plusses: keeping the expenses down (which implies infrequent trading); using an inexpensive source of research and using a plan that requires relatively little time and effort. Sounds like quite a challenging proposition, doesn't it? Fortunately, it is possible to get all of these fine attributes and obtain a stock portfolio that does remarkably well.

The Starters portfolios stick to large and well-known Canadian companies, since they are easy to keep track of (i.e., they are often in the press). Furthermore, these companies are not nearly as subject to instances of manipulation and fraud as smaller companies are. The motivation for seeking companies with large profits should be self-explanatory, since the conservative investor would like to see good profits today instead of the hoped-for, but often illusory, profits of tomorrow. Dividends are payments made by the company to stockholders. High payments indicate strength in a company (particularly in combination with large earnings). Price is a natural concern — obviously, you'd like to purchase at a low price and sell at a higher one. It's hard to forecast the selling price, so we'll try to compensate by making sure to buy on the cheap. Expenses will be kept in check by relying on the material presented here and infrequent trading.

Here's the Starter method:

- Talk with your financial planner to make sure that this is the right thing for you to do.
- Start with the stocks in the TSE 35 index, which is composed of 35 of the largest and most actively traded companies in the country (see Table 1).
- Look up the dividend yield (labeled "Yield"), price-to-earnings ratio ("P/E"), and price ("Close") of each of these companies in the *Globe and Mail*. Throw out any stock with a dividend yield of zero percent, or with a negative or zero P/E ratio. Such stocks pay no dividends or they have no profits.
- For each stock that remains, calculate its Value Ratio (VR): Divide its price-to-earnings ratio by its dividend yield. The lower the Value Ratio, the better. Low ratios imply high profits, high dividends and low prices.
- Create each portfolio.

  The Sensible Starter portfolio is composed of equal dollar amounts of each of the five lowest VR stocks.

  The Super Starter portfolio is composed of the lowest VR stock (so it isn't, strictly speaking, a portfolio).
- Buy the stocks through your low-cost financial planner or discount broker.

Table 1

Stocks in the TSE 35		
Abitibi-Consolidated (A)	Dofasco (DFS)	Placer Dome (PDG)
Alcan (AL)	Imasco (IMS)	Renaissance Energy (RES)
Bank of Montreal (BMO)	INCO (N)	Royal Bank (RY)
Bank of Nova Scotia (BNS)	Laidlaw (LDM)	Seagram (VO)
Barrick Gold (ABX)	Macmillan Bloedel (MB)	Suncor Energy (SU)
BCE Inc (BCE)	Magna International (MG.A)	Talisman Energy (TLM)
Bombardier (BBD.B)	Moore Corp (MCL)	TD Bank (TD)
Cdn. Occidental Petrol. (CXY)	National Bank (NA)	Teck Corp (TEK.B)
Canadian Pacific (CP)	Noranda (NOR)	Thomsom Corp (TOC)
Canadian Tire (CTR.A)	Nortel Networks (NT)	Transalta (TA)
CIBC (CM)	Nova Chemicals (NCX)	Transcanada Pipelines (TRP)
CN Rail (CNR)	Petro-Canada (PCA)	(See www.tse.com.)

- Wait for a year and sell your stocks, and go through steps 1 through 7 again.

That's the method. Check out Table 2 to see how it has performed over the past decade. The Sensible Starters portfolio chalked up an impressive average annual gain of 17.1 percent, which beat the index by 5.7 percent per year! Not only did the Sensible Starters perform well, but with a reasonable amount of diversification its annual returns managed to have higher highs (47.2 percent vs. 30.0 percent) and higher lows (–6.6 percent vs. –11.6 percent) than the index.

The Super Starters portfolio had a blistering 20.52 percent average annual gain, which was a remarkable 9.1 percent improvement on the index. However, since it contains only one stock, it suffered from a larger variation in returns. Its highest high was an amazing 79.6 percent gain, but its lowest low was a disappointing –25.9 percent. So although the Super Starters portfolio has done very well, it's only for those with a strong stomach.

You can estimate the total cost of the Sensible Starters method to be about $300 and $100 for the Super Starters (i.e., $25 per trade plus $50 for time and resources). These costs are equivalent to what an average Canadian equity fund would charge on a $15,000 portfolio and on a $5,000 portfolio, respectively.

The last row in Table 2 shows the result of a $25,000 initial investment in each portfolio (including commissions of $25 per trade). These results should help to motivate those interested in trying their own hands at stock picking, and hopefully will intrigue even the seasoned investor.

Table 2

Annual Percentage Return of the TSE 35 and the Starter Portfolios

Year	Sensible Starters	Super Starters	TSE 35
1988-1989	23.03%	13.81%	11.32%
1989-1990	19.02%	22.59%	21.89%
1990-1991	–0.51%	5.97%	–11.65%
1991-1992	46.86%	79.56%	11.01%
1992-1993	-3.02%	–25.93%	–3.58%
1993-1994	12.15%	28.83%	24.34%
1994-1995	–2.21%	1.84%	5.52%
1995-1996	14.84%	6.54%	14.47%
1996-1997	30.79%	15.34%	30.01%
1997-1998	47.20%	72.94%	16.38%
1998-1999	–6.55%	–9.68%	–0.09%
1999 to July 21	23.98%	34.43%	15.59%
Average :	17.13%	20.52%	11.43%
High :	47.20%	79.56%	30.01%
Low :	–6.55%	–25.93%	–11.65%
Beats the TSE35 :	8 times out of 12	7 times out of 12	
Growth of $25,000:	$145,408.92	$166,356.02	$84,125.78

7 The Rubber Meets the Road: *Building or Rebuilding Your Mutual Fund Portfolio*

IN THIS SECTION, I WILL WORK THROUGH A profiling system and look at some mutual fund case studies.

The first part of this chapter outlines a questionnaire that *Worth* magazine has allowed me to print here. This questionnaire is the result of an exclusive study with Roper/Starch Worldwide. I believe that the personality profiles that result from this questionnaire offer powerful insights into identifying which kind of portfolio is right for individual investors.

It's a simple exercise. Fill in your best responses to the questionnaire to determine your own "money personality." The results will provide the basis for building your best portfolio solution. You can then determine what kind of investment portfolio would be right for you.

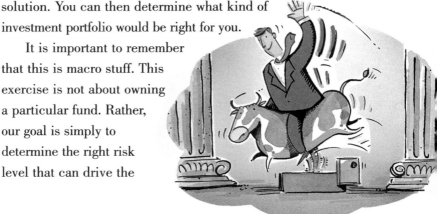

It is important to remember that this is macro stuff. This exercise is not about owning a particular fund. Rather, our goal is simply to determine the right risk level that can drive the best asset mix to meet your objectives. Later, we'll take a look at some case studies. Finally, we examine one investor's model portfolio, which we will redesign to match the investor's profile, and to "power up" his growth potential.

Duff's Tips

Small Investors Aren't as Bad at Choosing Stocks as Most People Think. They're Worse.

Not long ago, a U.S. study of 97,000 trades in 1000 randomly selected accounts from one discount brokerage firm demonstrated that people generally sell the stocks they should be buying and buy the turkeys they ought to be selling.

Does time eventually prove them right? Nope. The effect becomes even more pronounced as the time after the trade increases from four months to a year, and then to two years. This startling result, which is measured before commissions, argues strongly that mutual funds — with their professional management and efficient trading — are an excellent alternative for individual investors.

After Two Years

Stocks sold increased by	2.9%
Stocks bought declined by	0.7%
Difference	3.6%

The Questionnaire

An exclusive Worth/Roper study. Republished by permission of *Worth*.

A. Which expresses how you feel?

- I'd rather be safe than sorry in my investment decisions. 0
- I believe in taking financial risks. 1

If you answered 1, then you are a hunter.

If you answered 0, go on to question B.

B. Which do you agree with?

- When it comes to money, a person has to look out for himself or herself first. 0
- Even with financial matters, it is important to think of others before yourself. 1

If you answered 0, continue to question C.

If you answered 1, skip to question G.

C. Wealth makes a person more attractive.

(1 = disagree completely; 7 = agree completely)

1 2 3 4 5 6 7

If you answered 1, 2, 3, 4, or 5, continue to question D.

If you answered 6 or 7, then you are a striver.

D. Which expresses how you feel?

- I most enjoy buying luxury items. 0
- I most enjoy buying things that are practical and sensible. 1

If you answered 0, then you are a splurger.

If you answered 1, then skip to question F.

E. With money, I feel that it is more important to plan for the future than to enjoy what I have now.

(1 = disagree completely; 7 = agree completely)

1 2 3 4 5 6 7

If you answered 1, 2, or 3, then you are a nester. If you answered 4, continue to question F. If you answered 5, 6, or 7, then you are a gatherer.

F. How do you feel about assessing your options when it comes to buying life insurance?

1. Quite competent
2. Somewhat competent
3. Uncertain
4. At a loss

If you answered 1, 2, or 3, then you are a gatherer. If you answered 4, then you are a nester.

G. My top priority is to get ahead financially.

(1 = disagree completely; 7 = agree completely)

1 2 3 4 5 6 7

If you answered 1 or 2, then you are an idealist. If you answered 3 or 4, then continue to question H. If you answered 5, 6, or 7, then you are a protector.

H. Rate your competence when choosing an investment.

1. Quite competent
2. Somewhat competent
3. Uncertain
4. At a loss

If you answered 1 or 2, then you are a protector.

If you answered 3 or 4, then you are an idealist.

Write your money personality here

________________.

For a discussion of what each money personality means, see the sidebar on page 71.

Money Personality

Whatever your money personality, of course, your current financial situation will also determine the components of your portfolio.

Now take what you've learned about yourself and let's look at our Portfolio Builder chart on page 80.

For example, let's say that you have learned that you are a "hunter." You'll see your money personality profiled, and designated by a colour bar on the risk/return arc.

Below, I have identified a model asset allocation for you. This portfolio is the result of our "optimization analysis." This sophisticated financial engineering looks at historic returns, risk, and the correlation between different kinds of investments to determine which mix would have been best, historically, to achieve the highest return possible from one of the five levels of risk.

The Efficient Frontier

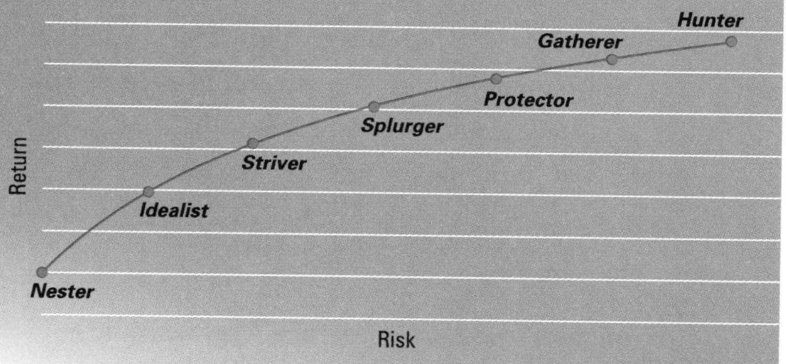

Hunter
Gatherer
Protector
Splurger
Striver
Return
Idealist
Nester
Risk

	Nester	Idealist	Striver	Splurger	Protector	Gatherer	Hunter
Canadian Equity	20	20	20	25	25	25	25
US Equity	10	10	20	20	20	20	20
International Equity	0	0	0	10	20	30	40
Bonds	35	45	55	40	30	20	10
Cash	35	25	5	5	5	5	5
Best Year*	26%	29%	36%	37%	38%	41%	42%
Worst Year*	–1%	–2%	–5%	–8%	–10%	–13%	–14%
Biggest Drop	5%	5%	7%	12%	15%	19%	20%
Months to recover	7	14	18	20	21	22	23
% of time this portfolio lost money*	1%	1%	5%	8%	9%	11%	11%

*(12 month rolling return)

If you need investment money within the next two to three years, or if you are especially bearish, your model portfolio will need to be tweaked to be more conservative (left on the scale).

If you are very bullish, or have many years to invest, you may want to lean to the right of your recommended model, just to customize the asset mix for your personal situation.

The optimization that I've used for this book and that I use in my work is special because it doesn't use traditional risk measures to quantify the pain of risk. My system uses some complex formulas to derive a common sense assessment of a fund's risk of loss — how often, how likely, how severe, how long to recover. This is what dramatically sets apart this strategic asset allocation system from others which use standard deviation — an old-fashioned idea of risk — as the basis for measuring risk.

Model Portfolios

Forget age minus your shoe size. Today's more sophisticated methods allow for deep, introspective psychological profiling. And that's more than mumbo-jumbo. We've been looking at how values, habits, and goals influence your satisfaction with a given investment portfolio. Since future market returns aren't known (but historic relationships and risk are), we can develop an asset allocation whose risk profile is right for you.

Younger Investor — Average Aggressiveness

Nicole, 23 years old, recently received about $100,000 through an insurance settlement. Her job provides her with enough income to support her lifestyle. Nicole is in a 39 percent marginal tax bracket. She doesn't know a lot about investing, but she's eager to learn and wants to put her money to work. While she is willing to take some risks, a drop of 10 to 12 percent in the value of her investments is about as much as she can handle. Nicole says that if there was another major crash, she wouldn't be comfortable buying more, but she definitely wouldn't sell. We've assessed her as a Splurger.

Profiles of Each Money Personality

Nesters This type of person doesn't care much about managing money. Nesters equate money with comfort, not security. They aren't interested in leaving money for their kids, but rather in living for today. These individuals really don't have much in the way of investments and just want to get by. Nesters do not believe that a person's wealth is equated with his or her worth.

Idealists Idealists are generous, thrifty people who don't much care for money. They wouldn't be devastated by a losing investment — but then again they're not that likely to be involved much in investing. For them money means security, not happiness.

Strivers Strivers are controlled by money and would feel terrible if they lost a nickel. For these individuals, money equals happiness. They believe that luck or connections produce wealth. The striver is not a big saver and generally isn't sophisticated in financial or investment matters.

Splurgers Splurgers buy luxuries. They are also quite risk-averse. These individuals are hunters but without the financial acumen. They appreciate those who appreciate the best, and aren't very practical.

Protectors Protectors put others first. They are financially savvy and have adequate insurance, or more. They are competent, stable, and think of others first in financial affairs.

Gatherers Gatherers do not have the highest income, but are miserly and wise in many ways. They look out for themselves, are conservative investors, and can afford to recognize and embrace long-term risk in investing. Gatherers are usually comfortable with their ability to choose investments. For them, money equals security.

Hunters Hunters are high-income individuals who are aggressive about making, spending, and investing their money. Sometimes hunters are extravagant, and they generally equate money with happiness, achievement, or power. Hunters feel comfortable choosing investments and believe that it takes intelligence and guts to produce wealth.

Her target asset allocation is as follows:

- Canadian equities 25%
- U.S. equities 20%
- International equities 10%
- Fixed income 40%
- Cash 5%

Based on Nicole's situation and investor profile, here's the portfolio we've recommended for her:

$20,000	Bissett Canadian Equity
$ 9,000	Mawer New Canada
$20,000	Maxxum American Equity
$40,000	McLean Budden Fixed Income
$11,000	Templeton Growth

January 1997 to August 31, 1999:

Average MER:	1.4%
Average annual return:	12.78%
Best year:	32.5%
Worst year:	–6.74%
% of time lost money:	12.77%
Biggest drop:	–14.87%
Time to recover:	15 months

Older Investors — More Conservative

John and Mary Ann are both 63. They are retired, and each is in a 26 percent tax bracket. They have a combined portfolio worth $400,000, all in RRSPs. Their income is sufficient for their modest lifestyle. However, they are not comfortable taking much risk at all. John and Mary Ann don't ever want to lose more than six percent of their portfolio's value at any one time, and they would be almost unwilling to lose money over a one-year period. They would be happy with a seven percent annual return, as long as their risk criteria were met. We've assessed them as Nesters. As such, their target asset allocation is as follows:

- Canadian equities 20%
- U.S. equities 10%

- International equities 0%
- Fixed income 35%
- Cash 35%

Their current portfolio, while it isn't bad, costs them 1.75 percent in annual expenses and could expose them to a 14 percent drop in value:

$120,000	90 day T-bills
$ 48,000	First Canadian Asset Allocation
$ 40,000	First Canadian US Growth
$100,000	PH&N Dividend Income
$ 55,000	PH&N Short Term Bond and Mortgage
$ 37,000	Royal & Sun Alliance Balanced

Based on Mary Ann and John's situation and investor profile, here's the portfolio we've recommended for them. It calls for some simple, no-cost switches in their RSP, and offers substantial cost savings.

$120,000	90 day T-bills
$ 88,000	First Canadian Dividend
$155,000	PH&N Bond
$ 37,000	Royal & Sun Alliance US Equity

January 1997 to August 31, 1999:

Average MER:	0.9%
Average annual return:	10.16%
Best year:	21.22%
Worst year:	–2.29%
% of time lost money:	0.71%
Biggest drop:	–6.37%
Time to recover:	11 months

Case Study

Let's walk through a case study of a portfolio, rebuilt for a client I'll call Steve. Steve's responses to the questionnaire revealed that he is a Hunter. In terms of business and personal background, Steve runs a family business wholesaling vegetables, and is very confident and well informed on financial matters. He reads *The Globe and Mail* every

Three Things Some Fund Managers Won't Tell You

1. "I got my clock cleaned by missing the bank rally earlier in the year, so now I'm really swinging for the fences. I need to take some extra risks with the fund if I'm going to make my bonus for the year."
2. "I wish I had never let the marketing department talk me into launching this narrow-mandate sector fund. Sector funds sell, so now I've got a bundle to invest, but I can't sell out of this sector, and I'm bearish."
3. "I hope investors don't flood me with redemptions; I've got some big positions in illiquid stocks that I just couldn't unload in a hurry."

Three Things Your Advisor Won't Tell You

1. ***"I make great money but I'm cheaper than you think."*** Your advisor is your friend. It's natural for investors to haggle over the commissions that they pay, but instead people should be haggling for funds with lower management expenses. That way, investors would save money, year after year.
2. ***"I'm really a marketing pro — not a money manager."*** The mantra for the brokerage business today is "gathering assets." This is a good thing: it keeps advisors focused on dealing with relationships, understanding individual client needs, and providing education and service. All that leaves little time to keep up with all the mountains of research on individual stocks and sectors. Don't expect your financial advisor to see a crash coming. Expect him or her to have understood your psyche and to have structured your account to withstand a crash.
3. ***"I'd prefer to liquidate your portfolio up front, and then invest the proceeds."***
   Any advisor stands to make more if you bring in a portfolio of cash than if you bring a portfolio of good mutual funds, good dividend-paying stocks, and quality bonds. Advisors get paid to put you into new stuff, which is often hot stuff and is often unproven. But good financial advisors have your best interests at heart, so be wary when someone advises you to "sell everything."

day — studying for investment opportunities and following up on matters of general business. He earns good money and is aggressive about how he makes and spends that money. He considers himself to be somewhat extravagant and generally equates money with happiness, achievement, and power.

For Steve, who has about half of his investments within his RRSP, the best portfolio would be one way over to the right of the efficient frontier: the Hunter portfolio. Here's the asset mix from page 69: 40 percent international stock, 20 percent U.S. stock, 25 percent Canadian stock, and 15 percent in bonds and cash.

Steve's long-term horizon, low need for liquidity, and financial savvy suggest that he can withstand tough times in the market. In fact, Steve says he looks forward to a pullback so that he can have the opportunity to go and pick up some more funds.

Although he's not wildly bullish about the market right now, he has faith in the idea that being an owner of companies is far more lucrative than being a loaner to banks and others or just holding fixed income investments. Historically, the Hunter's asset mix has had the following risk characteristics (the stats for other money types are shown in the table on page 69):

Best Year: 30%
Worst Year: –11%
Biggest Drop: –16.5%
Time to recover from that slide: 16 months
% of the time one-year returns were negative: 9.2%
(using data back to 1987)

Remember that we haven't even begun to discuss specific mutual funds yet for Steve — because it doesn't really matter that much. The asset allocation is what really drives his returns. After I suggested the right type of portfolio (the asset allocation) for Steve and showed him the downside risk associated with an aggressive allocation, Steve confirmed that he was comfortable with assuming that much risk. So after getting his buy-in, I drafted the following list of funds for him.

In his RRSP he already owned $50,000 in funds from Mackenzie and Sceptre. Outside his RRSP he owned funds from GT Global, AGF, Trimark, and Templeton. Steve works with a financial advisor.

To achieve the ideal asset allocation targeted above, we needed only to make switches within his current families.

The Basics of Steve's Situation

Here are some of the basic ideas I kept in mind for Steve that apply for most other people.

1. We want to keep his fixed-income stuff inside his RRSP where it will be sheltered from its normally heavy tax burden.
2. We want to maximize the foreign content within the RRSP. If that foreign exposure plus the foreign stuff outside his registered plan doesn't add up to the target foreign exposure we identified in the

personality type, then we'll just have to get more foreign exposure inside his RRSP — beyond the government's 20 percent limit. One way to do that is through the use of fully foreign, fully RRSP-eligible funds that use derivatives. (Canada Trust, Global Strategy, and C.I. all have good choices here.) Steve didn't need to go with derivatives because he had so much savings outside his plan that he could fill up his global shopping basket there. For another option, look back at "Getting More Foreign Content Inside Your RRSP," in Chapter 4.

3. Like many people, Steve had too much in bond funds — which, frankly, are a rip in this interest rate environment (with interest rates so low, a bond fund's expenses gobble up too much of its yield right off the top).
4. Where switches are necessary, I try to first look at the tax bill he might have to pay to sell a position. Second, I try to find a good fund in the same family. Only after failing with that would I make a new sell recommendation for someone. Steve's money was all in good fund families, so the tweaking we had to do was just to improve his asset mix — we had to buy more equity funds.

The Rebuild

Here's the recommended portfolio of the best funds for Steve. The process we are describing here is just a simplified version of what you can do with the Portfolio Rebuilder worksheet to follow.

	Current Holdings		Changes Needed to Get the Right Asset Mix and Own Great Funds
RRSP Holdings	$40,000	Industrial Income	Switch to Ivy Canadian
	10,000	Sceptre International	Hold
Non-RRSP Holdings	$15,000	Trimark Income Growth	Switch to Trimark Fund
	10,000	AGF Canadian Bond	Switch to AGF Asian Growth
	10,000	GT Global Health Care	Hold
	15,000	Templeton Global Smaller Companies	Hold
Total	**$100,000**		

How to Buy in a Rich Market

Pre-authorized chequing (or PAC) plans are boring. I know. You sign up for one of these automatic monthly mutual fund purchase programs for, say, $500 a month and — yawn — you get the benefit of automatic good timing. Grade-school math shows that your fixed-dollar purchase amount goes to buy more units of the fund when prices are low and fewer when the fund is on a tear.

It's hardly a new idea, but it remains one of the most important ways to achieve success in mutual funds — systematically.

Which is, in fact, the opposite of what most people are doing today. My research shows that investors do a poor job of buying and selling mutual funds. They buy high, and too often they panic and sell when the market drops.

So for those bored with the simplistic PAC plan, here's a twist that will make your pulse quicken. It's an accelerated PAC plan.

To do it, you manually alter the pace of the purchase program according to market circumstances — spending more money when the fund is down and less when it's up.

I can't find much literature on accelerated dollar-cost averaging, but it's got lots of sex appeal, especially in a rich market. Historically this strategy would have done even better than regular fixed dollar-cost averaging, which is really saying something, because regular PAC plans are already so effective. In fact, averaging in over time almost always beats a lump sum investment — and with less risk, since not all of your capital is at stake during those first couple of years.

This new strategy accentuates the benefits of the original PAC plan concept.

You step up the program when prices are low by altering the amount of the debit from your bank account.

It's a contrarian move, because buying more as prices fall means going against the market consensus. It works only if you have a long-term view that things will turn around. But then again, if you weren't bullish about the fund over the long term, why own it at all?

And vice versa. You keep on buying when things are high — but you buy less. You reduce the amount of your original fixed-dollar PAC plan.

My twist is called the triple play. To do it, you triple the amount of your monthly purchases when prices are depressed. And you cut back the pace of your buying to one-third of the normal clip when prices are surging. Under normal circumstances, you just put in the normal amount.

To determine thresholds for "normal" and "surging," use the fund's one-year return as a yardstick. (When the one-year return is extremely strong or weak, it's often a negative indicator of future performance.)

If it's in negative territory, triple a $500 monthly purchase to $1500 a month, and leave it that way until the one-year return goes back into plus territory. That way, you really burn through your cash reserve of, say, $10,000 when prices are down — gobbling up units at off-peak prices.

When the one-year return is flying high (above 10 percent) you just slow down, trimming the purchases back to one-third of your original monthly figure. In the case of our $500 normal purchase, the trimmed-back amount would be $167 per month.

Averaging in Beats a Lump Sum Investment

Annual Return Comparison (for a $10,000 Investment)

Begun At	Lump Sum	Triple Play
Market top (8/87)	8.7%	12.0%
Market bottom (11/90)	14.8%	16.2%

Based on TSE 300 total return index

There are a few caveats to point out. First, don't let the pursuit of this strategy knock you too far away from what is a sensible overall asset mix for you. You could spin your wheels pouring money into an Asian fund now, but find by Christmas that your asset mix is so offside, any market pullback could really hurt. The strategy is best used to purchase aggressive equity funds up to the weighting that's appropriate. Then you stop.

Second, bear in mind that it takes a little work to set up one of these programs. Your advisor needs a limited power of attorney to alter the monthly purchase amount. Or, if you're doing it on your own, you'll need to pay attention to the fund's returns, then call to change the purchase amount. So the benefits only make sense with a large investment — say $50,000 or $100,000 or more.

Still, the lesson for investors is a simple one. The best time to invest is when you have the money. But to reduce risk, don't pile into the most aggressive equity fund right after it's had a run.

Portfolio Rebuilder

Current Situation				Target Asset Allocation*		
Current Asset List $	**%**	**Asset Class**	**Item**	**%**	**Asset Class**	**Change Required (+/–%)**
TOTAL		Cdn. Equity			Cdn. Equity	
		US Equity			US Equity	
		Int'l Equity			Int'l Equity	
		Bonds			Bonds	
		Cash			Cash	
$ ______	____	**Totals** ______		____		

Mutual Fund Analysis					Notes
Overall Performance (# of stars)	Grade In		Biggest Drop	Time to Recover	i.e., Cost to Sell, or Same-Family Switch Ideas
	Up Markets	Down Markets			

* from FundMonitor downside risk optimization
** considered half Cdn. Equity, half bond

8 How to Pick 'Em:

The FundMonitor System

The "Star" Score Rewards Great Performance

Overall performance: ★★★★★

If you've read the preceding chapters' examination of fund performance, you'll already know that when I go looking for this year's best funds, I'm going beyond a summary of the past year's returns.

Every fund in my FundMonitor Profiles listing has earned its place as one of the best in its fund category. Naturally, some of these funds score higher than their peers, so I've designed a ranking system that provides more specific scoring for the individual funds.

You'll notice that — like Michelin restaurant reviewers — I have used a "star" system to designate the very best performers. Each of the best funds is scored — with a maximum of five stars — on its comparative monthly rankings against peer funds.

If you are interested in a ranking for a fund that doesn't qualify as one of my FundMonitor Profiles picks, check the Ultimate Tables toward the end of the book, where I have gathered some basic research on the most popular and interesting funds.

The "star" scoring system only measures performance based on the fund's average monthly ranking. And while this provides an objective measure of performance, it's still a rather limited perspective. To make your most informed investment choice, you must supplement the star score with more qualitative data about consistency, risk, efficiency, and style.

Qualifier 1: Consistency of Performance

To qualify for my FundMonitor Profiles list, a fund must demonstrate consistency: consistent performance in good and bad markets, as well as consistency of people — that is, the people guiding the fund. The ideal, of course, would be a fund that ranked in the top "quartile" (the top 25 percent in its category) in every calendar year for the past 35 years, and whose manager and research team never changed. Although that ideal fund doesn't exist, you get the idea.

Let's examine these consistency factors:

Consistent Performance

Consistency
Year-by-year quartile ranking of this fund against only similar rivals
Total Return:

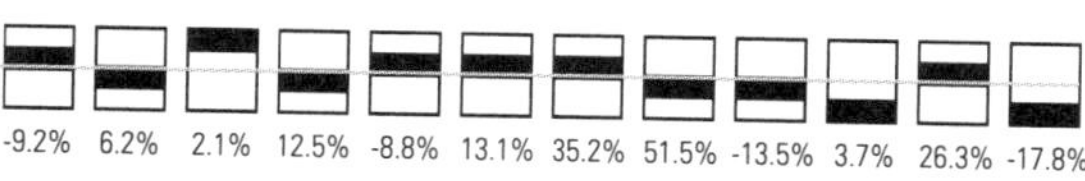

The average monthly ranking system evaluates a fund's performance history — usually since inception. My system compensates for the fact that different funds have vastly different histories. For example, if you consider that the past several years have represented the longest bull market in history, you can expect that some funds introduced during this time have had a pretty spectacular run of positive performances. An older fund that has weathered a few rough years in the beginning may not sport such a high compound return as does a younger fund.

I overcame this unfairness by deconstructing my average monthly ranking formula — examining the performance rankings of each of my profiled funds relative to those in the same group for a given number of recent time periods. The series of vertical boxes you see illustrates how the fund performed compared to its peers — for the years 1989 to 1998, and through to August 1999.

This is shown graphically as a matrix, with each column representing a calendar year (moving chronologically from left to right), and with each row representing the "performance quartile" for the time period.

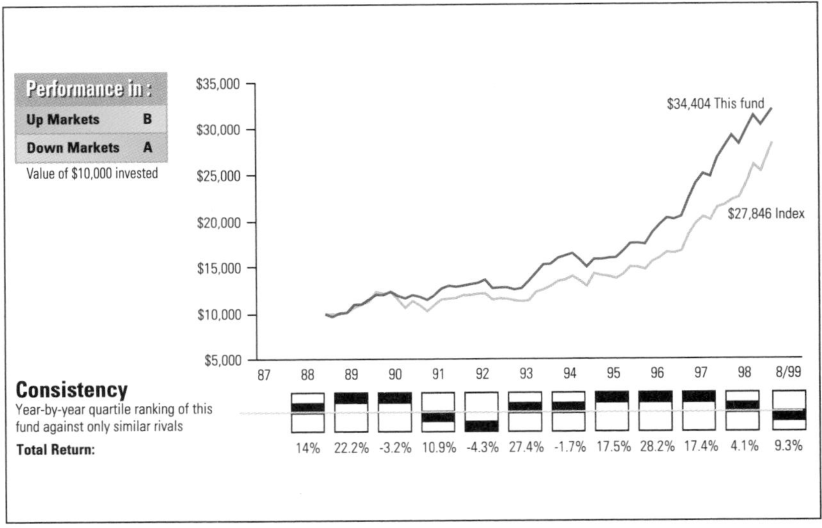

A key benefit of comparing performance over discrete (that is, non-overlapping) time periods is that it allows us to see how similar funds fared in good and bad markets.

For some very valuable insight, take a moment to compare the performance graph carefully with the consistency grid. You may see instances where the markets were down and even the performance of the fund was down, but where it still scored in the top quartile in its category. That suggests that the fund performed well in a downturn. Support for such a conclusion would come in the form of a down market grade of "A."

Look, also, for meaningful trends in a fund's performance over time. You may see that the performance of a highly ranked fund has declined over the past few years. (That was certainly true, for example, with some funds from Trimark and Altamira, before both families rocketed back to the top ever since the summer meltdown of 1998.) Or you may see that an average-ranked fund has lately picked up. Either observation may influence your investment decision.

Choosing Talent

Is it talent or luck? Some fund managers make the headlines with their spectacular performances. Does that mean that we should seek out these stars and throw our money behind them?

Not necessarily. I'd be willing to bet that the fund manager who posted the 100 percent-plus performance last year can't repeat that performance in the future.

But I do think that talent exists. I believe that some fund managers consistently outperform their counterparts in other funds. And I think that, overall, a long-term investor (and that's most of us) will do well to remain with a manager, or team, that has done well in the past.

There are talented managers out there today, but it takes some homework to find them. Look for a manager who consistently beats the market — whether the market is going up or down. Look for depth of talent in the whole management team that supports the fund. And look for evidence that sound research is informing the team's decisions. Or, let me look for you. I've gone through this process for every fund and have presented my conclusions in this book.

Consistent Management

Behind every great mutual fund performance is a dedicated group of professionals. Most investors like to put a face to their fund. They want to know something about the person or team that they are entrusting with their money. They intuitively understand that their success rests on the people factor. For this reason, watch out for frequent changes, or turnover, of management teams. When people leave, your fund becomes a different entity. In the profiles that follow, I've identified the lead manager(s) of each of my FundMonitor choices.

Finding the Good Managers and Avoiding the Bad

It takes some homework to find a talented manager, but it is possible to identify the consistently good ones. Talented managers have the following characteristics:

- they consistently beat the market;
- they are supported by a management team that demonstrates both talent and depth (it takes more than a "star" manager to run a successful fund);
- they make consistent use of sound research as part of the decision-making process.

Bad managers are easier to identify. These fund companies or individuals exhibit all the opposite characteristics of the best managers — and usually in abundance. Look for these danger signs:

- fund performance that is consistently below par, compared to its peers, or performance that swings wildly between hot and cold;
- high turnover of managers or support team members. This is a reliable indicator of an unsupportive environment, poor compensation, and/or an ineffective management structure;
- funds with high fees (often a warning signal for an ineffective structure);
- an absence of a support "team," or a shortage of analysts. You can't beat first-hand research, but you need the resources to do it effectively.

It is also important to note that a change in management does not necessarily require a switch out of your fund. In fact, my research indicates that you're better off remaining with your existing fund than following your manager to another fund. But long-term consistency of a management team is always a good sign. So if you're hunting for funds yourself, do some research. Find out how long the management team has been together and who owns a piece of the firm (and can reasonably be expected to remain). This is valuable information.

Here's a quick tip: These are five fund families with a big lineup of good funds. Their products are widely available in Canada through advisors. While some of the funds in these families are better than others, if you build a portfolio around the core holdings of these fund families, you're in good hands:

- Bissett
- Fidelity
- Mackenzie
- Templeton
- Trimark.

Behind Every Star Is a Management Firm

When we talk about a "fund manager," we usually think about the one person whose smiling photograph dominates advertising and fund communications. But these lead managers couldn't operate without the support of a team that works collaboratively to make investment decisions.

Are some firms better than others? Absolutely. Here are some guidelines for identifying a superior company.

Been around the block a few times.

Look for a fund company that's been around for at least ten years. History has shown that the economy takes about that length of time to go through a full cycle of recession, recovery, and growth. (Okay, this cycle is a little longer.) If the company has survived a full cycle, it will probably be around for a while.

Lots of money under management.

Sure, there are lots of small firms with hot little funds, but you can't beat the advantages of a good asset base. Companies with lots of money in their funds can afford to hire the best managers, they can support them with the best resources, and they have the buying power to get the best deals on significant blocks of stocks, for example. When we think of "big," we're referring to total assets of $3 billion or more for bond managers, and at least $1 billion for equity managers.

Managers stick with the company.

While there's no reason to panic if your longtime fund manager suddenly leaves (see above), a revolving door of managers is a bad sign. In general, a company should not lose more than one senior investment professional every five years. Turnover both creates and reflects problems; if fund managers are jumping ship, you should be asking some pointed questions.

Managers live where they invest.

Who is likely to know more about what is happening in southeast Asia — the guy in a Bay Street office or the woman living and working in Singapore? I've heard the arguments for and against, but I believe that fund managers who buy stocks or bonds in overseas markets can get a much better feel for opportunities and threats if they are living where they invest. Look for a firm that has offices or advisors located in the markets where it is doing business.

Minimum red tape in management structure.

Granted, it is difficult for the average investor to know how the management structure of a company affects the fund managers, but I have looked at this situation fairly closely in most fund companies. I like to see a firm that gives its individual fund managers complete and immediate authority to make buy and sell transactions as they see fit (provided, of course, that they meet the fund's mandate). A bureaucratic structure is seldom a good thing for managers. When opportunity knocks suddenly, you want to answer the door without having a committee meeting first.

Qualifier 2: Appropriate Risk

Since my system for evaluating mutual funds is based on past performance, it makes sense that the highest-flying funds (the ones that took the most risk) would have the highest rates of return over time. But that doesn't make them the most appropriate funds for investors.

In this book, I am presenting a fresh approach to measuring risk. In the FundMonitor Profiles and Ultimate Fund Tables (a summary of most of the available funds), you will find more detailed information about risk than you've ever seen before. I have augmented each fund's performance with information about the risk that they have taken to achieve that performance.

One of my ways of measuring risk is simple. If we are all going to fall in love with a fund's past performance, then why not study, measure, and compare its past risk? How has it done in tough times? How much did it lose in its biggest slide? And how long did it take to recover? I've also looked at how a currency-sensitive fund — such as a foreign fund — has performed during the tough times when the Canadian dollar is appreciating against foreign currencies.

This notion of downside risk measured in a common-sense way is all too rare in Canada. It should be an essential part of not only choosing mutual funds for Canadians, but also of setting our expectations about what we can expect in future tough periods from any given fund.

I may be a bit of an agitator, but I've been urging Canadian regulators to make mandatory disclosures about a fund's past risk. I believe that this information should be conveyed in common-sense ways such as how often a fund did worse than a simple benchmark such as the five-year GIC. Or how often a fund lost money. Most fund companies don't want to publicize that information, because so few funds (even the good ones) manage to outperform the benchmark, or to earn consistent, double-digit returns without setbacks.

These companies would doubtless prefer if investors simply bought funds based on the long-term rates of return. But I believe that an investor who is better informed about what is likely to happen in tough times is more likely to exhibit behaviour that is congruent with good, successful, long-term results.

Qualifier 3: Efficiency

The third feature that distinguishes my FundMonitor picks is efficiency, or the total level of expenses charged by a fund. Here I am talking about the management expense ratio: a percentage figure that represents the sum of all management fees and other expenses.

I believe that the whole concept and terminology of management fees is downright misleading and shouldn't be allowed. For example, I've had money managers tell me that their fund charges only "reasonable fees" of 2.25 percent. I call their bluff and respond, "But wait, the management expense ratio is 2.6 percent! That's well above average and your fund's performance has been pretty mediocre."

How High Annual Expenses Make Loads Pale by Comparison

Consider this. Ten years ago you made a $10,000 investment, and it's been netting 13 percent annually in a fund that charges a management expense ratio of 2.3 percent. (This is not unrealistic, by the way. Over the past 10 years, most funds have performed at about 13 percent, and 2.3 percent is the average management expense ratio.)

Your $10,000 initial investment will have accrued and paid out something like $5000 in management expenses over that period. That's big dough! Now you see why fund managers make so much money.

Even though your investment has an ending value after 10 years of something over $30,000, you've paid a stunning amount of money for management expenses.

What does this tell us? Stop fretting over the cost of loads. They're a one-time expense, and really represent only a tiny portion of the overall fees we're paying in the funds we buy.

Their response is usually something inane, like "Yes, well, but our management *fees* are low." That's nonsense.

As we discussed in chapter 2, the management expense ratio (MER) is the only measure that includes all charges and is therefore the only one to focus on. The MER is the number included in most newspaper listings of performance. And performance is always, by law, net of the management expense ratio.

Now that I've said all this, let me emphasize that I would happily recommend funds with very high expense ratios — if they offered a very high future net return even after paying the big fees. Keep in mind, however, that a pricey fund's high expenses are kind of guaranteed. The high return really isn't.

All else being equal, I would choose a fund with lower expenses over a comparable fund that charges a bundle year-in and year-out.

Qualifier 4: Style

The style of a fund helps to achieve the stated investment objectives, and offers you an important selection tool in choosing the right funds for your personal portfolio.

Our style analysis can tell you whether a fund is aggressive or tame, and can predict its likely performance in different market environments. Two funds with very similar approaches, which hold similar

New Strategies for Being Thrifty

Don't pay for active management of bonds.
Just buy coupons, or for heaven's sake, if you're gonna buy a bond fund, buy a cheap one (with an MER under, say one percent.) See chapter 6 for more on this issue.

Avoid expensive funds-of-funds.
Never, never, never pay three percent or more for a wrap account.

Ask your full-service advisor for access (with part of your money) to low-fee fund families like PH&N, Scudder, Bissett, and GBC.

Consider indexing for a part of your equity portfolio.

Write a letter to Paul Martin saying you'd like to be able to buy U.S. funds, or call and add your message to my audio petition: 1-888-ASK-DUFF (extension 1999).

stocks for similar reasons and sell them at the same time, will undoubtedly have extremely similar performances. Their return pattern will be identical in good times and bad, which means that they'll provide almost no diversification from one another and would therefore be bad complements.

You can begin to see why the selection of each fund must be weighed in the context of your overall portfolio. (Look back at my discussion of diversification in Chapter 4.) But as you go through my Fund-Monitor Profiles, watch for the different concepts in style analysis, and the way that channels into a single, overall view of a fund's investment style. My style concepts are well founded in the academic world and are applied by my research team on Canadian mutual funds in an exclusive way for readers of this book.

This first approach is **holdings-based style analysis**. This involves examining the portfolio to determine which style its management employs. In equity funds, for example, holdings-based style analysis would do a simple quantitative review on the stocks in the portfolio. In a fund that typically comprised conservative stocks (with very low price-to-earnings (P/E) ratios and very low price-to-book value (P/BV) ratios and slow growth), then holdings-based style analysis would suggest that that fund was a "value fund."

Value and growth represent opposite ends of a continuum of the price in the underlying stocks. Researchers have proven that value and growth styles perform differently enough to allow for legitimate diversification among and between the two approaches. A growth portfolio's holdings would reveal (on average) much higher valuations in terms of P/E ratios and P/BV ratios and so on. Growth stock investing is generally considered a somewhat more aggressive approach than value investing.

But since both value and growth are terms that tend to have positive connotations, the trouble with holdings-based style analysis is that every fund is in the middle, claiming to be at both ends of the value-growth continuum. Everyone wants to be a value investor, but we all want to claim that we own growth companies. Unfortunately, few investors actually have the discipline to be one or the other. That's not bad, but it certainly is frustrating for investors who are trying to diversify among and between hundreds of different mutual fund choices.

This dilemma is one of the key reasons I've embraced a second kind of style analysis. Returns-based style analysis is an approach that examines the performance pattern of the fund over the past few years versus other funds and indexes. This approach is not concerned with what the portfolio contains now or in the past. Rather, it simply makes inferences from the return pattern about what is likely in the portfolio or what approach the manager is likely to have been taking. **Returns-based style analysis**, which I've added to augment our holdings-based style analysis, offers important clues about what style a fund really employs. Technically speaking, it is a co-variance analysis of how a fund has performed versus other funds and indexes — with a very high correlation suggesting a near match in investment approach.

In Chapter 3 I explained how well this discrete-return system of mine has done for readers of my books over the years. So, naturally, the reason I continue to use it is that the system actually works. When scored using a simple average ranking like mine, funds that were good in the past are more likely to be good in the future.

In some categories, the system's biggest benefit isn't that it helps to pick the best funds, but that it helps you identify and avoid the worst ones.

Together, these two forms of style analysis helped me arrive at the overall style of a fund. For details on how to read the style grid in the FundMonitor review legend, read on. Chapter 9 will provide detailed background to our systems.

9 The Best of the Best:

FundMonitor Profiles for 2000

THIS IS REALLY THE MEAT OF THE BOOK. It's where we profile 66 established funds that have proven that they are consistently good performers. Each fund has its own full-page fact sheet.

These funds had to clear some high hurdles to make it on to my list. While I've offered some of my own personal, subjective comments about each of the funds, it's a ruthlessly scientific, quantitative system that actually chooses and analyzes these funds. To reach this level, each fund had to demonstrate consistent, high average monthly ranks in the past — compared only to its closest peers. If a fund failed to make these rankings, it was cut. It's that simple.

To further refine the list for your needs, read through the profiles. Each one will provide a glimpse of some of the intimate details — even the scary stuff — on each

for more information

www.fundmonitor.com

I'll take just a moment to tell you a bit about my Web site.

In addition to this book, I have developed a "living book" on the Internet, which can be personalized for your needs. My new Web site can take you further than the pages of this book, but with all the same principles.

On your first visit to the site, be sure to register so that you can take advantage of all the premium services (see page 58).

The site offers all of the fund research data tables you see at the back of this book, and even more. But the real bonus is that all of this information can be ranked and sorted, based on your own criteria. It's an amazing service, and I'm indebted to my Web wizards, who told me it was possible and then made it happen.

You will also find an online questionnaire, designed to help you identify an optimized asset allocation that's right for you. And if you register yourself for a personalized review, you can have your own personal home page on the FundMonitor site. Your page will greet you with performance monitoring of your real or hypothetical model portfolio. It's available to every investor who signs up for the FundMonitor service (for which there is a fee).

You can make changes online. You can find free fund research. You can do anything you like. There is also a chat room, so you can share your questions and concerns with other readers online.

It's informative and it's fun. I look forward to seeing you there!

fund. For example, you'll find out how risky it's really been. Or what style it really employs. (Forget about the manager's claims of being a "value investor"! That's hogwash, if the stocks in the fund are expensive.)

In each essay, you'll find more qualitative information. That's where I'll mention more important issues such as major management changes. If a fund makes the list based on my quantitative, objective analysis, then it stays on the list, even if the management has undergone a change. But I'll let you know about it. You see, most manager changes involve just a small change at the top. Often, another team member takes over. For example, that's what happened with the Ivy Funds, where Jerry Javasky took over the reins from departed Gerry Coleman, who cut loose and went to C.I. That's a pretty subtle management change. Consequently, I'll do the math to determine which funds have had the best past performance, and I'll just give you an overview of what's been happening with the fund.

Each portion of the review page is designed to help you identify critical information fast. Here's an introduction to what it all means.

Up top, you'll see the fund name and a little Canadian flag if it's fully RRSP eligible ( ). If it's counted only as foreign content for your RRSP, then the flag will look like this . The team that's specifically responsible for this fund will be shown here along with the name of their investment firm. It's important to know who's running the fund. The management firm that employs the manager is shown here — and it's not always the same as the fund company. Sometimes the fund company has arranged for a sub-advisor: an unrelated firm that they've hired to run the fund. I think subs are slightly better, because if they really stink, it's easier to fire them than it is to fire an entire team within your own company.

You'll notice that every fund that has made my Fund Profiles list has been given a certain number of stars. The star rating system that I use represents the AMR (Average Monthly Rank) of each fund against similar funds. That means, for example, that international equity funds are only compared to other international equity funds. This type of rating system allows me to get a better idea of how a fund has performed against its peers.

Keep in mind, though, that the star rankings only represent each fund's monthly rank since its inception. They do not take into account a fund's management changes, level of risk, etc. Those are totally separate variables for each fund, and make up a different aspect of the Fund Profile.

In other words, a fund that has an overall performance rating of four stars should not necessarily be replaced with a fund that has received a five-star rating. The system wasn't meant to be that refined. It's merely meant to show that some funds have done better than others.

The performance chart simply represents the value of a $10,000 initial investment (with all dividends reinvested) since inception for the fund or since 1987 — whichever came first. A benchmark for each type of fund is shown to help investors get an idea of how an unmanaged rival index did in comparison with this fund.

The star rating includes more history than can be shown graphically on these pages. Terrific performance in the 80s can inflate a fund that looks weak lately.

There are three important questions I ask when rating a mutual fund: How has it performed in up markets? How has it performed in down markets? And, finally, what is its management expense ratio (MER)? Although there are other determining factors when evaluating a fund, the answers to these questions go a long way toward predicting future returns.

The MER is pretty easy to find out, because every fund company discloses it in their annual report. But a fund's performance in up and down markets is impossible to find, because nobody calculates it. I do, since I think it's really helpful to know what to expect from your fund if the market takes a sudden downturn.

You may be wondering how I differentiate between up and down markets. I consider a down market one that endures at least a 10 percent drop from peak to trough. Any other market is considered an up market.

My grading system is designed to be easy to understand. A group of selected funds is broken down into quartiles. Their rank is represented with a mark of A, B, C, or D (A being the top 25 percent and D being the bottom).

Consistency

My distinctive column graphs show consistency at a glance. This is the first thing I look at in gauging any fund's past performance. Each vertical box represents a single calendar year. If the top quarter of the box is shaded, then the fund did better than a vast majority of its rivals.

It placed in the top quartile of its class, meaning that it did better than 75 percent of its peers. Because these boxes are non-overlapping, they don't suffer from the typical distortions you'll find in compound return calculations, where one blockbuster year can skew a whole decade's worth of only mediocre results.

Why Quartile Rankings Change

Historic quartile comparisons with my book this year are a bit different from prior years. That's because I'm using a much more refined system to do real apples-to-apples comparisons.

It's always been important to my way of measuring mutual funds to be sure to compare only similar funds, to see which do best, and to test for consistency. But now data from Portfolio Analytics allows us to group funds in a way that is very specific. A fund that always has lots of big banks, for example, can now be categorized and rated against only similar funds. That way, we find the best of the bank-heavy funds. This more refined system is more fair because even a relatively weak bank-heavy fund would look great lately in comparison to a fund that, as a matter of policy, always has lots of smaller cyclical companies. Truth is, the latter fund would be punished by lumping it with the bank-heavy fund, what with the explosion in bank share prices over the last year or so.

These more refined peer groups neutralize for style and compare only funds with very similar approaches. That way the best funds from each approach will rise to the top — rather than all the funds from one hot approach rising to the top.

Accurate Returns

How are you doing? It's important to know, so you can know whether you've goofed. But calculating your personal rate of return has been a boondoggle for the investment industry for these three reasons:

1. It's complicated. Cash flows into and out of the funds represent a measurement challenge. Even the industry is up in arms over the best formula to use in portraying an individual's own personal rate of return. The industry has settled on something called the Modified Dietz method, which is just a kind of internal rate of return calculation.

2. It's controversial. Some studies (like the one shown on page 67) show that people just don't do that well in the market. Showing your account holders how badly they've done with your advice is like taunting them.

3. It's expensive. The data required, in terms of historical cost information, from every account holder and on every security, is huge. And, of course, the firm needs the date on which the security was purchased, and every penny earned in income since the fund or stock was bought. It all adds up to a nightmare of details.

The solution: Buy Quicken (the bestselling software program), and update the value of your funds yourself. Or use the service offered to buyers of this book: free access to the FundMonitor Shadow Account system on the Web. By registering at our Web site, you can input your own holdings and cost information, then change them anytime. The application will calculate your personal rate of return. Not just once, but anytime.

And it will keep you abreast of any changes, with its built-in Portfolio Alert feature. All it does is e-mail a message out to you whenever your account is slumping, based on criteria you can set. The rate of return calculations are updated daily at 7 p.m. EST, to incorporate the day's changes. So you can see how you've weathered any market pullback.

The Beardstown Ladies' investment club should have had a performance calculator. You remember them, right? They're the older women from Beardstown, Ohio, who've been featured as investment whizzes on *Sixty Minutes* and other shows. They've sold almost a million copies of their how-to guides. But the 10-year 23 percent annual return they claim on the books' covers is a mistake: They only made 9 percent a year.

Oops.

Here is your temporary password for access to Duff Young's FundMonitor site at www.fundmonitor.com:

```
Login ID:    reader

Password:    JU4ANCEK8
```

Funds Profiled (in alphabetical order)

The Honourable Mentions List

These fine funds barely missed making the cut when we calculated fund performance and drew up this year's FundMonitor Profiles list.

Canadian Balanced:

McLean Budden Balanced

AIM GT Canada Income Class

International Balanced:

Fidelity Global Asset Allocation

Universal World Asset Allocation

Canadian Bond:

Altamira Bond

Lotus Bond

International Bond:

Altamira High Yield Bond

C.I. Global High Yield

Canadian Equity:

Maritime Life Canadian Equity (A&C)

Sceptre Equity Growth

Canadian Small Cap Equity:

Talvest Millenium Next Generation

Bissett Small Cap

Dividend:

Canada Trust Dividend Income

IRIS Dividend

International Equity:

AGF International Value

Fidelity International Portfolio

U.S. Equity:

MD U.S. Equity

OIQ Ferique American

Regional Equity — Asia:

CDA Pacific Basin (KBSH)

C.I. Pacific

Regional Equity ,— Europe:

Hongkong Bank European Growth

Scudder Greater Europe

Regional Equity — Emerging Markets:

Spectrum United Emerging Markets

Elliott & Page Emerging Markets

Sector Equity — Science & Technology:

Green Line Science & Technology

Sector Equity — Resource:

Green Line Resource

Labour:

C.I. Covington

Vengrowth

Fidelity Canadian Asset Allocation Fund

Managed by: Dick Haberman

From: Fidelity Investments Canada Ltd.

RRSP Eligible: 

Overall performance: ★★★★★

Performance in:	
Up Markets	–
Down Markets	–

Value of $10,000 invested

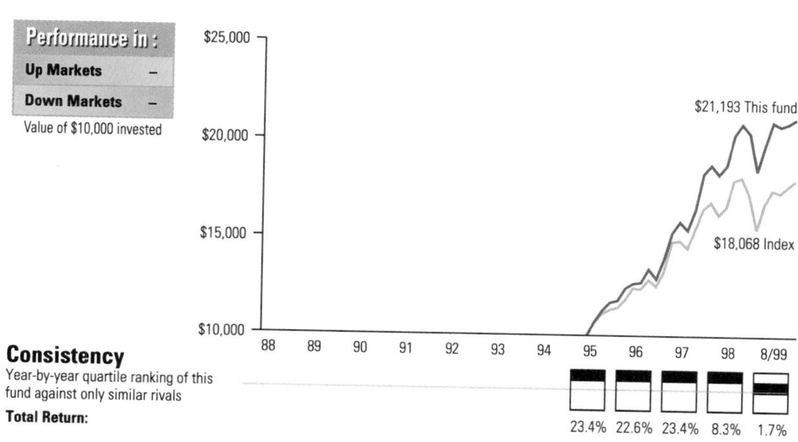

Consistency
Year-by-year quartile ranking of this fund against only similar rivals

Total Return: 23.4% 22.6% 23.4% 8.3% 1.7%

Risk

% of time fund has lost money over 12-month period	2%
Biggest drop	-11%
Months to recover	7

Efficiency

For every $100	$2.41
which for this class is	Avg

Fit (Investment style)

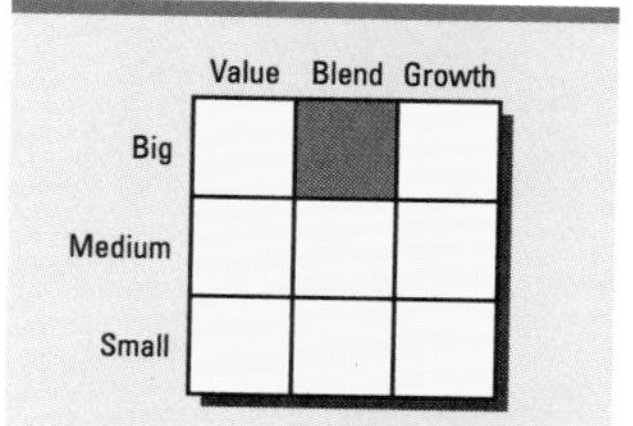

Opinion

This huge fund really is different from its peers in so many ways. It's got way, way more diversification by security, by sector, and by manager than any other fund in the country. And it's got way more talent behind it.

So it really does stand alone in bragging about adding value, say, on the fixed income side — where exposure to corporate bonds allows the fund to avoid making daring bets on interest rates. Or in stocks, where the fund isn't shy about putting some money into small caps. Even on the international side, there's a multi-manager approach that is one of the finest in the world. All of these enhancements mean more work for the team. And only Fidelity can do them all and do them well: from credit research on bonds, to company visits on small caps to regional analysts in far-away markets, the team does it all.

Together it adds up to stellar performance and incredible simplicity. Just don't buy this fund if you've already got 10 different funds in your portfolio. That's overdiversification — and it'll doom you.

Common Sense Asset Builder III Fund

Managed by: Jerry Javasky

From: Mackenzie Financial Corporation

RRSP Eligible: 

Overall performance: ★★★★★

Performance in:	
Up Markets	A
Down Markets	D

Value of $10,000 invested

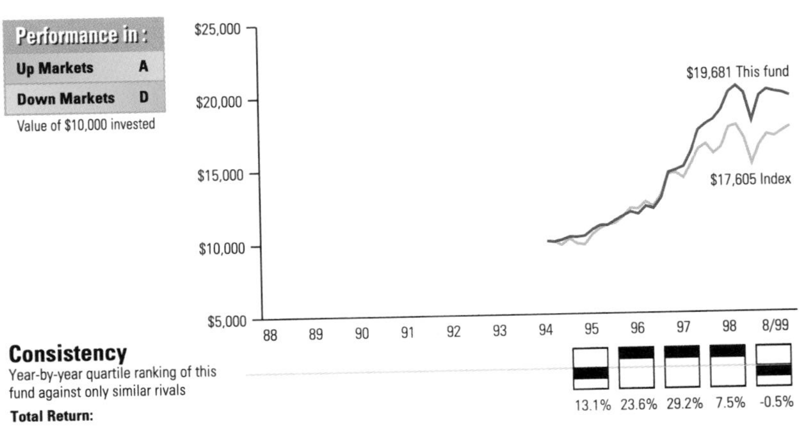

Consistency
Year-by-year quartile ranking of this fund against only similar rivals

Total Return:

Risk

% of time fund has lost money over 12-month period	3%
Biggest drop	-13%
Months to recover	NA

Efficiency

For every $100	$2.25
which for this class is	Avg

Fit (Investment style)

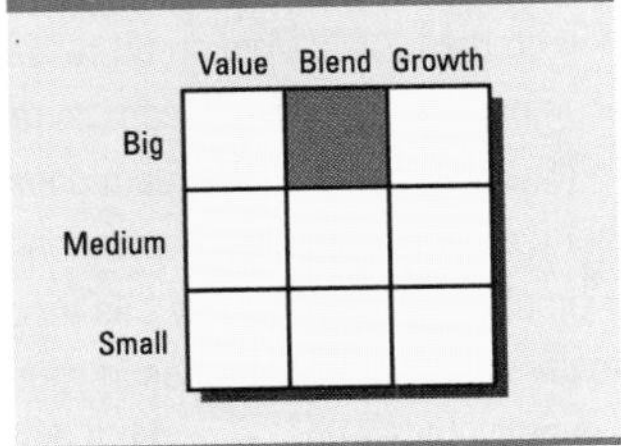

Opinion

With about half the fund in bonds this is a middle-of-the-road balanced fund. But the banks and utilities have been a drag this year as higher rates have crimped the strategy that worked so well for so long.

Canadian Balanced

Bissett Retirement Fund

Managed by: Michael A. Quinn

From: Bissett and Associates Investment Management Ltd.

RRSP Eligible: 

Overall performance: ★★★★½

Performance in:	
Up Markets	A
Down Markets	D

Value of $10,000 invested

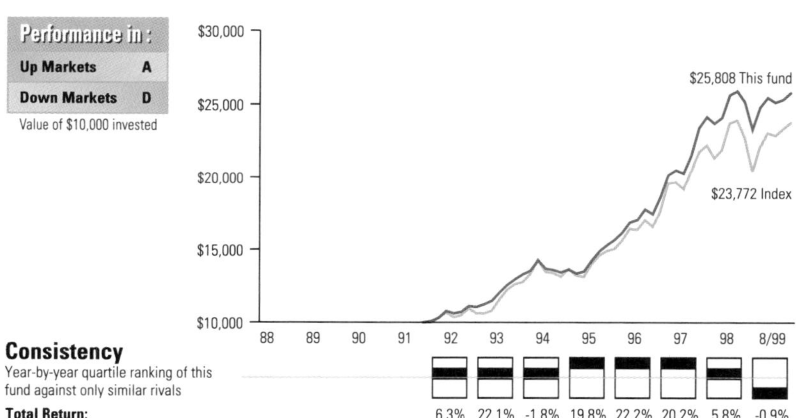

Consistency
Year-by-year quartile ranking of this fund against only similar rivals

	92	93	94	95	96	97	98	8/99
Total Return:	6.3%	22.1%	-1.8%	19.8%	22.2%	20.2%	5.8%	-0.9%

Risk

% of time fund has lost money over 12-month period	11%
Biggest drop	-12%
Months to recover	NA

Efficiency

For every $100	$0.23
which for this class is	Low

Fit (Investment style)

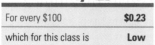

	Value	Blend	Growth
Big	■		
Medium			
Small			

Opinion

If you're a do-it-yourselfer and you want to do it simply, then this fund is a nice one-decision pick. It's a rare beast: an actively managed fund that doesn't try to time markets and doesn't charge much.

Like several in the Bissett family, though, this fund's missed out on the recovery in 1999 by missing out on the hottest areas of the market: the momentum stocks. Also, the bonds haven't helped, despite a basically conservative philosophy on managing fixed income. They were a little long when the market went south, a little too heavy in corporates when the spreads fattened, and a little too domestic when the loonie surged.

The fund is just a collection of other Bissett funds with a thin extra layer of management expenses added in. Think total costs for the underlying funds, plus 0.23 percent for the packaging. But Quinn does a good job of tweaking the proportions of the other funds in this portfolio for that extra fee.

Canadian Balanced

Phillips Hager & North Balanced Fund

Managed by: David Heal

From: Phillips Hager and North Investment Management

RRSP Eligible: 

Overall performance: ★★★★★

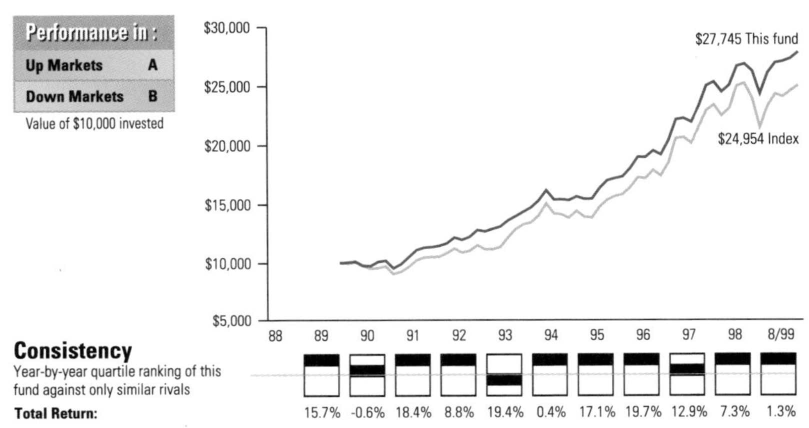

Risk

% of time fund has lost money over 12-month period	6%
Biggest drop	-12%
Months to recover	8

Efficiency

For every $100	$0.88
which for this class is	Low

Fit (Investment style)

	Value	Blend	Growth
Big		■	
Medium			
Small			

Opinion

When I beat up on balanced funds for their premium pricing and passive management, I'm talking about the other 230 names in the category. A handful, like this one, really do stand out as excellent choices.

This favourite of mine is a gem for more than just its low fees. (It costs only 0.88 percent annually to own). It's also one of the best actively managed funds around, with success in every area — from asset mix to duration management and stock selection. PH&N's investment team has done well with some broad themes over the years, like the financials they've held based on an early vision of the boomer trend. As well, they've seen restructuring and diminished inflation before others knew these trends were possible.

Lately the religion has been cyclicals. Yup, the tired, cheap old companies that dig, drill, and cut their way to prosperity a few times each decade. This fund owned them well in early 1999 — before they took off. But this is a big trend, they think.

Too, the fund has benefited over time from exposure to corporate bonds through yield enhancement, even though the rate calls haven't been bang on this year.

Canadian Balanced

NAL–Investor Balanced Growth Fund

Managed by: Brian Dawson

From: McLean Budden Limited

RRSP Eligible: 

Overall performance: ★★★★

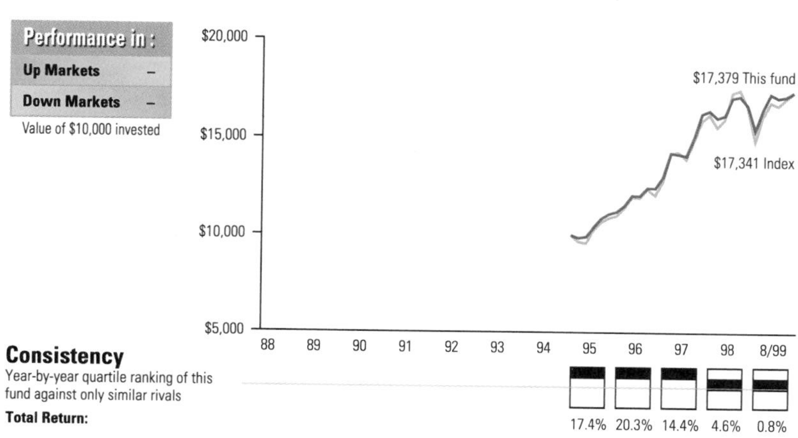

Consistency
Year-by-year quartile ranking of this fund against only similar rivals

Total Return: 17.4% 20.3% 14.4% 4.6% 0.8%

Risk

% of time fund has lost money over 12-month period	8%
Biggest drop	-12%
Months to recover	8

Efficiency

For every $100	**$2.40**
which for this class is	**Avg**

Fit (Investment style)

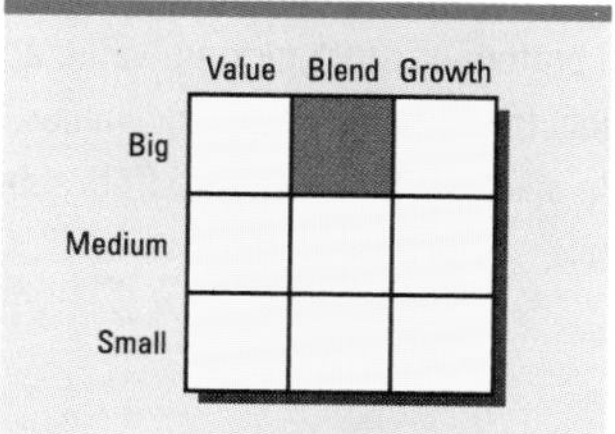

Opinion

McLean Budden manages this fund for Manulife, and performance has been good. Of course, you can save 1.25 percent annually simply by going direct to McLean Budden.

Canadian Balanced

Global Strategies Income Plus

Managed by: Tony Massie

From: Global Strategy Financial Inc.

RRSP Eligible: 

Overall performance: ★★★½

Performance in:	
Up Markets	A
Down Markets	D

Value of $10,000 invested

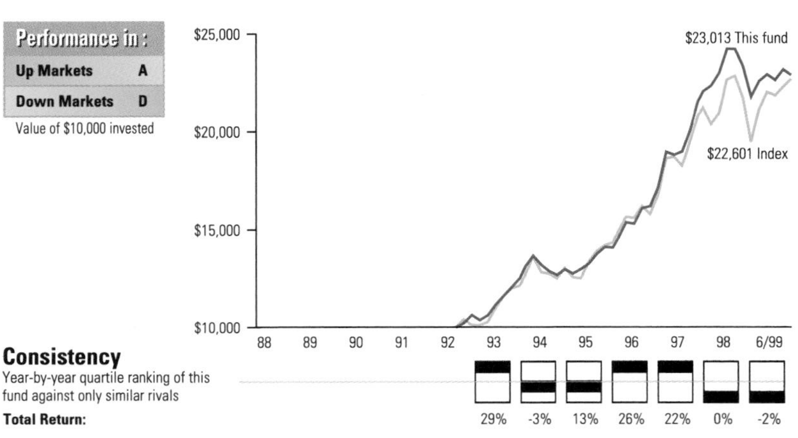

Consistency
Year-by-year quartile ranking of this fund against only similar rivals

	93	94	95	96	97	98	6/99
Total Return:	29%	-3%	13%	26%	22%	0%	-2%

Risk

% of time fund has lost money over 12-month period	19%
Biggest drop	14%
Months to recover	NA

Efficiency

For every $100	$2.37
which for this class is	Med

Fit (Investment style)

	Value	Blend	Growth
Big	■		
Medium			
Small			

Opinion

Tony Massie likes to buy good value, so it's no surprise that he is nuts about Canada—the currency and the stocks. He says there are tons of great values in Canada and he is so optimistic on the Loonie that he has trimmed foreign content down to almost nothing. He's focusing on a smaller number of stocks (from 130 last year to about 75 now), and earlier this summer took some profits on the banks. More recently he's been spending some cash and finding some bargains in the trees. Massie runs this more tactical offering by first doing some macro analysis to get a handle on the direction of the overall economy. Then, he complements that with old-fashioned bottom-up stock picking. Value-added has come mainly from scooping up good values on the equity side and, to a lesser extent, from subtle shifts in asset mix.

ICM Balanced Fund

Managed by: Brian Thomas

From: Lincluden Management Limited

RRSP Eligible: 

Overall performance: ★★★★

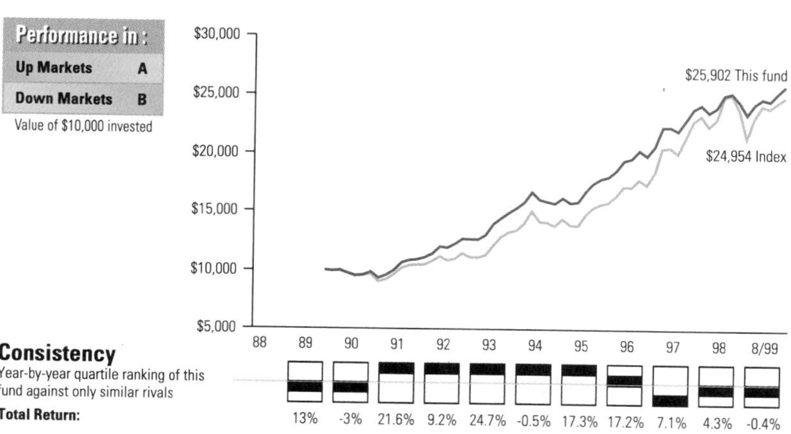

Risk

% of time fund has lost money over 12-month period	16%
Biggest drop	-17%
Months to recover	19

Efficiency

For every $100	$0.17
which for this class is	Low

Fit (Investment style)

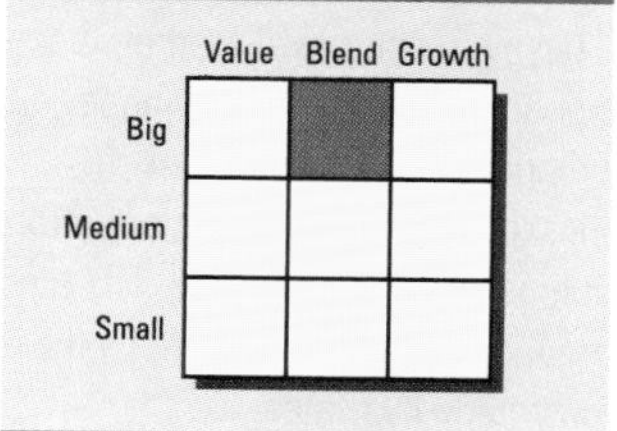

Opinion

Integra Capital Management is the rarest kind of money manager: a clever marketer.

You see, Integra says that the problem with most firms is that they employ a particular style and investment discipline rigorously, following that style through its inevitable ups and downs. Investors will invariably get whipsawed by the single-style approach and its inherent lack of diversification.

So instead of having its own money managers in-house, Integra simply markets the money management services of two outside firms, which employ very different approaches. That way, Integra's clients get built-in style diversification from the top-down: thematic, macro work done by Gryphon Investment Counsel and the more contrarian, value approach used by Lincluden of Oakville.

One problem with these funds is that the management fees are charged directly to the unitholder's account, so the performance results you see here are really gross figures. That helps them look better when compared to regular mutual funds' net returns. Like I said, they're clever marketers.

Trimark Income Growth Fund

Managed by: Robert Krembil

From: Trimark Investment Management Inc.

RRSP Eligible: 

Overall performance: ★★★★★

Performance in :	
Up Markets	A
Down Markets	C

Value of $10,000 invested

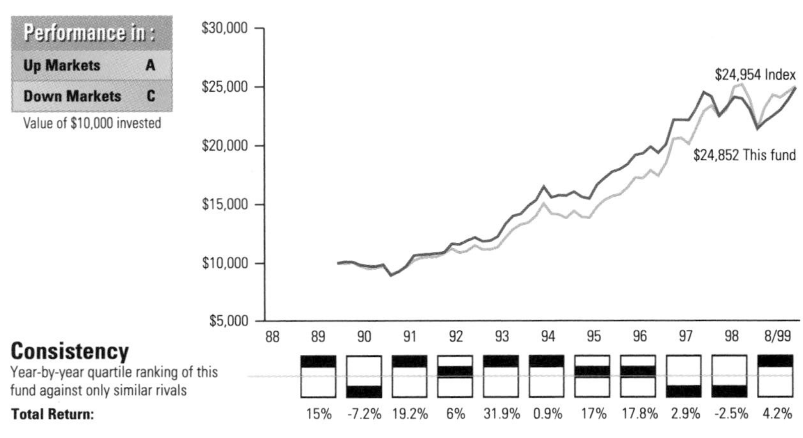

Consistency
Year-by-year quartile ranking of this fund against only similar rivals

Total Return:	89	90	91	92	93	94	95	96	97	98	8/99
	15%	-7.2%	19.2%	6%	31.9%	0.9%	17%	17.8%	2.9%	-2.5%	4.2%

Risk

% of time fund has lost money over 12-month period	15%
Biggest drop	-15%
Months to recover	22

Efficiency

For every $100	$1.56
which for this class is	Low

Fit (Investment style)

	Value	Blend	Growth
Big		■	
Medium			
Small			

Opinion

Forgive this fund for its two bad years and you'll see one of the best gems in the country. Understand what happened and you'll appreciate the true nature of the approach at Trimark.

For 15 years the fund had remarkably consistent returns. Its biggest loss ever was 15 percent. It charges just 1.56 percent a year.

Also, the fund tries never to make a big score by being entirely right on an interest rate call or an asset allocation decision. Instead, the idea is to add value over time with incremental wins to protect capital first and grow it second.

That's where Trimark fell off track. Former equity manager Vito Maida was too early in dumping banks and buying resources. Together, these twin errors compounded — not to lose money, but to lose ground against the competition.

Of all possible active management errors, this one seems least harmful over time. The fund's stunning turnaround was made possible by the weighting decisions made by Maida.

GWL Growth & Income (M) DSC

Managed by: Jerry Javasky

From: Mackenzie Financial Corporation

RRSP Eligible: 

Overall performance: ★★★½

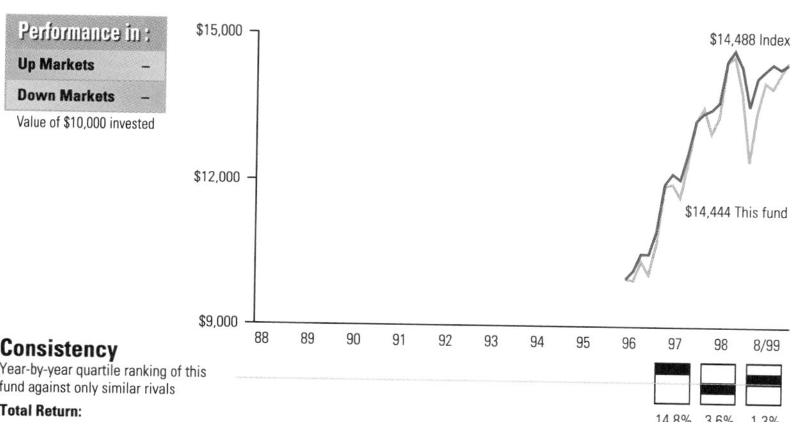

Consistency
Year-by-year quartile ranking of this fund against only similar rivals

Total Return: 14.8% 3.6% 1.3%

Risk

% of time fund has lost money over 12-month period	13%
Biggest drop	-9%
Months to recover	NA

Efficiency

For every $100	$2.38
which for this class is	Avg

Fit (Investment style)

	Value	Blend	Growth
Big		■	
Medium			
Small			

Opinion

Mackenzie runs this confusing clone for a bunch of marketing half-wits at Great West. They cleverly put the (M) on to make it clearer. Yeah, their lineup is crystal clear.

On a more serious note, this is a clone of the Ivy Growth & Income Fund. That means you'll find big-cap stocks and lots of cash in it. That also means the fund roared when banks were raging, but has slowed since.

International Balanced

C.I. International Balanced Fund

Managed by: Bill Sterling

From: C.I. Fund Management

RRSP Eligible: 

Overall performance: 

Performance in:	
Up Markets	–
Down Markets	–

Value of $10,000 invested

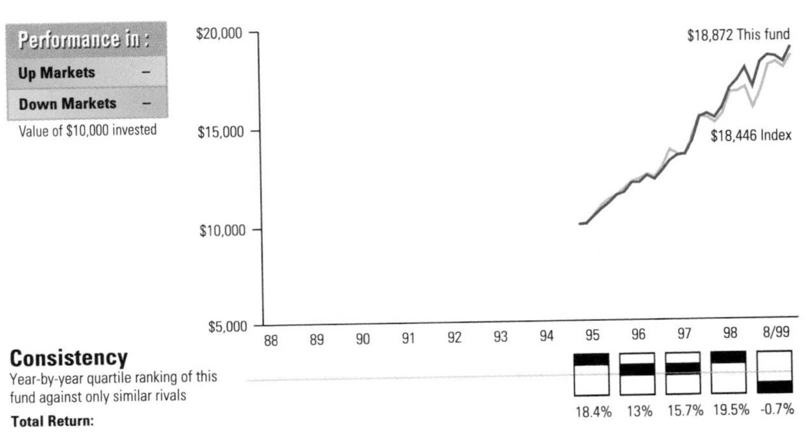

Consistency
Year-by-year quartile ranking of this fund against only similar rivals

Total Return: 18.4% 13% 15.7% 19.5% -0.7%

Risk

% of time fund has lost money over 12-month period	0%
Biggest drop	-5%
Months to recover	3

Efficiency

For every $100	$2.44
which for this class is	Avg

Fit (Investment style)

	Value	Blend	Growth
Big		■	
Medium			
Small			

Opinion

It's tough to find a better thematic bet for your future than this set of international balanced funds. This fund uses a similar approach to CI's Global Boomernomics Fund and both are quite similar to their fully RSP-eligible clones.

The concept is strong. Take a global guru in macro economic thinking (that's Sterling, a Harvard Ph.D. and former chief economist with Merrill Lynch), then marry him up with a team known for fundamental bottom-up research.

Together, the team manages the asset mix decision and stock selection with a bent toward being conservative and avoiding disaster. That's why the fund is best suited for people who aren't looking to shoot the lights out.

If you owned only one fund, this would be a decent choice because it's got more diversification than most: by asset class, by geography, by capitalization, and by investment style. The team focuses on growth at a reasonable price and seldom misses out on rallies in growth or value stocks.

International Balanced

FMOQ Investment Fund

Managed by: Guy Normandin

From: T.A.L. Investment Counsel Ltd.

RRSP Eligible: 

Performance in:	
Up Markets	A
Down Markets	B

Value of $10,000 invested

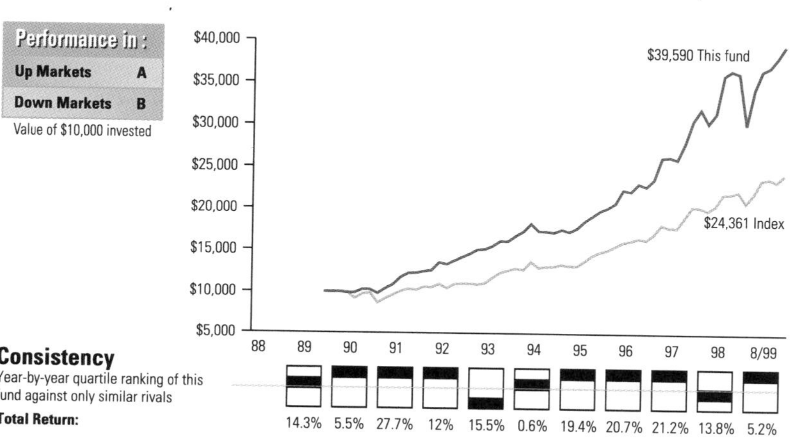

Consistency
Year-by-year quartile ranking of this fund against only similar rivals

Total Return:

89	90	91	92	93	94	95	96	97	98	8/99
14.3%	5.5%	27.7%	12%	15.5%	0.6%	19.4%	20.7%	21.2%	13.8%	5.2%

Risk

% of time fund has lost money over 12-month period	7%
Biggest drop	-19%
Months to recover	9

Opinion

This fund has a great track record versus its peers; but its peers are balanced funds, and this one can hardly be called that — it holds virtually no bonds. But with a dirt-cheap MER and great returns, who would complain?

Efficiency

For every $100	$0.64
which for this class is	Low

Fit (Investment style)

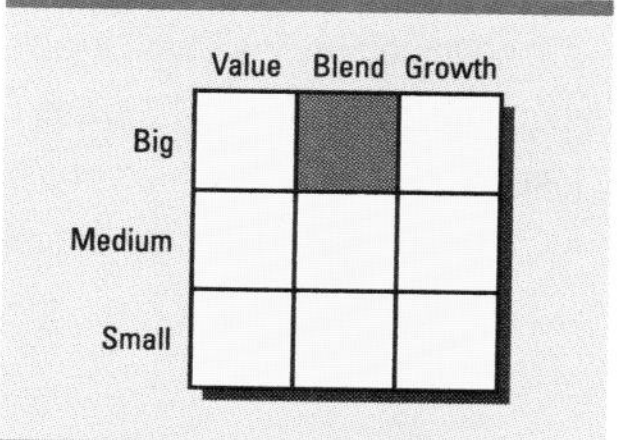

AGF American Tactical Asset Allocation Fund

Managed by: Kathy Taylor

From: Barclays Global Investors

RRSP Eligible: 

Overall performance: ★★★★★

Performance in:	
Up Markets	B
Down Markets	–

Value of $10,000 invested

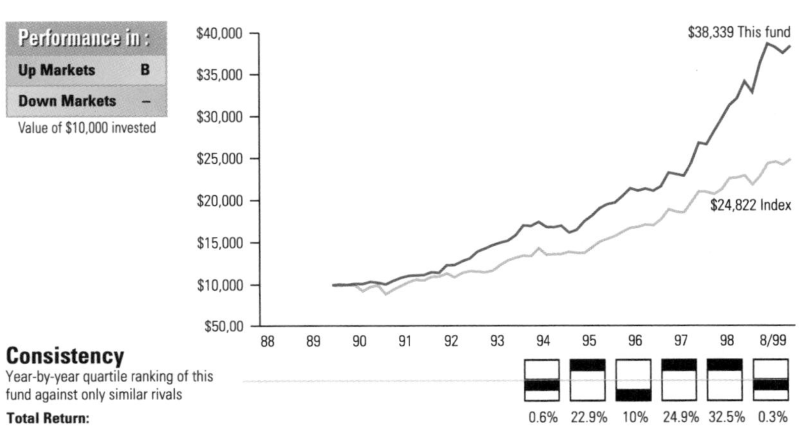

Consistency
Year-by-year quartile ranking of this fund against only similar rivals

Total Return:	94	95	96	97	98	8/99
	0.6%	22.9%	10%	24.9%	32.5%	0.3%

Risk

% of time fund has lost money over 12-month period	2%
Biggest drop	-7%
Months to recover	11

Efficiency

For every $100	$2.56
which for this class is	Avg

Fit (Investment style)

	Value	Blend	Growth
Big		■	
Medium			
Small			

Opinion

Proving yet again that there is merit to at least one kind of market timing, this quant-heavy fund has posted yet another stellar year of performance since its last appearance in this book.

It's a great fund that takes advantage of disparities in relative value between stocks, bonds, and cash. The focus is on being out of the bad assets, though that sometimes does mean getting into them while they're still uncomfortably cheap. The approach is geared not so much to making buckets of money as simply to achieving equity returns without full equity risk. Make no mistake about it, though; this team is good.

They've done incredibly well with asset mix shifts both big and small. Plus, to gain stock exposure, they just hold the index, instead of picking individual names, which has been a blessing as big index stocks have soared.

McLean Budden Fixed Income Fund

Managed by: Bill Giblin

From: McLean Budden Limited

RRSP Eligible: 

Overall performance: ★★★★

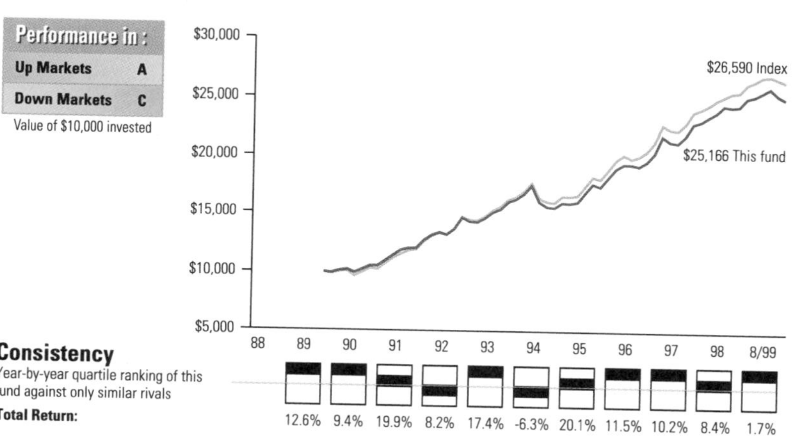

Risk

% of time fund has lost money over 12-month period	7%
Biggest drop	-12%
Months to recover	15

Efficiency

For every $100	$0.80
which for this class is	Low

Fit (Investment style)

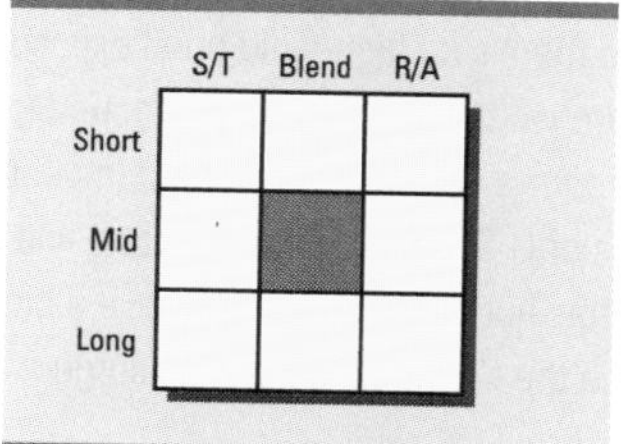

Opinion

Do you know if the new Highway 407 bonds are a good deal?

Me neither. That's why I think there's a role for a credit team in a fixed income portfolio: to pick up yield by identifying the right corporate issues. This inexpensive fund benefits from having the kind of depth that allows for tons of credit research, so that the managers can add some "positive carry," as it's called, by being overweight in corporate and provincial bonds.

Beyond that, this team manages the interest rate decision effectively — adding value consistently. Both the sector exposure and the rate call, however, are managed within fairly narrow constraints just so there are no surprises.

That's why this is a better bet than buying individual bonds on your own — something we often recommend in place of owning the hundreds of rotten, expensive bond funds that compete with this fine offering.

Canadian Bond

Beutel Goodman Income Fund

Managed by: Bruce Corneil

From: Beutel Goodman & Company Ltd.

RRSP Eligible: 

Overall performance: ★★★★

Performance in:	
Up Markets	A
Down Markets	D

Value of $10,000 invested

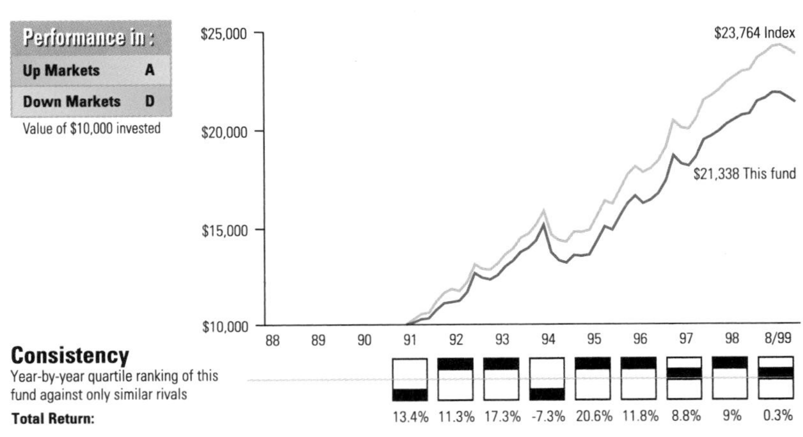

Consistency

Year-by-year quartile ranking of this fund against only similar rivals

	91	92	93	94	95	96	97	98	8/99
Total Return:	13.4%	11.3%	17.3%	-7.3%	20.6%	11.8%	8.8%	9%	0.3%

Risk

% of time fund has lost money over 12-month period	9%
Biggest drop	-14%
Months to recover	18

Efficiency

For every $100	$0.67
which for this class is	Low

Fit (Investment style)

	S/T	Blend	R/A
Short			
Mid			■
Long			

Opinion

This is an institutional product all the way. That's why you have to love it. It costs only 0.62 percent annually to own, so it's miles ahead of most bond funds and all balanced funds.

This fund is actively managed, and managed well, at that. Bruce Corneil and the team add value in three ways: first, by getting the duration call right. Then they try to get into the right mix of long- and short- or mid-term bonds to achieve that target duration. Finally, they like to carry some high-grade corporate paper to goose yield a bit.

It's all done within fairly narrow constraints to keep a lid on risk. So you won't find big, bold rate calls. And there's no high-yield bond exposure. Heck, there isn't even any currency action in here. That's rare for a Canadian bond fund (most play U.S. treasuries or U.S. pay Canadian issues) and the absence has hurt relative performance a bit this year, since the Canadian dollar has surged.

Trimark Advantage Bond Fund

Managed by: Patrick Farmer

From: Trimark Investment Management Inc.

RRSP Eligible: 

Canadian Bond

Performance in:	
Up Markets	–
Down Markets	–

Value of $10,000 invested

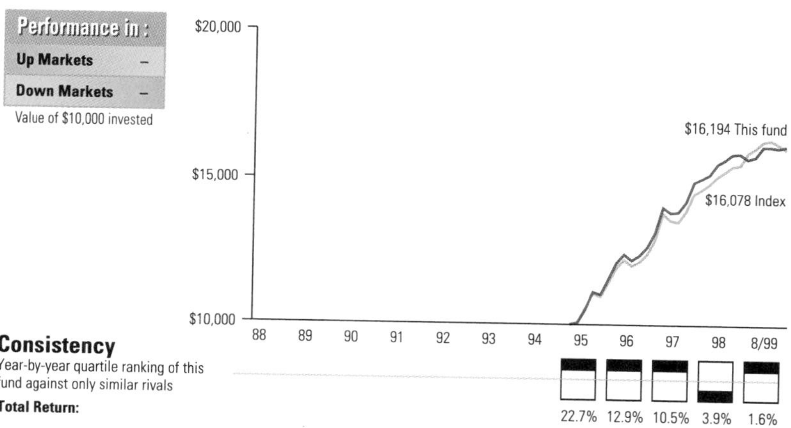

Consistency

Year-by-year quartile ranking of this fund against only similar rivals

Total Return: 22.7% 12.9% 10.5% 3.9% 1.6%

Risk

% of time fund has lost money over 12-month period	0%
Biggest drop	-3%
Months to recover	5

Efficiency

For every $100	$1.24
which for this class is	Low

Fit (Investment style)

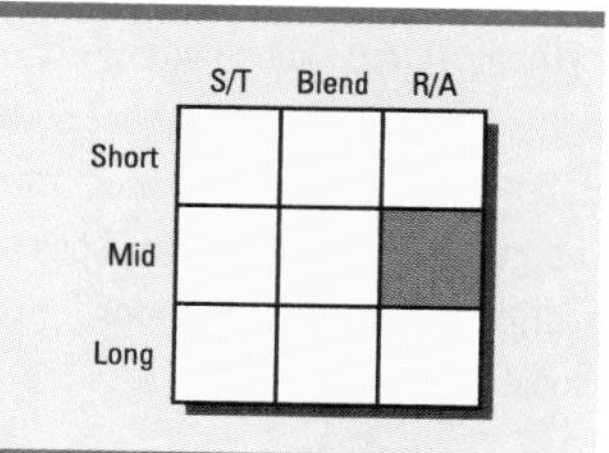

Opinion

Pat Farmer has always had a few advantages over his peers. But low fees had never been one of them. That is, until the firm decided, four years ago, to launch a unique product in Canada: a broker-sold corporate bond fund that has reasonably low fees. The doubly different fund has indeed earned a role in investors' hearts because of its good returns.

Corporate issues are becoming a bigger part of our market, since our government isn't running big deficits anymore. And with more and more savers looking for conservative interest-bearing instruments, corporate bonds are becoming the vehicle of choice. This area now makes up 20 percent of the ScotiaMcLeod Universe Bond Index, twice what it was a few years ago. Looking at shorter terms and higher yields than governments, they're more like a bottom-up stock research exercise than a big call on interest rates. Hence the success Trimark has at adding value in this area.

Fidelity Emerging Markets Bond Fund

Managed by: John Carlson

From: Fidelity Investment Canada Ltd.

RRSP Eligible: 

Overall performance: ★★★★★

Performance in:	
Up Markets	A
Down Markets	–

Value of $10,000 invested

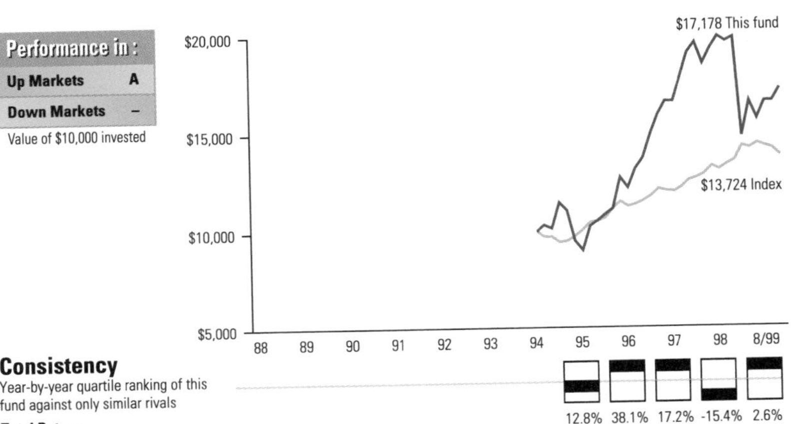

Consistency
Year-by-year quartile ranking of this fund against only similar rivals

Total Return: 12.8% 38.1% 17.2% -15.4% 2.6%

Risk

% of time fund has lost money over 12-month period	33%
Biggest drop	-28%
Months to recover	NA

Efficiency

For every $100	$2.34
which for this class is	High

Fit (Investment style)

	S/T	Blend	R/A
Short			
Mid		■	
Long			

Opinion

Yes, emerging markets debt behaves more like stocks than bonds.

And yes, this fund is a wild beast of a bond fund. But the story here is one of diversification and the role specialized fixed income can play in a portfolio. The fund has the unique charm of being both risky and risk reducing. That's because it's negatively correlated with domestic fixed income assets — which simply means that it tends to zig when our bonds zag. So yes, you can achieve smoother returns in your overall portfolio by adding this bumpy bond fund.

But keep in mind that sovereign debt of emerging nations, like those in Latin America, favoured by this fund, do have lots of sensitivity to commodity prices. So this fund can sometimes behave like a resource fund — which underscores its difference from most bond funds. But if you're chock full of funds that drill for their earnings, look for your fixed income exposure elsewhere.

Guardian Foreign Income Fund

Managed by: Laurence Linklater

From: Dresdner RCM Global Investors

RRSP Eligible: 

Overall performance: ★★★★½

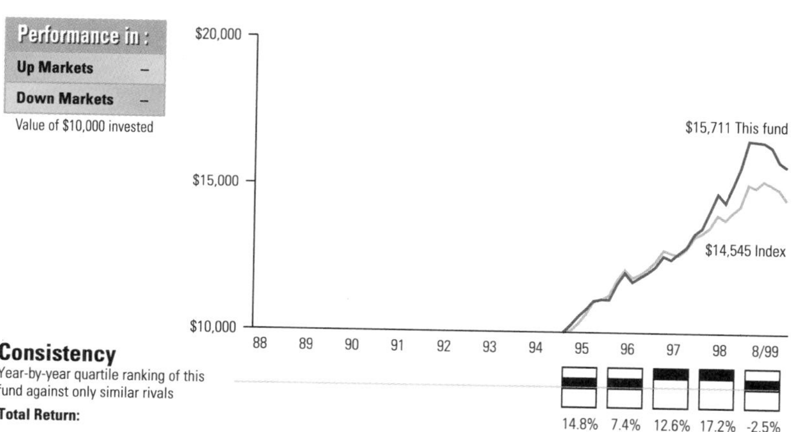

Risk

% of time fund has lost money over 12-month period	0%
Biggest drop	-8%
Months to recover	NA

Efficiency

For every $100	$2.04
which for this class is	Avg

Fit (Investment style)

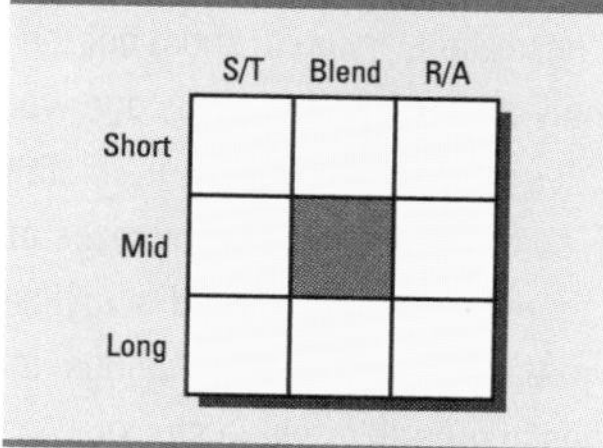

Opinion

We continue to like this solid, but dull, RSP-eligible foreign bond fund. It's mostly a diversification play. But that's the point. Interest rate cycles around the world are out of sync, so just because bond yields in Canada are rising right now doesn't mean you have to suffer bond market losses.

The foundation for the argument is a good one: Foreign bonds offer excellent diversification. But the argument is a bit flawed. Here's why. While interest rate cycles do vary widely around the world, sudden rate spikes affect every nation instantaneously. That means that you do get diversification with a fund like this, but you don't get insulated from the kind of calamity we had in 1994, when U.S. Fed hikes killed the world's bond markets.

Linklater's done well lately with a continued bet on the greenback as the Euro has slid. But with Treasuries getting pinched, the fund can find itself with currency gains offsetting market losses.

CI International Balanced RSP Fund

Managed by: Bill Sterling

From: BEA Associates Inc.

RRSP Eligible: 

Overall performance: ★★★★★

Performance in:	
Up Markets	–
Down Markets	–

Value of $10,000 invested

Consistency

Year-by-year quartile ranking of this fund against only similar rivals

	95	96	97	98	8/99
Total Return:	18.4%	13%	15.7%	19.5%	-0.7%

Risk

% of time fund has lost money over 12-month period	0%
Biggest drop	-5%
Months to recover	4

Efficiency

For every $100	$2.43
which for this class is	Avg

Fit (Investment style)

	S/T	Blend	R/A
Short		■	
Mid			
Long			

Opinion

Here's an established leader in a category you'll hear more about this season. Because of clever work by some Bay Street lawyers, a new breed of funds is being created to clone popular existing foreign funds but offer full RRSP eligibility.

This four-year-old sweetheart of a fund uses a slightly different technique to achieve its foreign content from some of the newer offerings, but does so without much discernable drag on returns, something the new breed may find tough.

Together, the team manages the asset mix decision and stock selection with a bent toward being conservative and avoiding disaster. It's best for people who aren't necessarily trying to shoot out the lights.

If you only owned one fund, this one wouldn't be a bad pick. It's well diversified: by asset class, by geography, by capitalization, and by investment style. The team focuses on a blend of styles called growth at a reasonable price, and seldom misses out on rallies in growth or value stocks.

AIC Diversified Canada Fund

Managed by: Michael Lee-Chin

From: AIC Limited

RRSP Eligible: 

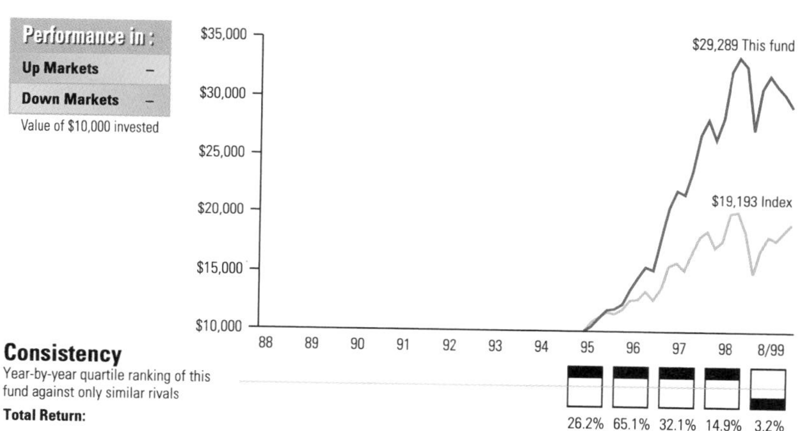

Canadian Equity

Risk

% of time fund has lost money over 12-month period	11%
Biggest drop	-19%
Months to recover	NA

Efficiency

For every $100	$2.27
which for this class is	Avg

Fit (Investment style)

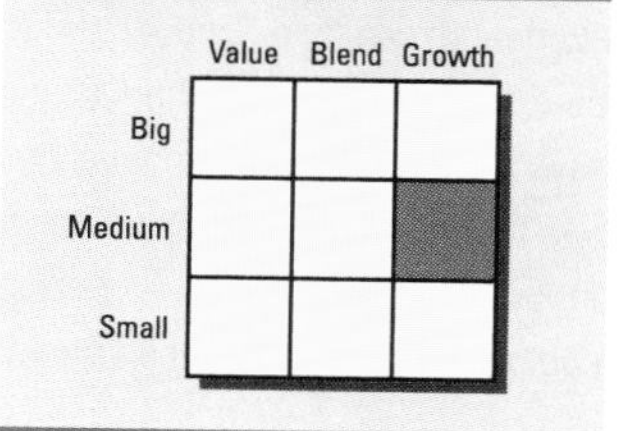

Opinion

The numbers for this fund have been unbelievable: top-quartile results for every one of the last four calendar years. But I'm not wild about it.

Being that much better than the pack comes from just plain old being different from the pack. This fund *is* different. Despite the word "diversified" in its name, the fund is largely a passive sector play on the financial services industry that AIC likes so much. This fund, of course, is not supposed to be a sector fund like AIC Advantage and Advantage II, but it still keeps more than half its asset in financial services companies.

Such a bet will always work out in one of two ways: very well or very badly. That's okay, as long as you know about it going in. And of course, there's the issue of active management. While the team at AIC do work hard to pick the stocks to buy, they pretty much turn passive once they own them — their way of paying homage to the tax-deferring billionaire icon they mimic, Warren Buffett.

Scudder Canadian Equity Fund

Managed by: Philip S. Fortuna

From: Scudder, Stevens & Clark Inc.

RRSP Eligible: 

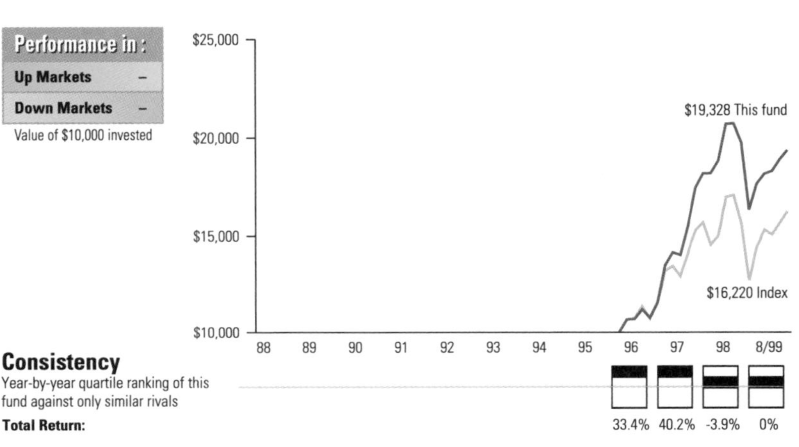

Risk

% of time fund has lost money over 12-month period	33%
Biggest drop	-21%
Months to recover	NA

Efficiency

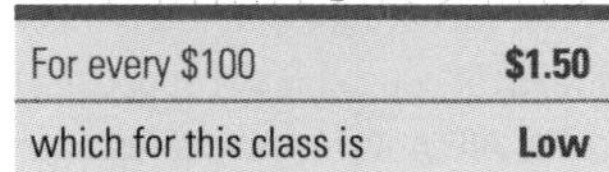

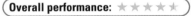

For every $100	**$1.50**
which for this class is	**Low**

Fit (Investment style)

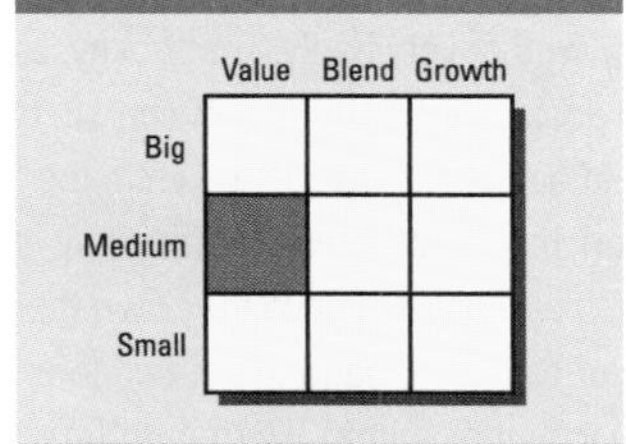

Opinion

Phil Fortuna and his San Francisco-based team use a proprietary "black box" quantitative model that constantly analyzes stocks to search for disparities in relative value. The idea is to generate good returns by capitalizing on factors known to create opportunity — like a company trading at the low end of its historic relative price/cash flow ratio or something.

All the funds at Scudder are unique and compelling — for more than just their low fees. This U.S. powerhouse is really one of the world's best money management shops. In funds like this one, their approach is so hard and analytic that it makes other money managers who rely on gut feel look like astrologers.

The new deal to combine Scudder and Maxxum and distribute funds through Investors Group and London Life is a great move. It combines two tiny fund families that have killer lineups with some real distribution. But don't kid yourself — prices are going straight up for the new clones of funds like this one.

Standard Life Canadian Dividend Fund

Managed by: Peter Hill

From: Standard Life Portfolio Management

RRSP Eligible: 

Overall performance: ★★★★★

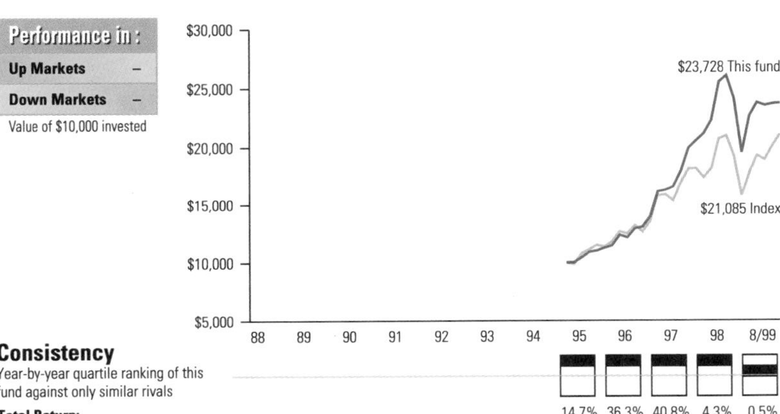

Canadian Equity

Risk

% of time fund has lost money over 12-month period	13%
Biggest drop	-26%
Months to recover	NA

Efficiency

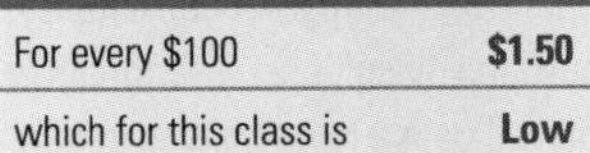

For every $100	$1.50
which for this class is	Low

Fit (Investment style)

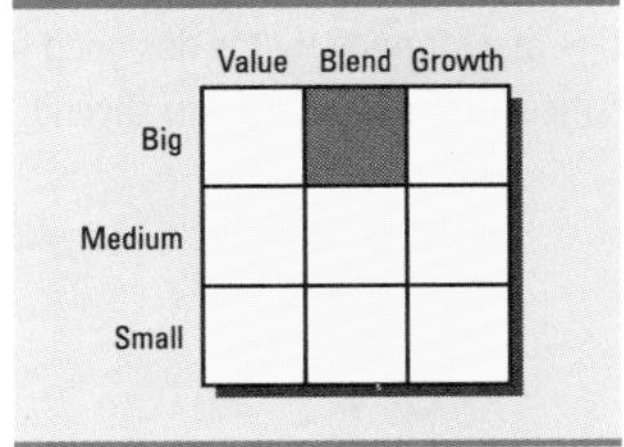

Opinion

From a powerhouse insurer based in Edinburgh comes this meek little Canadian equity fund. Despite its title, we classify it as a Canadian equity fund, not a dividend offering; the yield is only a small part of this fund's total return — which has been excellent no matter what category you call it.

Though it suffered a setback in '99, the fund has earned impressive, consistent results without ever taking sector bets. In fact, there's a policy to never exceed five percent of the TSE sector weight in any one group, and to be in at least 11 of the 14 TSE subgroups at all times. So everything you've seen in outperformance comes from good stock-picking and, to a lesser extent, the edge gained by having lower fees than most.

This year the Montreal-based team of 14 responsible for the fund and the $15 billion they manage alongside it did miss out on a big win in commodities. They owned some cyclical names, but not enough of the deep resource plays. So think of it this way: It's a conservative equity fund that might miss out on some upside at times, but will always protect against steep declines.

Industrial Alliance Stocks Fund

Managed by: Luc R. Fournier

From: Industrial Alliance Life Insurance Co.

RRSP Eligible: 

Overall performance:

Performance in:	
Up Markets	A
Down Markets	B

Value of $10,000 invested

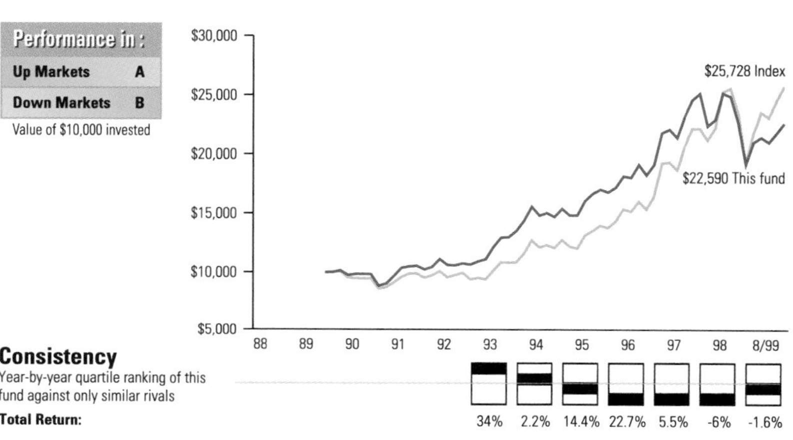

Consistency
Year-by-year quartile ranking of this fund against only similar rivals

Total Return: 34% 2.2% 14.4% 22.7% 5.5% -6% -1.6%

Canadian Equity

Risk

% of time fund has lost money over 12-month period	19%
Biggest drop	-29%
Months to recover	NA

Efficiency

For every $100	$1.82
which for this class is	Low

Fit (Investment style)

	Value	Blend	Growth
Big	■		
Medium			
Small			

Opinion

Here's a stock fund with a long history of cyclical returns. Right now it's very much off cycle: It's had a few years in the tank. But my system is quantitative, meaning that it ranks this fund over its history, versus everybody else. This naturally gives a great deal of weight to the seven-year streak the fund had, starting in about 1988 (not shown), when it beat the pants off most of its rivals with great consistency. And its low MER certainly hasn't hurt. The foreign exposure here is achieved with a large holding in a Templeton pooled fund. Other than that, though, you'll see big names in here from a broad spectrum of the Canadian securities landscape — everything from big golds to big banks — in a strategy that is designed to provide diversification first and growth second.

First Canadian Dividend Fund

Managed by: Michael Stanley

From: Jones Heward

RRSP Eligible: 

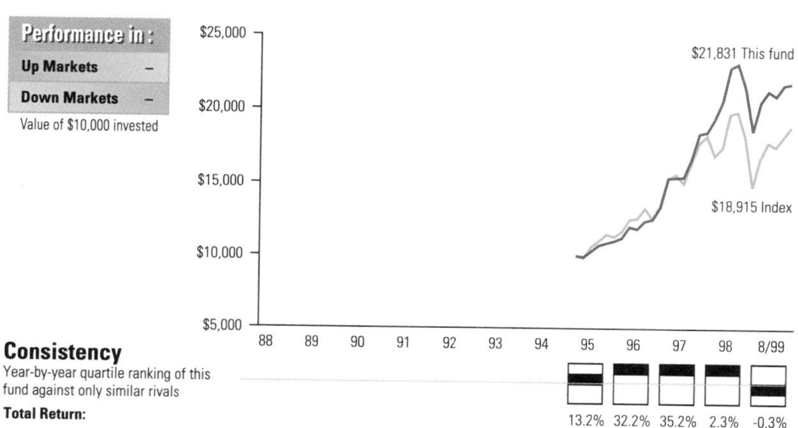

Risk

% of time fund has lost money over 12-month period	11%
Biggest drop	-22%
Months to recover	NA

Efficiency

For every $100	$1.67
which for this class is	Low

Fit (Investment style)

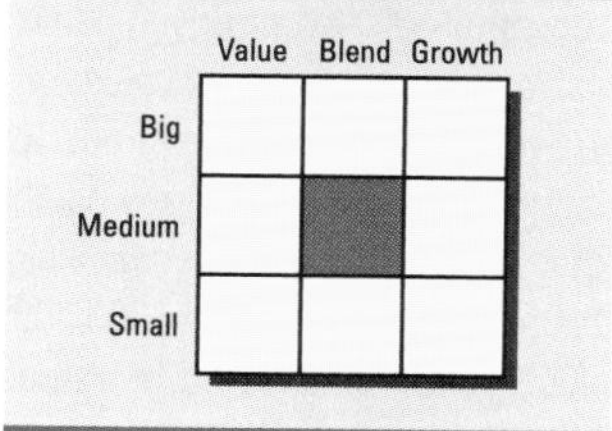

Opinion

Michael Stanley knows the right way to make money in Canada's perennially lagging stock market. He buys conservative stocks that grow their dividends over time. It's a simple formula that works.

This fund is mostly a common stock fund. All of its holdings do pay dividends, of course; just not the high dividends you'd get from preferred shares. There are no bonds, which is a plus for taxable investors.

The fund has succeeded through its strategic decision to own, then trim, then repurchase bank shares. Only over the final of these three decisions has the timing been off a little. The banks are getting thumped at the time of writing, hurting Stanley's relative performance. But he makes a strong case for real value now, saying the banks' common stock yields are today something like 60 percent of what ten-year government of Canada bonds yield. Traditionally, that's augered well for the share price performance of this important group, which drives the performance of this fund.

ABC Fundamental Value Fund

Managed by: Irwin A. Michael

From: I.A. Michael Investment Counsel Ltd.

RRSP Eligible: 

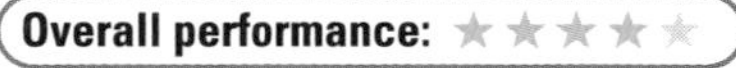

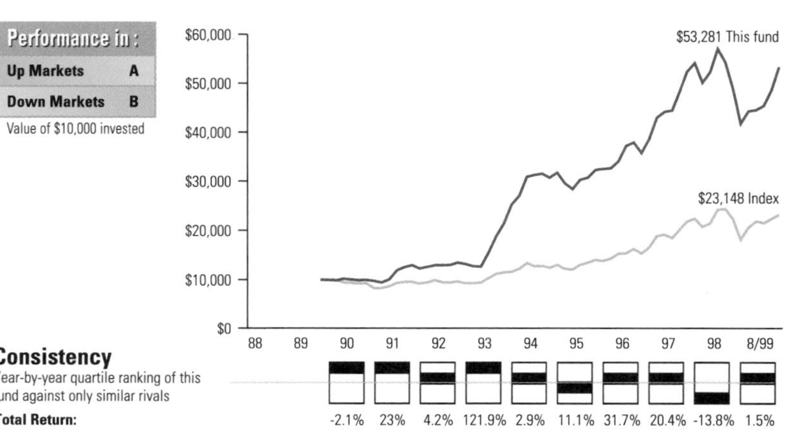

Risk

% of time fund has lost money over 12-month period	21%
Biggest drop	-31%
Months to recover	NA

Efficiency

For every $100	$2.00
which for this class is	Low

Fit (Investment style)

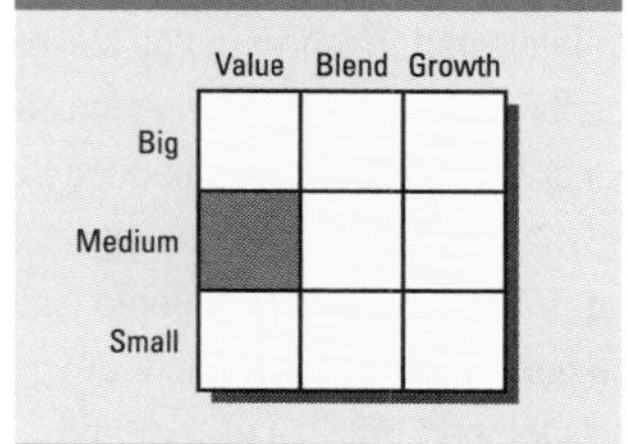

Opinion

It's happened before and it'll happen again. A legendary manager gets whacked with a severe downturn by simply having been a little early in some companies that really ought to be trading for more. Some people think the smart guy turned stupid. But he's certain that he's right about the real value, and boom! Eventually it happens: The fund rockets ahead because of appreciation in the very stocks that were killing it.

It happened for Irwin Michael in this fund, which cratered 31 percent last year during the summer meltdown. He understands the delicate balance between knowing when to buy dirt-cheap stocks and — just as important — knowing when to punt. His rebound has topped the charts with wins in cable stocks, takeover targets, event-driven names, and even defensive plays. He does the valuation work, but then he lives and breathes the Street, following its ever-changing psychology and staying ahead of the shifts that can derail funds for years. I highly recommend this fund for anyone with $300,000 and up. That way, you'll have enough left over after this firm's $150,000 minimum to diversify into another style.

Bissett Canadian Equity Fund

Managed by: Michael A. Quinn

From: Bissett and Associates Investment Management Ltd.

RRSP Eligible: 

Overall performance: ★★★½

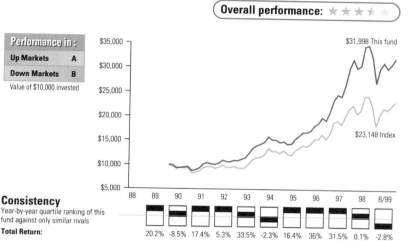

Performance in:	
Up Markets	A
Down Markets	B

Value of $10,000 invested

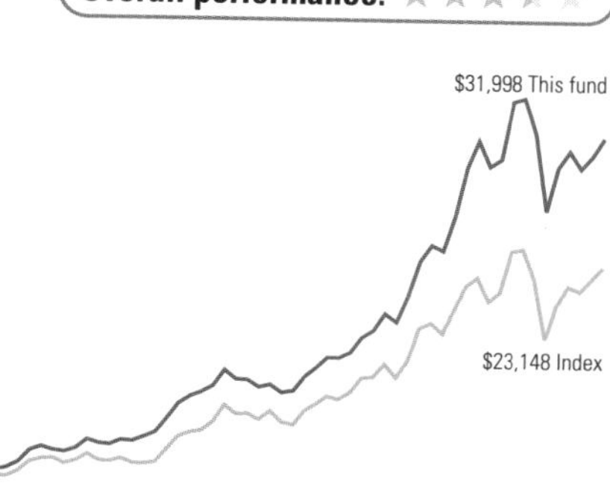

Consistency
Year-by-year quartile ranking of this fund against only similar rivals

	89	90	91	92	93	94	95	96	97	98	8/99
Total Return:	20.2%	-8.5%	17.4%	5.3%	33.5%	-2.3%	16.4%	36%	31.5%	0.1%	-2.8%

Risk

% of time fund has lost money over 12-month period	19%
Biggest drop	-26%
Months to recover	23

Efficiency

For every $100	$1.18
which for this class is	Low

Fit (Investment style)

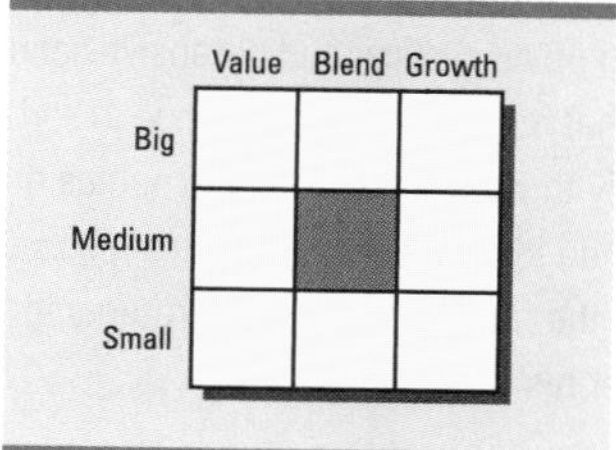

Opinion

This mostly bigger-cap fund did well throughout the messy meltdown in '98 by being more focused on value than ever before. Plus, the fund has had less exposure to smaller-cap stocks than usual. But it didn't own the super stocks that have led the rebound. Names like TD Bank, Seagram, and Nortel simply don't meet this team's screens for financial quality and earnings sustainability. And since they don't play the momentum game, they, like many, have been punished (in a relative sense) for missing these important high flyers.

The already low MER of this fine fund has actually come down lately. And on the stock side, better things are surely ahead. The demutualization of Canada's bigger insurance companies leaves this team with a strong advantage: They've always outperformed in the rate-sensitive sector because they understand the importance of the balance sheet in financial companies.

Canadian Equity

Trimark Canadian Fund

Managed by: Robert Krembil

From: Trimark Investment Management Inc.

RRSP Eligible: 

Overall performance:

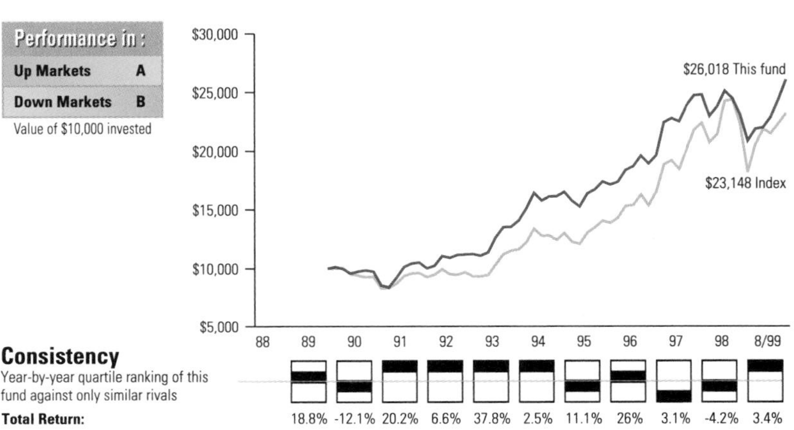

Risk

% of time fund has lost money over 12-month period	14%
Biggest drop	-23%
Months to recover	17

Efficiency

For every $100	$1.52
which for this class is	Low

Fit (Investment style)

	Value	Blend	Growth
Big		■	
Medium			
Small			

Opinion

No fund recommendation has drawn more fire and fury than this one. I've recommended the fund every year since 1994. I'm proud that I maintained and even upgraded my position in 1998, when thousands of broker cold calls went out screaming "sell." Finally the closing chapter is now being written on a period of erratic relative performance designed to do exactly what the firm says it has always stood for: protecting capital first and growing it second.

Former manager Vito Maida did great with this fund in the face of huge cash inflows during his first 21 months on the job. Then came the fateful decision to punt the banks — a year too early. Worse, he loaded up on cyclical and defensive securities in a move that most said was a change in style. Ultimately those are precisely the names that soared. And it's his legacy of cyclical picks that have powered the fund to top-quartile returns in 1999 — even after his departure.

AGF Dividend Fund

Managed by: Gordon H. MacDougall

From: Connor Clark & Lunn Investment Management Ltd.

RRSP Eligible: 

Overall performance: 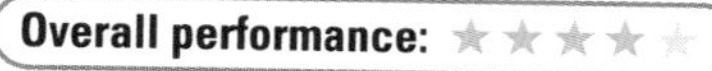

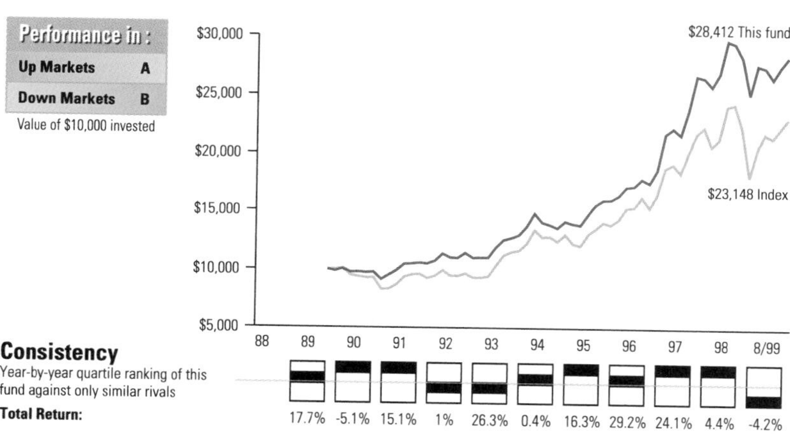

Risk

% of time fund has lost money over 12-month period	**15%**
Biggest drop	**-19%**
Months to recover	**NA**

Efficiency

For every $100	**$1.87**
which for this class is	**Low**

Fit (Investment style)

	Value	Blend	Growth
Big		■	
Medium			
Small			

Opinion

This fund is in the general Canadian equity category because it doesn't buy preferred shares and it is therefore not correctly compared to dividend funds that seek tax-advantaged income (the ideal mandate of funds bearing the name "dividend").

It's a conservative growth fund that makes judicial use of asset allocation to mitigate risks and is heavy on the fundamental research to search for names that embody a blend of value and growth.

What's remarkable is that the Vancouver-based team is consistently able to find companies that are both financially strong (with average financial coverage ratios that are well above the TSE 100) and fundamentally cheap. Lately, they've been in the big-cap resource area.

Because this fund never buys little exploration companies and high-tech start-ups, the fund did miss out on the early 1999 party to some degree — which is to be expected for a conservative offering like this.

Guardian Growth Equity Fund

Managed by: John Priestman

From: Guardian Capital Inc.

RRSP Eligible: 

Overall performance: ★★★★★

Performance in:	
Up Markets	A
Down Markets	C

Value of $10,000 invested

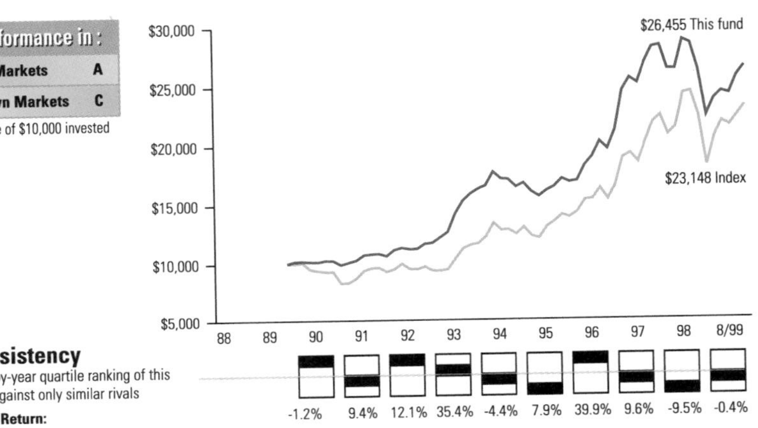

Consistency

Year-by-year quartile ranking of this fund against only similar rivals

Total Return:

90	91	92	93	94	95	96	97	98	8/99
-1.2%	9.4%	12.1%	35.4%	-4.4%	7.9%	39.9%	9.6%	-9.5%	-0.4%

Risk

% of time fund has lost money over 12-month period	23%
Biggest drop	-28%
Months to recover	NA

Efficiency

For every $100	$2.17
which for this class is	Avg

Fit (Investment style)

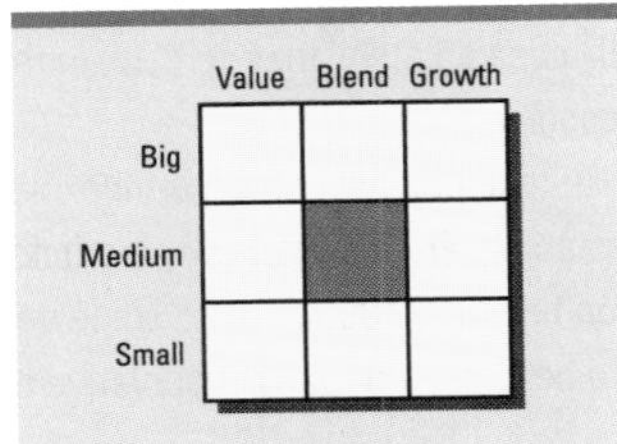

Opinion

Every three years or so, it seems that this quality fund kicks butt. The fact that their relative performance seems to gyrate gives a false impression that their investment approach does too.

In fact, the fund is a tightly focused play on a handful of three dozen firms that can participate in what manager John Priestman sees as a very strong period for worldwide growth. He reckons that strength will continue for consumers, exporters, and non-North American economies.

He's been wrong before with thematic views that were early — like his call on banks two years ago. But he seems to be correct so far with this list of mostly bigger cap financial and resource names.

Remember to buy on a front load at Guardian to get substantially lower annual expenses. This fund is called "classic," which means you'll pay a small front-end load and save 0.68 percent a year in fees. That's a bargain.

Standard Life Equity Fund

Managed by: Peter Hill

From: Standard Life Portfolio Management

RRSP Eligible: 

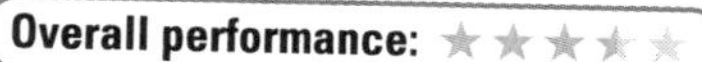

Performance in :	
Up Markets	A
Down Markets	D

Value of $10,000 invested

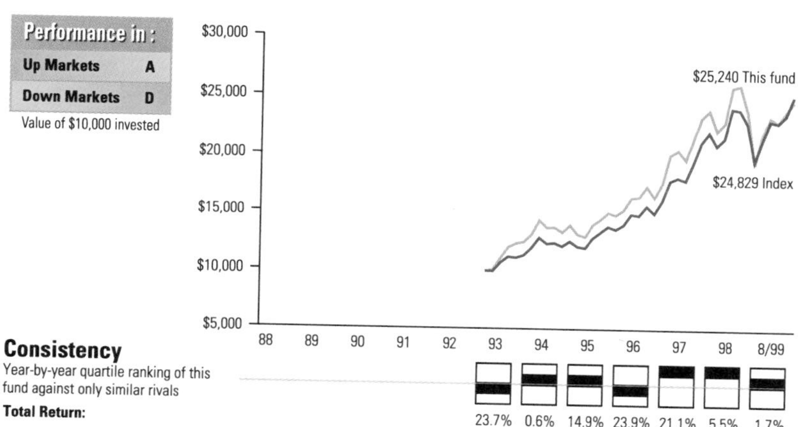

Consistency
Year-by-year quartile ranking of this fund against only similar rivals

Total Return:

93	94	95	96	97	98	8/99
23.7%	0.6%	14.9%	23.9%	21.1%	5.5%	1.7%

Canadian Equity

Risk

% of time fund has lost money over 12-month period	13%
Biggest drop	-21%
Months to recover	13

Efficiency

For every $100	$2.00
which for this class is	Avg

Fit (Investment style)

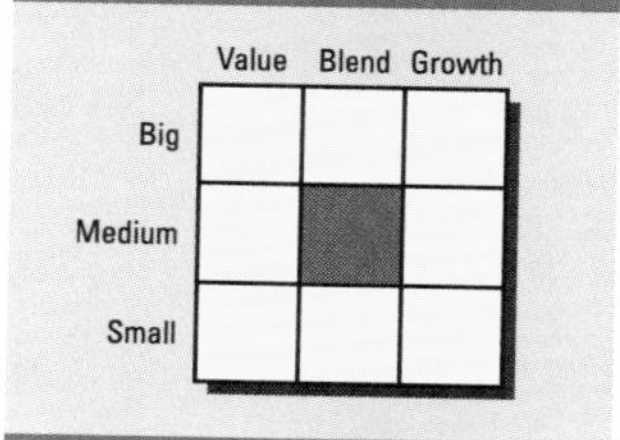

Opinion

You just had to know that with all the market action lately being concentrated in the huge stocks that dominate the index, index investing was going to become hotter than ever. Yup; many of the bums in this market are the courageous few who rolled the dice and did not buy Nortel or BCE (which together account for 22 percent of the TSE). This is not one of those courageous few. It's an actively managed fund, sure. But it operates with a style pension funds like to call "active core," which means that it doesn't deviate heavily from index weights.

It's been a great time for big cap active core managers, and this "no surprises" fund is no exception. Without ever taking sector bets, the fund has consistently come up with excellent results. As with Standard Life Canadian Dividend, there's a policy in place never to exceed five percent of the TSE sector weight in any one group. So everything you've seen in outperformance comes from good stock picking and, to a lesser extent, the edge gained by having lower fees than most funds have.

Principal Growth Fund

Managed by: Michael Lawton

RRSP Eligible: 

Overall performance: ★★★★★

Performance in:	
Up Markets	A
Down Markets	A

Value of $10,000 invested

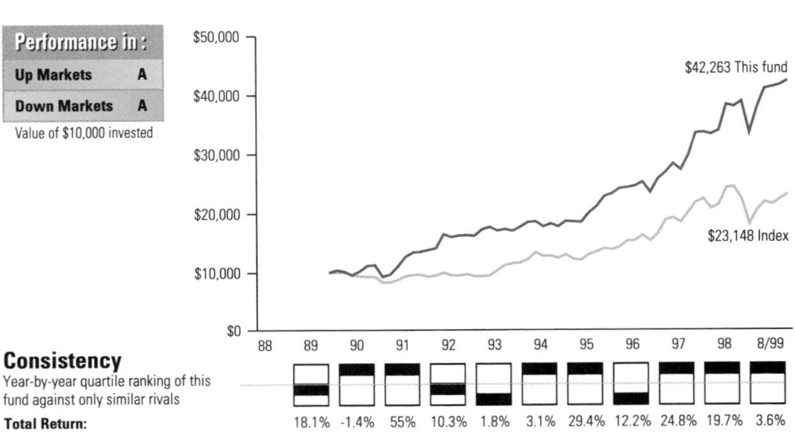

Consistency
Year-by-year quartile ranking of this fund against only similar rivals

	89	90	91	92	93	94	95	96	97	98	8/99
Total Return:	18.1%	-1.4%	55%	10.3%	1.8%	3.1%	29.4%	12.2%	24.8%	19.7%	3.6%

Risk

% of time fund has lost money over 12-month period	5%
Biggest drop	-19%
Months to recover	7

Efficiency

For every $100	$0.50
which for this class is	Low

Fit (Investment style)

	Value	Blend	Growth
Big			
Medium			■
Small			

Opinion

A good fund if you can get your hands on it. It's a great performer in all market conditions and the MER is dirt cheap.

I confess that I don't know jack about this western-based firm. So the problem is that I don't know if the indicated fees are the total fees. This means I need to investigate direct charges to the investor account — something to be wary of.

Fidelity Canadian Growth Company Fund

Managed by: Alan R. Radlo

From: Fidelity Investments Canada Ltd.

RRSP Eligible: 

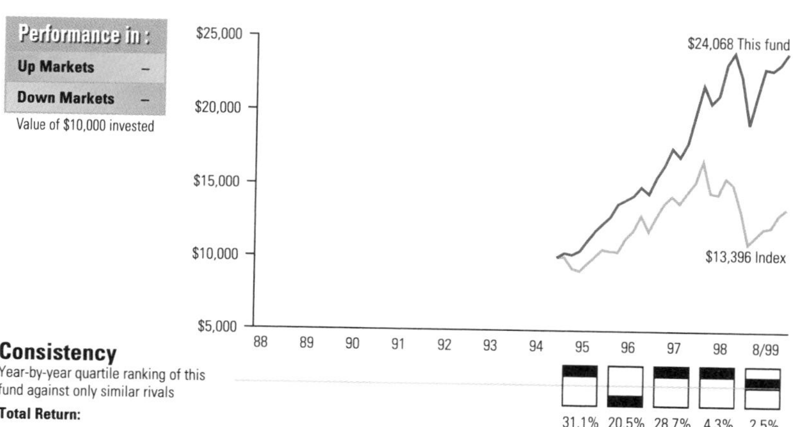

Risk

% of time fund has lost money over 12-month period	14%
Biggest drop	-20%
Months to recover	NA

Efficiency

For every $100	$2.45
which for this class is	Avg

Fit (Investment style)

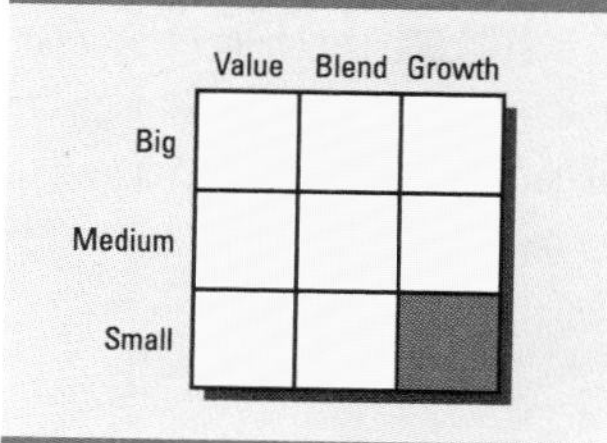

Opinion

Radlo's terrific performance in this fund's first three years depended on limited exposure to resource stocks, which were in the tank and his fundamental research showing that Quebec was full of fabulous, fast-growing cheap companies.

But weakness in the first half of 1999 was caused by concerns over valuations, leaving Radlo uneasy about spending money. At writing, he still had about 20 percent in cash. In a strong market that's a real drag. For part of the year (when rocks were running) he missed out on the hottest area of the small cap marketplace — the resource names.

Those two weaknesses were simply outweighed by old-fashioned acumen in stock-picking. With something like 130 names in the fund most of the time, there are always standouts. Lately, they've been in communications and technology, but don't think of this as a sector fund. It's more of a broad play on relative valuations and inefficiencies in the small cap arena.

GBC Canadian Growth Fund

Managed by: Scott Taylor

From: Pembroke Management Ltd.

RRSP Eligible: 

Overall performance: ★★★★

Performance in:	
Up Markets	A
Down Markets	A

Value of $10,000 invested

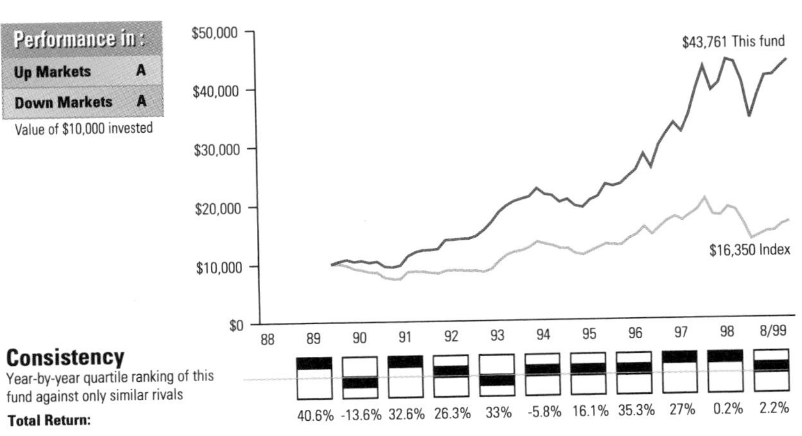

Consistency
Year-by-year quartile ranking of this fund against only similar rivals

Total Return:	40.6%	-13.6%	32.6%	26.3%	33%	-5.8%	16.1%	35.3%	27%	0.2%	2.2%

Risk

% of time fund has lost money over 12-month period	22%
Biggest drop	-27%
Months to recover	NA

Efficiency

For every $100	$1.89
which for this class is	Low

Fit (Investment style)

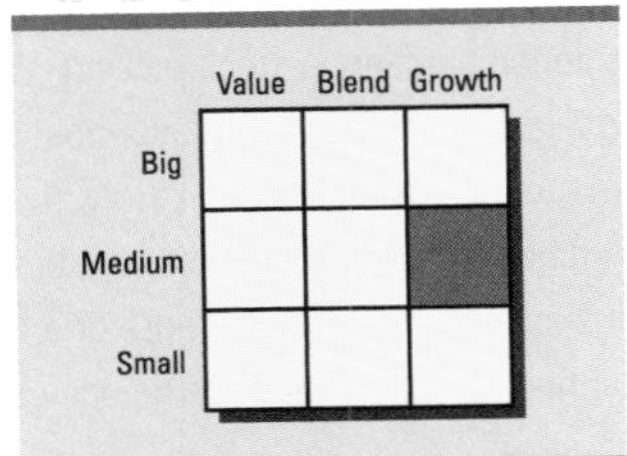

Opinion

If the Canadian mutual fund investor ever gets really sophisticated, this fund company is going to soar. They simply offer better products at better prices, with better service, than any other company in Canada. They're still relatively unknown to the retail public because they haven't advertised in years.

This fund's broad mix of technology, drugs, telecom and a little resources makes it decidedly more growth-oriented than many of its peers. And that does itself impose a degree of risk. But overall, the fund has beat 75 percent of its peers in bear markets — a remarkable achievement for a fund that's always right at the top of the charts in good times.

There's a $100,000 minimum investment with GBC and the funds are available through brokers, so before you get sucked into some crappy wrap account for high net worth investors, ask about this fine offering.

Canadian Equity — Small and Mid Cap

Mawer New Canada Fund

Managed by: Martin D. Mawer

From: Investment Management

RRSP Eligible: 

Overall performance:

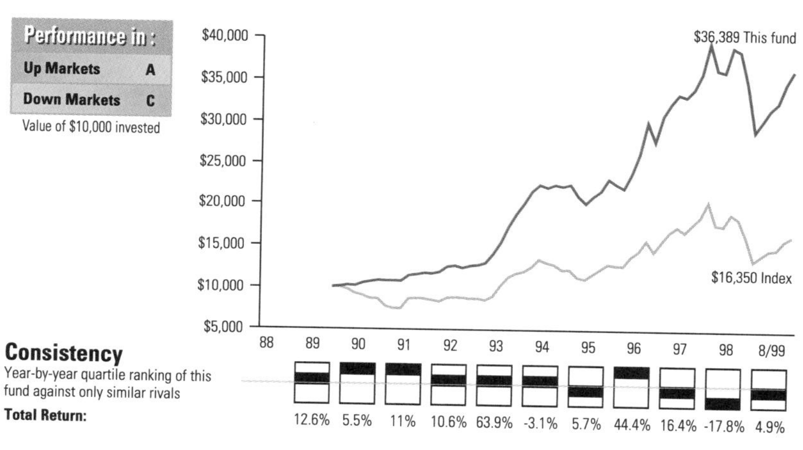

Risk

% of time fund has lost money over 12-month period	15%
Biggest drop	-27%
Months to recover	NA

Efficiency

For every $100	$1.57
which for this class is	Low

Fit (Investment style)

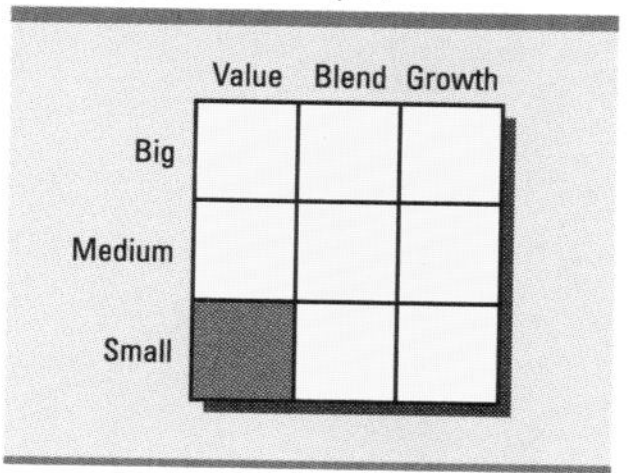

Opinion

This fine fund has gone through a tough time over the last couple of years, but that all seems to be coming to an end. In last year's book, I wrote about how Bill MacLaughlan had expressed real concerns about the risk posed by small-cap stocks. He felt that they could suffer in any stock downturn and were not particularly attractive at that time. Six months later small-cap stocks had underperformed by a mighty 20 percentage points. Not surprisingly, MacLaughlan has done well with the fund in this environment.

It's important to mention, though, that this fund lost its prior manager at the end of 1996, and during 1997 liquidated some of the long-held wins previous manager Leigh Pullen had accumulated. Those realizations added up to a distribution at the end of 1997 of almost 30 percent of the fund's value, heavy by any stretch of the imagination. Overall, with this fund you can expect great management at a low MER — two factors that make this pick highly attractive to smart investors.

MetLife MVP Growth Fund

Managed by: Susan Blanchard

From: AMI Partners

RRSP Eligible: 

Overall performance: ★★★★★

Performance in:	
Up Markets	A
Down Markets	B

Value of $10,000 invested

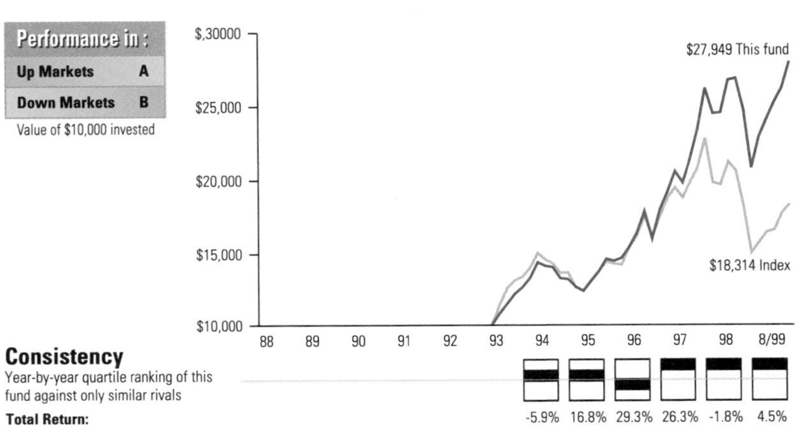

Consistency
Year-by-year quartile ranking of this fund against only similar rivals

Total Return: -5.9% 16.8% 29.3% 26.3% -1.8% 4.5%

Risk

% of time fund has lost money over 12-month period	24%
Biggest drop	-24%
Months to recover	NA

Efficiency

For every $100	$2.49
which for this class is	Avg

Fit (Investment style)

	Value	Blend	Growth
Big			
Medium			
Small			■

Opinion

Great numbers for this Susan Blanchard-run fund. Without banks and with a wad of cash uninvested, it's been all stock-picking to get to this achievement. Thank some technology wins.

That's the good news. The bad news is that Mutual Life (now called Clarica) has taken over all of MetLife's individual insurance business, and has closed off this fund to new investors. It remains open to new sales from existing unitholders. AMI is still the manager on this fine fund, which by now bears the name Clarica MVP Growth.

Talvest Small Cap Canadian Equity Fund

Managed by: Sebastian van Berkom

From: Van Berkom and Associates Inc.

RRSP Eligible: 

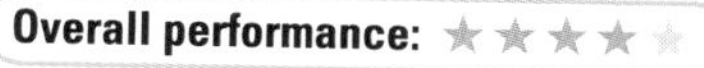

Performance in :	
Up Markets	A
Down Markets	C

Value of $10,000 invested

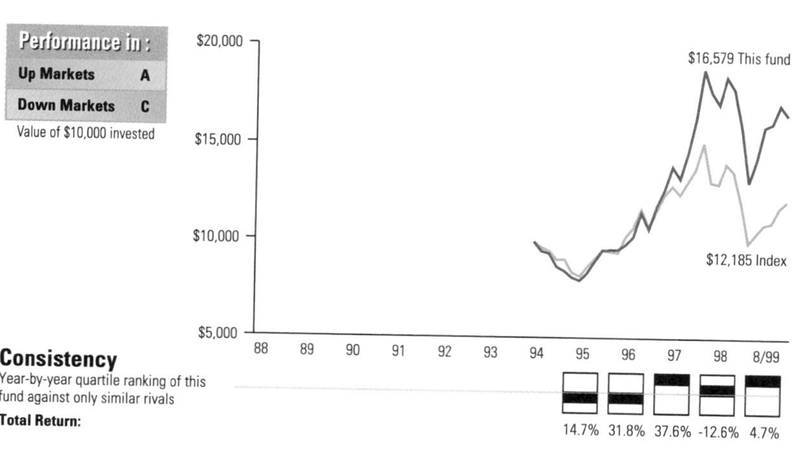

Consistency
Year-by-year quartile ranking of this fund against only similar rivals

Total Return: 14.7% 31.8% 37.6% -12.6% 4.7%

Risk

% of time fund has lost money over 12-month period	29%
Biggest drop	-31%
Months to recover	NA

Efficiency

For every $100	$2.54
which for this class is	Avg

Fit (Investment style)

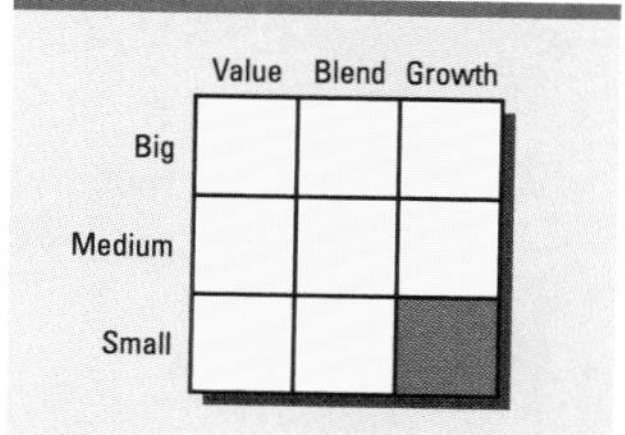

Opinion

Small cap managers usually either buy tons of different companies to reduce the risk of being wrong with any one name, or they buy very few so that they can have the time to focus and understand each better.

Van Berkom has chosen the latter approach. And he gets even more time to focus on his short list of 50 or so companies because he has such low turnover — only about 25 percent annually. But the one trick in concentrated funds — especially ones with a buy and hold (and hold) approach — is that you've got to pick the right companies. Look at names like TLC The Laser Centre, JDS Uniphase and C.I. Fund Management to get an idea of what kind of quality you're getting here: Many of the fund's holdings get taken over because Van Berkom buys stocks the way executives buy companies. Hence the appeal of his holdings to acquisitors.

Now's a great time to finally consider making this one of your core families. It's got strength in stocks and bonds, both in Canada and abroad.

Hongkong Bank Dividend Income Fund

Managed by: Jim Gilliland

From: HSBC Asset Management Canada

RRSP Eligible: 

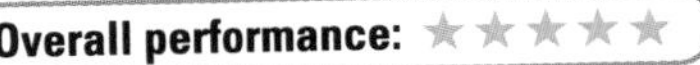

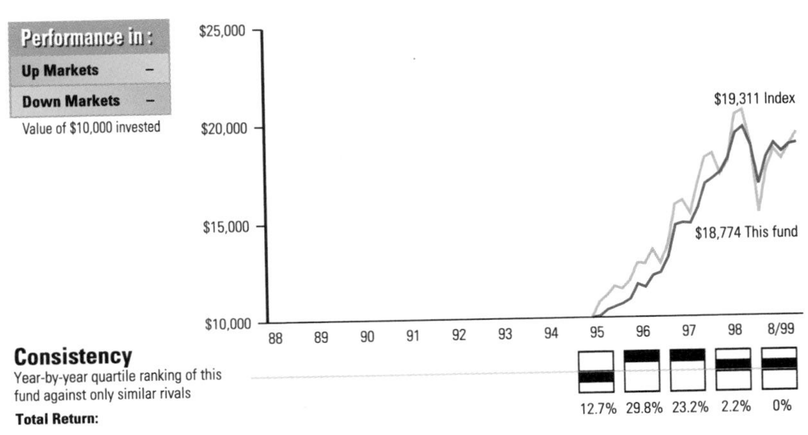

Risk

% of time fund has lost money over 12-month period	16%
Biggest drop	-17%
Months to recover	NA

Opinion

This fund is cheap and owns a boatload of excellent banks, utilities, and pipelines. Oh, and performance has been spectacular. Jim Gilliland has outdone himself with this no-load offering.

Efficiency

For every $100	$1.85
which for this class is	Avg

Fit (Investment style)

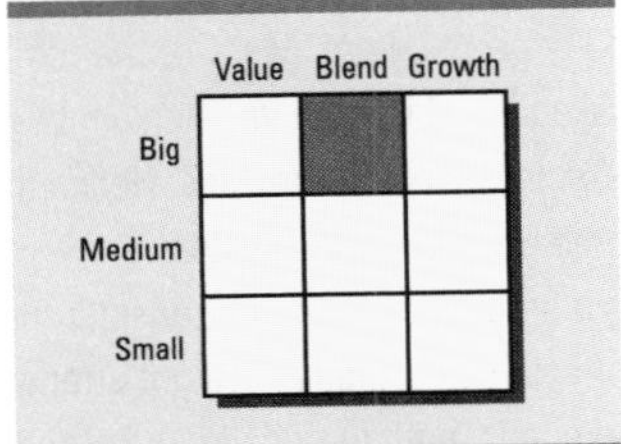

Altamira Dividend Fund

Managed by: Ian M.H. Joseph

From: Altamira Management Ltd.

RRSP Eligible: 

Performance in:	
Up Markets	–
Down Markets	–

Value of $10,000 invested

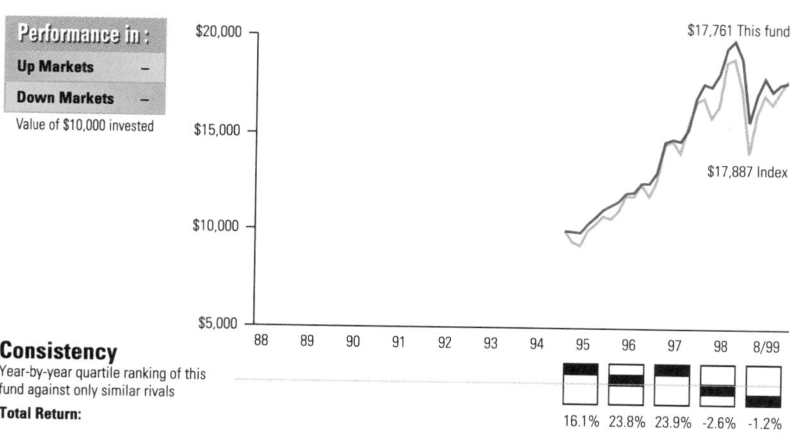

Consistency
Year-by-year quartile ranking of this fund against only similar rivals

Total Return: 16.1% 23.8% 23.9% -2.6% -1.2%

Risk

% of time fund has lost money over 12-month period	23%
Biggest drop	-20%
Months to recover	NA

Efficiency

For every $100	$1.62
which for this class is	Low

Fit (Investment style)

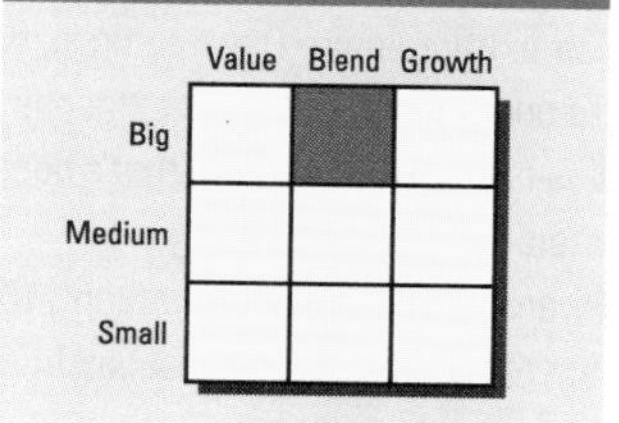

Opinion

This fund has stumbled badly in 1999 when compared to its peer group, in part because its peer group is such a grab-bag of everything from pure stocks funds that call themselves dividend funds to pref share funds that are full of bonds.

The problem is only relative. This big cap is a great fund in terms of absolute performance, risk profile, fees, and rate sensitivity. And it's got far more actual tax-advantaged yield than most in the dividend fund category. That means you really ought to hold the fund outside your RSP or RIF — to maintain the tax advantages.

But with 40-odd percent in pref shares, the fund sometimes has trouble keeping up with its competitors in strong markets. So don't own it to keep up with the competition. Own it to earn steady yield today and modest growth of income over time — without losing the farm if rates rise.

Altamira is absolutely cleaning up in the areas of index funds, technology funds, and domestic stocks.

BPI Global Opportunities Fund

Managed by: Daniel R. Jaworski

From: BPI Global Asset Management LLP

RRSP Eligible: 

Overall performance: ★★★★★

Performance in:	
Up Markets	–
Down Markets	–

Value of $10,000 invested

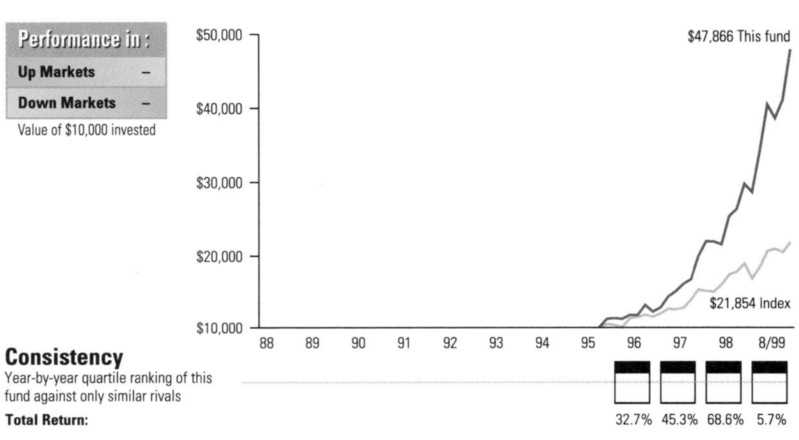

Consistency
Year-by-year quartile ranking of this fund against only similar rivals

	96	97	98	8/99
Total Return:	32.7%	45.3%	68.6%	5.7%

Risk

% of time fund has lost money over 12-month period	0%
Biggest drop	-10%
Months to recover	2

Efficiency

For every $100	$2.44
which for this class is	Avg

Fit (Investment style)

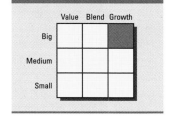

	Value	Blend	Growth
Big			■
Medium			
Small			

Opinion

It's a little cruel and unfair to recommend this superstar in a listing of the best mutual funds in the country. The fund is perhaps the hottest vehicle ever available domestically, having doubled a couple of times in just over three years since inception. Learning of its merit is cruel because you'll have to pony up a cool $150,000 to get in.

It's a hedge fund. Yup, like the sexy offshore kind that are just for the super-rich and usually have minimums of $5 million or more. It uses short-selling in combination with long positions to build a portfolio that is, in some ways, really conservative. In fact, it hasn't ever lost money over a three-month period. Stock-picker extraordinaire Dan Jaworski, who heads BPI's operation in Orlando, is the one responsible for this big cap growth fund that's done well in areas like telecoms and technology.

You'll want to have much more than $150,000 to diversify the rest of your portfolio away from this unusual fund.

Bissett Multinational Growth Fund

Managed by: Fred E. Pynn

From: Bissett and Associates Investment Management Ltd.

RRSP Eligible: 

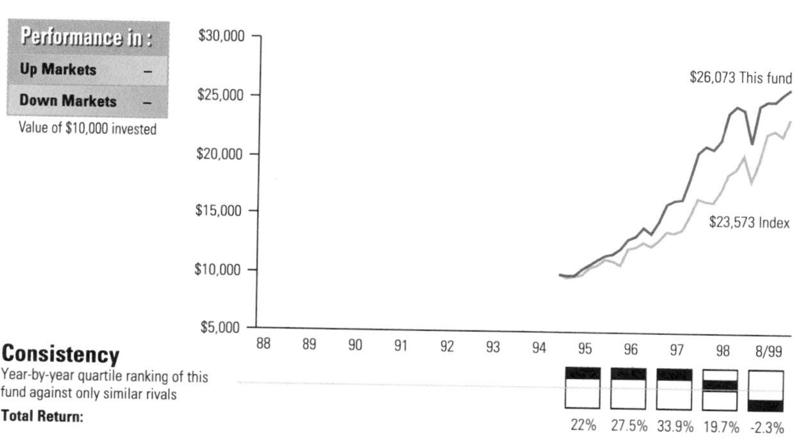

Risk

% of time fund has lost money over 12-month period	0%
Biggest drop	-12%
Months to recover	5

Efficiency

For every $100	$1.34
which for this class is	Low

Fit (Investment style)

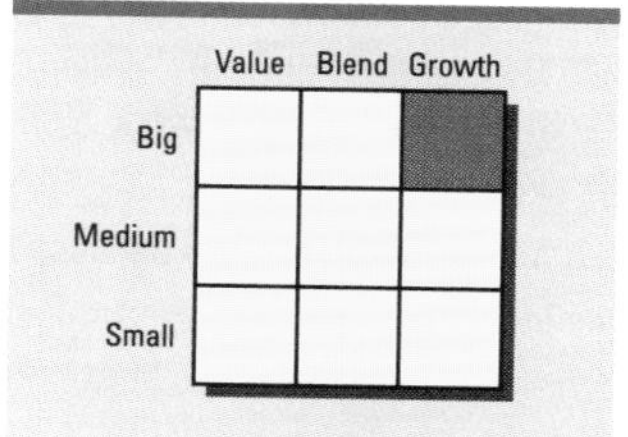

Opinion

Who can argue with the numbers? Plus-twenty percent returns in each of its four full calendar years. An MER under a buck forty. First or second quartile every year since inception. Fast five-month recovery time in the last quasi-bear market.

But despite the impressive quantitative details, my feelings aren't that positive for this fund.

The fund is unique versus its global peers in many ways. It's got a full 20 percent invested in Canada (but that's coming down). It's full of U.S. big caps. And it only gets its somewhat limited non-North American exposure through New York-traded American Depository Receipts (or ADRs). True, they're equivalent to the foreign stock they represent, but are scarcer.

All the U.S. exposure helps explain the great past performance — the U.S. has been the hottest market on earth. But this fund is so conservative that it could really miss out on rallies in small caps, emerging markets, and Asia — three areas that just aren't available under the present structure of this fund.

Global Strategy World Companies Fund

Managed by: Oscar Castro, Chris Jenkins

From: Montgomery Asset and Rothschild Asset

RRSP Eligible: 

Overall performance: ★★★★½

Performance in:	
Up Markets	–
Down Markets	–

Value of $10,000 invested

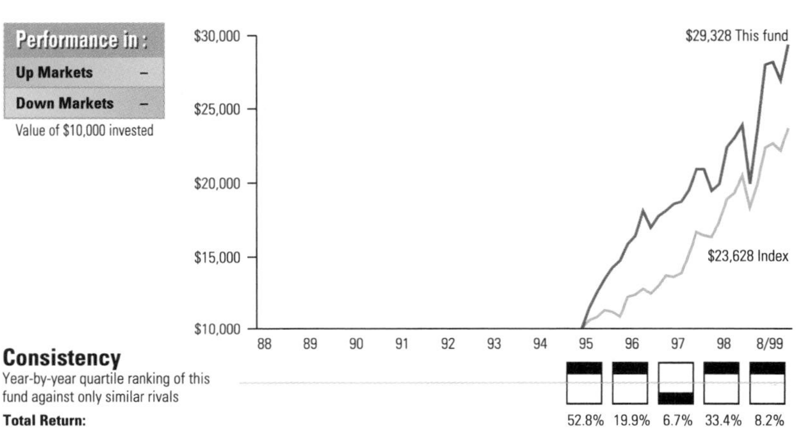

Consistency

Year-by-year quartile ranking of this fund against only similar rivals

	95	96	97	98	8/99
Total Return:	52.8%	19.9%	6.7%	33.4%	8.2%

Risk

% of time fund has lost money over 12-month period	2%
Biggest drop	-16%
Months to recover	4

Efficiency

For every $100	$2.65
which for this class is	Avg

Fit (Investment style)

	Value	Blend	Growth
Big			■
Medium			
Small			

Opinion

Making its debut on this list, this newer fund is the picture of what you should look for in a global equity offering. It's the result of a collaboration with Montgomery, a bottom-up tech-savvy research shop, and Rothschild, a top-down currency and interest rate kind of a shop.

This fund avoids country bets by setting minimum and maximum exposure constraints on the country decision. And then Montgomery focuses on five themes: 1. Euro dynamics — liberalization, privatization, and the Euro. 2. Digital convergence — telecom, TV, media, and e-commerce. 3. Alternative power, especially for vehicles. 4. Outsourcing — in manufacturing and service industries. 5. Concept retailing — things like IKEA that work in one country and will likely work elsewhere.

I'm such a fan of the approach because the math backs up its intuitive appeal. This portfolio owns faster-growing companies and has better downside protection than any index.

International Equity

Maxxum Global Equity Fund

Managed by: Helen Young Hayes

From: Janus Capital Corp

RRSP Eligible: 

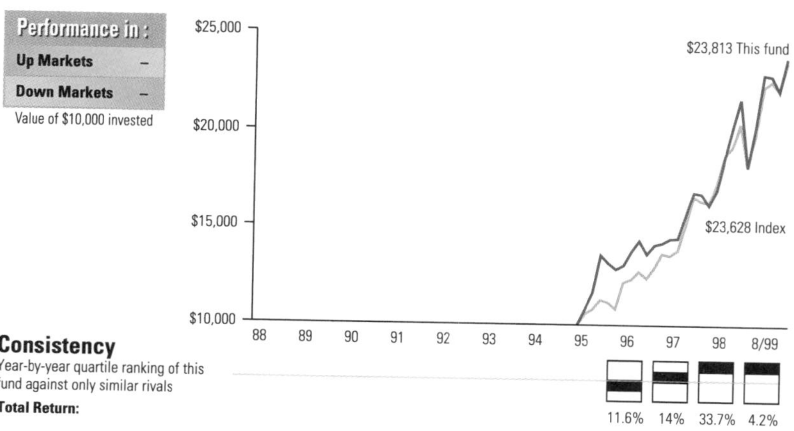

Risk

% of time fund has lost money over 12-month period	0%
Biggest drop	-16%
Months to recover	4

Efficiency

For every $100	$2.50
which for this class is	Avg

Fit (Investment style)

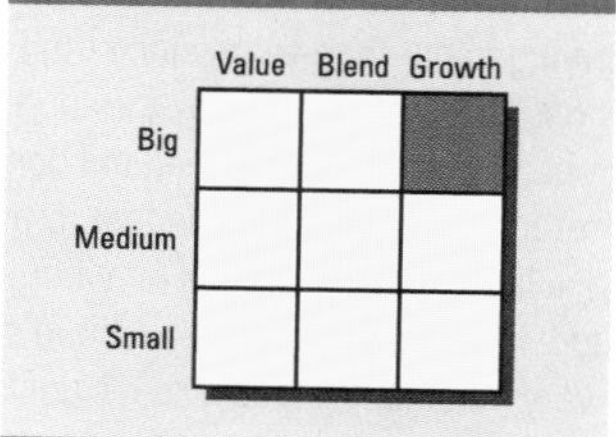

Opinion

Helen Young Hayes is smart and tough. Just like this fund. It invests overseas the old-fashioned way — by kicking tires and trying products. The Denver-based team responsible for the fund is famous for the degree to which they delve into a company's affairs to get an understanding of whether its products are any good, whether its competitors are catching up, and whether its management can do what it sets out to do.

Behind it all is a fiery Yale graduate who competes in triathlons and wins kudos for simply finding better companies. She was named Morningstar's fund manager of the year in 1997 and (unlike the usual aftermath of such an honour) went on to perform even better afterward.

You'll want to be a part of this fund family, not just for its connection to great managers in Denver, but because of its connections around the world. Maxxum is now a part of Scudder, which has formed a distribution deal with Investors Group and London Life.

Templeton International Stock Fund

Managed by: Donald F. Reed

From: Templeton Management Limited

RRSP Eligible: 

Overall performance: ★★★★

Performance in:	
Up Markets	A
Down Markets	D

Value of $10,000 invested

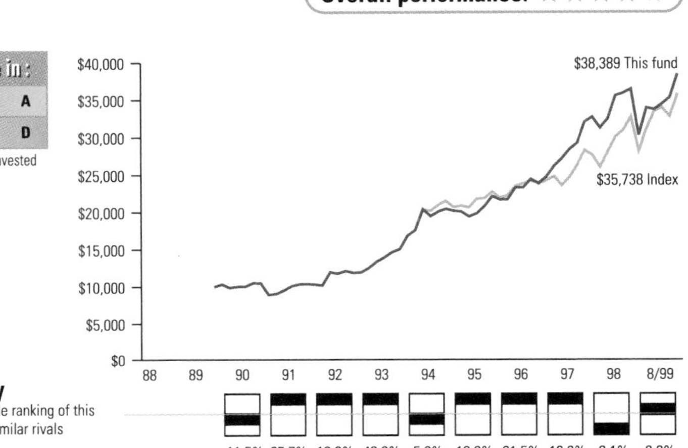

Consistency
Year-by-year quartile ranking of this fund against only similar rivals

	90	91	92	93	94	95	96	97	98	8/99
Total Return:	-11.5%	25.7%	12.2%	48.2%	5.2%	12.2%	21.5%	16.3%	8.1%	0.9%

Risk

% of time fund has lost money over 12-month period	14%
Biggest drop	-17%
Months to recover	10

Efficiency

For every $100	$2.46
which for this class is	Avg

Fit (Investment style)

	Value	Blend	Growth
Big	■		
Medium			
Small			

Opinion

This too has rebounded from a slump in '98 brought on by a stubborn refusal on the part of the whole team at Templeton to avoid the big cap momentum plays that powered the market that year. Things have been more normal in 1999, with a resumption of the long-term trend that value stocks beat growth.

But think that you're getting diversification from the Templeton Growth Fund by buying this baby; this fund's mandate has a constraint against investing in the United States, but the rest of the portfolio is identical to that of its aforementioned worldwide sister fund.

Two thirds of the portfolio is invested in Europe. That's added value over the past few years. The European stocks have done well, but given some of that back on currency losses in the Euro — a trend that isn't worth worrying about long-term, since the Euro's weakness adds gas to exporters held by the fund. Still, don't own a European fund with this one, and don't think that the great returns earned so far can last forever. Even Templeton is leery of making calls on where the market's headed. It's tougher to identify cheap stocks in what is a very rich market today, so it's unlikely that share prices are set to surge any time soon.

MD Growth Investment Limited

Managed by: Jeff Everett

From: Templeton Management Limited

RRSP Eligible: 

Overall performance: ★★★★

Performance in:	
Up Markets	A
Down Markets	B

Value of $10,000 invested

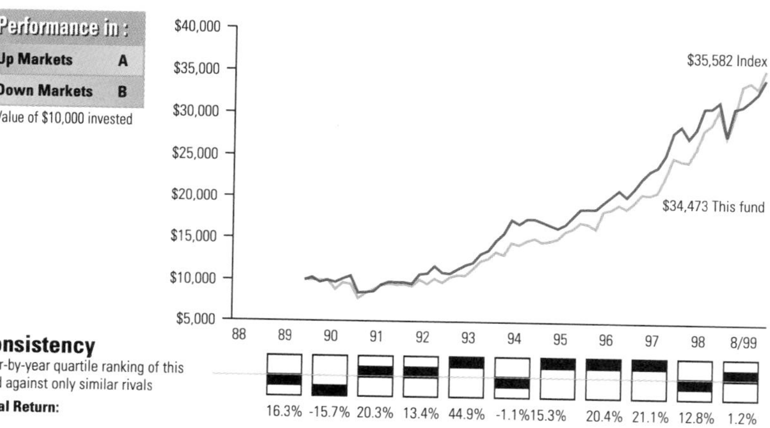

Consistency
Year-by-year quartile ranking of this fund against only similar rivals
Total Return:

Risk

% of time fund has lost money over 12-month period	18%
Biggest drop	-43%
Months to recover	37

Efficiency

For every $100	$1.28
which for this class is	Low

Fit (Investment style)

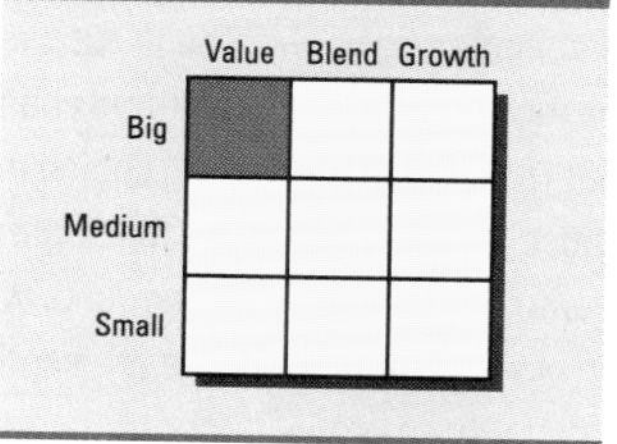

Opinion

This great fund is only available to physicians and their families. If you're a doctor with savings to invest, you've got to believe in the Templeton discipline and the importance of razor-thin fees. So go ahead and buy this fund, which is really just a cheaper clone of the Templeton Growth Fund (which, at 1.97 percent annually, is already pretty inexpensive). This fund is 0.69 percent lower than Templeton Growth every year. Cutting your international equity costs by one third is an easy way to keep your overall MER down to a nice lean level.

Keep two things in mind, though. First, you do need diversification. This fund has a very distinct style — one that's occasionally out of favor. So buy a growth fund to go with it. Second, if you like or need advice, ask for it. Both MD and independent advisors will be happy to provide advice on taxes, financial planning, and whatnot — even though each will have opposing biases about where the rest of your money should go.

Scudder Global Fund

Managed by: William E. Holzer

From: Scudder Stevens & Clark Inc.

RRSP Eligible: 

Overall performance: ★★★★★

Performance in:	
Up Markets	–
Down Markets	–

Value of $10,000 invested

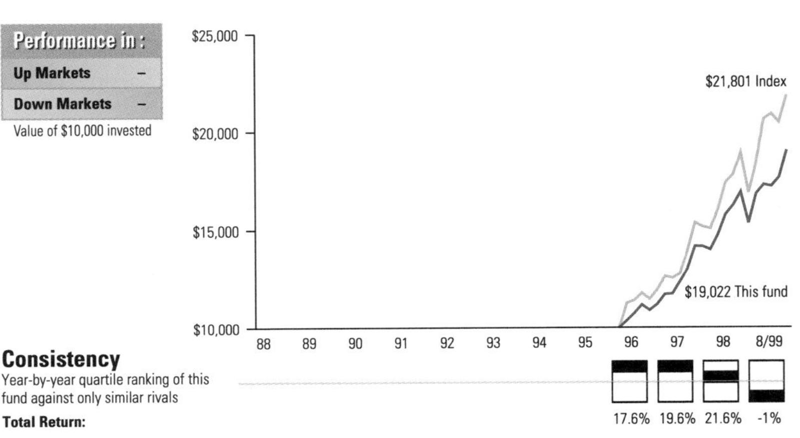

Consistency
Year-by-year quartile ranking of this fund against only similar rivals

Total Return: 17.6% 19.6% 21.6% -1%

Risk

% of time fund has lost money over 12-month period	0%
Biggest drop	-9%
Months to recover	4

Efficiency

For every $100	$1.75
which for this class is	Low

Fit (Investment style)

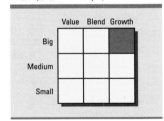

	Value	Blend	Growth
Big			■
Medium			
Small			

Opinion

Bill Holzer and his team are among the new breed of investment managers who are reorganizing their research to allow all analysts to better understand their sectors. That's because his analysts don't have sectors per se. Usually, you get a Germany analyst, a U.K. guy, a Canadian expert, and so on. But at Scudder, this team is very new age: It's not top-down, necessarily. It's just different. It's theme-driven. After first identifying themes, like deregulation of the telecom industry, restructuring and outsourcing in the manufacturing world, or whatever, the team then drills down to find beneficiaries of the trends. The analysts become focused on how a trend will have far-reaching implications — through suppliers, inputs, consumers, and the distribution channel.

It's neat research and it's being copied more and more because it makes sense. It's made great money, too, for investors in this fine fund, which is just barely old enough to make the 36-month cutoff for inclusion in these profile pages.

Green Line Global Select Fund

Managed by: Robert Yerburry

From: Perpetual Portfolio Management Inc.

RRSP Eligible: 

Overall performance:

Performance in :	
Up Markets	A
Down Markets	D

Value of $10,000 invested

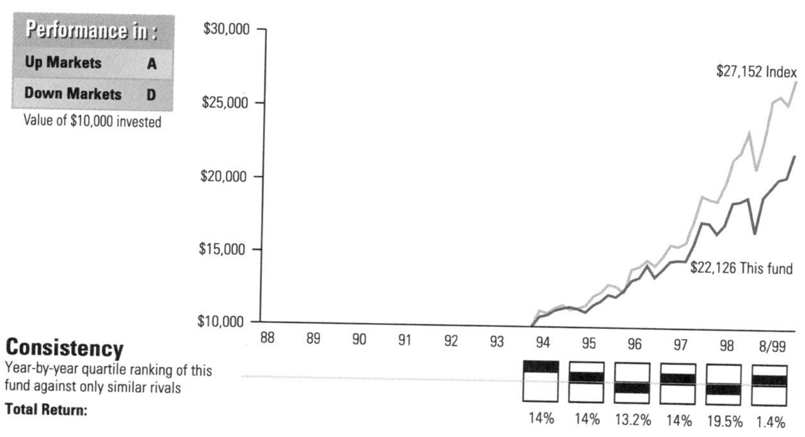

Consistency

Year-by-year quartile ranking of this fund against only similar rivals

Total Return:

Risk

% of time fund has lost money over 12-month period	1%
Biggest drop	-12%
Months to recover	3

Efficiency

For every $100	$2.33
which for this class is	Avg

Fit (Investment style)

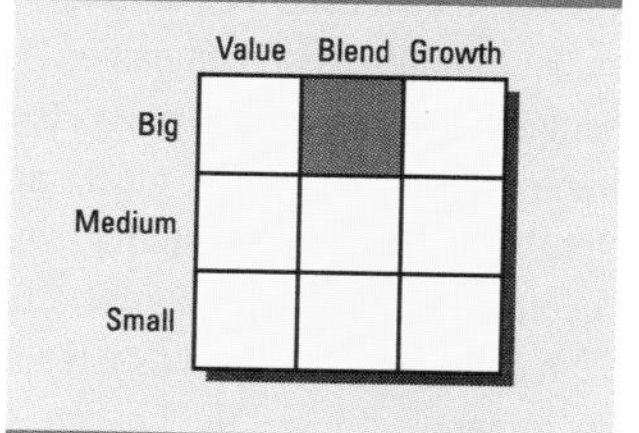

Opinion

Perpetual is one of the best-known names in retail fund management in the U.K.

With 22 portfolio managers, they really can credibly claim to do all the top-down asset allocation work, and to do fundamental research on the 300 to 400 companies typically held in this portfolio.

The firm is a bit of a paradox in many ways. Most firms that make the top-down asset mix decision first are big country rotators, something that seldom works out well. But Bob Yerbury and his team make only gradual asset mix shifts, and their country tilts aren't wild.

The high-turnover fund tends to throw off plenty of taxable capital gains, something that's not too pleasant outside an RSP. But it's a steady money maker in all kinds of different environments. Lately, the wins have come from increased exposure to Japan, especially, and also to the rest of Asia. But owning mid cap stocks in the U.S. has hurt relative performance in what's been a go-go period for U.S. mega-cap stocks.

Trimark Fund

Managed by: Robert Krembil

From: Trimark Investment Management Inc.

RRSP Eligible: 

Overall performance:

Performance in:	
Up Markets	A
Down Markets	C

Value of $10,000 invested

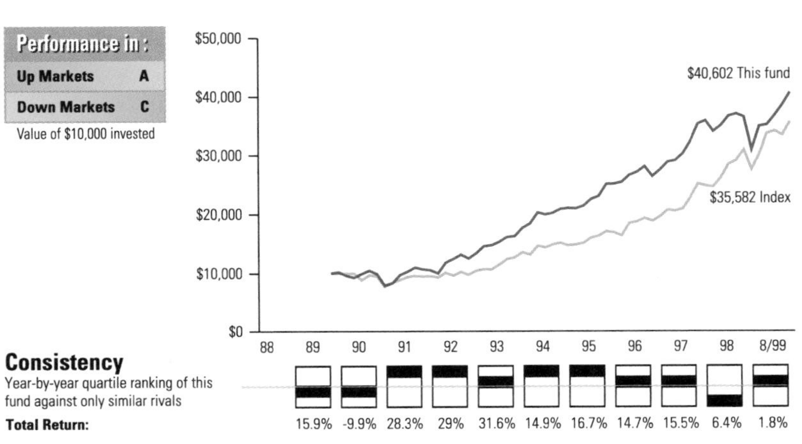

Consistency
Year-by-year quartile ranking of this fund against only similar rivals

Total Return:	89	90	91	92	93	94	95	96	97	98	8/99
	15.9%	-9.9%	28.3%	29%	31.6%	14.9%	16.7%	14.7%	15.5%	6.4%	1.8%

Risk

% of time fund has lost money over 12-month period	12%
Biggest drop	-29%
Months to recover	18

Efficiency

For every $100	$1.52
which for this class is	Low

Fit (Investment style)

	Value	Blend	Growth
Big			■
Medium			
Small			

Opinion

Trimark didn't invent the approach of doing a ton of company-specific homework on each holding, but they sure have perfected it. Although U.S. exposure has been a great win for this fund, a case can be made that the global exposure is achieved through the purchase of U.S. businesses that acquire the better part of their income from overseas. The contrarian bet in Trimark Fund right now focuses on a lightening up on the fast-running European market, which has done so well for the fund in its recent past. There is some concern about the U.S. market as well — it's been so hot that the fund managers are taking a lot of profits there and investing a great deal in Japan. The increased exposure to Japan comes not just through export companies like Sony, but also domestic ones like Matsushita Electric and the brokerage firm Nomura. These stocks are a new direction for the fund, a play on a turnaround in the domestic economy. And, for that matter, a turnaround in the perception of Japan as a leader in management, manufacturing, and finance.

Templeton Growth Fund

Managed by: Mark G. Holowesko

From: Templeton Galbraith & Hansberger Ltd.

RRSP Eligible: 

Overall performance: ★★★½

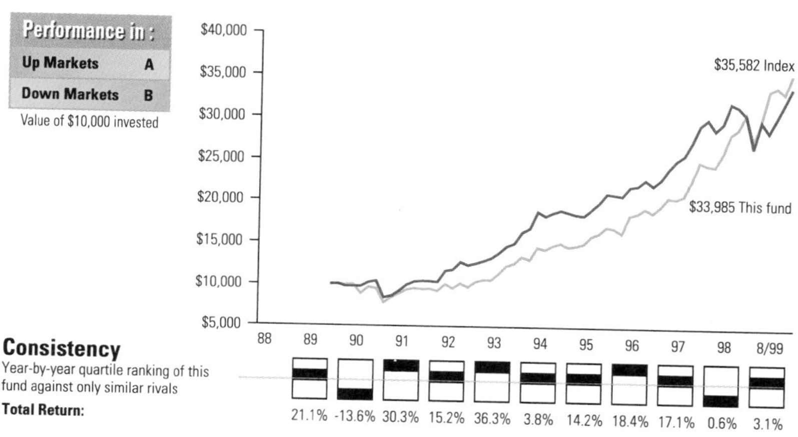

Risk

% of time fund has lost money over 12-month period	16%
Biggest drop	-27%
Months to recover	22

Efficiency

For every $100	$1.97
which for this class is	Low

Fit (Investment style)

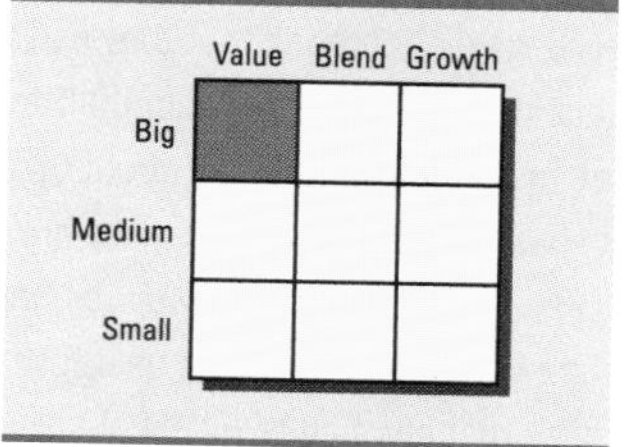

Opinion

After a tough year in 1998, the entire research team from Templeton sat down together to ask themselves if their old-fashioned value approach was simply out of touch.

Clearly, their style was out of touch — at least for a period, as big glamour stocks roared ahead, leaving lots of active managers looking dumb. But the managers seem to have matured from the exercise. They redoubled their conviction that being contrarian is the only way to make money over time. And they concluded that, while early, the firm was right to buy the cheap stocks they chased right into the toilet in '98, in what has proven to be the most disparate market on record: A year when value stocks (of any cap) lagged higher P/E names by an unbelievable 31 percent. Of course, now the tide has turned for cheap stocks — as well as commodity names. The fund's trailing twelve-month P/E ratio is half that of the benchmark index today — a major contributor to the '99 turnaround.

Standard Life International Equity

Managed by: Peter Hill

From: Standard Life Portfolio Management

RRSP Eligible: 

Overall performance: ★★★★★

Performance in:	
Up Markets	–
Down Markets	–

Value of $10,000 invested

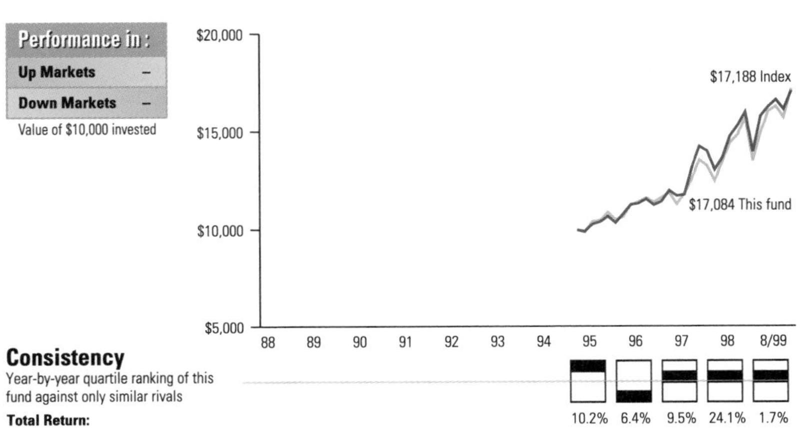

Consistency
Year-by-year quartile ranking of this fund against only similar rivals

	95	96	97	98	8/99
Total Return:	10.2%	6.4%	9.5%	24.1%	1.7%

Risk

% of time fund has lost money over 12-month period	2%
Biggest drop	-12%
Months to recover	4

Efficiency

For every $100	$2.00
which for this class is	Avg

Fit (Investment style)

	Value	Blend	Growth
Big		■	
Medium			
Small			

Opinion

The 45 investment professionals in the U.K. and the 14 in Montreal add up to a team that's packaged its famously conservative institutional approach in this fund for retail investors.

I like the approach because it's not so big on massive country hopping (which is common among the worst international funds). Not that it's completely constrained, either. The fund can wiggle its way into deviations from the MSCI index weights, something that's managed to add value in this fund over time.

It's a big cap fund and it uses U.S.-traded American Depository Receipts (or ADRs) for its exposure to foreign stocks. That limits the fund somewhat, because it means that they can't buy a foreign stock unless it also trades in the States, or unless they bend their rules. Only about 65 percent of the U.K.-based research team's picks are available as ADRs, so the Canadian team has had to pick many of their own stocks over the past few years — something it's managed quite nicely, thank you.

International Equity

Greystone Managed Global Fund

Managed by: Robert L. Vanderhooft

From: Greystone Capital Management Inc.

RRSP Eligible: 

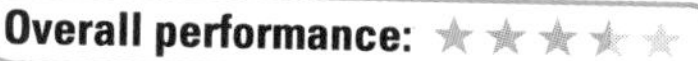

Performance in:	
Up Markets	A
Down Markets	D

Value of $10,000 invested

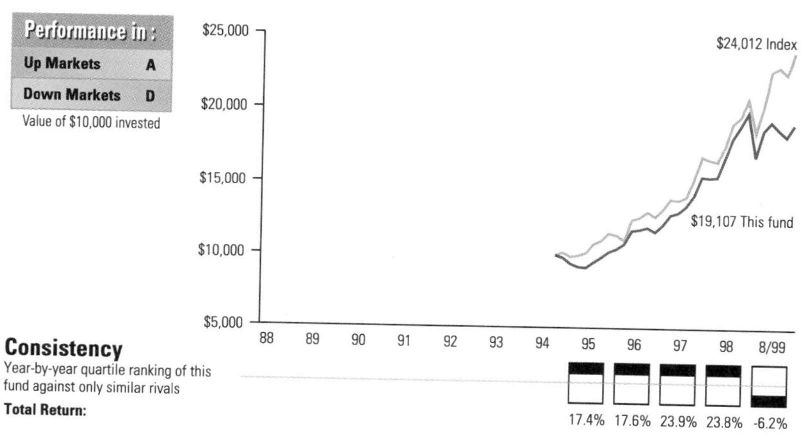

Consistency
Year-by-year quartile ranking of this fund against only similar rivals

Total Return: 17.4% 17.6% 23.9% 23.8% -6.2%

Risk

% of time fund has lost money over 12-month period	7%
Biggest drop	-15%
Months to recover	4

Efficiency

For every $100	$2.46
which for this class is	Avg

Fit (Investment style)

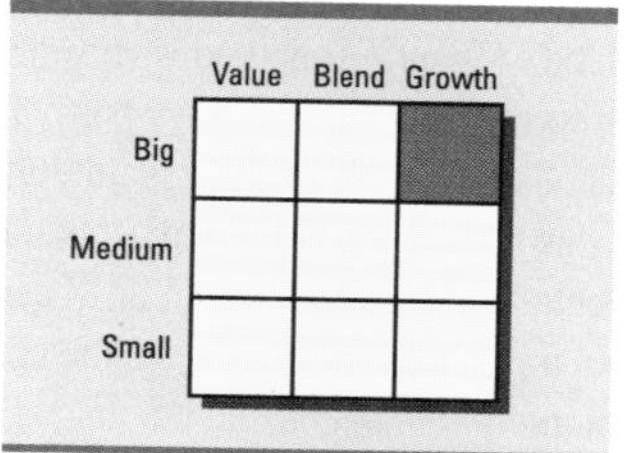

Opinion

It'll take $10,000 to get started in this fund. Past performance has been quite good and up market scores are top-notch. This fund is soon to become part of the Guardian family of funds.

Maxxum American Equity Fund

Managed by: Warren Lammert

From: Janus Capital Corp.

RRSP Eligible: 

Overall performance: ★★★★★

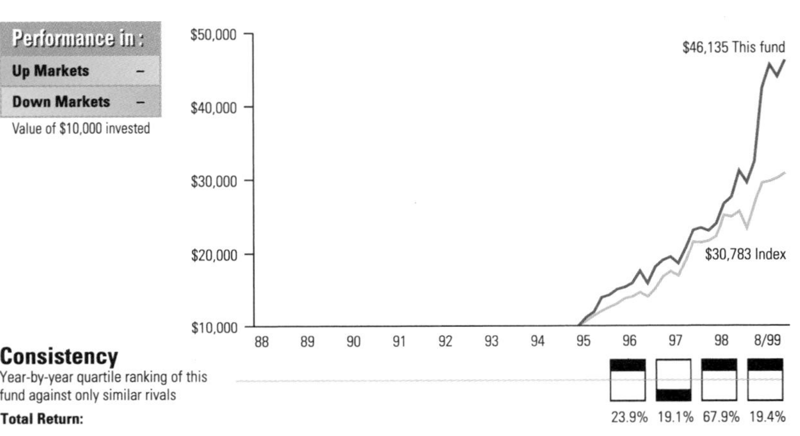

Risk

% of time fund has lost money over 12-month period	0%
Biggest drop	-12%
Months to recover	3

Efficiency

For every $100	$2.50
which for this class is	Avg

Fit (Investment style)

	Value	Blend	Growth
Big			■
Medium			
Small			

Opinion

If you like Internet stocks, you'll love this fund. Its biggest holding is Amazon.com, the online book seller whose market cap continues to astound market watchers. The company loses money on every book it sells, but I like to joke that its secret is that they make it up on volume.

The performance from this most recent Internet mania has juiced returns of this newer fund so much that its quantitative score beats out other great U.S. equity funds that have appeared in the book for years. But this fund is a two-edged sword. Fully 30 percent of its holdings are in the technology area. And many of those names are in the most frenzied part of the market — the Net stocks. And that's what will determine the fund's fate — for better or worse.

One thing's for sure. This fund is very different from its competitors. The U.S. technology-heavy funds available here in Canada are generally sector funds or small caps. But this baby is big cap and diversified. Plus, it's a fundamentally driven fund — not one based on momentum trading. And the fund is allowed to go up to 30 percent international, making it a unique hybrid.

Royal & Sun Alliance U.S. Equity Fund

Managed by: Ted Francis

From: Royal Insurance

RRSP Eligible:

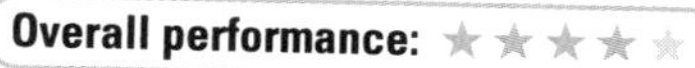

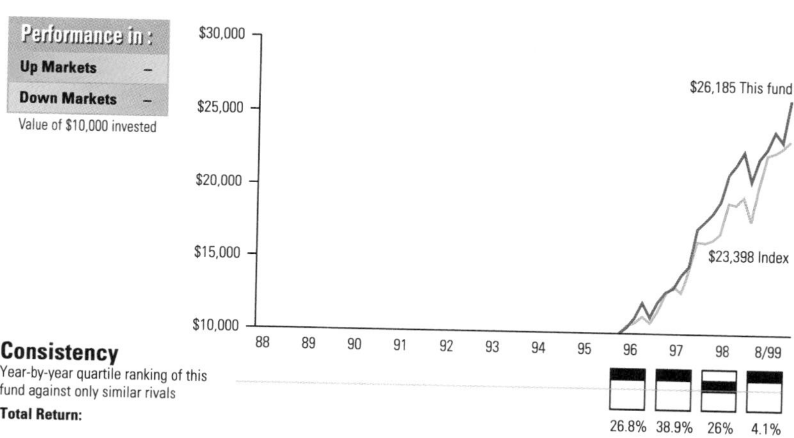

Risk

% of time fund has lost money over 12-month period	0%
Biggest drop	-9%
Months to recover	4

Efficiency

For every $100	$2.60
which for this class is	High

Fit (Investment style)

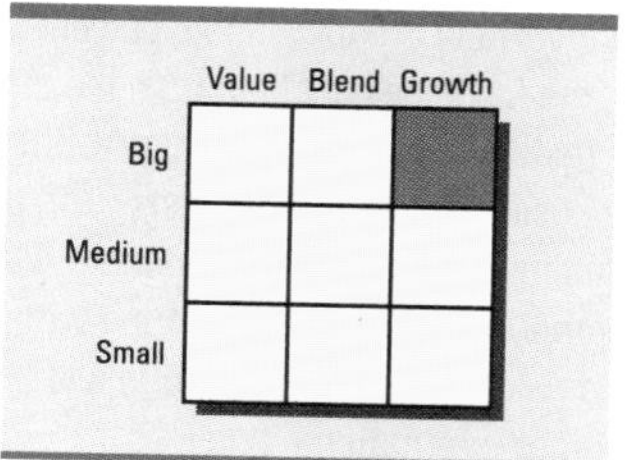

Opinion

A super fund, run by Ted Francis, managed out of the U.K. He looks for growth at a reasonable price and this has led to many technology names that have paid off well. Check out the track record. Unbelievable.

U.S. Equity

AIM Pacific Growth Fund

Managed by: Andrew Callender

From: INVESCO

RRSP Eligible: 

Overall performance: ★★★★★

Performance in:	
Up Markets	–
Down Markets	–

Value of $10,000 invested

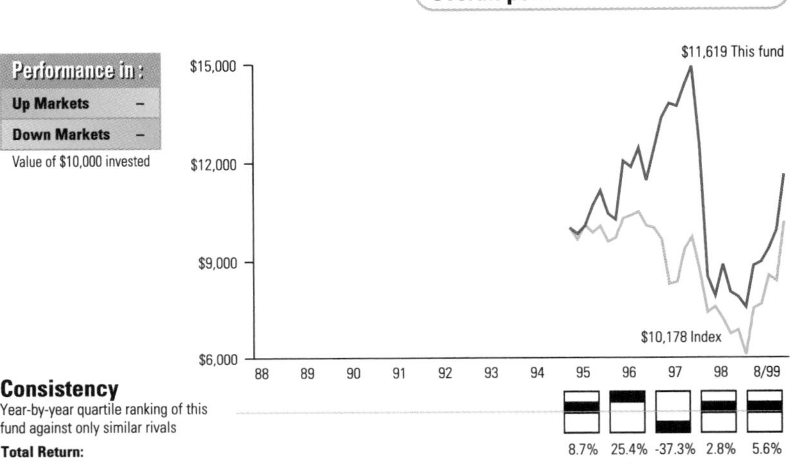

Consistency
Year-by-year quartile ranking of this fund against only similar rivals

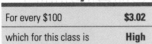

Total Return:	95	96	97	98	8/99
	8.7%	25.4%	-37.3%	2.8%	5.6%

Risk

% of time fund has lost money over 12-month period	33%
Biggest drop	-50%
Months to recover	NA

Efficiency

For every $100	$3.02
which for this class is	High

Fit (Investment style)

	Value	Blend	Growth
Big			■
Medium			
Small			

Opinion

Here's a fund that's had mixed results in a category that's gone through one of the wildest rides investors here have ever seen. This fund suffered more than most in the currency-induced downturn two years ago. But then a big move into financial stocks just at the bottom last year helped power a big uptick in performance. Results have been hot and cold in '99, owing mostly to country picks (Japan's done well) and interest rate fears (those financial stocks are getting slaughtered).

The fund is a bit Japan-centric. Manager Andrew Callender is based in Tokyo and has been for what must seem like forever. And the fund's mandate allows it to hold up to 50 percent in Japan, way more than most in its peer group. With 25 percent in Japan at writing, the fund has benefited from the announced corporate restructurings in that country. But will Japanese business actually cut costs? The answer will determine the fate of this fund more than most.

Remember that this is a small fund with a big MER and a risky region. So be sure to use it only to augment other international holdings.

Fidelity Far East Fund

Managed by: K.C. Lee

From: Fidelity Investments Canada Ltd.

RRSP Eligible: 

Overall performance: ★★★★

Performance in:	
Up Markets	A
Down Markets	A

Value of $10,000 invested

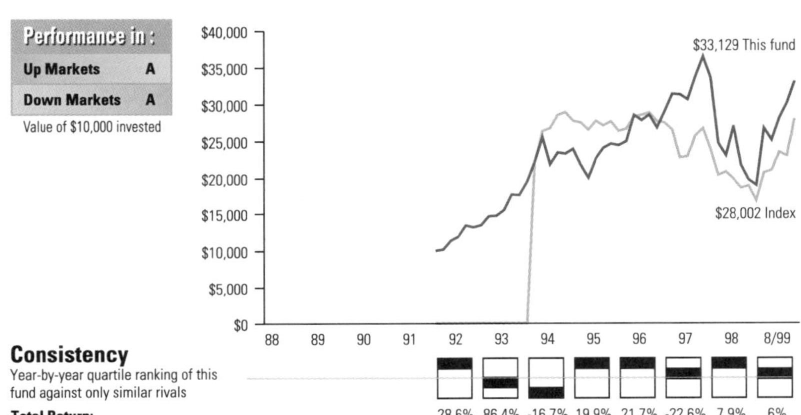

Consistency
Year-by-year quartile ranking of this fund against only similar rivals

	92	93	94	95	96	97	98	8/99
Total Return:	28.6%	86.4%	-16.7%	19.9%	21.7%	-22.6%	7.9%	6%

Risk

% of time fund has lost money over 12-month period	23%
Biggest drop	-54%
Months to recover	NA

Efficiency

For every $100	$2.86
which for this class is	Avg

Fit (Investment style)

	Value	Blend	Growth
Big	■		
Medium			
Small			

Opinion

K.C. Lee has been a skillful steward of this fund through treacherous times. And his conviction runs high; He had the courage two years ago to maintain huge exposure to Hong Kong while other fund managers bolted.

Despite the market's roller coaster, he's maintained relatively steady returns at the head of the pack. But I still can't figure out whether he's taking more risk or less than the other Asian funds available.

For example, he's still holding on to Hutchinson Whampoa, HSBC, and Cheung Kong, his top three holdings, whose aggregate value adds up to just over half the fund's total value. (This exposure is due to appreciation; fund regulations say that no more than 10 percent of a fund's value can be invested in any single security.) These each represent a terrific play on China in the next century, but that's a lot of risk.

I recommend this fund. But I don't get the sense that Lee thinks now's the time to buy. He's as concerned about valuations as he's ever been.

Universal European Opportunities Fund

Managed by: Tim Stevenson

From: Henderson International

RRSP Eligible: 

Overall performance: ★★★★½

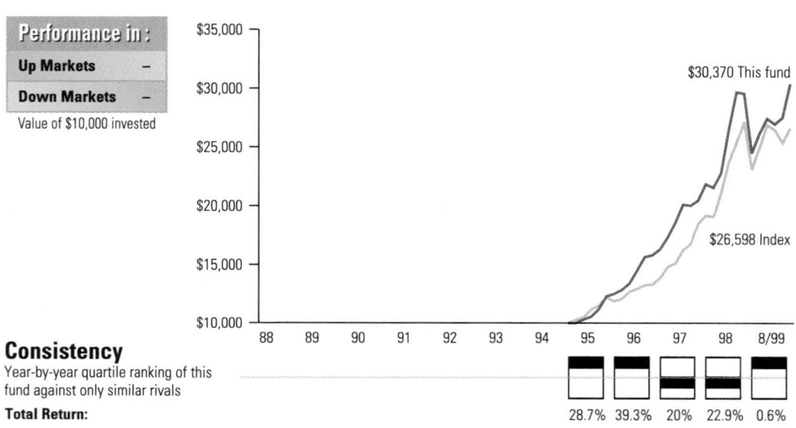

Risk

% of time fund has lost money over 12-month period	6%
Biggest drop	-17%
Months to recover	NA

Efficiency

For every $100	$2.43
which for this class is	Avg

Fit (Investment style)

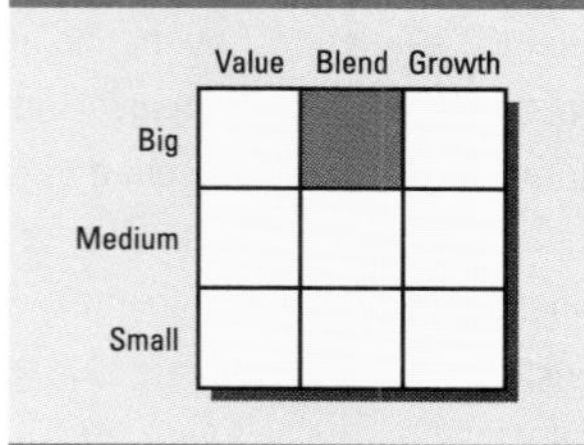

Opinion

The team at Henderson in London has done well, overall, since inception. But a couple of softer years forced the team to consider their mistakes.

They concluded that their style had to change. They realized that true value investing doesn't always work in Europe because some companies value traps, protected from takeovers by legislation. And with earnings growth tougher to come by in Europe in recent years, it's become doubly important to find good companies that can grow in any environment. While Henderson won't pay rich multiples, the style has changed to have more of a sensitivity to growth.

They've cut the number of names in the fund nearly in half, and half of those embody what you'd call a growth-at-a-reasonable-price quality. Small cap exposure hurt last year, as did unhedged exposure to a slumping European currency. But the themes of restructuring, contrarian situations, and true value plays will add to those GARP holding to leave this diversified fund a little broader in scope. Remember that this fund owns big companies in small emerging European markets and many smaller companies in the big markets.

Green Line European Growth Fund

Managed by: Patricia Maxwell-Arnot

From: Credit Suisse Asset Management

RRSP Eligible: 

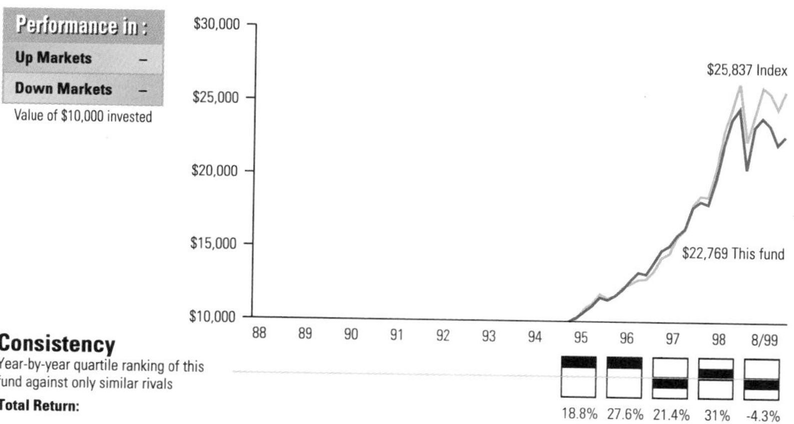

Risk

% of time fund has lost money over 12-month period	4%
Biggest drop	-16%
Months to recover	NA

Efficiency

For every $100	$2.58
which for this class is	Avg

Fit (Investment style)

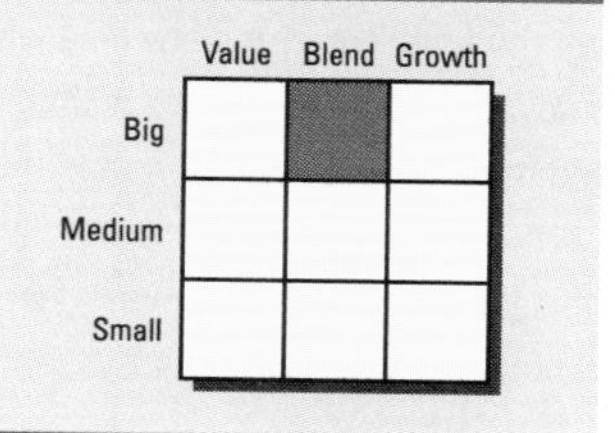

Opinion

This fund missed the white-hot telecom sector last year with a near-fatal early move into industrial stocks whose value was compelling and whose appeal lay largely with its fit in their big-picture scenario.

Credit Suisse runs money using a macro scenario approach that first forecasts the big picture. From that initial view, everything else can be determined. Their bullish growth model was right, but early. Because of it, the first part of '99 proved disastrous as the market became polarized: big cap glamour growth stocks (like telecoms and drugs) surged. And everything else got left behind.

Luckily, they were saved (as usual) by great country selection. No big bets, mind you. Just enough overweight in this or that market to add value without risking everything. Recent moves include big wins in France and Italy.

GreenLine remains one of the best fund families in Canada, which is remarkable for a bank. Despite its stumble, this fund is a strong part of their lineup.

Fidelity European Growth Fund

Managed by: Thierry Seroro

From: Fidelity International Ltd.

RRSP Eligible: 

Overall performance: ★★★★★

Performance in:	
Up Markets	A
Down Markets	B

Value of $10,000 invested

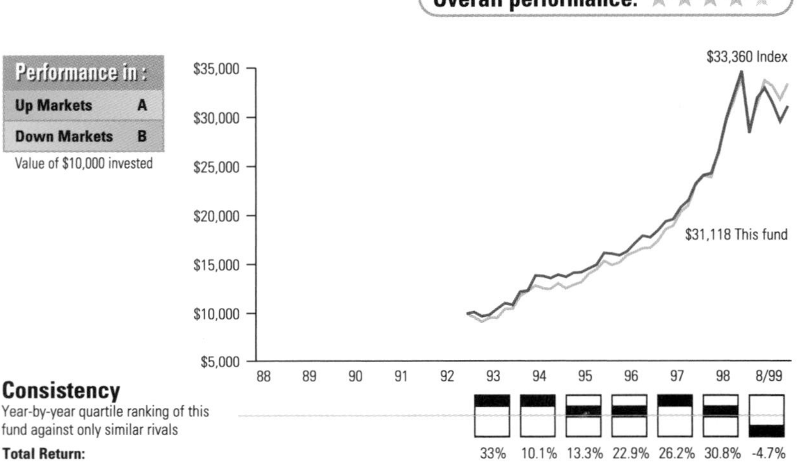

Consistency
Year-by-year quartile ranking of this fund against only similar rivals

	93	94	95	96	97	98	8/99
Total Return:	33%	10.1%	13.3%	22.9%	26.2%	30.8%	-4.7%

Risk

% of time fund has lost money over 12-month period	**4%**
Biggest drop	**-18%**
Months to recover	**NA**

Efficiency

For every $100	**$2.60**
which for this class is	**Avg**

Fit (Investment style)

	Value	Blend	Growth
Big		■	
Medium			
Small			

Opinion

Serero 's a great manager who's been at Fido for nearly a decade. But the cyclicals have been on fire in early 1999, and growth managers like Serero and former manager Sally Walden (who's still involved with this fund) have been left behind.

The theory is that the only way to make real money over time in Europe is through firms that actually create real growth over time. Not through country timing, asset allocation, or stock-picking in cyclicals. Better to focus on technology and change — to get an edge over other research houses.

One example is telecommunications, a sector that's been very good to investors in this fund. Why worry about the Euro like everybody else when the makers of new telecommunications technology are so insulated from currency woes. In fact, they benefit from it.

So in this year's Euro-induced weakness, this weak fund remains an excellent pick.

BPI Emerging Markets Fund

Managed by: Pablo Salas

From: BPI Global Asset Management LLP

RRSP Eligible: 

Overall performance: 

Performance in:	
Up Markets	–
Down Markets	–

Value of $10,000 invested

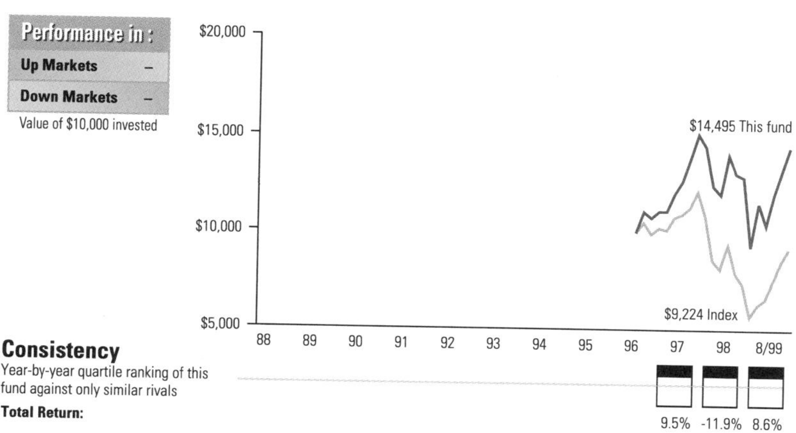

Consistency
Year-by-year quartile ranking of this fund against only similar rivals

Total Return: 9.5% -11.9% 8.6%

Risk

% of time fund has lost money over 12-month period	46%
Biggest drop	-38%
Months to recover	NA

Efficiency

For every $100	$2.61
which for this class is	Low

Fit (Investment style)

	Value	Blend	Growth
Big		■	
Medium			
Small			

Opinion

With eight top-notch investment professionals in the Orlando office, manager Pablo Salas has real muscle on his side. And with a 31 percent return in the first half of 1999, he had momentum working for him as well.

Many of the premises on which the massive secular growth estimates were founded have proven accurate. Freer trade, more-prudent fiscal management, an emerging middle class, and improving technology have all borne fruit as investment bets. But currency meltdowns have left two severe hangovers: first in Mexico, then in Thailand. Going forward, there's reason to believe in the benefits of the forced austerity these nations have endured. Like Canada, with its weak currency and huge deficits, these countries have tightened their belts and dug their way out of trouble.

Salas has a knack for value and an understanding of telecoms, two factors that have helped him score big relative numbers on this fund.

Regional Equity — Emerging Markets

Scudder Emerging Markets Fund

Managed by: Joyce E. Cornell

From: Stevens & Clark Inc.

RRSP Eligible: 

Overall performance: ★★★★½

Performance in:	
Up Markets	–
Down Markets	–

Value of $10,000 invested

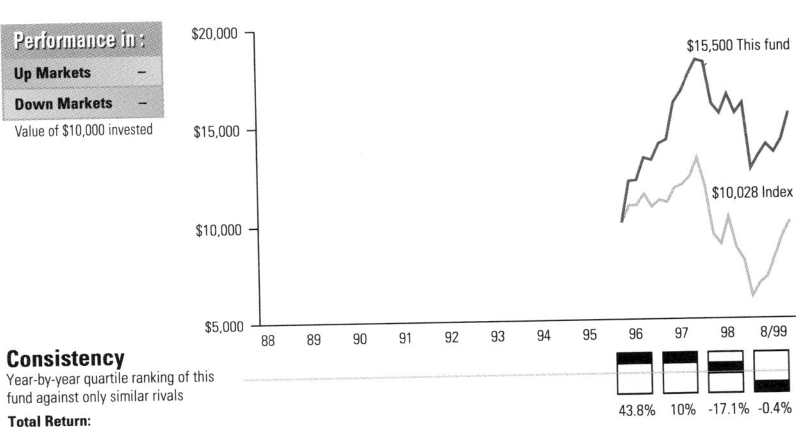

Consistency
Year-by-year quartile ranking of this fund against only similar rivals

Total Return: 43.8% 10% -17.1% -0.4%

Risk

% of time fund has lost money over 12-month period	51%
Biggest drop	-30%
Months to recover	NA

Efficiency

For every $100	$2.50
which for this class is	Low

Fit (Investment style)

	Value	Blend	Growth
Big		■	
Medium			
Small			

Opinion

This tiny fund has only $15 million in it, barely enough to make trades feasible. The top-down approach that worked so well in the fund's first couple of years has been a disappointment so far in 1999. Cornell and the team missed Asia and Latin America, the two biggest wins in competitors' portfolios this year. Instead, they've had lots (I mean lots) of exposure to central Europe and the Middle East.

The approach is very macro, seeking first to identify political climates that are conducive to market strength, then to look for government fiscal policies that support long-term economic growth. These ingredients found a country gets on the focus list and the analysts get to work.

The fund did enjoy some lift from the strength in oil during 1999, but it wasn't enough to offset the weakness in country selection. I'm going to hold off on my recommendation, although it did meet the quantitative screens to place second in its peer group, since most of its 41-month history was filled with a consecutive winning streak.

Sector Equity — Natural Resources

Maxxum Natural Resource Fund

Managed by: Jacqueline Pratt

From: MAXXUM Group

RRSP Eligible: 

Overall performance: ★★★★

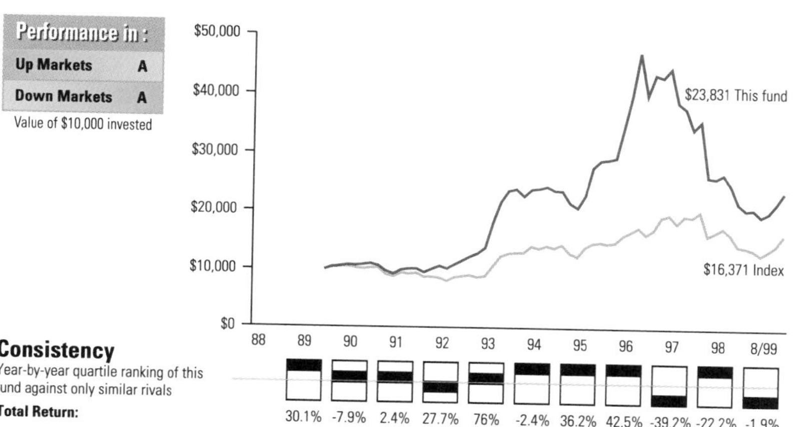

Risk

% of time fund has lost money over 12-month period	38%
Biggest drop	-64%
Months to recover	NA

Efficiency

For every $100	$2.25
which for this class is	Low

Fit (Investment style)

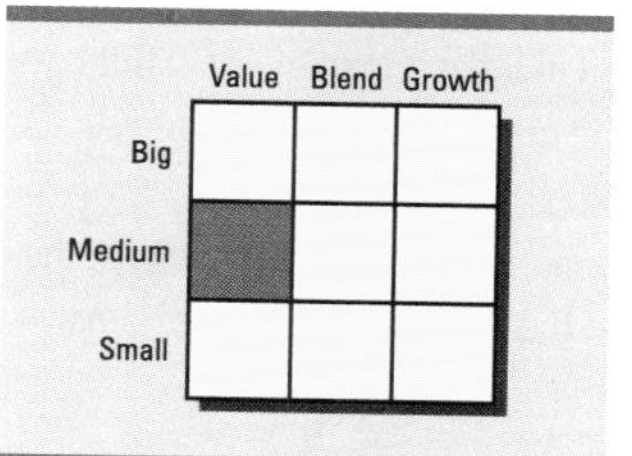

Opinion

With newsletters urging investors to dump their resource funds after the recent bloodbath, I'm more inclined than ever to urge you to buy this and other good funds — cheap.

Sector Equity — Science & Technology

Altamira Science & Technology

Managed by: Ian Ainsworth

From: Altamira Management Ltd.

RRSP Eligible: 

Overall performance: ★★★★★

Performance in:	
Up Markets	–
Down Markets	–

Value of $10,000 invested

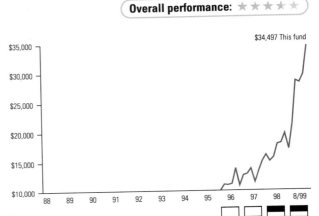

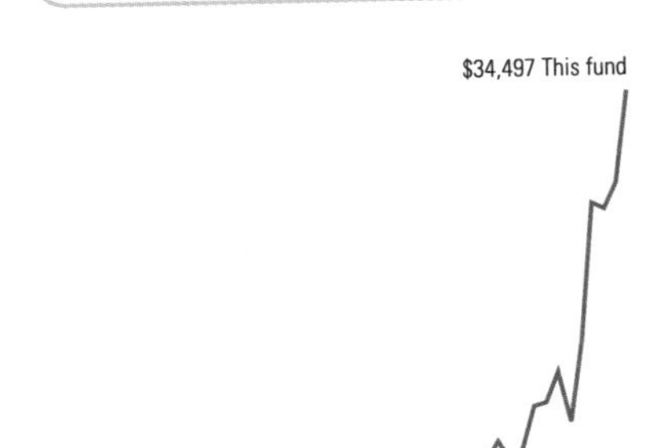

Consistency
Year-by-year quartile ranking of this fund against only similar rivals

Total Return:

96	97	98	8/99
13%	17.3%	65.6%	14.3%

Risk

% of time fund has lost money over 12-month period	5%
Biggest drop	-21%
Months to recover	13

Efficiency

For every $100	$2.36
which for this class is	Low

Fit (Investment style)

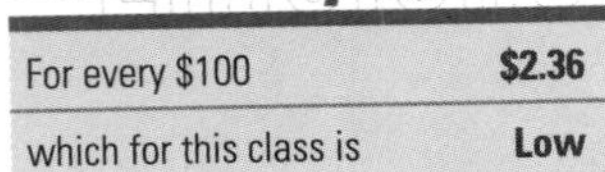

	Value	Blend	Growth
Big			■
Medium			
Small			

Opinion

As targeted plays, sector funds offer the best bang for the buck in any booming area. And they offer a somewhat lower-risk way to play a boom.

But investors tend to chase them after they've been wildly hot. Then these latecomers often turf the funds after a downturn, forgetting that they trend they were trying to play was a long-term secular growth trend.

If you want a hot fund like this because you like its mix of big and small caps, of hardware and software, of life sciences and telecoms, then own it for good. There is tremendous potential from technology in the coming years, and yes, sure, it's already discounted in today's market price. But betting on growth and managing it with a professional is a good strategy.

And remember, the extra decisions, the extra taxes, and the fees make this an expensive fund to trade.

First Ontario Fund LSVCC

Managed by: Allan Crosbie

From: Crosbie & Co.

RRSP Eligible: 

Overall performance: ★★★★

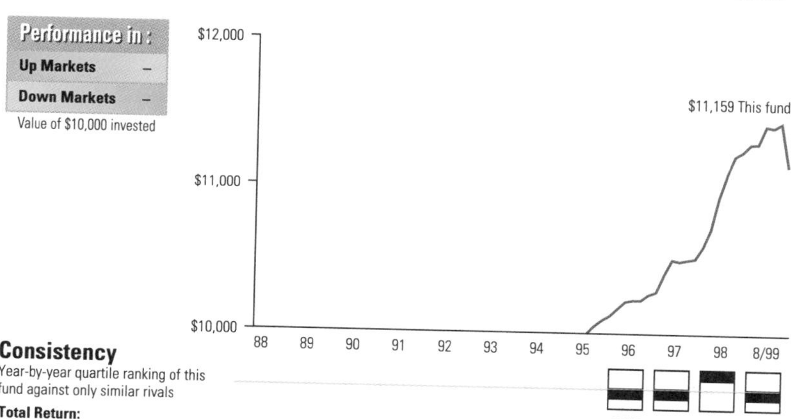

Labour

Risk

% of time fund has lost money over 12-month period	0%
Biggest drop	-3%
Months to recover	3

Efficiency

For every $100	$4.75
which for this class is	Avg

Fit (Investment style)

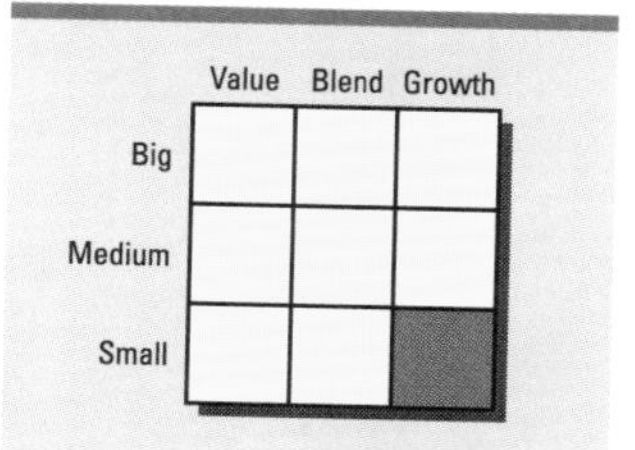

Opinion

Managers of LSIF have to do an incredible amount of work; the manager of this one, Ken Delaney, is no exception. He looks for firms with progressive human resource practices and has been quite successful in his selections.

Canadian Equity

Crocus Investment Fund

Managed by: James Umlah

From: Crocus Investment Management

RRSP Eligible: 

Overall performance: ★★★★

Performance in:	
Up Markets	–
Down Markets	–

Value of $10,000 invested

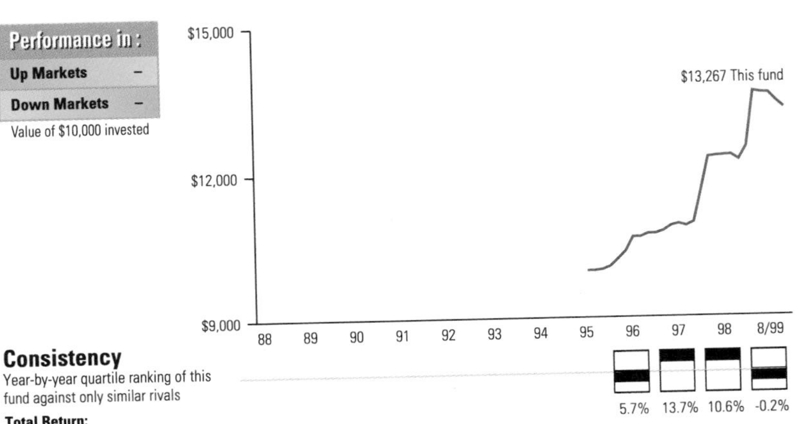

Consistency
Year-by-year quartile ranking of this fund against only similar rivals

Total Return:

Risk

% of time fund has lost money over 12-month period	0%
Biggest drop	-2%
Months to recover	NA

Efficiency

For every $100	$3.78
which for this class is	Low

Fit (Investment style)

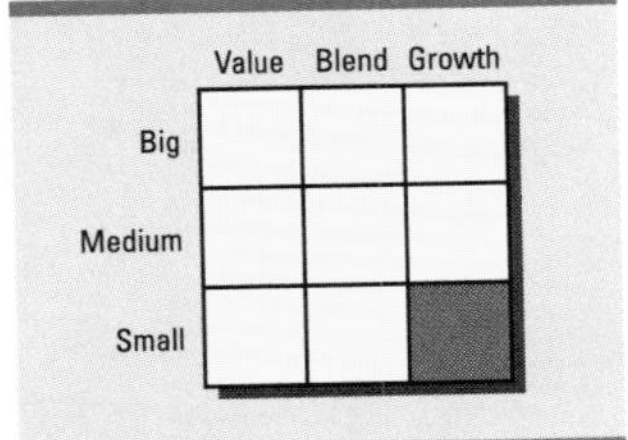

Opinion

Although this labour-sponsored fund is off a bit this year, it certainly has had a good run. About half of the total assets are in businesses that promote employee ownership. This fund is only available in Manitoba.

10 The Ultimate Fund Tables

THE ULTIMATE FUND TABLES GIVE YOU THE latest information available at time of printing. Here you'll find information that you won't find anywhere else — the good and the bad.

You'll also find a key feature in the Ultimate Fund Tables. Realizing that new investors may be intimidated by a mass of numerical data, I've given you the statistics translated into a short, factual comment, based on the following characteristics of each fund:

- age
- past performance
- performance in bull *and* bear markets
- comparison to index.

Obviously, the comments may not tell the whole story, but I hope they serve as useful pointers for potential investors, and complement the statistical figures that are the real meat of the Ultimate Fund Tables.

Overall performance: ★★★★★

As with my Chapter 9 profiles, each commentary begins with a star ranking of the fund's overall performance. This is a good guideline to whether the fund merits further investigation.

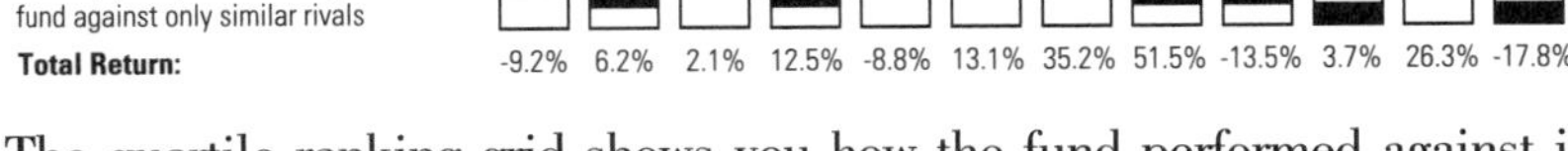

The quartile ranking grid shows you how the fund performed against its peers over each calendar year. Look for funds which stay in the top two quartiles most of the time. This measurement strategy is a better indicator than looking at year-over-year returns, because it is an effective measure in good times as well as bad. If the fund performs in the top two quartiles, its returns may have been low, but it performed better than similar funds.

You'll also find my Management Expense Ratio (MER) stoplight graphic, which offers a guideline to the fund's ongoing expenses. A red light indicates that the fund's MER is in the top one-third of funds of its type. A yellow designates a fund with an MER in the average range, and a green light signifies a fund which is a bargain relative to its peers.

Because I think every investor should have some key information on a fund's darkest hours, I've identified the percentage of times the fund has lost money over any twelve-month period.

I'll also tell you how low the fund has ever gone — its biggest drop. (This isn't information that the fund company is willingly going to share in its marketing materials.) You'll also see how long it took the fund to recover from its worst low; the recovery period is measured from the point at which it began the decline to the point at which it had recovered that original price. Our team at FundMonitor refers to it as the fund's "time under water."

Does a long time "under water" mean that you should reject a fund? Not necessarily. In fact, Canada's best-performing fund over the last decade spent four years of that decade under water as a result of the crash of 1987. Should you be aware of the risk? Absolutely.

Welcome to the Ultimate Fund Tables!

Legend: ★ = overall past performance vs. similar funds (5 ★ max). Boxes show the quartile performance for a fund each calendar year vs. only similar funds (1 is the best score possible). ● = high; ○ = average; and ● = a fund with low expenses.

Consistency: Overall Past Performance	Fund Name	Type	90	91	92	93	94	95	96	97	98	Aug. '99	Risk: Up	Down	% of Time Losing $	Biggest Drop	Date	No. of Mo's to Recover	Efficiency: MER	
★★★★½	**20/20 Aggr Global Stock**	Fgn Eq								4	2	1	NA	NA	3%	–20%	8/31/98	8	3.64	●
They've taken profits in Europe and boosted Asian exposure as the Far East picture improves somewhat. They expect that Asia's continued economic strength will lead to better than expected global growth for 1999.																				
★★★	**20/20 Aggressive Growth**	US Eq					3	2	4	3	1	1	A	B	19%	–20%	7/31/98	5	2.55	○
Richard Driehaus looks at earnings momentum, but complements that by adding in rigorous fundamental analysis to determine the sustainability of earnings and the timeliness of prospective stocks. Does well in down markets.																				
★★★½	**20/20 Cdn Resources**	Nat Res	3	3	3	3	3	1	1	2	4	2	B	C	44%	–59%	12/31/80	147	2.80	●
Oil and gas firms continue to be the focus of this fund, so it's missed the party in the forest. But if Bob's right, strong demand from Asia's continuing recovery and continued global growth will juice the whole sector.																				
★★	**20/20 Emerg Markets Value**	Fgn Eq						4	3	4	2	1	D	D	58%	–57%	9/30/94	NA	3.57	●
Hong Kong and Brazil make up a combined 28% of this portfolio, which have been big wins for this fund. Stock selection is the strength of the Brandes team, and this $33 million fund has seen performance improve in 1998 and 1999.																				
★★★	**20/20 Latin America**	Fgn Eq						4	1	3	4	4	C	NA	46%	–66%	10/31/97	NA	3.24	●
Peter Gruber has this fund fully invested and near three quarters of that is in Brazil. He expects the Latin markets to outpace the huge US and European markets in the coming 2 to 3 years. Then again, he's been saying that for a while.																				
★★	**20/20 Managed Fut Value**	Spec Eq								1	4	1	NA	NA	46%	–70%	2/28/98	NA	3.00	○
John Di Tomasso hit a major brick in the wall last February and has dropped 60% since then. The fund uses options – not futures – which is problematic since he has to be right not just on direction, but on timing too. A very contrarian fund.																				
★½	**20/20 RSP Aggr Smaller Co**	Cdn Eq								4	4	3	NA	NA	53%	–31%	5/31/98	NA	2.73	●
The rapid-fire trading style of this Chicago-based firm works brilliantly in every deep, liquid market around the world. But Canada is not a deep, liquid market. While we love the Driehaus style, it seems fitting that AGF's Ferguson will take over.																				
★★½	**20/20 RSP Aggressive Equ**	Cdn Eq					4	1	1	4	3	3	B	D	39%	–33%	5/31/98	NA	2.47	○
This is the sister to the RSP Aggressive Smaller Companies fund. The fund remains closed to new investments. Gerard Ferguson's lower turnover and more value-biased style will be more suitable to this market and the smaller stocks that this fund holds.																				
★★½	**A.P.P.Q. Equilibre**	Bal					4	1	3	2	3	1	C	D	25%	–11%	2/28/94	15	0.86	●
Spotty performance overall and poor showings in bull and bear markets. The big positive here is an expense ratio of just 0.85% annually.																				
★★★★	**ABC American-Value**	US Eq								1	3	4	NA	NA	33%	–23%	5/31/98	14	2.00	●
Since inception, Irwin Michael has more than doubled his benchmark, the Russell 2000. With this strict value discipline, he has done well in a market dominated by big growth stocks. As of mid-year, 1/3 of the fund was sitting in cash.																				
★★★½	**ABC Fully-Managed**	Bal	1	3	4	1	1	1	1	3	4	1	B	B	17%	–18%	5/31/98	13	2.00	○
Many of Irwin Michael's stock positions have been the target of takeovers, and that's good news for unitholders of this fund. More than 1/3 of the fund was sitting in cash in June.																				
★½	**Acadia Balanced**	Bal						4	2	4	4	4	NA	NA	39%	–29%	10/31/97	NA	2.42	●
This fund has been very unimpressive with bottom quartile performance in every year, except 1996. Its 2.42% MER hasn't helped matters any. Nor have its biggest holdings – Nortel and BCE, two of the nation's hottest stocks.																				
★★★★	**Acuity Pooled Cdn Bal**	Bal					2	2	1	1	1	4	A	D	18%	–19%	7/31/98	NA	2.99	●
Ian Ihnatowycz & Hugh McCauley run this institutional fund which requires a minimum investment of $150k and carries a management fee of 1%. The fund's a solid performer but has been hit hard in down markets.																				

Legend: ★ = overall past performance vs. similar funds (5 ★ max). Boxes show the quartile performance for a fund each calendar year vs. only similar funds (☐ is the best score possible). ● = high; ● = average; and ● = a fund with low expenses.

Consistency: Overall Past Performance	Fund Name	Type	Risk: Up	Down	% of Time Losing $	Biggest Drop	Date	No. of Mo's to Recover	Efficiency: MER
★★★½	**Acuity Pooled Cdn Equity**	Cdn Eq	A	D	20%	–23%	5/31/98	8	0.00
The techno-craze that has been driving the US has spilled over into Canada, and this fund has been riding that wave with holdings in Canadian tech firms like ATI, and some big US stocks like Microsoft and Cisco.									
★★	**Acuity Pooled ConsAsst All**	Bal	D	D	38%	–16%	7/31/98	NA	0.00
Want a smaller dose of hot stocks? Try this kinder, gentler version of the Acuity approach. It's got the hot stocks that have done well, but also has some bonds to steady the swings. Yogen Fruz and some income trusts have hurt, but it'll come back.									
★★	**Acuity Pooled Env Sci&Tec**	Fgn Eq	B	B	18%	–21%	5/31/98	8	0.00
This in an institutional version of the Clean Environment Canadian Equity Fund, one we like. But this one requires a minimum investment of $150k and carries a management fee of just 1%.									
★★★	**Acuity Pooled Glo Bal**	Bal	C	NA	22%	–12%	7/31/98	5	0.00
Like its domestic-only cousin, this balanced product requires $150k, costs just over 1% and owns lots of income trusts. But this one's got some global exposure. It's got the hot stocks that have done well, but also has some bonds to steady the swings.									
★★½	**Acuity Pooled Glo Equity**	Fgn Eq	C	D	20%	–23%	7/31/98	6	0.00
This is an amazing fund because of its global mandate, global peer group and domestic wins. Yes, great small cap technology companies exist here in Canada. Just check out the winning names in the fund: ATI, GEAC, Open Text, Silent Witness.									
★★★	**AGF American Growth**	US Eq	B	A	17%	–49%	2/28/73	77	2.78
Steve Rodgers believes that the current environment of robust economic growth, technological efficiencies and low inflation justify present market valuations. He focuses on large caps and likes to hold for 5 years.									
★★½	**AGF Asian Growth Class**	Fgn Eq	B	D	39%	–59%	2/29/96	NA	3.03
After a horror show of a performance in the Asian depresion, the fund is back on top with exposure to more mature markets in the region. Today's risk is one of US interest rates, with so much of the portfolio relating to property in Hong Kong.									
★★★	**AGF Canadian Stock Fund**	Cdn Eq	B	C	25%	–28%	5/31/98	NA	2.46
Martin Hubbes is having an impact since the birth of this new fund from the merged AGF Cdn Stock and AGF Cdn Growth. What's neat is that he's managed to achieve both big cap conservative positioning and exposure to hot mid cap names.									
★★★½	**AGF Cdn Tact Asset All**	Bal	B	B	11%	–15%	6/30/98	10	2.42
Barclays uses a quantitative model to actively manage the asset mix on this opportunistic fund. The bond weighting has hurt in '99 but the huge-cap stocks have helped keep the fund ahead of its peers.									
★★½	**AGF China Focus**	Fgn Eq	NA	NA	62%	–57%	8/31/97	NA	3.49
A narrow mandate hurts this tiny fund, as does its 57% slide during the Asian depression. It really is a focused way to play the biggest growth story of the next century, though, so if you're fearless, this is the ride of a lifetime.									
★★★½	**AGF Euro Asset Allocat**	Bal	A	NA	10%	–18%	8/31/98	11	2.56
Warren Walker's decision to be almost 100% in equities ensured full participation in Europe's unprecedented bull market, and the recent foresight to increase cash has protected investor's gains. An excellent fund.									
★★★	**AGF European Growth**	Fgn Eq	A	D	10%	–21%	8/31/98	NA	3.03
John Arnold and Rory Flynn look for bargains. Not 'blood in the streets' bargains. Just good businesses that are misunderstood, or are at the cusp of change. That means they've missed out on this year's shift to European darlings of steady growth.									
★★½	**AGF Germany Class**	Fgn Eq	NA	NA	11%	–22%	8/31/98	NA	2.99
Unless you're really bullish on Germany, a better approach for investing in Europe is through a more diversified fund. Although performance has been good, its narrow focus and higher MER make it more vulnerable to any setback.									
★★★★★	**AGF Germany Class M**	Fgn Eq	NA	NA	9%	–21%	8/31/98	NA	NA
This fund does get some diversification from other European countries, but its narrow mandate suggests investors should not overload on this specialty fund.									

Legend: ★= overall past performance vs. similar funds (5 ★ max). Boxes show the quartile performance for a fund each calendar year vs. only similar funds (□ is the best score possible). ● = high; ● = average; and ● = a fund with low expenses.

Consistency			Performance Trend										Risk						Efficiency
Overall Past Performance	Fund Name	Type	90	91	92	93	94	95	96	97	98	Aug. '99	Up	Down	% of Time Losing $	Biggest Drop	Date	No. of Mo's to Recover	MER
★★★½	**AGF Growth & Income**	Bal	□	□	□	□	□	□	□	□	□	□	A	A	21%	–27%	11/30/73	44	2.50 ●
A bottom-up approach to picking growth stocks, a bit of tactical asset allocation and a willingness to get into speculative junior technology plays all make this a wilder balanced fund than most; hence its good but erratic relative performance.																			
★★★	**AGF Growth Equity**	Cdn Eq	□	□	□	□	□	□	□	□	□	□	D	D	29%	–54%	12/31/80	55	2.80 ●
Tons of names that include not just the resource patch, but more and more technology issues, are what keep this aggressive fund from getting thumped at every turn. Manger Bob Farquharson is bullish on both the economy and the emerging technology.																			
★★	**AGF High Income Fund**	Div	□	□	□	□	□	□	□	□	□	□	D	A	1%	–6%	2/28/94	13	1.68 ●
Few managers have called the bond market as well as this one, Clive Coombs. But this fund is constrained to short and mid term bonds, which hardly allow for participation in any rally. A third of the fund sits in pref shares to goose income after tax.																			
★★★★½	**AGF International Stock**	Fgn Eq									□	□	NA	NA	7%	–15%	8/31/98	3	2.98 ●
This newer fund has had a great start. It's the non-North American version of the AGF International Value Fund, also managed by a superstar value team at Brandes in San Diego. There's plenty of expsoure here to mature companies in emerging markets.																			
★★★½	**AGF International Value**	Fgn Eq	□	□	□	□	□	□	□	□	□	□	A	A	6%	–14%	8/31/98	3	2.77 ●
As the bull market changes, it becomes more selective – and more ideal for the San Diego-based team at Brandes. They've blown the doors off their competitors for years, but now are doing so with exposure to Japan and to cheap oil and gas stocks.																			
★★★★	**AGF Japan Class**	Fgn Eq				□	□	□	□	□	□	□	A	B	31%	–38%	2/28/90	48	3.07 ●
Conservative stock-picking with an eye for value has helped this fund eke out gains in a wretched bear market. The Northwestern MBA running the fund from Tokyo is worried that recent enthusiasm toward Japan may be overdone.																			
★★★	**AGF RSP Intl Equity All**	Fgn Eq					□	□	□	□	□	□	B	D	16%	–17%	8/31/98	7	2.45 ●
This fund maintains full RRSP eligibility by investing in foreign equity index futures. Decent results in up markets, but passive strategies usually lose in down markets.																			
★★★½	**AGF Special U.S. Class**	US Eq	□	□	□	□	□	□	□	□	□	□	A	A	23%	–51%	2/28/73	46	2.86 ●
A big move into e-commerce has juiced this sleeper in '99, its first wake-up since Steve Rodgers took over in '96. It's a risky portfolio, but Rodgers says how could it be any more risky than the big-cap glamour stocks that are so pricey today?																			
★★½	**AGF World Balanced Fund**	Bal					□	□	□	□	□	□	D	NA	20%	–21%	6/30/90	19	2.46 ●
Even after pulling back the equity weighting to 74%, the fund remains way tilted toward stocks. That's helped as bonds have suffered in '99. But missing Asia and Japan has wiped out all the gains and more from good asset class and stock selection.																			
★★½	**AGF World Equity Class**	Fgn Eq							□	□	□	□	NA	NA	3%	–16%	8/31/98	10	3.07 ●
Steve Way runs this fund for AGF and uses a top-down quantitative model that searches for undervalued markets. Performance has been weak in recent years since the model typically overweights emerging markets.																			
★★★½	**AIC Advantage**	Cdn Eq								□	□	□	NA	NA	27%	–30%	9/30/87	44	2.26 ●
After getting whacked with a 20% loss in the year ended June 30/99, the fund is looking less like a financial services fund. Huge declines in permanent holdings like Newcourt haven't helped. Today just 4 of its top 10 stocks are in financial services.																			
★★★★	**AIC Income Equity Fund**	Cdn Eq									□	□	NA	NA	13%	–14%	7/31/98	7	2.38 ●
This is a pricey, dicey income fund. It's for people who want income but don't need capital protection. That said, after the drubbing it's taken the fund can only rebound in the remainder of 1999.																			
★★★½	**AIC Value**	US Eq		□	□	□	□	□	□	□	□	□	A	C	10%	–26%	3/31/90	11	2.28 ●
By avoiding Internet stocks, the fund hopes to avoid any market risk. But owning huge glamour stocks in a frothy market isn't exactly safe. Top holding Merrill Lynch is now unwittingly in the 'net business. And Coke's sky-high price has gone flat.																			
★★½	**AIC World Equity**	Fgn Eq					□	□	□	□	□	□	C	D	24%	–23%	8/31/98	NA	2.38 ●
This fund excludes North America but is similar otherwise to AIC Advantage. Over half of the fund in European financial & wealth management companies, a promising sector. But we're more positive on this fund than its sisters because of better valuations.																			

Legend: ★= overall past performance vs. similar funds (5 ★ max). Boxes show the quartile performance for a fund each calendar year vs. only similar funds (□ is the best score possible). ● = high; ● = average; and ● = a fund with low expenses.

Consistency			Performance Trend										Risk						Efficiency	
Overall Past Performance	Fund Name	Type	90	91	92	93	94	95	96	97	98	Aug. '99	Up	Down	% of Time Losing $	Biggest Drop	Date	No. of Mo's to Recover	MER	
★★	**AIM American Premier Fund**	US Eq			□	□	□	□	□	□	□	□	D	C	7%	–14%	8/31/95	15	2.93	●
The Denver-based trio at Invesco that took over in 1996 have kicked butt with a momentum trading approach to part of this big cap growth fund. Credit core holdings in health care, technology and telecom market leaders.																				
★★½	**AIM Canadian Balanced**	Bal				□	□	□	□	□	□	□	D	C	5%	–14%	6/30/98	7	2.59	●
Sure, it charges way, way more than most. And true, it had a horrible record for a long time. But this puppy's on a roll now, with the move to Denver-based management at Invesco and a somewhat aggressive approach to asset allocation.																				
★★½	**AIM Canadian Premier Fund**	Cdn Eq		□	□	□	□	□	□	□	□	□	C	C	16%	–25%	6/30/98	11	2.69	●
No, it's not managed from Canada. And no, it hasn't had a good track record. And no, frankly, its fees aren't even close to reasonable. But with killer stock selection since taking over, Clas Olsson has trumped his rivals.																				
★★½	**AIM European Growth Fund**	Fgn Eq				□	□	□	□	□	□	□	C	B	14%	–20%	8/31/98	5	2.93	●
With 90% of the focus on bottom-up growth stock picking, the fund has missed the recent move in cyclicals to some degree – a rare exception to the excellent performance since Invesco took over in June of 1996.																				
★★★	**AIM Glo Health Sciences**	Spec Eq					□	□	□	□	□	□	B	NA	3%	–15%	2/28/94	11	2.64	●
Hot sector, hot story, hot new manager. Just don't put too much of your portfolio into this narrow-mandate fund. It's kind of a global fund, but 70% is in the US. It's kind of a broad sector, but there's only a few dozen names. And it's kind of hot lately.																				
★★	**AIM GT America Growth**	US Eq						□	□	□	□	□	NA	NA	11%	–22%	7/31/98	5	2.92	●
This is a mid-cap earnings momentum style of management, one that's ideally suited to the current environment, except that mid caps haven't been hot. The new team took over in March 1999 and have already turned performance around.																				
★★★	**AIM GT Canada Growth Cl**	Cdn Eq						□	□	□	□	□	NA	NA	18%	–24%	6/30/98	13	2.42	○
San Francisco-based Derek Webb really has figured out how to run an earnings momentum fund in the tiny Canadian market: stay clear of small caps. Though this fund does own some, it's got no constraints. So when Imasco's hot, he's there.																				
★★★★	**AIM GT Canada Income Cl**	Div								□	□	□	NA	NA	44%	–20%	6/30/98	NA	2.10	○
Blue-chip stocks, option-writing for income and a third of the portfolio in income trusts; that's the formula. It is paying high current income with decent capital stability, but this fund won't score capital gains over time. That's the trade off.																				
★½	**AIM GT Glo Infrastructure**	Spec Eq						□	□	□	□	□	NA	NA	4%	–13%	8/31/98	5	2.78	●
What's neat about this global sector fund is that it's really a number of sector funds together, with a number of common themes. Like telecommunications, residential housing development, cement and heavy industry: all ready to roll with world growth.																				
★★★★½	**AIM GT Glo Nat Resources**	Nat Res						□	□	□	□	□	NA	NA	39%	–43%	11/30/97	NA	2.96	●
Very few Canadian investors choose global resource funds, assuming that Canada must have the best companies in every sector at the best prices. But this fund proves that's not true. Still, if all your money's inside your RRSP, look elsewhere.																				
★★★½	**AIM GT Global Grwth & Inc**	Fgn Bd						□	□	□	□	□	NA	NA	7%	–8%	1/31/99	NA	2.78	●
Don't confuse this Global Growth & Income with the Canadian version. New manager Michael Lindsell does no option-writing and holds no income trusts. This is just a docile balanced fund with blue chip stocks and sovereign bonds.																				
★★	**AIM GT Global Health Care**	Spec Eq								□	□	□	NA	NA	22%	–15%	3/31/97	4	2.75	●
This fund is cheaper to own than its sister fund, the AIM Global Health Sciences, but is likely to be merged into the latter. It has a worse track record, but the same manager, holdings and approach.																				
★★½	**AIM GT Global Telecom**	Spec Eq						□	□	□	□	□	NA	NA	15%	–23%	6/30/96	13	2.78	●
Think more than just telecom here. Think "convergence" of cable, Internet, telephone and wireless. Mike Mahoney owns hardware providers, service firms and monopoly companies that own the 'pipe' going into people's homes.																				
★★★★½	**AIM GT Latin Amer Growth**	Fgn Eq						□	□	□	□	□	NA	NA	37%	–51%	8/31/97	NA	2.94	○
Here's one of the real standouts in a sector people no longer feel passionate about. But the fundamentals are good for Latin America – as good as they were in 1994. It's just that now we know the region is heavily affected by global currencies and rates.																				

Legend: ★ = overall past performance vs. similar funds (5 ★ max). Boxes show the quartile performance for a fund each calendar year vs. only similar funds (▭ is the best score possible). ● = high; ● = average; and ● = a fund with low expenses.

Consistency			Performance Trend										Risk						Efficiency	
Overall Past Performance	Fund Name	Type	90	91	92	93	94	95	96	97	98	Aug. '99	Up	Down	% of Time Losing $	Biggest Drop	Date	No. of Mo's to Recover	MER	
★★½	**AIM International Value**	Fgn Eq											D	B	27%	–23%	8/31/90	32	2.95	
The same firm has been running this fund since 1996, but name changes have made that difficult to follow. By pursuing a stodgy value approach in a hot market for value stocks, the Atlanta-based team have missed the boat.																				
★★	**All-Canadian Capital**	Cdn Eq											D	A	18%	–45%	2/28/73	65	2.00	
How much punishment can one fund (or investor) take. This ultra-defensive fund is well-prepared for armageddon, with cash and gold certificates and gold stocks. But it's been prepared forever. What a pig.																				
★★	**All-Canadian Compound**	Cdn Eq											D	A	19%	–46%	2/28/73	65	0.00	
Ditto here. A weak fund from a family that offers no bench strength. This one isn't worth your time. As to why no MER shows up, I can only assume that they're disincluding it in the performance calculations as well, a horrible thought.																				
★★	**All-Canadian Resources**	Nat Res											D	A	40%	–52%	8/31/87	79	2.00	
If for some reason you really, really want an All-Canadian fund, buy this one, but then again, why would you really, really want an All-Canadian fund?																				
★★★	**AltaFund Investment**	Cdn Eq											B	D	33%	–40%	10/31/97	NA	2.43	
Lead manager David Taylor is gone now after a move to diminish this fund's historically high resource bias, but the focus on finding good opportunities in Western Canada will remain. Oil and gas exposure has helped lately, as has a value tilt.																				
★★½	**Altamira Asia Pacific**	Fgn Eq											B	C	66%	–58%	11/30/94	NA	2.41	
As one would expect, this fund is dominated by Japan and Hong Kong. Relative performance has been quite good but a bit inconsistent. Now that Asia appears to be back on solid ground, things look promising for this fund.																				
★★½	**Altamira Balanced**	Bal											D	C	26%	–26%	8/31/87	66	2.00	
There's great diversification on the equity side of this fund because four of the top ten holdings are actually other Altamira funds. Performance has been close to average.																				
★★★★	**Altamira Capital Growth**	Cdn Eq										N/A	NA	NA	18%	–27%	7/31/87	24	2.00	NA
A well diversified, TSE 35-esque fund that has finally started to peel its performance off the floor after a couple of bad years. If Ian Joseph can get this fund back in line with its historical performance, watch out!																				
★★★★	**Altamira Equity**	Cdn Eq											A	B	13%	–33%	10/31/97	NA	2.33	
This is almost a completely new fund since being taken over by the three current managers. Resources are no longer a main staple. They have put a major focus on bank stocks but many of their technology plays have paid off big time.																				
★★★	**Altamira European Equity**	Fgn Eq											B	C	5%	–18%	8/31/98	NA	2.38	
Here's a well diversified fund managed offshore with a big chunk of its money invested in the U.K. Performance has been consistently above average.																				
★★½	**Altamira Glo Diversified**	Bal											C	D	25%	–36%	9/30/87	99	2.00	
This "global" fund has almost a 50% weighting in the U.S. Altamira began managing this fund in-house in 1997 in attempt to boost poor performance.																				
★★★	**Altamira Global Discovery**	Fgn Eq											NA	NA	49%	–51%	8/31/97	NA	3.08	
Emerging markets have been rough territory over the past few years and the top-down approach used by manager Vincent Fernandez has not helped performance a great deal. Mexico and South Africa account for 1/4 of the fund.																				
★★★★	**Altamira Growth & Income**	Bal											A	B	18%	–28%	10/31/97	NA	1.40	
Shauna Sexsmith has chosen to fill over 3/4 of this fund with "conservative" Canadian equities. Even this is somewhat aggressive for a balanced fund. Five-year performance has been unspectacular, but lately, many of her picks have been on fire.																				
★★★★	**Altamira High Yield Bond**	Fgn Bd											NA	NA	6%	–9%	8/31/98	7	1.94	
Though he likes to buy emerging markets debt, Barry Allan likes buying bonds denominated in G7 currencies. He sticks to mid-term issues and is now about equally exposed to the loonie and the greenback.																				

Legend: ★ = overall past performance vs. similar funds (5 ★ max). Boxes show the quartile performance for a fund each calendar year vs. only similar funds (□ is the best score possible). ● = high; ● = average; and ● = a fund with low expenses.

Consistency			Performance Trend										Risk						Efficiency
Overall Past Performance	Fund Name	Type	90	91	92	93	94	95	96	97	98	Aug. '99	Up	Down	% of Time Losing $	Biggest Drop	Date	No. of Mo's to Recover	MER
★★★	**Altamira Intl RSP Index**	Fgn Eq											A	NA	NA	–4%	5/31/99	1	0.50 ●
Though we believe there is lots of room to add value on the international scene, it's tough to argue with this cheap passive alternative. Boston-based State Street runs this index offering and you won't find any fund cheaper than 0.5% in this country.																			
★★★½	**Altamira Japanese Opport**	Fgn Eq						□	□	□	□	□	NA	NA	66%	–41%	11/30/94	56	2.49 ●
Performance has taken off since this fund's lows in 1998. Being in the right industries (industrial products and financial companies) has helped superb bottom-up stock picking in the battered Japanese smaller-cap arena by manager Mark Grammer.																			
★★★	**Altamira N.A. Recovery**	Cdn Eq					□	□	□	□	□	□	C	D	35%	–28%	5/31/98	NA	2.35 ●
The key to Dave Taylor's approch is finding hidden value in the Canadian and U.S. markets. He invests in everything from consumer products to resources. If there are cheap stocks in an industry, Dave will probably find them.																			
★★½	**Altamira Precious Metal**	Nat Res						□	□	□	□	□	NA	NA	66%	–73%	6/30/96	NA	2.38 ●
This fund really took it on the chin beginning in mid-1996 and it has a long way to go before making any sort of recovery. With gold hitting historic lows on a regular basis, it will take spectacular stock picking to keep this fund above water.																			
★★★	**Altamira Resource**	Nat Res	□	□	□	□	□	□	□	□	□	□	D	B	42%	–54%	3/31/97	NA	2.34 ●
Foreign exposure has been reduced by manager Craig Porter and a lot of money has been put into the oil and gas sector. Craig is very busy putting back the pieces after the bottom fell out of the commodities market last year.																			
★★½	**Altamira Select American**	US Eq				□	□	□	□	□	□	□	C	C	12%	–23%	5/31/98	13	2.32 ●
Mediocre performance are two words that can sum up this fund's performance. However, now that small and mid cap stocks are starting to wake up, the manager's GARP philosophy and restructuring plays should bode well in this beaten-down arena.																			
★★★	**Altamira Special Growth**	Cdn Eq	□	□	□	□	□	□	□	□	□	□	A	A	28%	–35%	10/31/97	NA	1.80 ●
Sue Coleman hasn't fared too well with this fund. Not only have small caps been losers, but the fund's relative performance has been somewhat shabby. Coleman's leave of absence will see colleague Alex Sasso take over this fund for the next year.																			
★★★	**Altamira US Larger Co**	US Eq					□	□	□	□	□	□	B	C	2%	–12%	8/31/98	3	2.33 ●
Here's a big cap fund with an emphasis on tech issues. Cisco, IBM and Microsoft are some of its biggest holdings. The manager likes to set scenarios for the future and buy companies based on his outlook. Short-term performance has been fantastic.																			
★★½	**Apex Asian Pacific**	Fgn Eq						□	□	□	□	□	C	B	53%	–44%	5/31/96	NA	2.80 ●
This smaller fund is quite good in down markets but there are several better far east funds.																			
★★½	**Apex Balanced Fund (AGF)**	Bal	□	□	□	□	□	□	□	□	□	□	C	A	19%	–30%	11/30/73	43	3.00 ●
This AGF-managed fund has lots of good names but we're not sold on it, thanks to lacklustre performance. How come? Killer fees make this and any other balanced fund a joke at this level in this interest rate environment.																			
★★½	**Apex Canadian Gro (AGF)**	Cdn Eq	□	□	□	□	□	□	□	□	□	□	D	A	24%	–32%	10/31/97	NA	3.00 ●
Another AGF-managed fund, this one has fared quite well recently. Manager Martin Hubbes really favours financial services in this fund, a group that has been up and down lately.																			
★★★	**Associate Investors**	Cdn Eq	□	□	□	□	□	□	□	□	□	□	C	A	22%	–34%	4/30/81	23	1.50 ●
A nice conservative stock fund based on old-fashioned bottom-up research, patient accumulation and disciplined selling. All this, and reasonable fees to boot. Softness lately is due to the pipes, banks and utes that had been so strong for so long.																			
★★	**Atlas Am LargeCap Grth**	US Eq	□	□	□	□	□	□	□	□	□	□	D	B	12%	–24%	9/30/87	42	2.51 ●
A good combination of technology and industrial stocks has not been helping the performance of this fund too much. Hopefully the manager's GARP philosophy will start paying dividends soon.																			
★★½	**Atlas American Advantage**	Bal						□	□	□	□	□	NA	NA	9%	–14%	7/31/98	9	2.55 ●
Here's a fund with some all-American names, like 3M, McDonald's, Du Pont and Boeing. Unfortunately, overall performance has been less all-American lately.																			

Legend: ★= overall past performance vs. similar funds (5 ★ max). Boxes show the quartile performance for a fund each calendar year vs. only similar funds (□ is the best score possible). ● = high; ● = average; and ● = a fund with low expenses.

Consistency			Performance Trend										Risk						Efficiency
Overall Past Performance	Fund Name	Type	90	91	92	93	94	95	96	97	98	Aug. '99	Up	Down	% of Time Losing $	Biggest Drop	Date	No. of Mo's to Recover	MER
★★½	**Atlas Canadian Balanced**	Bal											D	A	9%	–9%	2/28/94	13	2.18
Manager Len Racioppo always ensures that this fund's US exposure is maximized. The Canadian equity holdings are mainly TSE 35-type names, dominated by financial services stocks.																			
★½	**Atlas Cdn Emerging Growth**	Cdn Eq											NA	NA	46%	–49%	10/31/97	NA	2.61
Gene Vollendorf at Bissett recently took over this fund and he is definitely a pro. As the small-cap market continues to come out of the doldrums, watch for this fund to shine.																			
★★★	**Atlas Cdn Large Cap Grth**	Cdn Eq											B	C	31%	–27%	8/31/87	23	2.42
Fred Pynn from Bissett uses a purely bottom-up approach to selecting stocks. He looks for companies that have good growth prospects and are reasonably priced. One of Fred's favourite sectors is Industrial products.																			
★★	**Atlas Cdn Large Cap Value**	Cdn Eq											NA	NA	22%	–26%	5/31/98	NA	2.55
This would be a better fund if the manager maximized its foreign exposure. The mainly large-cap portfolio is sprinkled with plenty of great names like JDS Uniphase, Qualcomm and Imasco.																			
★★½	**Atlas Cdn Small Cap Value**	Cdn Eq											NA	NA	30%	–37%	11/30/97	NA	2.66
BonaVista is a firm that really emphasizes value, and they show off their skill with this fund. A heavy weighting in oil and gas has boosted the fund's near-term performance. Look for this fund to almost always be fully invested.																			
★★★	**Atlas European Value**	Fgn Eq											B	D	5%	–17%	8/31/98	NA	2.58
There are lots of European telecom companies in this fund, a fact that has definitely helped performance. Europe is not as hot now as it has been but the management of this fund is very talented so we expect good things.																			
★★½	**Atlas Global Value**	Fgn Eq											C	C	10%	–13%	5/31/98	7	2.70
There was a pretty high cash weighting in this fund for a time, which probably should have been in the red-hot US market, an area that has been significantly under-represented. This high-cost fund has picked right up lately, though.																			
★★★	**Atlas Latin American**	Fgn Eq											C	NA	45%	–47%	2/28/94	41	2.95
Latin America has been a wild ride recently but the managers of this fund have done extremely well. There are significant holdings in telecommunications companies and Argentina, Brazil and Mexico are the country favorites.																			
★★★½	**Atlas Pacific Basin Value**	Fgn Eq											B	A	71%	–37%	9/30/94	58	2.90
This Pacific fund uses a top-down approach to map out what contries have the best growth prospects. Next, manager David Marvin searches for the best companies in each country and he continues to be very successful with this technique.																			
★★★	**AZURA Balanced**	Bal											NA	NA	5%	–10%	8/31/98	8	2.28
Do not buy this fund. Unlike most funds of fund that offer some relief from the natural double-layering of fees, this family really does whack you twice. You could build and monitor this portfolio of these exact funds yourself for zero in extra fees.																			
★★★	**AZURA Balanced RRSP**	Bal											NA	NA	35%	–17%	5/31/98	NA	2.29
This fund is doomed by double fees. Do not buy it. Unlike most funds of funds that offer some relief from the natural double-layering of fees, this family really does whack you twice.																			
★½	**AZURA Conservative**	Bal											NA	NA	16%	–4%	6/30/98	5	2.03
The only thing worse than paying fees twice is paying them twice with no added value and for a balanced portfolio – where fees are doubly important in a yield enviornment like the one we've got now.																			
★★½	**AZURA Growth Fund**	Fgn Eq											NA	NA	19%	–17%	5/31/98	13	2.29
There are fine funds inside this offering. So why pay another couple of bucks in expenses to own them? It just doesn't make sense. Buy the funds, not the bundle.																			
★★	**AZURA Growth RRSP Pooled**	Cdn Eq											NA	NA	39%	–24%	5/31/98	NA	2.29
Really, I can't say it strongly enough: Do not buy this fund. It adds a whole new layer of fees on top of the MERs for the undelying funds – a fatal flaw. The funds and portfolios are okay. So just buy them.																			

Legend: ★ = overall past performance vs. similar funds (5 ★ max). Boxes show the quartile performance for a fund each calendar year vs. only similar funds (☐ is the best score possible). ● = high; ● = average; and ● = a fund with low expenses.

Consistency: Overall Past Performance	Fund Name	Type	90	91	92	93	94	95	96	97	98	Aug. '99	Risk: Up	Down	% of Time Losing $	Biggest Drop	Date	No. of Mo's to Recover	Efficiency: MER
★★★	**Barreau Quebec Balanced**	Bal											C	A	6%	–10%	2/28/94	15	0.78 ●
Cheap, cheap, cheap. And conservative, with a down-market score that's to die for. This fund is managed by Bolton Tremblay out of Montreal.																			
★★	**Bell Group RRSP Balanced**	Bal											D	D	21%	–10%	5/31/98	NA	1.15 ●
Despite its low fees, this private fund has had dismal performance across the board.																			
★★½	**Bell Group RRSP Equity**	Cdn Eq											D	D	21%	–33%	10/31/97	NA	2.65 ●
This tiny private offering has very high fees and below-average performance. Exposure to some cyclical stocks has helped turn the numbers around so far in 1999.																			
★★	**Beutel Goodman Amer Equ**	US Eq											D	D	13%	–18%	5/31/98	NA	2.48 ●
The value approch used by Tor Williams has not been favoured by Wall Street over the past few years. Even with the resurection of many so-called value stocks, this fund has still lagged. A high MER doesn't help this fund's case.																			
★★★	**Beutel Goodman Balanced**	Bal											C	D	12%	–12%	5/31/98	NA	2.07 ●
Maximum foreign exposure has not made this fund a winner. A heavy oil and gas weighting has helped recent performance, but better balanced funds are available elsewhere.																			
★★	**Beutel Goodman Cdn Equity**	Cdn Eq											D	D	27%	–24%	5/31/98	NA	1.99 ●
In all markets, this fund has been unspectacular. The long term value focus has been a drag, to be sure, in these growth days. But even the bank exposure was too little too late. Ditto for oil and gas. Beutel's a fine firm, but this fund is no find.																			
★★★	**Beutel Goodman Intl Equ**	Fgn Eq											B	D	30%	–19%	6/30/98	13	2.84 ●
This well diversified fund has the UK and Japan as its biggest holdings. Performance had been off a bit until cyclicals started kicking again in early 1999. It's a big cap fund with developed markets only and some real kick in good times.																			
★★★½	**Beutel Goodman Small Cap**	Cdn Eq											NA	NA	23%	–22%	5/31/98	14	2.29 ●
A strict value discipline. A short, concetrated list of stocks. A fundamental, research-driven process. That's the way to find gems in Canada's less-than-perfectly-efficient small cap market. Denis March finds real bargains in real growing companies.																			
★★	**Bissett American Equity**	US Eq											D	B	11%	–33%	9/30/87	44	1.44 ●
Jeff Morrison tries to stay within the S&P 100 for this fund. A GARP approach is utilized for this fund of 40 to 50 stocks. A thematic approach is taken when selecting stocks but performance has been subpar.																			
★★★½	**Bissett Dividend Income**	Div											A	C	15%	–15%	6/30/98	NA	1.31 ●
Fred Pynn finds and sticks with companies that are compounding growth internally thanks to a consistently improving ROE. He tries to uncover growth at a reasonable price. Nearly 30% of this fund is in preferred shares.																			
★★	**Bissett Intl Equity**	Fgn Eq											NA	NA	5%	–14%	8/31/98	4	2.00 ●
Fleming focuses on a bottom-up style. Dividend growth, debt to equity ratios, dividend yields and overall valuations are considered before any trades are made. Suprisingly, a 25% weighting in Japan has not made this fund a winner yet this year.																			
★★★★	**Bissett Small Cap**	Cdn Eq											A	D	26%	–36%	11/30/97	NA	1.78 ●
Gene Vollendorf recently took this fund over and increased the target capitalization of its holdings. Hopefully this will bring performance to decent levels. Gene's a good manager and the fund has a low MER, so expect good things in the future.																			
★★½	**BNP (Canada) Equity**	Cdn Eq											C	D	20%	–25%	5/31/98	NA	2.13 ●
This is sort of a wimpy fund that doesn't seem to deviate much from index weightings in an effort to never be on the bottom (or the top) of the charts. It is mediocre in every regard, despite its exposure to the stocks that have been the index darlings.																			
★★★	**BPI Amer Small Companies**	US Eq											C	A	30%	–41%	8/31/87	63	2.55 ●
Industrial products account for over 40% of this fund's money. Manager John Bichelmeyer is the picture of the bottom-up value approach. A long list of holdings improves diversification, but dilutes gains on hot names like Qualcomm.																			

Legend: ★ = overall past performance vs. similar funds (5 ★ max). Boxes show the quartile performance for a fund each calendar year vs. only similar funds (□ is the best score possible). ● = high; ○ = average; and ● = a fund with low expenses.

Consistency			Performance Trend										Risk						Efficiency	
Overall Past Performance	Fund Name	Type	90	91	92	93	94	95	96	97	98	Aug. '99	Up	Down	% of Time Losing $	Biggest Drop	Date	No. of Mo's to Recover	MER	
★★★	**BPI American Equity Value**	US Eq	□	□	□	□	□	□	□	□	□	□	B	B	4%	–13%	8/31/98	3	2.51	●
Financial services account for almost 30% of this fund. But the biggest gas comes from tech stocks like Microsoft, Cisco and Lucent. Still, it is a value fund and it has done well in both good and bad markets by focusing on market leaders.																				
★★½	**BPI Canadian Equity Value**	Cdn Eq	□	□	□	□	□	□	□	□	□	□	D	B	29%	–27%	4/30/98	NA	2.53	●
Kevin Klassen has been at the helm of this fund since late 1998 and he has almost turned the entire thing over. Gone are the small caps and private placements, doubling average cap. But still performance hasn't turned around yet.																				
★★★½	**BPI Canadian Resource**	Nat Res	□	□	□	□	□	□	□	□	□	□	A	A	36%	–68%	6/30/96	NA	2.83	●
A weighting of over 30% in oil and gas has made this fund a winner so far this year. Bob Lyon tries to find the hidden gems in the resource sector that show great growth prospects and he has been doing a fine job since taking over for Fred Dalley.																				
★★½	**BPI Cdn Small Companies**	Cdn Eq	□	□	□	□	□	□	□	□	□	□	B	B	41%	–52%	3/31/97	NA	2.62	●
Small caps are still dead in the water, despite a little sign of breath in '99. But standouts in oil and gas, plus some technology names have helped spark a turnaround after two tough years for long-time hero Steve Misener.																				
★★½	**BPI Dividend Income Fund**	Div	□	□	□	□	□	□	□	□	□	□	C	B	10%	–11%	6/30/98	NA	1.50	●
This is a real dividend fund. Not that common-stock crap you usually see in this category. A real, conservative fund with lean expenses and a focus on growing after-tax income over time without much capital risk. A quality fund with enduring appeal.																				
★★★	**BPI Global Equity Value**	Fgn Eq	□	□	□	□	□	□	□	□	□	□	B	A	15%	–30%	9/30/87	32	2.44	○
The Orlando-based team responsible for this fund since 1994 has done so many things right: Country weights, currency exposure and more. But all that is just luck, because it was all a result of a basic mandate to own dominant industry players.																				
★★★	**BPI Global Small Co**	Fgn Eq					□	□	□	□	□	□	A	D	25%	–23%	5/31/98	13	2.35	○
With rigid screens, management interviews and clear price targets, Pablo Salas and the rest of the 7-person Orlando-based team take on the world of underfollowed names. The idea is to buy great firms with leadership positions and rapid growth rates.																				
★★★★½	**BPI Income & Growth Fund**	Bal									□	□	NA	NA	14%	–13%	6/30/98	7	2.51	●
This is another pricey balanced fund that just won't cut it over time in this rate environment. With a short duration on the bonds (something you could buy yourself), there's just not enough yield to provide decent income, despite good stock picks.																				
★★★★★	**BPI Intl Equity Value**	Fgn Eq									□	□	NA	NA	7%	–15%	8/31/98	5	2.51	●
Here's the non-North American version of Dan Jaworski's Global Equity Value fund. With no US, it's no surprise that the absolute returns have been lower. But from a diversification standpoint this fund is a gem for people with big US holdings.																				
★★★	**C.I. American**	US Eq				□	□	□	□	□	□	□	B	D	0%	–10%	7/31/98	5	2.41	○
Bill Priest still has a pile of consumer stocks – now comprising over 56% of this portfolio. Despite the 'D' grade in down markets, this fund dropped only half as much as the S&P 500 during the summer decline in 1998.																				
★★½	**C.I. American RSP**	US Eq							□	□	□	□	NA	NA	0%	–13%	7/31/98	4	2.38	○
Using derivatives, this fund achieves full RRSP eligibility, which is a real benefit for people whose savings are all tied up in their registered plans. But there is a cost to the convenience: A performance hit that's subtle but never ending.																				
★★★½	**C.I. Canadian Balanced**	Bal					□	□	□	□	□	□	B	D	6%	–15%	6/30/98	7	2.33	○
John Zechner is quite conservatively positioned with just 38% in stocks and 22% in cash. On the equity side, he's got healthy exposure to Canadian technology (which has worked out well) and an above-average dividend yield just under 2%.																				
★★★	**C.I. Canadian Growth**	Cdn Eq					□	□	□	□	□	□	C	D	10%	–28%	6/30/98	10	2.38	○
Zechner's back. After a few tough years of being too conservative, he's now in the zone with winners in everything from cable and communication stocks to oil and gas and Internet plays. He trades 'em quick, though, so these names will be gone soon.																				
★★★½	**C.I. Canadian Income**	Bal						□	□	□	□	□	NA	NA	9%	–12%	5/31/98	8	1.85	○
With a bargain MER of well under 2 bucks and hot stock picking since having been too early on the cyclical names, this fund offers a real deal for investors. Its active asset allocation is imperfect, but is designed to protect capital – a noble goal.																				

Legend: ★ = overall past performance vs. similar funds (5 ★ max). Boxes show the quartile performance for a fund each calendar year vs. only similar funds (□ is the best score possible). ● = high; ○ = average; and ● = a fund with low expenses.

Consistency			Performance Trend										Risk						Efficiency	
Overall Past Performance	Fund Name	Type	90	91	92	93	94	95	96	97	98	Aug. '99	Up	Down	% of Time Losing $	Biggest Drop	Date	No. of Mo's to Recover	MER	
★★★½	**C.I. Emerging Markets**	Fgn Eq				□	□	□	□	□	□	□	B	A	35%	–31%	10/31/94	57	2.78	○
One of the biggest winners since the market's free fall in late 1994, this New York-managed fund offers some of the best fundamental research on emerging markets in the country, without too much concern over size and trading ability.																				
★★★	**C.I. Global**	Fgn Eq	□	□	□	□	□	□	□	□	□	□	B	A	20%	–23%	9/30/87	44	2.49	○
Boomer-guru Bill Sterling is the strategist behind this fund these days, but it's really a team product. That means it benefits from Bill Priest's valuation and accounting research, Greg Dilberto's country research and a slew of industry specialists.																				
★★	**C.I. Global Equity RSP**	Fgn Eq					□	□	□	□	□	□	D	D	18%	–14%	2/28/94	23	2.47	○
Here is a very different approach to RRSP-eligible foreign exposure. This fund makes little use of index futures but rather gets exposure to individual foreign stocks with a special type of derivative. Returns here have been underwhelming.																				
★★★★	**C.I. Global High Yield**	Fgn Bd						□	□	□	□	□	NA	NA	26%	–21%	5/31/98	NA	2.19	●
Hedging helped this fund protect its gains in 1999, after a rough spell during the summer meltdown in '98. Mostly sovereign issues here represent a more secure way to play the economies of developing nations with diversification – and income.																				
★★	**C.I. Latin American**	Fgn Eq						□	□	□	□	□	D	NA	49%	–52%	8/31/97	NA	2.77	●
Lead manager Emily Alejos took over leadership of this struggling fund early in 1998 with hopes of a turnaround. The bulk of the portfolio is invested in Mexico and Brazil as Alejos feels these are the strongest and most liquid of Latin countries.																				
★★★★	**C.I. Pacific**	Fgn Eq	□	□	□	□	□	□	□	□	□	□	D	B	24%	–51%	8/31/97	NA	2.52	●
Terry Mahoney's appointment as lead manager is not major news since he's been co-manager since 1990. Country decisions have been inconsistent. Take Japan, for instance. They owned it when it sucked and turfed it too early, missing the huge rebound.																				
★★★	**C.I. Sector American**	US Eq				□	□	□	□	□	□	□	B	C	0%	–10%	8/31/98	4	2.46	○
You've just gotta know to trade out of this after years like '99 may prove to be: Years where gains are big and assets didn't grow much. That's when distributions are likely to be biggest – so switch to the Sector Short Term Fund.																				
★★	**C.I. Sector Canadian**	Cdn Eq	□	□	□	□	□	□	□	□	□	□	D	C	36%	–29%	9/30/89	47	2.43	○
Want to avoid the stiff taxes of the John Zechner approach? This is your fund. But you'll have to trade out of it before distributions – by going to another C.I. Sector fund. Trading within this Sector structure is tax-free. Holding is not.																				
★★½	**C.I. Sector Emerg**	Fgn Eq				□	□	□	□	□	□	□	D	B	37%	–31%	10/31/94	57	2.83	○
The tax structure here works for frequent traders – which is a strategy, I guess, in a fund that swings this wildly. Trading within the C.I. Sector structure is tax-free. But holding is not because they still pay distributions to unitholders regularly.																				
★★★	**C.I. Sector Global Shares**	Fgn Eq	□	□	□	□	□	□	□	□	□	□	C	A	14%	–14%	8/31/90	9	2.54	○
Trading within the C.I. Sector structure is tax-free. But holding is not because they still pay distributions to unitholders regularly. By matching the returns of its underlying fund pretty consistently, this fund proves that it pays to beat the tax man.																				
★★★★½	**C.I. Sector Global Tele**	Spec Eq								□	□	□	NA	NA	0%	–15%	8/31/98	3	2.45	○
You know the telecom sector's on fire. You know that a global approach is best for diversification. You know this team rocks. But you may not know that this fund can and will still pay distributions to unitholders on D-day. So switch out beforehand.																				
★★	**C.I. Sector Hsbgr Asian**	Fgn Eq						□	□	□	□	□	NA	NA	67%	–69%	9/30/94	NA	2.82	○
Don't count Hansberger out because of recent softness. This is a superb firm that's doing everything right. Their picks will explode over time. This structure allows heavy traders to move around within the Sector funds without triggering a tax event.																				
★½	**C.I. Sector Hsbgr Euro**	Fgn Eq				□	□	□	□	□	□	□	D	D	24%	–22%	6/30/98	NA	2.53	○
I'm big on a European rebound. I'm big on only recommending these Sector funds to people who understand that if, on distribution day, you are sitting in a Sector fund that pays distributions, you're gonna get whacked. Own CI Sector Short Term on D-day.																				
★½	**C.I. Sector Latin Amer**	Fgn Eq						□	□	□	□	□	NA	NA	45%	–52%	8/31/97	NA	2.82	○
If you're gonna trade a wild fund like this, then this Sector strucure is the only way to do it. You've just gotta know to trade out of this after years when gains were big and assets didn't grow. That's when distributions are likely to be biggest.																				

Legend: ★ = overall past performance vs. similar funds (5 ★ max). Boxes show the quartile performance for a fund each calendar year vs. only similar funds (□ is the best score possible). ● = high; ● = average; and ● = a fund with low expenses.

Consistency			Performance Trend										Risk						Efficiency
Overall Past Performance	Fund Name	Type	90	91	92	93	94	95	96	97	98	Aug. '99	Up	Down	% of Time Losing $	Biggest Drop	Date	No. of Mo's to Recover	MER
★★★	**C.I. Sector Pacific**	Fgn Eq											B	B	33%	–52%	8/31/97	NA	2.57
The fund's been soft for years thanks to inconsistent country picks. Too early selling Hong Kong, too early owning Japan and more. But this Sector structure allows heavy traders to move around within the Sector funds without triggering a tax event.																			
★★★	**Caldwell Associate**	Bal											B	D	19%	–26%	5/31/98	NA	2.48
Only twice this decade has Tom Caldwell missed fully participating in a bull market. That's not such a crime for this, a conservative balanced fund. We like this fund, but point out that it and all balanced funds clipping a couple of points are pricey.																			
★★	**Caldwell International**	Fgn Eq											D	NA	15%	–18%	5/31/98	11	2.76
Some teeny tiny funds goose performance with a lucky hit on some obscure name that no institution could ever buy. But this is an actual big cap fund. We don't recommend this one, but do like the others in the family.																			
★★★	**Camaf: Cdn Anaesth Accum**	Cdn Eq											B	A	26%	–35%	3/31/73	58	2.68
Convenient access to a billion dollar money manager you've never heard of, Laketon Invesment Management. With 9 pros, the Toronto firm does 150 company interviews annually and spends 70% of in-house research effort on field trips.																			
★½	**Cambridge Amer Growth**	US Eq											D	B	37%	–32%	11/30/93	51	4.60
Horribly cyclical. Unbelievably expensive to own. Occasional, explosive performance. That's about it to summarize this fund. It's a strange offering from a strange firm. Manager Raoul Tsakok has been buying some respectable big caps lately, though.																			
★★	**Cambridge Americas**	Fgn Eq										N/A	NA	NA	23%	–33%	8/31/87	52	4.71
This is a US fund no matter how you cut it. Some may want to compare it against Latin America funds, but that's exceedingly generous. There's a little Latin World exposure here, but not much.																			
★★½	**Cambridge Balanced**	Bal											D	A	22%	–68%	6/30/96	NA	4.37
What's this? A balanced fund that charges 4.37% and doesn't make good net returns for investors? Unbelievable! Bonds yield just over 5%, so my God, you gotta figure a balanced fund like this would earn something for investors. Ha!																			
★★★½	**Cambridge China**	Fgn Eq											NA	NA	82%	–66%	4/30/95	NA	4.71
A ridiculous fund company, to be sure. But this fund (which is awful) is probably one of their better choices. It does offer exposure to speculative names in a speculative, potentially huge market. So when China moves, this baby will sizzle.																			
★★	**Cambridge Global**	Fgn Eq											D	C	26%	–70%	10/31/96	NA	4.95
No, no. This fund doesn't just charge almost 5% a year in expenses. It also buys country funds, which themselves charge a healthy couple of per cent a year. Despite occassional sporadic wins, this fund just doesn't deserve your money.																			
★★½	**Cambridge Growth**	Cdn Eq											D	A	29%	–75%	6/30/96	NA	4.41
If your idiot cousin lost his job at Mac's Milk and took up day-trading, he'd probably wind up with a portfolio just like this: Rotten penny stocks with crazy promises and unfulfilled potential, clouded by the occasional win.																			
★½	**Cambridge Pacific**	Fgn Eq											D	D	45%	–86%	9/30/87	NA	6.04
There are some decent holdings here. But despite the usual capital markets law that says buy low, this turkey is unlikely to rebound from its heart-thumping 86% nose dive. Its MER is climbing – to 6.04% lately.																			
★½	**Cambridge Precious Metals**	Nat Res											NA	NA	100%	–86%	10/31/96	NA	4.40
Here's one area where a wildman-cum-speculator can probably do well: in the gossipy world of junior mining stocks in and around the VSE. But the fund should only do well when metals are on the move, which they were earlier this year.																			
★★½	**Cambridge Resource**	Nat Res											C	C	42%	–86%	6/30/96	NA	4.37
Even with oil and gas on fire, tree takeovers and lots of broad-based strength in resources, this pig hasn't participated. Too bad, really. Because it's been the one kind of market that a guy like this could actually make any money: Speculative excess.																			
★★	**Cambridge Special Equity**	Cdn Eq											D	A	59%	–77%	6/30/96	NA	4.48
A rebound from its 77% nosedive isn't reason to jump aboard this fund. It's just too wacky. Yes, some technology names have moved. And yes, there were some wins in golds. But don't buy this fund. Now or ever.																			

Legend: ★ = overall past performance vs. similar funds (5 ★ max). Boxes show the quartile performance for a fund each calendar year vs. only similar funds (□ is the best score possible). ● = high; ● = average; and ● = a fund with low expenses.

Consistency			Performance Trend										Risk						Efficiency
Overall Past Performance	Fund Name	Type	90	91	92	93	94	95	96	97	98	Aug. '99	Up	Down	% of Time Losing $	Biggest Drop	Date	No. of Mo's to Recover	MER
★★★	**Canada Life Asia Pacific**	Fgn Eq							□	□	□	□	NA	NA	64%	−36%	8/31/97	23	2.40 ●
It looks a lot like the Hansberger Asian Fund because it is the Hansberger Asian management team. That means a core value discipline, any cap approach and long holding periods. But with this fund, you get a bargain MER.																			
★★★	**Canada Life Cdn Equity**	Cdn Eq	□	□	□	□	□	□	□	□	□	□	C	A	22%	−27%	7/31/81	19	2.25 ●
Okay, this one's a bit of a yawn. The approach at newly-merged Laketon Investment Management is decidedly fundamental. But this is really a core holding (read inability to deviate much from index weights) so there are few surprises here.																			
★★★½	**Canada Life European Equ**	Fgn Eq							□	□	□	□	NA	NA	3%	−19%	8/31/98	5	2.40 ●
This one's managed by Tom Tibbles at Hansberger with an eye to cheap, cheap stock picking. That's worked better in the market downturn in Europe lately, as has the mid cap focus and currency management. But the approach will shine brighter over time.																			
★★★	**Canada Life Managed**	Bal	□	□	□	□	□	□	□	□	□	□	B	C	16%	−12%	5/31/98	8	2.25 ●
Poor Gary Kondrat of what's now Laketon Investment Management. Great bond calls and stock selection are muted by fees. Balanced funds that are half in bonds at 5.5% can't charge 2.25% and still add value. This one has, but barely.																			
★★★½	**Canada Life US & Itl Equ**	Fgn Eq	□	□	□	□	□	□	□	□	□	□	A	B	12%	−23%	9/30/87	18	2.40 ●
The heavy mandated allocation to the States has helped the fund as the US market has extended a record 17-year bull market. The managers continue to add value through stock selection in addition to the extra return they get from pure luck.																			
★★	**Canada Tr Emerging Mkts**	Fgn Eq							□	□	□	□	NA	NA	47%	−53%	8/31/97	NA	2.95 ●
Schroder, a British firm, is responsible for this popular offering. They use a broadly diversified approach to mitigating risk that includes a blend of valuation and growth characteristics, with an obvious eye out for potential political and other risks.																			
★★	**Canada Tr Special Equity**	Cdn Eq	□	□	□	□	□	□	□	□	□	□	B	B	34%	−36%	10/31/97	NA	2.14 ●
With a bottom-up stock selection routine and a top-down thematic model, this fund has suffered from inconsistent messages in what's been a rotten environment. Newish manager Linda Pallin is doing better now with Nelvana and QLT, plus some oil stocks.																			
★★½	**Canada Trust AmeriGrowth**	US Eq					□	□	□	□	□	□	C	D	3%	−16%	7/31/98	4	1.27 ●
Since it's invested in US$, this RSP-eligible US fund has underperformed its US$ benchmark consistently, but by less than you might think. Why they pursue this policy is beyond me, because otherwise the fund's a gem.																			
★★	**Canada Trust AsiaGrowth**	Fgn Eq						□	□	□	□	□	D	C	64%	−45%	2/28/94	NA	2.40 ●
This fund maintains full RRSP eligibility by investing in futures contracts of Southeast Asian markets and Japan. But the fund hasn't had the pick up you'd expect from its huge weighting in Japan and the fact that the Japanese market's been on fire.																			
★★★½	**Canada Trust Balanced**	Bal	□	□	□	□	□	□	□	□	□	□	B	B	12%	−12%	6/30/98	12	2.08 ●
Protecting capital first, growing it second. That's the motto for this steady pup. It uses a top-down thematic model to help with asset mix and sectors, then applies an army of analysts on the stock selection side.																			
★★½	**Canada Trust EuroGrowth**	Fgn Eq						□	□	□	□	□	C	D	13%	−17%	8/31/98	NA	2.08 ●
This fund invests in futures contracts on European indexes to achieve full RRSP eligibility. That's good. It owns a disproportionate share of bigger cap stocks. That's good too. But currency management adds a dicey element, though it's done well lately.																			
★★★★	**Canada Trust Glo Asst All**	Bal										□	NA	NA	0%	−8%	8/31/98	3	2.60 ●
Newer fund with a top-down asset allocation model that is, as it should be, fixated on the Fed's moves. That means that this fund hopes to get the big picture right. So right that they can justify rich fees without even trying to pick individual stocks.																			
★★★	**Canada Trust Intl Equity**	Fgn Eq A	□	□	□	□	□	□	□	□	□	□	B	C	23%	−20%	8/31/98	5	2.41 ●
Active stock selection here at a bargain price. This is one of CT's better choices. It's got a multi-manager approach, the highlights of which are the Boston-based team at Scudder (who do Europe and the US) with a big cap blend style.																			
★★	**Canada Trust North Amer**	Fgn Eq	□	□	□	□	□	□	□	□	□	□	D	B	25%	−38%	2/28/73	70	2.27 ●
Active management of stocks in Canada and the US make this a funny hybrid. It lags US funds, and clobbers Canadian ones. But it's not really International, either. No matter, the big cap focus has blessed Claude King in his 3 years on the job.																			

Legend: ★= overall past performance vs. similar funds (5 ★ max). Boxes show the quartile performance for a fund each calendar year vs. only similar funds (□ is the best score possible). ● = high; ○ = average; and ● = a fund with low expenses.

Consistency: Overall Past Performance	Fund Name	Type	Performance Trend: 90	91	92	93	94	95	96	97	98	Aug. '99	Risk: Up	Down	% of Time Losing $	Biggest Drop	Date	No. of Mo's to Recover	Efficiency: MER	
★★★	**Canada Trust Stock Fund**	Cdn Eq	□	□	□	□	□	□	□	□	□	□	B	C	22%	–27%	5/31/98	NA	1.83	○
By owning big cap stocks from a variety of industries, the fund has benefited from the move to cyclicals in '99. But missing the banks a year earlier still haunts this potentially good fund. It charges little, has a good team and a sensible approach.																				
★★★★½	**Canada Trust U.S. Equ Ind**	US Eq									□	□	NA	NA	0%	–11%	8/31/98	2	0.75	●
This is the best US index fund from CT. It's got skinny fees, a top-notch index pro advising it and very little tracking error. And it doesn't suffer from any of that currency nonsense that plagues other products in the family.																				
★½	**Canada Trust US Equity**	US Eq		□	□	□	□	□	□	□	□	□	D	D	8%	–13%	7/31/98	4	2.18	○
Why pay more than 2 bucks in fees for active management of big cap shares when the family offers a better choice that charges just one third the MER?																				
★★★★★	**Canadian Imperial Equity**	Cdn Eq										□	NA	NA	57%	–27%	6/30/98	13	2.00	○
TAL's Real Trepanier is a growth manager who pays attention to valuations. He's not afraid to pull the trigger on a stock he feels is too pricey. His stocks are limited to TSE 300 names but has a good mix of big stable firms and small growth stocks.																				
★★★★	**Canso Canadian Equity**	Cdn Eq									□	□	NA	NA	27%	–16%	5/31/98	11	2.00	○
Performance has been good for this obscure $1.2 million fund. Lead manager John Carswell insulated this fund well from the 1998 summer meltdown by holding a good chunk of cash and lots of high-yielding securities like income trusts.																				
★★	**Capital All Vent LSVCC**	Spec Eq							□	□	□	□	NA	NA	43%	–15%	7/31/96	NA	5.29	●
We love this small fund because of its grass roots research and technology focus. The J-curve says that all venture capital pools will show poor returns in the first three years or so but will then explode as the few real gems take off.																				
★★★	**Capstone Balanced Trust**	Bal	□	□	□	□	□	□	□	□	□	□	C	A	15%	–19%	5/31/84	12	2.00	○
Great numbers from a great firm with a long, long history picking stocks for Canadians. Yup, that's Canadian General Investments – the advisor on this pup. The approach is inherently conservative with a blend approach and no cap constraints.																				
★★½	**Capstone International**	Fgn Eq	□	□	□	□	□	□	□	□	□	□	C	C	18%	–19%	7/31/98	6	2.00	●
This too is managed by Michael Smedley at Canadian General Investments, a fine firm that just hasn't done as well overseas, despite its willingness to delve even into emerging markets in what's been a superb time for them.																				
★★★½	**CCPE Diversified**	Bal	□	□	□	□	□	□	□	□	□	□	B	B	13%	–13%	5/31/98	11	1.35	●
A dirt cheap fund with some good numbers – thanks to manager Dave Knight at Knight, Bain, Seath & Holbrook. This one's restricted, though, to members of CCPE. Like many, these group funds are an excellent deal because of the access to top counsellors.																				
★★★	**CCPE Global Equity**	Fgn Eq							□	□	□	□	NA	NA	2%	–12%	8/31/98	3	1.95	●
Okay, so fees aren't everything. This one's been uninspiring so far, despite its reasonable MER. Fees do matter over time, but so does active management. Better choices do exist within this fund family.																				
★★★	**CCPE Growth**	Cdn Eq	□	□	□	□	□	□	□	□	□	□	C	B	26%	–23%	5/31/98	13	1.35	●
Geoff Watters and Mike Stanley from Jones Heward run this restricted access fund with a blend style and a bigger-cap focus. They've proven it to be a consistent winner for members in all but the hottest market environments.																				
★★★½	**CCPE U.S. Equity**	US Eq							□	□	□	□	NA	NA	0%	–13%	8/31/98	3	1.75	○
It's a bird! It's a plane! It's Clark Kent managing this fund from Gotham! Well, not quite. His name is Kent Clark, but his firm (Goldman Sachs) is a superstar of the institutional world with research that makes money managers dizzy.																				
★★	**CDA Aggressive Equity (A)**	Cdn Eq						□	□	□	□	□	D	D	34%	–34%	10/31/97	NA	1.00	●
Think mid cap focus and long term growth. Think dirt cheap pricing just for dentists. Think of all the dentists who try to do this themselves! Don't bother. You can't replicate this diversification, this upside or this approach – even with E*Trade.																				
★★★	**CDA Balanced (KBSH)**	Bal	□	□	□	□	□	□	□	□	□	□	B	A	16%	–25%	4/30/81	22	0.97	●
Hey, doc! If you don't own this, maybe you need a check up. Low cost access to new managers Knight, Bain, Seath & Holbrook – a standout firm that's known for great pension numbers. A superb balanced fund for dentists.																				

Legend: ★ = overall past performance vs. similar funds (5 ★ max). Boxes show the quartile performance for a fund each calendar year vs. only similar funds (▭ is the best score possible). ● = high; ● = average; and ● = a fund with low expenses.

Consistency: Overall Past Performance	Fund Name	Type	Risk: Up	Risk: Down	% of Time Losing $	Biggest Drop	Date	No. of Mo's to Recover	Efficiency: MER	Comment
★★★	**CDA Common Stock (A)**	Cdn Eq	C	A	24%	–33%	11/30/73	56	0.97	I know, I know. Low fees don't help in the short term when the manager misses the banks. But Altamira's call on cyclicals proved fortuitous and the fund's on fire again. So if you're a dentist, seek professional help with this fine fund.
★½	**CDA Emerging Markets (K)**	Fgn Eq	NA	NA	77%	–54%	6/30/96	NA	1.45	Bill Viera at institutional firm KBSH has a great track record in Asia and in developed markets. This fund has been a pig because there's just no money in it. A half a million bucks or so does not a convenient account make.
★★★½	**CDA European (KBSH)**	Fgn Eq	NA	NA	7%	–19%	8/31/98	4	1.45	Again, low cost access for dentists to KBSH, a great firm. Their focus on industry-leading growth stocks in Europe is good. But their measly $5 million in this fund doesn't seem to have been a plus, you might say. We love the CDA family, so be patient.
★★★½	**CDA International Equ (K)**	Fgn Eq	NA	NA	5%	–16%	8/31/98	4	1.45	Another tiny international fund from KBSH here, this dentists-only offering employs a growth style that tilts larger names, making this fund a decent complement to the other CDA global equity fund managed by Templeton.
★★★★½	**CDA Special Equity (K)**	Cdn Eq	NA	NA	29%	–29%	11/30/97	16	1.44	You name the hot smaller or mid cap stock and this fund's probably owned it. It's a relatively tight list of terrific stocks trading at still-reasonable prices. The kind of companies you didn't know Canada had. All in a cheap wrapping for dentists.
★★½	**Cdn Medical Disc LSVCC**	Spec Eq	NA	NA	40%	–17%	4/30/98	NA	4.71	Closed to new investors. A killer labour fund with long term appeal. The next few years will see big realized gains in a portfolio that the accountants haven't yet bothered to mark up.
★½	**Cdn Venture Opport LSVCC**	Spec Eq	NA	NA	69%	–50%	3/31/94	NA	5.34	Goodman & Co. took over this dog at the end of 1996 and have done very well since then. This is a labour fund, so holders are stuck with it. But you can see that when a fund like this sells a holding, its markup is immediate and incredible.
★★★	**CentrePost Balanced**	Bal	C	D	23%	–15%	5/31/98	14	1.00	This is a sleeper of a fund whose conservative rate anticipation style has kept it golden in the drubbing of 1999. But that aversion to making big calls is a blessing only to very conservative clients. If you want aggressive bond action, look elsewhere.
★★½	**CentrePost Canadian Equ**	Cdn Eq	C	D	37%	–30%	5/31/98	NA	1.00	Rick Hutcheon's having a big year in what's been a long time coming for this fund, which is only available to hospital employees.
★★★	**CentrePost Foreign Equity**	Fgn Eq	B	D	0%	–15%	7/31/98	4	1.75	Available to hospital employees only, this fund has earned good returns in up markets. It charges a skinny MER, which doesn't hurt.
★★★	**Chou Associates**	US Eq	B	B	18%	–18%	9/30/89	18	1.86	Francis Chou is a professional money manager who works for a big insurance company. He started this tiny fund company on the side 13 years ago – for fun.
★★★	**Chou RRSP**	Cdn Eq	B	B	17%	–16%	12/31/89	25	2.02	With only $4 million or so in assets, you'd think this fund is not even a player. But it tromps big, brand name funds again and again – in good markets and bad. Its biggest mistake ever is missing the commodity stock rallies in '93 and '99.
★★★★	**CI Covington Fund LSVCC**	Spec Eq	NA	NA	2%	–3%	2/28/98	15	4.41	We remain huge supporters of Grant Brown and the hands-on team at Covington. The fund's recent wins still don't fully account for all the unrealized gains in this superb portfolio.
★★★	**CIBC Balanced Fund**	Bal	B	B	14%	–14%	6/30/98	10	2.27	TAL is well known for its active asset mix decision models that are used to manage this CIBC offering. Lead manager Jean Guy Desjardins has turned this fund around to above average performance with good stock picks and astute shifts in asset mix.

Legend: ★ = overall past performance vs. similar funds (5 ★ max). Boxes show the quartile performance for a fund each calendar year vs. only similar funds (☐ is the best score possible). ● = high; ● = average; and ● = a fund with low expenses.

Consistency			Performance Trend										Risk						Efficiency
Overall Past Performance	Fund Name	Type	90	91	92	93	94	95	96	97	98	Aug. '99	Up	Down	% of Time Losing $	Biggest Drop	Date	No. of Mo's to Recover	MER
★★½	**CIBC Canadian Resources**	Nat Res											NA	NA	56%	–49%	2/28/97	NA	2.35
Paul Wong has a thing for quality. So it's no wonder that he'll miss the occasional frothy market like that of spring '99. No one can predict commodity prices, so Wong figures he must either chase momentum or just buy great businesses. It's that simple.																			
★★★	**CIBC Capital Appreciation**	Cdn Eq											B	D	25%	–24%	5/31/9	13	2.40
Virginia Wai-Ping is one tough customer. By digging deep into the companies she scouts, she uncovers more than most Bay Street types. But that's what's needed in managing an aggressive all-cap fund. This one's been on a tear since she took over.																			
★★★★★	**CIBC Cdn Small Companies**	Cdn Eq											NA	NA	0%	–26%	6/30/98	10	2.00
Virginia Wai-Ping is at her best in this small cap fund because small caps are less efficienctly priced, meaning that there's more room for adding value with a big call. It's a new fund with big wins from a variety of names and a reasonable MER.																			
★★½	**CIBC Core Canadian Equity**	Cdn Eq											D	C	33%	–27%	6/30/98	NA	2.25
A shorter list of 65 stocks and an active hand explain this fund's remarkable turnaround over the past few years under the new leadership of Real Trepanier. With big wins in CGI and TLC The Laser Centre, plus some big cap names, it's been on fire.																			
★★★	**CIBC Dividend Fund**	Div											B	D	24%	–20%	6/30/98	NA	1.97
This is simply a conservative stock fund. It produces a decent after tax income compared with most common stock funds, to be sure. But the idea here isn't so much current income as growth of income over time.																			
★★★½	**CIBC Emerging Economies**	Fgn Eq											NA	NA	39%	–39%	8/31/97	NA	2.69
Nicholas Applegate runs this fund on behalf of CIBC with a view towards broad diversification by country and industry. Bigger, more liquid stocks are held in smaller markets. You'll find more diversification by industry here than in most of the peer group.																			
★★★★★	**CIBC Energy Fund**	Nat Res											NA	NA	56%	–51%	10/31/97	NA	2.35
Okay, sure. Oil has been on fire. But this is a tighly constrained fund. The manager can't buy any other sector. He does try to avoid making the big commodity call, though, by owning oil service companies, for example. And trying to find great management.																			
★★	**CIBC European Equity**	Fgn Eq											NA	NA	6%	–16%	8/31/98	NA	2.48
A very, very big cap fund in an area the manager still thinks offers lots of potential through restructuring and improved efficiencies. But performance has been soft so far and the fees are rich for this bank-sold fund that comes without an advisor.																			
★★★	**CIBC Far East Prosperity**	Fgn Eq											D	A	63%	–44%	1/31/94	NA	2.69
Duncan Mount was early on Japan in '98. Correct, but early. That's the risk you take with an active manager in Asia whose top-down country work produces the critical decision. He was right in selling the tigers in '97, wrong on Hong Kong in '98 etc.																			
★★½	**CIBC Global Equity**	Fgn Eq											C	B	11%	–16%	8/31/90	16	2.55
Forget about the history pre-1996. That was before TAL Investment Counsel was bought by the Commerce and appointed to run this and other house funds. The TAL team is top-notch, and has cleaned up since taking over this pup.																			
★★★	**CIBC Global Technology**	Spec Eq											NA	NA	9%	–20%	8/31/98	3	2.58
The idea here is to get a diversified play on the large theme of innovation in the world today. That means going beyond pricey net stocks – to networking, hardware, software and telecom names. It means you'll need an iron gut, but growth rates are huge.																			
★★★★½	**CIBC Japanese Equity**	Fgn Eq											NA	NA	39%	–28%	8/31/97	23	2.46
Hong Kong-based Duncan Mount was a little early with the exporters in 1998, a move that marks the only blemish in this fund's history. The fund will rock if indeed Japanese industry follows through with announced restructurings – and layoffs.																			
★★★★½	**CIBC N.A. Demographics**	US Eq											NA	NA	0%	–16%	7/31/98	5	2.45
There are a few North American equity funds around. And a couple of boomer-related concept funds. Both are a great idea. But both are tricky to benchmark. If you lack US exposure, this is a nice way to get it in a growth-style fund.																			
★★½	**CIBC U.S. Equity Index**	US Eq											C	C	0%	–12%	8/31/98	3	0.90
CIBC's index lineup has come a long way in a couple of years. This is an attactive passive fund because it's professionally-monitored, unhedged and relatively cheap to own.																			

Legend: ★= overall past performance vs. similar funds (5 ★ max). Boxes show the quartile performance for a fund each calendar year vs. only similar funds (□ is the best score possible). ● = high; ● = average; and ● = a fund with low expenses.

Consistency			Performance Trend										Risk						Efficiency
Overall Past Performance	Fund Name	Type	90	91	92	93	94	95	96	97	98	Aug. '99	Up	Down	% of Time Losing $	Biggest Drop	Date	No. of Mo's to Recover	MER
★★★★	**CIBC U.S. Index RRSP Fund**	US Eq								1	1	2	NA	NA	0%	–10%	8/31/98	2	0.90 (low)
A first-generation RRSP-eligible foreign index fund with most of its money in T-Bills and a little in index futures to give the whole portfolio the feel of being fully invested in the US. Expect new, pricier versions of this concept to flood the market.																			
★★½	**CIBC U.S. Small Companies**	US Eq							3	3	4	3	NA	NA	27%	–23%	5/31/98	13	2.45 (average)
Yes, the US market has been on fire. But no, this fund hasn't. Don't sweat it. All the action in the US has been in mega caps and net stocks. This is a concept growth portfolio with compelling valuations in an overlooked segment of the market.																			
★★★★	**Clarington Global Comm**	Spec Eq								1	2	2	NA	NA	0%	–22%	8/31/98	4	2.90 (high)
You will not find many better telecom managers than Oscar Castro, based in the UK, who runs this fund for Montgomery. The idea is to get a diversified play on a very broad theme: Convergence. He owns hardware, software and network companies.																			
★★★	**Clean Environment Bal**	Bal				1	4	4	1	1	4	4	B	D	25%	–19%	6/30/98	NA	2.52 (high)
Bonds have bombed and this fund has only 12% or so in bonds. So this fund should have clobbered its peers in '99, right? Wrong. A big one-quarter of the fund in income trusts wiped out much of the gains from great stocks like Open Text, ATI and Nortel.																			
★★★	**Clean Environment Equity**	Cdn Eq				1	4	2	2	1	3	4	A	D	27%	–28%	5/31/98	NA	2.52 (average)
Frozen yogurt may taste better than forest products or oil, but in this market it's the aftertaste that counts. Long-time holding YogenFruz has been whacked in this fine fund just at a time when commodities (which are absent here) are running.																			
★★★	**Clean Environment Itl Equ**	Fgn Eq					3	3	2	2	3	1	B	C	28%	–25%	6/30/98	NA	2.51 (high)
The team at Acuity really do have the right idea: They look for companies that are doing things right for the new world. A world where demand exists from consumers and business for better, cleaner processes. They buy innovative companies.																			
★★★½	**Co-operators Balanced**	Bal			3	2	2	1	2	1	4	4	A	D	20%	18%	5/31/98	NA	2.04 (average)
This seg fund with a reasonable MER is indeed rare. But it got pinched by the rate increases in '99 and by missing some hot sectors on the equity side. The fund uses a top-down sector rotation style and buys big and mid cap stocks.																			
★★½	**Co-operators Cdn Equity**	Cdn Eq			3	3	2	4	3	2	3	3	C	D	22%	–27%	5/31/98	NA	2.05 (average)
Being too conservative in the oil patch is no sin. But in this environment it can cost a fund dearly. This is a seg fund from a good firm, but it's never really lived up to its potential – or at least it hasn't in the last couple of years.																			
★★★½	**Co-operators U.S. Equity**	US Eq						1	1	1	4	4	A	D	23%	–39%	5/31/98	NA	2.09 (average)
After three incredible years, Milt Burns is on the bottom of the pile here because he isn't loaded to the gills with technology stocks. He understands the trends and all, he's just got a value discipline that this market hates right now.																			
★★★½	**Common Sns Asset Bldr I**	Bal						2	2	1	1	4	B	C	4%	–9%	6/30/98	6	2.09 (average)
A conservative balanced fund with good numbers offered through Primerica Life Insurance of Canada. It's almost identical to the Ivy Growth and Income Fund from Mackenzie, which is also managed by Jerry Javasky.																			
★★★★	**Common Sns Asset Bldr II**	Bal						2	1	1	1	4	A	C	6%	–12%	6/30/98	NA	2.25 (average)
With about half the fund in bonds this is a middle-of-the-road balanced fund. But the banks and utilities have been a drag this year as higher rates have crimped the strategy that worked so well for so long.																			
★★★★	**Common Sns Asset Bldr IV**	Bal						4	1	1	1	3	A	D	13%	–15%	6/30/98	NA	2.25 (average)
About 75% equities in this more aggressive fund that still goes under the 'balanced' category. But equity weights can go higher, since the manager (Mackenzie's Jerry Javasky) is still not fully invested.																			
★★★★	**Common Sns Asset Bldr V**	Bal						3	1	1	2	3	A	D	13%	–15%	6/30/98	NA	2.26 (average)
They call it a balanced fund, but there's only about 7% in bonds. Good thing, because bonds are in the tank this year. Too bad the banks are too. Still, there are some cash reserves of about 15%, but that could get spent any time.																			

Legend: ★= overall past performance vs. similar funds (5 ★ max). Boxes show the quartile performance for a fund each calendar year vs. only similar funds (☐ is the best score possible). ● = high; ● = average; and ● = a fund with low expenses.

Consistency			Performance Trend										Risk						Efficiency
Overall Past Performance	Fund Name	Type	90	91	92	93	94	95	96	97	98	Aug. '99	Up	Down	% of Time Losing $	Biggest Drop	Date	No. of Mo's to Recover	MER
★★½	**Concordia Equity**	Cdn Eq											C	D	27%	–24%	5/31/98	NA	2.27
Yield Management Group manages this on behalf of the insurance company with an eye toward big caps and a fairly conservative approach that's been perfect. Being light on the biggest cap darlings of the TSE has hurt relative performance lately.																			
★★★½	**Concordia Special Growth**	Cdn Eq											A	C	30%	–34%	10/31/97	NA	2.27
This is a small cap fund now managed by Yield Management Group, a Toronto-based institutional firm. It's a tight, eclectic list of value stocks – like real estate holdings, consumer names and high tech/telecoms.																			
★★½	**Concordia Strategic Bal**	Bal											NA	NA	26%	–16%	5/31/98	NA	2.04
This is a fund of funds that optimizes the balance of various other Concordia funds. But don't worry, there's no double dipping on fees. The fees on the underlying funds are rebated to the fund, which then charges its relatively cheap MER.																			
★★★½	**Cormel Balanced**	Bal											B	B	6%	–10%	6/30/98	6	0.92
A bright fund for electricians in la Belle Province, managed by Bolton Tremblay. Expenses are dirt cheap and performance has been good in all market conditions.																			
★★½	**COTE 100 Amerique**	US Eq											B	D	31%	–34%	5/31/98	NA	1.38
Despite its name and classification, this fund is holding a substantial position in Canadian stocks (over 2/3). The fund's mandate doesn't impose restrictions since it's classified as a foreign content holding.																			
★★★½	**COTE 100 EXP**	Cdn Eq											B	C	23%	–28%	5/31/98	NA	2.60
The EXP might stand for exporters expanding and having expertise – but whatever it is, it's pretty good. The lack of resources has hurt the fund this year, but the holdings are all dynamic, fast-growing companies.																			
★★	**COTE 100 REA-action**	Cdn Eq											NA	NA	42%	–28%	6/30/98	NA	2.60
Quebec growth stocks here in a unique mix that's not easily benchmarked. Peer group comparisons shown are to the general category of Canadian equities. But these comparisons are a little harsh given the fund's unique mandate.																			
★★★	**COTE 100 REER**	Cdn Eq											A	D	30%	–33%	5/31/98	NA	1.41
The same portfolio as several other Cote 100 funds, but with fees that are just about half what the others charge.																			
★★½	**Cundill Cdn Sec. Ser. A**	Cdn Eq											C	A	26%	–27%	8/31/89	48	2.04
Lots of trees and rocks in a cheapskate approach to stock picking that uncovers things no growth fund would ever own. That, and the compelling returns, make this contrarian fund worth consideration, especially for conservative folk.																			
★★★	**Cundill Value Fund Ser A**	Fgn Eq											B	B	15%	–54%	2/28/73	60	2.01
Performance has picked up over the past year for this fund because of its big exposure in Japanese and UK equities. But Peter Cundill has missed the greatest rally of all time in US stocks, pulling down his long term numbers.																			
★★½	**Desjardins Amer Market**	US Eq											NA	NA	0%	–10%	8/31/98	3	1.97
Canagex manages this Desjardins offering and uses a hybrid approach of direct stock investments, in addition to making extensive use of derivatives to maintain full RRSP eligibility.																			
★★½	**Desjardins Balanced**	Bal											C	C	21%	–15%	5/31/98	NA	1.92
Strategic asset allocation means that they pick a good long term mix and stick with it. So far, the fund hasn't overwhelmed. But Canagex deserves a second look. This steady pup targets a typical institutional 60/40 mix of stocks/fixed income.																			
★★	**Desjardins Divers Audac**	Bal											NA	NA	14%	–11%	5/31/98	11	1.89
This is more conservative than the Desjardins Balanced fund since it targets a 50/50 stock/fixed income split. It buys lots of mortgage-backed securities for fixed income, and uses a Desjardins Int'l fund for foreign equity exposure.																			
★½	**Desjardins Divers Moder**	Bal											NA	NA	5%	–6%	5/31/98	7	1.78
A consistent laggard with more than half its portfolio in mortgage-backed paper. The target equity component is only about 30% in this fund, which makes it hard to match performance with an equity-heavy group. It consequently held up well in 1998.																			

Legend: ★= overall past performance vs. similar funds (5 ★ max). Boxes show the quartile performance for a fund each calendar year vs. only similar funds (□ is the best score possible). ● = high; ● = average; and ● = a fund with low expenses.

Consistency			Performance Trend										Risk						Efficiency	
Overall Past Performance	Fund Name	Type	90	91	92	93	94	95	96	97	98	Aug. '99	Up	Down	% of Time Losing $	Biggest Drop	Date	No. of Mo's to Recover	MER	
★½	**Desjardins Divers Secur**	Bal							□	□	□	□	NA	NA	0%	–3%	7/31/98	4	1.69	●
The objective of this fund is to avoid losing money over any one-year period. In doing so, you risk not making much money over any period. Less than 20% in stocks and half in bonds make this a balanced fund with no gas.																				
★★★½	**Desjardins Dividend**	Div						□	□	□	□	□	A	D	20%	–18%	5/31/98	NA	1.92	●
Banks and other exposure to common shares like the utilities have helped performance to remain steady and predictable. But the summer was tough on big cap funds like this and rising rates in 1999 have kept this and other funds under water.																				
★★½	**Desjardins Environment**	Cdn Eq	□	□		□	□	□	□	□	□	□	C	D	21%	–26%	5/31/98	NA	2.12	●
If you want your money to do good, do it with a good specialty green manager – not a stock screen imposed as a constraint. Canagex screens for Canadian firms that make significant contributions to maintaining or improving the environment.																				
★★½	**Desjardins Equity**	Cdn Eq	□	□	□	□	□	□	□	□	□	□	C	B	29%	–32%	11/30/73	30	1.92	●
Keeping a big cap (TSE 100 focused) fund like this ahead of its peers in this crazy market has been a handful. This fund lags when BCE and Nortel take off, since they make up like 20%+ of the index.																				
★★★	**Desjardins Growth**	Cdn Eq						□	□	□	□	□	C	C	22%	–29%	5/31/98	NA	1.92	●
Canagex does a good job on this mid cap fund. They've scored some big wins in 1999 in technology and cyclical stocks. This a well diversified fund that makes no big sector bets, and fees are low for this category.																				
★★★	**Desjardins High Potential**	Cdn Eq										□	NA	NA	67%	–22%	6/30/98	NA	2.16	●
Here's a theme-driven fund that looks for stocks that can benefit from long-term economic trends. Canadian technology currently dominates this fund's holdings with picks like BCE, Nortel, Cogeco Cable and TD Bank.																				
★★★	**Desjardins International**	Fgn Eq	□	□	□	□	□	□	□	□	□	□	D	B	16%	–45%	2/28/73	62	2.20	●
Canagex took over management in 1995, and the fund has suffered since that time. They've been affected in 1999 by underweighting Asia and the US, and overweighting Europe. Historically, they've held up well during bear markets.																				
★★	**Desjardins Quebec Fund**	Bal	□	□	□	□	□	□	□	□	□	□	D	A	8%	–49%	6/30/97	NA	1.95	●
This is a balanced fund that is limited to bonds and stocks of Québec-based issuers. In Canada's relatively small market, such a constraint severely limits the universe of eligible securities to a very narrow list.																				
★★½	**Desjardins World Wide Bal**	Bal								□	□	□	NA	NA	0%	–5%	8/31/98	2	2.17	●
This global balanced fund does what few money managers do – it actively manages the currency. Canagex does this using currency futures. The fund maintains full RRSP eligibility by using financial derivatives rather than direct foreign exposure.																				
★★★	**DGC Entertain Vent LSVCC**	Spec Eq						□	□	□	□	□	NA	NA	30%	–6%	2/29/96	4	5.60	●
This fund has done well, despite a very narrow mandate. I'll admit that I never expected much from the fund, but cede its success.																				
★★½	**Dominion Equity Resource**	Nat Res	□	□	□	□	□	□	□	□	□	□	B	B	52%	–63%	8/31/87	70	2.60	●
It's been a tough environment for this old oil and gas fund but the turnaround in the energy sector has put the "+" back in its performance numbers. The fund has done well against other resource funds during bear markets.																				
★★★	**Dundee Fund of Funds**	Bal	□	□	□	□	□	□	□	□	□	□	C	C	21%	–19%	10/31/97	NA	0.52	●
The Goodman team's more active style sometimes adds value and sometimes doesn't for this fund of funds. Don't forget that this small MER is tacked on top of the fees of the underlying Dundee funds.																				
★★★	**Dynamic Americas**	US Eq	□	□	□	□	□	□	□	□	□	□	B	A	17%	–24%	9/30/87	22	2.35	●
Narrow leadership in the huge US market left many managers trailing the index, but it also left many stocks with attractive valuations. Anne McLean is loading up on just those types of stocks – namely in entertainment, consumer electronics, and technology.																				

Legend: ★= overall past performance vs. similar funds (5 ★ max). Boxes show the quartile performance for a fund each calendar year vs. only similar funds (□ is the best score possible). ● = high; ● = average; and ● = a fund with low expenses.

Consistency: Overall Past Performance	Fund Name	Type	Performance Trend: 90	91	92	93	94	95	96	97	98	Aug. '99	Risk: Up	Down	% of Time Losing $	Biggest Drop	Date	No. of Mo's to Recover	Efficiency: MER
★★	**Dynamic Canadian Growth**	Cdn Eq											C	D	33%	–36%	8/31/8	65	0.00 ●
Pre-1999 numbers on this fund are not very relevant. Gone are the days when this fund was a small-to-mid cap resource heavy fund. Rohit Sehgal has transformed this fund to an earnings momentum large cap portfolio. He's a good manager who pulls no punches.																			
★★★½	**Dynamic Dividend**	Div											B	A	10%	–10%	6/30/98	NA	1.49 ●
Todd Beallor has been on this fund for over a year now, with good results. Yield is increasing and expenses are falling, thanks in part to holdings in the income trust area.																			
★★½	**Dynamic Dividend Growth**	Div											C	C	22%	–14%	10/31/97	NA	1.56 ●
David Goodman and Todd Beallor lead this more growth-oriented dividend fund which focuses on common stocks. Big banks and utilities are at the core of this fund, along with some cyclical holdings that have propelled the fund in '99.																			
★★★	**Dynamic Europe**	Fgn Eq											A	A	31%	–27%	8/31/98	NA	2.46 ●
Joe Evershed's once-hot portfolio was hurt in the summer 1998 decline, but he's counting on corporate restructurings and consolidations to set the stage for increased profitability and higher stock prices.																			
★★★½	**Dynamic Far East**	Fgn Eq											B	A	27%	–32%	7/31/97	23	3.37 ●
This fund is arguably the best-kept secret in its category. It has only $21 million in assets but it's well diversified (no big country bets), it includes Japan (many don't), and it's a top performer in down markets.																			
★★★	**Dynamic Fund of Canada**	Cdn Eq											A	B	24%	–33%	4/30/81	22	2.20 ●
About 30% of this portfolio (now run by David Goodman) is in resources, which explains the relative turnaround in performance in 1999. The fund boasts a good 2.4% dividend yield – about 1 percentage point above the index.																			
★★½	**Dynamic Global Partners**	Bal											D	NA	18%	–11%	8/31/97	17	2.52 ●
This tactical global balanced fund was heavily underweight the US market, a decision that has worked against them for a few years. About 2/3 of this portfolio is currently in stocks.																			
★★★★	**Dynamic Global Pre Metals**	Nat Res										N/A	NA	NA	86%	–59%	9/30/96	NA	2.88 ●
The manager shuffle at Goodman and Company resulted in Jonathan Goodman's focusing his duties on the specialty resource and metals funds. This fund is a great candidate for a dollar-cost-averaging plan.																			
★★★	**Dynamic Global Resource**	Nat Res											C	D	48%	–59%	3/31/97	NA	2.69 ●
Jonathan Goodman has put together a well diversified portfolio that is less concentrated on energy (now just 31%) than it once was. That explains the performance lag so far in 1999. A broad fund like this is a good way to play the resource sectors.																			
★★	**Dynamic International**	Fgn Eq											D	B	25%	–45%	10/31/87	75	2.50 ●
Spotty performance has been the theme for this Dundee offering. Regional specialists Anne McLean (US) and Joe Evershed (Europe) run this global portfolio, which has historically done well in bear markets.																			
★★★½	**Dynamic Partners**	Bal											B	A	15%	–8%	5/31/98	NA	2.29 ●
You likely won't see the gutsy bets that Norm Bengough once made with this fund. There is now a team of five portfolio managers officially navigating this leaky ship whose return to prominence may have already begun.																			
★★★½	**Dynamic Precious Metals**	Nat Res											B	A	49%	–68%	6/30/96	NA	2.55 ●
Earnings of many gold stocks are unaffected by the continually declining price of the yellow metal. Why? Because many have locked in prices at which they can sell gold, by participating in the forward market.																			
★★½	**E&P American Gth**	US Eq											C	A	16%	–49%	2/28/73	46	2.37 ●
Goldman Sachs uses a hybrid approach in this large cap fund. They keep the fund sector neutral (i.e., same sector mix as S&P 500). Then, they choose specific stocks by using a quantitative valuation model, complementing that with qualitative factors.																			

Legend: ★= overall past performance vs. similar funds (5 ★ max). Boxes show the quartile performance for a fund each calendar year vs. only similar funds (☐ is the best score possible). ● = high; ● = average; and ● = a fund with low expenses.

Consistency			Performance Trend										Risk						Efficiency
Overall Past Performance	Fund Name	Type	90	91	92	93	94	95	96	97	98	Aug. '99	Up	Down	% of Time Losing $	Biggest Drop	Date	No. of Mo's to Recover	MER
★★★½	**E&P Asian Growth Fund**	Fgn Eq											NA	NA	47%	–37%	8/31/97	23	3.55
Japan makes up 60% of this fund. This, of course, has elevated the performance of the fund but when times are tough the high MER is difficult to swallow. There's a pretty big focus on bank stocks in this one.																			
★★★	**E&P Balanced Fund**	Bal											C	C	19%	–12%	5/31/98	NA	2.11
Here's a conservative fund with lots of government debt. Stocks are purchased based on their valuations after a rigorous bottom-up analysis and most of them are big, safe companies.																			
★★★½	**E&P Emerging Markets Fund**	Fgn Eq											NA	NA	47%	–47%	8/31/97	NA	3.45
Steven Bates is finding lots of value in Mexico, Brazil and Asia. He own all sorts of companies from computer makers to steel makers. The fund also has around 7% of its money in the hot US market.																			
★★★	**E&P Equity Fund**	Cdn Eq											A	D	25%	–28%	5/31/98	NA	2.12
A heavily traded fund that was uncharacteristically behind the mark for the past few years – largely because they missed the big interest sensitives. Performance has since improved thanks to names like Nortel, TD and BCE.																			
★★★	**E&P Global Equity Fund**	Fgn Eq											NA	NA	2%	–16%	8/31/98	4	2.52
Ian Henderson loves technology and telecommunications companies both internationally and in the US. In fact, the US makes up almost half of this fund. Relatively low expenses and good performance make this an attractive fund.																			
★★½	**Empire Elite Asset Alloc**	Bal											D	D	16%	–15%	5/31/98	NA	2.46
This tactical asset allocation fund currently holds a rather neutral asset mix of 50% stocks and 50% bonds and cash. Vince Zambrano and his team have full flexibility to go 100% to any asset class if they choose. Overall, unimpressive so far.																			
★★★	**Empire Elite Balanced**	Bal											C	C	16%	–12%	5/31/98	NA	2.44
Min/max rules say no less than 40% and no more than 60% in either stocks or bonds. Our rules say why pay premium balanced fund fees for subtle shifts? Buy a cheap bond fund and then buy their equity fund.																			
★★★	**Empire Elite Equity**	Cdn Eq											B	A	22%	–32%	9/30/87	64	2.42
Ina Van Berkel's been gone for a couple of years now and this conservative pup just can't get over it. New guy Vince Zambrano uses a big cap blend approach, but heavy cash has hurt lately.																			
★★½	**Empire Elite Intl Growth**	Fgn Eq											C	A	11%	–12%	5/31/98	7	2.45
With lots of industry and geographic constraints, this fund has ironically underperformed by underweighting the US. It's ironic because there is no limit on how much can be invested in North America. A good performer during bear markets.																			
★★★½	**Empire Equity Growth**	Cdn Eq											A	B	25%	–24%	6/30/81	18	1.24
Investors can save 1.16% annually by buying this fund, rather than the back-end loaded Elite Equity in this family. It's worth paying a front load to save that much on fees each year. Note that Catharina Van Berkel is gone, though.																			
★★★½	**Empire Premier Equity**	Cdn Eq											A	A	21%	–36%	4/30/73	56	1.44
Again, low annual fees of 1.44% make this a much better deal than the Elite Equity fund (almost 1% better each year). Other than fees, there is no difference between this fund and Empire's other two large cap Canadian stock funds.																			
★½	**Enterprise Vent Cap LSVCC**	Spec Eq											NA	NA	68%	–27%	2/28/97	NA	6.60
Expenses for the most recent year were reported as 6.60%, mainly due to its tiny $6.7 million asset base. But at least all of investors' money is invested. The fund holds just 2% in cash. However, performance has been weak.																			
★★½	**Equit Life Seg Comm Stock**	Cdn Eq											C	B	26%	–40%	6/30/81	22	1.04
This McLean Budden-managed seg fund has had average performance. Like many Canadian equity funds, its big names include the banks, BCE and Nortel.																			
★★½	**Equitable Life Asset All**	Bal											NA	NA	15%	–15%	5/31/98	13	2.25
Equitable Life manages this fund in-house and makes use of index futures to gain access to foreign markets. At 2.25%, this fund is expensive and has had umimpressive performance.																			

Legend: ★ = overall past performance vs. similar funds (5 ★ max). Boxes show the quartile performance for a fund each calendar year vs. only similar funds (□ is the best score possible). ● = high; ● = average; and ● = a fund with low expenses.

Consistency			Performance Trend										Risk						Efficiency
Overall Past Performance	Fund Name	Type	90	91	92	93	94	95	96	97	98	Aug. '99	Up	Down	% of Time Losing $	Biggest Drop	Date	No. of Mo's to Recover	MER
★★	**Equitable Life Cdn Stock**	Cdn Eq											D	D	19%	–28%	5/31/98	NA	2.25
	McLean Budden has recently been appointed to replace Guardian and to turn around the performance of this $63 million portfolio. Effectively, this fund gives you McLean Budden in the form of a seg fund for 0.50% more annually.																		
★★★	**Equitable Life Int'l**	Fgn Eq											NA	NA	4%	–14%	8/31/98	4	2.75
	This derivatives-based fund uses index futures to gain foreign exposure and remain RRSP eligible. Returns were great for a short time, thanks to a nearly 60% exposure to the S&P 500 and good Asian exposure.																		
★★★½	**Ethical Balanced**	Bal											B	B	16%	–18%	5/31/98	NA	2.11
	Co-operators takes a top-down view to managing this fund. Asset mix is decided by using economic forecasts and return projections. Stocks are selected using a sector rotation style; bonds, a rate anticipation approach.																		
★★★	**Ethical Growth**	Cdn Eq											C	A	22%	–21%	5/31/98	NA	2.24
	Martin Gerber uses Connor Clark's two-way asset allocation strategy between stocks and cash. They've gone as high as 50% in cash in the past, and that's proven to add lots of value over time for unitholders of this ethical holding.																		
★★½	**Ethical N.A. Equity**	US Eq											D	A	20%	–26%	6/30/81	18	2.39
	NY-based Allicance Capital has 20 industry analysts looking for stocks of firms with strong earnings trends. This approach lead them to a bunch of big cap US tech stocks that have lead the US bull run. This fund could fall hard in down markets!																		
★★½	**Ethical Pacific Rim**	Fgn Eq											NA	NA	42%	–61%	8/31/97	NA	3.39
	The team at Singapore-based SGY Asset Management see many positives in the Far East economies well into 1999 and beyond. More than half of the fund is held in Australia (30%) and Hong Kong (25%), but Japan is specifically excluded.																		
★★	**Ethical Special Equity**	Cdn Eq											NA	NA	30%	–27%	10/31/97	NA	2.79
	Leigh Pullen holds a good mix of more established small caps, some micro caps and private placements. He manages risk by keeping well-diversified and by building a core of more established firms, limiting exposure to smaller riskier plays.																		
★★½	**FCMI Precious Metals**	Nat Res											D	B	39%	–20%	8/31/93	24	4.16
	This one has had decent performance but like many precious metals funds, up market performance has been bad. Watch out for the high MER.																		
★★	**Fidelity Capital Builder**	Cdn Eq											D	B	29%	–29%	5/31/98	NA	2.46
	Last year's manager change saw a shift away from the deep cyclicals and illiquid little stocks, which has helped somewhat. But so far, this fund can't catch a break. True North and Canadian Growth Company are better Fido choices.																		
★★★½	**Fidelity Emerg Mkts Ptl**	Fgn Eq											NA	NA	57%	–70%	3/31/97	NA	3.83
	Dave Stuart leads a team that decides country mix, then relies on Fidelity's regional specialists for specific stock picks. Stuart thinks Asian corporate earnings have some growing to do to catch up to current valuations. Bullish on Mexican telecoms.																		
★★★★½	**Fidelity Focus Cons Ind**	Spec Eq											NA	NA	0%	–12%	8/31/98	3	2.49
	Lead manager Doug Chase will gladly take the reasonably priced #2 company in an industry, rather than the pricey stock of an industry leader. High turnover means you should keep this fund inside your RRSP.																		
★★★★	**Fidelity Focus Fin Serv**	Spec Eq											NA	NA	7%	–20%	8/31/98	7	2.50
	Bob Ewing runs a fairly concentrated portfolio of big US financial stocks. You'll find recognizable names such as Citigroup, AIG, and Bank America. This fund's big US sister costs just 1.17% per year!																		
★★★★★	**Fidelity Focus Nat Res**	Spec Eq											NA	NA	64%	–25%	10/31/97	18	2.45
	Energy is the focus of this portfolio. Larry Rakers looks for good stocks using bottom-up analysis but also likes sectors with favourable economic fundamentals. This fund actually costs 0.05% less than its US sister.																		
★★★★	**Fidelity Glo Asset Alloc**	Bal											A	NA	10%	–9%	8/31/98	3	2.59
	Dick Habermann leads a trio of managers and makes the top-down calls on this fund. A heavy US equity weighting has helped it outperform most of its peers, along with astute asset mix shifts.																		

Legend: ★ = overall past performance vs. similar funds (5 ★ max). Boxes show the quartile performance for a fund each calendar year vs. only similar funds (☐ is the best score possible). ● = high; ● = average; and ● = a fund with low expenses.

Consistency			Performance Trend										Risk						Efficiency
Overall Past Performance	Fund Name	Type	90	91	92	93	94	95	96	97	98	Aug. '99	Up	Down	% of Time Losing $	Biggest Drop	Date	No. of Mo's to Recover	MER
★★★½	**Fidelity Growth America**	US Eq											A	C	2%	–12%	8/31/98	4	2.30
Brad Lewis lead Fidelity's quantitative team, which monitors about 3,000 stocks daily using their proprietary computer models. Turnover is high with distributions to match. Consistently an upper quartile performer.																			
★★★½	**Fidelity Intl Portfolio**	Fgn Eq											A	B	10%	–20%	8/31/90	16	2.58
US equities remain a substantial holding (about 50%) for this fund, which holds positions in 499 stocks. Dick Habermann's top-down view is combined with the bottom-up stock picking of Fidelity's regional specialists.																			
★★★½	**Fidelity Japanese Growth**	Fgn Eq											B	D	61%	–39%	7/31/94	60	2.92
Jay Talbot is now in charge of this fund, which is emphasizing electrial machinery firms such as Sony and Matsushita. He likes these kinds of companies because of the non-cyclical nature of their earnings.																			
★★★½	**Fidelity Latin Amer Grth**	Fgn Eq											B	NA	49%	–48%	8/31/97	NA	3.12
Mexico and Brazil make up 75% of this fund's exposure. This $68 million fund is expensive at 3.12%, but has done well in bull markets.																			
★★½	**Fidelity Small Cap Amer**	US Eq											B	C	23%	–22%	5/31/98	NA	2.54
Fidelity's massive computer model monitors 3,000 stocks daily and uses 60 quantitative factors to rank the stocks according to their relative attractiveness. Poor overall performance, but fees have fallen by 46 basis points in four years!																			
★★½	**First Cdn Asset Allocat**	Bal											D	C	18%	–13%	2/28/94	17	1.94
The Jones Heward team picks growth stocks but pays lots of attention to valuations. Macro factors dictate the asset mix and fixed income decisions. On the corporate bond side, they stick to banks and utilities to reduce risk.																			
★★½	**First Cdn Emerg Markets**	Fgn Eq											NA	NA	46%	–48%	8/31/97	NA	2.27
James Robertson leads the team at Edinburgh and is bullish on Latin America – especially Mexico due to its positive economic trends. Performance has been weak overall.																			
★★½	**First Cdn Equity Index**	Cdn Eq											B	D	30%	–28%	5/31/98	NA	1.23
When you can get an index fund for 0.50% annually, why bother with this fund? Index funds are commodities that are differentiated only by price. With a 1.23% MER, this fund is doomed to underperform.																			
★★	**First Cdn European**	Fgn Eq											NA	NA	11%	–18%	8/31/98	NA	2.02
Nearly one-third of this fund is invested in the huge UK market. Lead manager Sharon Fay is expecting strong economic growth to drive stock prices up further – especially cyclicals.																			
★★★½	**First Cdn Far East**	Fgn Eq											NA	NA	43%	–54%	8/31/97	NA	2.27
Strong earnings growth, falling interest rates and inflation are big reasons why Asia's recovery has been so strong. Lead manager Alistair Thompson has raised some cash by taking profits since earlier this year – nearly doubling cash to 20% in June.																			
★★½	**First Cdn Intl Equity**	Fgn Eq											D	A	14%	–14%	8/31/98	8	2.00
Edingburgh's Ian Rattray runs this Europe-heavy international fund. About 70% of the fund is in Europe and about 20% in Japan. That mix has hurt performance this year as Asia has been the hottest region since fall 1998. Good down market performance.																			
★★	**First Cdn Japanese**	Fgn Eq											NA	NA	76%	–50%	11/30/94	NA	2.20
Though Masato Degawa of JP Morgan expects weak economic numbers for the remainder of 1999, he's bullish on some of the larger companies that have a viable restructuring plan, a good competitive edge, and strong exports.																			
★★½	**First Cdn NAFTA Advantage**	Fgn Eq											NA	NA	22%	–25%	5/31/98	13	2.00
About half of this portfolio is in the US, with the other half split evenly between Canada and Mexico. Large caps are the focus in all three markets, while the Mexican exposure is what's propelled this fund so far in 1999.																			
★★★	**First Cdn Resource**	Nat Res											C	D	53%	–56%	3/31/97	NA	2.26
Gold content in this portfolio has been cut to less than half of just four months. This fund is less energy-oriented than most in this category, which accounts for its sub-par performance so far in 1999.																			

Legend: ★ = overall past performance vs. similar funds (5 ★ max). Boxes show the quartile performance for a fund each calendar year vs. only similar funds (☐ is the best score possible). ● = high; ● = average; and ● = a fund with low expenses.

Consistency			Performance Trend										Risk						Efficiency
Overall Past Performance	Fund Name	Type	90	91	92	93	94	95	96	97	98	Aug. '99	Up	Down	% of Time Losing $	Biggest Drop	Date	No. of Mo's to Recover	MER
★★½	**First Cdn Special Equity**	Cdn Eq											C	C	38%	–31%	5/31/98	NA	2.22
Consumer and cyclical stocks make up about one-third of this portfolio. Interestingly, foreign content (which is quite low in this portfolio) is filled mainly by investing in mid-cap SPDRs – an index participation unit covering the S&P 400 mid cap index.																			
★★★	**First Cdn US Growth**	US Eq											B	C	7%	–13%	8/31/98	3	2.18
You'll find lots of big names in this fully invested US equity portfolio. This, and all US equity funds, lost over 2.50% on currency alone during the second quarter of 1999.																			
★★	**First Heritage**	Nat Res											D	C	49%	–53%	2/28/97	NA	4.66
Expenses in this tiny $2.8 million fund are very rich and simply not worthwhile. The managers would have to pull of a pretty neat trick to add value over and above the nearly 5% MER.																			
★★★★	**First Tr Fin Inst Trust**	Cdn Eq											NA	NA	33%	–27%	7/31/98	NA	1.15
Unit Investment Trusts (UITs) are growing in popularity because of their relatively low fees and the strict buy and hold philosophy – the holdings don't change. These trusts have a five-year life, after which time the portfolios are folded.																			
★★★★★	**First Tr NA Tech 1997 C$**	US Eq											NA	NA	23%	–19%	10/31/97	12	1.15
Big problem with this structure in a non-registered account. When the series expires, Rev Can treats it as if you've cashed out completely (resulting in a taxable capital gain), even if you re-invest directly to a new series of the same fund.																			
★★★★½	**First Tr Pharma 1996 C$**	Spec Eq											NA	NA	0%	–14%	4/30/99	NA	1.05
This portfolio is filled with huge US and European drugmakers. Increased life expectancies, an aging population, and increased investment in drug research are trends that Chicago-based Niké Securities are betting will continue to grow profits.																			
★★★★½	**First Tr Pharma 1997 C$**	Fgn Eq											NA	NA	0%	–14%	4/30/99	NA	1.15
The 1999 series of funds won't be as attractive as in the past. Fees are rising by roughly 80 basis points (0.80 percentage points) on this fund and by a similar amount on all others in this family.																			
★★★½	**FMOQ Canadian Equity**	Cdn Eq											A	D	16%	–24%	6/30/98	NA	0.75
This Quebec-based fund has dirt cheap fees and good performance, lead by Denis Ouellet of TAL Investment Counsel. Ouellet holds a good mix of bigger and smaller companies and focuses on growth – but doesn't like to overpay.																			
★★★½	**FMOQ International Equity**	Fgn Eq											A	B	12%	–15%	7/31/94	28	0.81
FMOQ funds are only available to Quebec doctors, which explains the low fees. This fund uses index futures to gain global exposure. TAL's team makes country decisions and the currency is actively managed using currency futures.																			
★★★	**FMOQ Omnibus**	Bal											D	C	4%	–13%	7/31/98	9	0.62
This is a balanced fund that has had slightly above average performance overall. Some Canadian technology picks and a 15% US weighting have helped performance so far in 1999.																			
★★★	**Forester Gr: Balanced**	Bal											B	C	17%	–14%	5/31/98	NA	2.00
This is one of many segregated funds offered to members of the Independent Order of Foresters. A pretty standard portfolio full of TSE 100 companies and some mid-term government bonds. Performance has been inconsistent overall.																			
★★★½	**Forester Growth: Equity**	Cdn Eq											A	C	23%	–27%	5/31/98	NA	2.00
Overall performance has been good, but they've suffered more recently despite the focus of big cap names. This portfolio was hit hard, dropping 27% during last summer's meltdown.																			
★½	**GBC International Growth**	Fgn Eq											D	A	32%	–23%	8/31/90	36	1.81
Not the best fund in GBC's line-up. The team at Babson, Stewart & Ivory International have not been able work much magic with this fund. Stocks are typically held for 3 to 5 years and you'll need at least $100,000 to get into this fund.																			
★★½	**GBC N.A. Growth**	US Eq											D	D	23%	–31%	12/31/80	24	1.90
Roughly 20% of the portfolio is held in Healtheon, a recent pharmaceutical IPO. The stock is down more than 70% from its 52-week high. Despite that, performance has been good in 1999 thanks to good stock picks in technology and communications.																			

Legend: ★ = overall past performance vs. similar funds (5 ★ max). Boxes show the quartile performance for a fund each calendar year vs. only similar funds (□ is the best score possible). ● = high; ● = average; and ● = a fund with low expenses.

Consistency			Performance Trend										Risk						Efficiency	
Overall Past Performance	Fund Name	Type	90	91	92	93	94	95	96	97	98	Aug. '99	Up	Down	% of Time Losing $	Biggest Drop	Date	No. of Mo's to Recover	MER	
★★★	**GFM Emerg Markets Country**	Spec Eq							□	□	□	□	NA	NA	49%	–45%	8/31/97	NA	1.50	● low
This regional fund invests in other country funds, so be aware of the double-layering of fees. The 1.50% MER does not include fees on the underlying funds.																				
★★½	**GI Emerg Markets Country**	Spec Eq							□	□	□	□	NA	NA	51%	–44%	8/31/97	NA	2.70	● average
This offering managed by Barry Olliff invests in closed and open ended funds from all over the world. Performance has been lackluster during its brief history.																				
★★	**Global Strat Cda Grwth**	Cdn Eq				□	□	□	□	□	□	□	D	D	28%	–25%	5/31/98	NA	2.45	● average
Tony Massie is very bullish on Canada and the loonie. For this reason, he's keeping nearly all of this fund in Canada. He has reduced his holdings in financial stocks and boosted his holdings in trees.																				
★★½	**Global Strat Cdn Small**	Cdn Eq						□	□	□	□	□	NA	NA	32%	–43%	10/31/97	NA	2.64	● high
John Sartz is a skilled manager who keeps a relatively focused portfolio of no more than 50 stocks. Despite his value label, Sartz has relaxed his valuation criteria somewhat. Fees on this fund have dropped nearly 10 basis points over the past year.																				
★★	**Global Strat Dvr Euro**	Fgn Eq				□	□	□	□	□	□	□	C	C	16%	–16%	8/31/98	NA	2.47	● average
Rothschild's Richard Robinson emphasizes simplicity and control in this portfolio by not participating in overly complex derivatives strategies. The fund was hurt by a bullishness on the Euro, a sentiment that worked out exactly wrong in 1999.																				
★★★	**Global Strat Dvr World**	Fgn Eq						□	□	□	□	□	NA	NA	0%	–12%	8/31/98	3	2.27	● average
The Rothschild team takes a top-down view and focuses on picking countries in this derivatives-based fund. Global Strategy allows country weightings to deviate by about 10 percentage points. They joined the Japan party early, but only with 8% of this fund.																				
★★½	**Global Strat Europe**	Fgn Eq						□	□	□	□	□	NA	NA	9%	–17%	8/31/98	NA	2.63	● high
Contrary to the macro thinking that dominates many other GS funds, Chris Jenkins takes a more fundamental bottom-up approach to picking stocks for this fund. Outsourcing and alternative power (i.e., for vehicles) have produced good returns recently.																				
★★★½	**Global Strat Gold Plus**	Nat Res					□	□	□	□	□	□	B	C	54%	–77%	6/30/96	NA	2.68	● high
Unitholdes of this fund lost a staggering 77% at the trough. This fund has a long way to go to break even – it's still 2/3 below its 1996 peak. When times are good for gold and metals, this fund does do better than most.																				
★★★½	**Global Strat Inc Plus**	Bal				□	□	□	□	□	□	□	A	D	20%	–14%	5/31/98	NA	2.37	● average
Tony Massie's interest sensitive stocks have been hurt by the stiff beating banks took in the summer of 1998 and rate hikes in 1999. He still has a fairly concentrated stock portfolio which is heavily tilted towards bank and utility stocks.																				
★★½	**Global Strat US Equity**	US Eq						□	□	□	□	□	NA	NA	0%	–11%	7/31/98	4	2.52	● high
Global Strategy's concept combines Rothschild's top-down approach with Schroder's bottom-up stock picking philosophy. Sounds good in theory; hasn't added up to above-average performance. AIM was lifted from the fund last year.																				
★★★	**Global Strat Wrld Bal**	Bal						□	□	□	□	□	NA	NA	0%	–7%	8/31/98	3	2.35	● low
Guiness Flight's asset allocation expertise is teamed with Rothschild and Schroder on this offering. Performance has been good overall, but weak so far in 1999 thanks to missing out on Asia and some profit-taking in the US.																				
★★★½	**Global Strat Wrld Equ**	Fgn Eq						□	□	□	□	□	NA	NA	2%	–14%	8/31/98	4	2.57	● average
A healthy dose of big US stocks and a good chunk of the hot Japanese market have kept this fund ahead of most so far in 1999. However, this team has taken some profits in the US & Japan and boosted positions in Europe.																				
★★★★	**Goldfund Ltd**	Nat Res								□	□	N/A	NA	NA	50%	–71%	4/30/74	65	2.73	● low
This fund has nearly a quarter of its money in gold bullion and everybody knows how that's done lately. The rest of the fund is in smaller gold mining companies. A decent fund if your outlook on gold is different than the market's.																				

Legend: ★= overall past performance vs. similar funds (5 ★ max). Boxes show the quartile performance for a fund each calendar year vs. only similar funds (▀ is the best score possible). ● = high; ○ = average; and ● = a fund with low expenses.

Consistency			Performance Trend										Risk						Efficiency	
Overall Past Performance	Fund Name	Type	90	91	92	93	94	95	96	97	98	Aug. '99	Up	Down	% of Time Losing $	Biggest Drop	Date	No. of Mo's to Recover	MER	
★★½	**Goldtrust**	Nat Res	1	4	4	3	2	4	4	1	1	4	D	D	45%	–58%	10/31/80	71	3.16	●
Almost half of this fund is invested directly in gold bullion. The remainder is in smaller gold mining firms. A high MER plus a big drop in gold prices has hurt performance recently.																				
★★½	**Green Line Asian Growth**	Fgn Eq					2	3	2	2	3	4	C	B	49%	–57%	8/31/97	NA	2.59	●
The team at Darier Hentch will continue to underweight Hong Kong since they see better fundamentals elsewhere in the region. This underweighting has been a positive in 1999, as smaller markets in the region have been white hot.																				
★★★	**Green Line Balanced Grth**	Bal	4	4	3	4	3	1	1	2	2	3	C	B	17%	–12%	5/31/98	8	1.95	○
The economy is so strong that McLean Budden doesn't expect any significant market downturn. Interest rate fears, they think, will be overshadowed by strong corporate profits over the next year. Nonetheless, they are conservatively positioned.																				
★★½	**Green Line Balanced Inc**	Bal	4	3	4	4	4	3	2	2	3	4	C	D	18%	–12%	5/31/98	NA	1.95	○
This is a more conservative offering with added emphasis on income. Aside from just holding more in bonds, Sceptre has about 1/3 of that component in corporate issues. The higher bond weighting has hurt performance recently.																				
★★½	**Green Line Blue Chip Equ**	Cdn Eq	2	3	3	4	4	3	2	2	3	4	D	C	24%	–27%	5/31/98	NA	2.25	○
Net assets in this fund have more than tripled over the past seven years – a period that has seen a nearly 20 basis point (i.e., 0.20 percentage points) increase in the MER. Significant exposure to rate-sensitive stocks has hurt returns in 1999.																				
★★★½	**Green Line Cdn Equity**	Cdn Eq	3	3	3	1	4	4	2	1	4	1	A	C	33%	–29%	5/31/98	14	2.10	○
A healthy dose of energy stocks and a maximized foreign component helped John Weatherall post a brisk performance reversal (for the better) in 1999. This is a good core Canadian equity holding.																				
★★★	**Green Line Cdn Index**	Cdn Eq	4	2	4	2	2	2	2	3	2	2	B	C	31%	–28%	5/31/98	NA	0.80	●
TD's quant group manages this passive fund, which is now expensive in relative terms. Royal and Altamira both offer similar funds at 0.50% per year. The fund mirrors the TSE 300 and has done well in comparison to other Canadian stock funds.																				
★★★	**Green Line Dividend**	Div	1	1	2	4	2	4	1	1	3	3	C	B	21%	–23%	6/30/98	NA	2.00	○
This fund's equity emphasis lead us to reclassify this fund in the large cap Canadian equity category. A 20% weighting in income trusts keeps this fund yielding more than double the TSE 300.																				
★★★	**Green Line Emerging Mkts**	Fgn Eq				2	2	3	3	2	3	1	A	C	47%	–51%	8/31/97	NA	2.63	●
The team at Morgan Stanley Dean Witter run this fund and they're bullish on Asia and Mexico. A 50% weighting in Asia markets propelled this fund to the top of its class so far in 1999.																				
★★★	**Green Line Energy**	Nat Res						3	2	1	4	1	NA	NA	44%	–65%	10/31/97	NA	2.11	●
Margot Naudie is a fundamentalist who picks energy stocks based on her disciplined process emphasizing quality. Her patience and attention to valuations are big positives for unitholders of this fund.																				
★★½	**Green Line Intl Equity**	Fgn Eq				3	1	4	3	3	3	2	C	A	19%	–13%	8/31/98	11	2.33	○
A big European weighting (73%) hurt returns in 1999 as many markets in the region were rocked by US interest rate jitters. Schroder Capital advises this International equity fund – sans North America. Performance has been weak overall.																				
★★★½	**Green Line Japan Growth**	Fgn Eq						2	2	2	2	4	NA	NA	64%	–35%	5/31/96	NA	2.60	●
Restructuring is the biggest trend in corporate Japan, and Schroder Capital is counting on that to drive investment in the region and drive stock prices up higher. This portfolio has a notable presence of big export-oriented firms.																				
★★★	**Green Line Lat Amer Grwth**	Fgn Eq						2	3	1	2	1	NA	NA	36%	–45%	8/31/97	NA	2.60	●
Morgan Stanley is very bullish on Mexico, as evidenced by its 43% weighting in the portfolio. They are more cautious in Brazil, where there is concern about President Cardoso's ability to implement strict fiscal reforms.																				
★★★★½	**Green Line Prec Metals**	Nat Res						2	1	3	2	3	NA	NA	58%	–66%	6/30/96	NA	2.12	●
Margot Naudie holds a concentrated portfolio of both big and small companies. Her top 15 holdings make up nearly 2/3 of the total portfolio so she is taking big bets on quality firms like Barrick, Freeport, and Euro-Nevada.																				

Legend: ★= overall past performance vs. similar funds (5 ★ max). Boxes show the quartile performance for a fund each calendar year vs. only similar funds (Q1 is the best score possible). ● = high; ○ = average; and ● = a fund with low expenses.

Consistency			Performance Trend										Risk						Efficiency	
Overall Past Performance	**Fund Name**	**Type**	**90**	**91**	**92**	**93**	**94**	**95**	**96**	**97**	**98**	**Aug. '99**	**Up**	**Down**	**% of Time Losing $**	**Biggest Drop**	**Date**	**No. of Mo's to Recover**	**MER**	
★★★	**Green Line Resource**	Nat Res					Q1	Q2	Q2	Q4	Q3	Q1	C	D	58%	–58%	3/31/97	NA	2.12	●
In May, Margot Naudie said that the run-up in metals was premature, and she's been proven right. Substantial core holdings in big energy stocks have helped her stay ahead of most of her peers in 1999.																				
★★★½	**Green Line Science & Tech**	Spec Eq					Q1	Q2	Q4	Q4	Q2	Q2	A	NA	7%	–22%	5/31/98	6	2.58	○
A more cautious attitude in the near term lead the team at T. Rowe Price to take profits in the first quarter of 1999 and hold considerable cash for awhile. They've since reinvested much of that cash and are now fully invested in many big US names.																				
★★★	**Green Line US Mid-Cap Gro**	US Eq					Q1	Q2	Q1	Q4	Q2	Q4	A	D	0%	–19%	7/31/98	5	2.33	○
T. Rowe Price runs this clone of a US-based fund bearing the same name. In Canada you'll pay 2.33% per year, while its big US sister charges just 0.95% annually! Western Wireless and Circuit City have been big wins.																				
★★★	**Green Line Value**	Cdn Eq					Q3	Q2	Q1	Q3	Q3	Q4	B	D	33%	–28%	5/31/98	NA	2.10	○
Significant exposure to energy stocks made for a good start to the year, but increased exposure to big interest sensitive stocks (including lots of banks) has hurt more recently as we've seen upward pressure on interest rates.																				
★★★	**Greystone Managed Wealth**	Bal						Q4	Q3	Q1	Q1	Q3	C	D	13%	–11%	6/30/98	NA	2.50	●
This fund soon will be part of the Guardian family of funds but management won't change. A well diversified portfolio of stocks make up the majority of the holdings. Manager Rob Vanderhooft looks for quality companies with good growth prospects.																				
★★½	**Growsafe Cdn Equity**	Cdn Eq					Q2	Q2	Q3	Q4	Q1	Q1	C	D	12%	–26%	5/31/98	8	2.45	○
With a new manager and a new focus on emerging technology stocks that will power the next century, this fund has completely turned the corner. It's a potent mix of hardware, software, infrastructure and health care names – with potent performance.																				
★★½	**Growsafe Intl Balanced**	Bal					Q2	Q4	Q3	Q2	Q2	Q3	D	NA	2%	–7%	8/31/98	3	2.79	●
Yes, it uses derivatives to achieve full foreign exposure with full RRSP eligibility. But no, it's not risky. It's so not risky. Trouble is, it's just a dull balanced fund with foreign pay bonds and a little foreign index exposure that costs 2.5%.																				
★★★★	**Growsafe US 21st Century**	US Eq								Q3	Q1	Q1	NA	NA	0%	–15%	8/31/98	2	2.13	●
Here's a good product in the TA family: a growth fund that meets your needs for foreign exposure in an RSP and still delivers the goods in terms of performance. Remember though, that you'll need to add some non-North American holdings somewhere.																				
★★★½	**Growsafe US 500 Index**	US Eq							Q2	Q2	Q1	Q2	NA	NA	0%	–11%	8/31/98	2	2.13	○
It's a fully-foreign, fully-RRSP eligible US index fund with no leverage. That's an idea that works. You'll get expsoure to global leaders and get it deemed Canadian by RevCan.																				
★★★	**GS American Equity Fund**	US Eq								Q1	Q3	Q4	NA	NA	0%	–11%	7/31/98	4	2.76	●
Rothschild manages this fund for Investors Group and has about 40% in cyclical stocks. This fund does cost about 0.25% more than Global Strategy's own US equity fund and performances for both have been about average.																				
★★½	**GS Canadian Equity Fund**	Cdn Eq								Q3	Q4	Q4	NA	NA	45%	–24%	5/31/98	NA	2.78	●
Again, here you've got a more costly version of a Global Strategy fund. Tony Massie now has reduced interest sensitive exposure and boosted holdings in cyclical companies. That hasn't been enough to turn performance around in 1999.																				
★★★	**GS International Equity**	Fgn Eq								Q2	Q3	Q3	NA	NA	3%	–12%	8/31/98	4	2.76	●
Rupert Robinson manages this global fund, which holds more than 40% in the huge US market. Overweighting Europe and underweighting Asia (including Japan) has hurt performance recently.																				
★½	**GTS Canadian Protected**	Cdn Eq	Q1	Q3	Q1	Q4	Q2	Q4	Q4	Q4	Q1	Q1	D	B	8%	–6%	11/30/93	19	2.40	○
This team used to use popular mutual funds (from AGF and Trimark) for its Canadian equity exposure but now they use TSE 35 futures to better control equity exposure. Roughly 25% of this fund is invested in the family's other two funds.																				
★	**GTS First American**	US Eq			Q4	Q3	Q3	Q4	Q4	Q4	Q1	Q3	D	C	35%	–17%	9/30/98	NA	2.80	●
Using computer modelling and market timing, this fund aims to beat the S&P 500 by 6 percentage points annually over any three-year period. Not likely since it's had a very difficult time just beating most of its peers.																				

Legend: ★ = overall past performance vs. similar funds (5 ★ max). Boxes show the quartile performance for a fund each calendar year vs. only similar funds (1 is the best score possible). ● = high; ● = average; and ● = a fund with low expenses.

Consistency			Performance Trend										Risk						Efficiency
Overall Past Performance	Fund Name	Type	90	91	92	93	94	95	96	97	98	Aug. '99	Up	Down	% of Time Losing $	Biggest Drop	Date	No. of Mo's to Recover	MER
★★	**GTS Protected American**	Bal	1	4	3	2	1	4	4	4	1	3	D	A	14%	–12%	3/31/99	NA	2.30 ●
Proprietary computer models guide the managers' asset mix decision in this fund. But despite top-quartile performance in down markets and their objective of never having a losing year, this fund has historically lost money about 13% of the time.																			
★★½	**Guardian Amer Equity**	US Eq	3	1	1	2	1	2	4	4	4	1	C	A	18%	–38%	2/28/73	58	2.04 ●
Michael Rome (Lazard) took over leadership in early '98. He's a small cap specialist and has done very well so far in his tenure. Overall performance has been excellent in down markets.																			
★★	**Guardian Amer Equity Cl B**	US Eq							4	4	4	1	NA	NA	13%	–17%	10/31/97	14	2.64 ●
You'll save 60 basis points (0.60 percentage points) annually by choosing this fund's "classic units," which are bought on a front end basis. Michael Rome is particularly skilled in finding good small/mid cap stocks – which this fund emphasizes.																			
★½	**Guardian Cdn Bal Class B**	Bal							4	4	4	4	NA	NA	38%	–11%	5/31/98	NA	2.79 ●
A newer version of the original balanced fund with front or back load option. The biggest difference – this one is more expensive by a whopping 100 basis points.																			
★★½	**Guardian Cdn Balanced**	Bal	1	2	1	4	1	4	4	4	4	4	D	A	16%	–26%	12/31/80	29	1.62 ●
This fund is managed with a long-term focus and macro economic outlook; that is the most important influence in investment decisions. Resource stocks are big in the fund, especially those of oil and gas companies.																			
★★½	**Guardian Emerg Markets B**	Fgn Eq							2	3	4	3	NA	NA	69%	–49%	8/31/97	NA	2.92 ●
This is the same fund as the original Guardian Emerging Markets fund but the MER has been inflated. It is also available with a front or back-end load.																			
★★★½	**Guardian Emerging Markets**	Fgn Eq						1	2	3	4	3	NA	NA	48%	–48%	8/31/97	NA	1.77 ●
Manager James Donald has big money in Latin America and has done well with his South Korea holdings but the fund has lagged behind the majority of its peers. However, the extremely low MER has been a plus.																			
★★½	**Guardian Enterprise**	Cdn Eq	2	4	3	4	3	1	1	3	2	3	C	A	27%	–37%	10/31/97	NA	2.33 ●
The goal of the value driven approach used for this fund is to sniff out very cheap small cap names. Although the recent performance of small caps has been weak overall, this fund has lagged its competitors.																			
★★★	**Guardian Enterprise Cl B**	Cdn Eq							1	3	2	3	NA	NA	44%	–37%	10/31/97	NA	2.98 ●
This is the carbon copy of the original Enterprise fund with a higher MER attached to it.																			
★★★	**Guardian Global Equ Cl B**	Fgn Eq							2	4	1	2	NA	NA	0%	–16%	8/31/98	4	2.54 ●
Same as the original Global Equity fund, but a higher MER has been attached.																			
★★★	**Guardian Global Equity**	Fgn Eq	4	4	4	2	2	2	2	4	1	2	C	B	22%	–36%	2/28/73	45	1.82 ●
About 40% of this fund is in Europe, another 40% is in the US and the remaining 20% is divided between Asia and cash. Plenty of technology and telecom names are in this fund. It has lagged a bit due to its low Asian weighting.																			
★★★	**Guardian Global Small Cap**	Fgn Eq						2	4	3	2	4	NA	NA	50%	–48%	8/31/97	NA	2.60 ●
This one is very diversified – it holds over 100 stocks. Manager David Plants has put almost half of the money into tech, media and telecom names. The vast majority of the stocks are from the US and Europe but that hasn't helped performance.																			
★★★	**Guardian Gro Equity Cl B**	Cdn Eq							1	3	4	3	NA	NA	38%	–28%	5/31/98	NA	2.85 ●
Manager John Priestman has really made this a concentrated fund by holding only around 30 stocks. He puts a focus on larger cap names that are growing well. About a quarter of the fund is in financial services.																			
★★	**Guardian Intl Bal Class B**	Bal							3	3	4	1	NA	NA	6%	–7%	5/31/98	7	2.85 ●
Exactly the same fund as the original International Balanced. Oh, except for one thing – the MER is jacked up significantly.																			

Legend: ★ = overall past performance vs. similar funds (5 ★ max). Boxes show the quartile performance for a fund each calendar year vs. only similar funds (☐ is the best score possible). ● = high; ● = average; and ● = a fund with low expenses.

Consistency: Overall Past Performance	Fund Name	Type	Performance Trend: 90	91	92	93	94	95	96	97	98	Aug. '99	Risk: Up	Down	% of Time Losing $	Biggest Drop	Date	No. of Mo's to Recover	Efficiency: MER
★★½	**Guardian Intl Balanced**	Bal											D	A	13%	–10%	2/28/94	21	2.02
There is almost exactly a 50/50 split between bonds and stocks for this fund and almost all holdings from both asset classes originate in the US and Asia. Performance has been far less than spectacular.																			
★★½	**Guardian Monthly Div**	Div											D	A	18%	–9%	10/31/97	NA	1.33
It looks like a dog for the past few years because it's compared against thoroughbreds. Instead of common stocks, this actually holds prefs. You know, for income. It's the best conservative true dividend fund in the country.																			
★	**Guardian Monthly Div Cl B**	Div											NA	NA	44%	–10%	10/31/97	NA	1.93
Same as the original Monthly Dividend fund with the benefit of a higher MER.																			
★★	**GWL Balanced Fund (B) DSC**	Bal											NA	NA	23%	–13%	5/31/98	NA	2.49
Since the fall of 1998, this fund has been spending its cash picking up North American interest sensitive and resource stocks. The "B" in the fund's name means that Beutel Goodman manages this portfolio.																			
★★	**GWL Balanced Fund (B) NL**	Bal											NA		NA 26%	–13%	5/31/98	NA	2.73
This is the "no load" version of the Beutel Goodman managed fund. But make no mistake about it – this fund is "loaded" with a cumbersome expense ratio of 2.73% (0.25% more than the DSC fund).																			
★★½	**GWL Balanced Fund (M) DSC**	Bal											NA	NA	35%	–17%	10/31/97	21	2.59
Almost 60% of this fund's Canadian stocks are in cyclicals (and a big chunk in energy). This explains the relative performance boost this year. This fund is very expensive – especially since half the fund is in cash and shorter term bonds.																			
★★	**GWL Balanced Fund (M) NL**	Bal											NA	NA	35%	–17%	10/31/97	21	2.83
Again, it's not worth paying this much just to go no load. Plus, it's deceiving to label the more expensive product as the one with fewer sales fees. This is the costly way to go in this family.																			
★★★	**GWL Balanced Fund (S) DSC**	Bal											NA	NA	26%	–13%	5/31/98	NA	2.50
You'll have a 1.04% headstart every year if you choose Sceptre Balanced Growth over this pricey fund. Both are managed in the same fashion by the same Sceptre manager – Lyle Stein.																			
★★½	**GWL Balanced Fund (S) NL**	Bal											NA	NA	26%	–13%	5/31/98	NA	2.74
Unless you need creditor protection or estate guarantees, this fund is simply too expensive to make it worthwhile – even under the direction of Lyle Stein, a fine manager.																			
★★½	**GWL Canadian Equ (G) DSC**	Cdn Eq											NA	NA	25%	–34%	5/31/98	NA	2.34
Exposure to energy and technology has added up to top-quartile performance for this in-house managed fund. Nortel and BCE, which have been on fire for a couple of years, make up 16% of this fund.																			
★★½	**GWL Canadian Equ (G) NL**	Cdn Eq											C	B	28%	–34%	5/31/98	NA	2.58
There is a cost to everything. To buy funds in this family without deferred sales charges (DSC), you'll have to fork out an extra 0.25% in fees – each year!																			
★★½	**GWL Cdn Resources (A) DSC**	Nat Res											NA	NA	68%	–58%	10/31/97	NA	3.01
Veteran AGF resource specialist Bob Farquharson runs this GWL version. Nearly half of the portfolio is invested in energy stocks, with positions in gold and metals making up another quarter of the fund. Fees on this fund are super high.																			
★★	**GWL Cdn Resources (A) NL**	Nat Res											NA	NA	68%	–58%	10/31/97	NA	3.25
Despite having highly skilled management at the helm, this fund is destined to lag its peers since it's so darn expensive.																			
★★★½	**GWL Cdn Rl Est 1 (G) DSC**	Real											NA	NA	4%	–3%	9/30/94	20	2.70
This is one of only three remaining fund in this category that invests directly in property. Half of the portfolio is in Ontario with another 40% held out west. Occupancy rates are high and they focus on office buildings to generate returns.																			

Legend: ★ = overall past performance vs. similar funds (5 ★ max). Boxes show the quartile performance for a fund each calendar year vs. only similar funds (□ is the best score possible). ● = high; ○ = average; and ● = a fund with low expenses.

Consistency			Performance Trend										Risk						Efficiency	
Overall Past Performance	Fund Name	Type	90	91	92	93	94	95	96	97	98	Aug. '99	Up	Down	% of Time Losing $	Biggest Drop	Date	No. of Mo's to Recover	MER	
★★½	**GWL Cdn RI Est 1 (G) NL**	Real						□	□	□	□	□	NA	NA	52%	–26%	7/31/90	NA	2.94	●
Again, about a quarter point more annually to go no load. So after 7 years when the DSC would expire anyway, you've probably spent much, much more in fees.																				
★★★	**GWL Divers (G) DSC**	Bal						□	□	□	□	□	NA	NA	13%	–14%	5/31/98	11	2.35	○
This is a fund of funds, holding other GWL-managed seg funds to gain exposure to different asset classes. Performance has been about average with stronger performance lately coming from GWL's resource-heavy Canadian equity fund.																				
★★½	**GWL Diversified (G) NL**	Bal	□	□	□	□	□	□	□	□	□	□	D	A	14%	–14%	5/31/98	11	2.59	●
Performance of this fund lags its DSC sister. Why? The DSC version has sales charges that apply if you sell out, while this one costs more on an annual basis.																				
★★½	**GWL Equity (M) DSC**	Cdn Eq								□	□	□	NA	NA	23%	–14%	6/30/98	NA	2.54	●
Just like the flagship Mackenzie Ivy Canadian, this Jerry Javasky-managed GWL fund is sitting on a pile of cash. Heavy exposure to interest sensitive stocks, low cyclical exposure, and a lot of cash have added up to a poor showing in 1999.																				
★★	**GWL Equity (M) NL**	Cdn Eq								□	□	□	NA	NA	26%	–15%	6/30/98	NA	2.78	●
With all that cash sitting there, this fund's 2.78% MER will be an anchor on returns. Go DSC in this family, or better yet go directly to Mackenzie to get this same fund (Ivy Canadian) and save more than 0.45% annually.																				
★★★	**GWL Equity Fund (S) DSC**	Cdn Eq								□	□	□	NA	NA	42%	–27%	5/31/98	NA	2.51	●
About 1/3 of this fund sits in interest sensitive stocks and has hurt performance this year due to interest rate fears. Managed by Sceptre, this fund is too expensive – by about 1% annually compared to Sceptre's own funds.																				
★★★	**GWL Equity Fund (S) NL**	Cdn Eq								□	□	□	NA	NA	42%	–27%	5/31/98	NA	2.75	●
An extra 0.25% annually just to avoid a DSC schedule. It's just not worth it in most cases.																				
★★½	**GWL Equity Index (G) DSC**	Cdn Eq						□	□	□	□	□	NA	NA	25%	–34%	10/31/95	21	2.17	○
It's laughable that an index fund could charge so much. It's doomed – do you hear that? – *doomed* to underperform. Yes, worse funds exist. But some of them might do well someday. This one won't.																				
★★½	**GWL Equity Index (G) NL**	Cdn Eq	□	□	□	□	□	□	□	□	□	□	C	C	32%	–28%	5/31/98	NA	2.40	○
Even higher fees to go no load mean even more certain doom for this pig.																				
★★★½	**GWL Equity/Bond (G) DSC**	Bal						□	□	□	□	□	NA	NA	21%	–19%	5/31/98	NA	2.37	○
GWL has spent their cash and boosted Canadian equity exposure. And now this fund is fully invested. A good offering in the whole messy GWL line up.																				
★★★	**GWL Equity/Bond (G) NL**	Bal	□	□	□	□	□	□	□	□	□	□	B	C	19%	–19%	5/31/98	NA	2.61	●
Again, about a quarter point more annually to go no load. So after 7 years when the DSC would expire anyway, you've probably spent much, much more in fees.																				
★★	**GWL Growth & Inc (A) DSC**	Bal								□	□	□	NA	NA	42%	–25%	10/31/97	NA	2.58	●
Since last fall, AGF's Gerard Ferguson has become more bullish on Canadian stocks – at the expense of cash and bonds. Not much of a premium to get AGF on this GWL seg fund, which is quite active in its asset mix decisions.																				
★★	**GWL Growth & Inc (A) NL**	Bal								□	□	□	NA	NA	42%	–25%	10/31/97	NA	2.82	●
There is just too much overlap in this family. You've got "Growth & Income," "Diversified," and "Equity/Bond." Despite some fundamental differences but they are not much different really.																				
★★★	**GWL Growth & Inc (M) NL**	Bal								□	□	□	NA	NA	16%	–10%	6/30/98	NA	2.60	●
This, like GWL's other Growth and Income funds, is managed by Jerry Javasky of Mackenzie. And like Mackenzie's own Ivy Growth & Income fund, this one's sitting on a pile of cash (about 18%).																				

Legend: ★ = overall past performance vs. similar funds (5 ★ max). Boxes show the quartile performance for a fund each calendar year vs. only similar funds (☐ is the best score possible). ● = high; ● = average; and ● = a fund with low expenses.

Consistency			Performance Trend										Risk						Efficiency	
Overall Past Performance	Fund Name	Type	90	91	92	93	94	95	96	97	98	Aug. '99	Up	Down	% of Time Losing $	Biggest Drop	Date	No. of Mo's to Recover	MER	
★★½	**GWL Growth Equity (A) DSC**	Cdn Eq											NA	NA	42%	–33%	10/31/97	NA	2.98	●
Lead manager Bob Farquharson has scored some points this year with his holdings in technology and deep cyclicals. We're big fans of Farquharson's work but he'll have to work pretty darn hard to add value, over and above the 3% MER.																				
★½	**GWL Growth Equity (A) NL**	Cdn Eq											NA	NA	42%	–33%	10/31/97	NA	3.22	●
At nearly 3.22% annually, this fund will have a tough time adding value over time. Investors who want this fund are better off going DSC in this same family or go straight to AGF to buy the Canadian Growth Equity fund.																				
★★★★½	**GWL Int'l Opport (P) DSC**	Fgn Eq											NA	NA	8%	–23%	8/31/97	11	2.95	●
Boston-based Putnam is the manager on this fund, and they've done a nice job – despite the high fees. It's an all-cap, non-North American equity fund that's had success underweighting big European markets while emphasizing Japan and Asia.																				
★★★★½	**GWL Int'l Opport (P) NL**	Fgn Eq											NA	NA	8%	–24%	8/31/97	11	3.19	●
Putnam uses a growth apporach to picking its 150 stocks but they will pull the trigger if valuations get too high. Be careful about holding this fund outside of your RRSP/RRIF since turnover is high – as is the potential for significant taxable distributions.																				
★★★★	**GWL Intl Equity (P) DSC**	Fgn Eq											NA	NA	2%	–18%	8/31/98	10	2.60	●
The team at Putnam thinks that Japan's economic uptick won't last. They're expecting an economic contraction (negative growth) for calendar 1999. At the end of May, most of their Japanese positions were significantly trimmed.																				
★★	**GWL Larger Co (M) DSC**	Cdn Eq											NA	NA	39%	–25%	5/31/98	NA	2.58	●
Mackenzie's Neil Lovatt uses a blended style to manage this fund. He looks for sectors that are undervalued, then searches hard for solid companies with clean financials and good growth prospects. It sounds real nice, but it just hasn't worked well.																				
★★	**GWL Larger Company (M) NL**	Cdn Eq											NA	NA	39%	–25%	5/31/98	NA	2.82	●
Neil Lovatt's approach hasn't been very successful with this fund and with fees approaching 3%, that's likely to prove a heavy burden on returns.																				
★★½	**GWL N.A. Equity (B) DSC**	Fgn Eq											NA	NA	35%	–22%	5/31/98	NA	2.50	○
Despite its mandate, this is really more like a Canadian stocks fund – less than 20% in US stocks, 12% in cash, and the rest in Canadian stocks. That also explains why the fund's done better in 1999.																				
★½	**GWL N.A. Equity (B) NL**	Fgn Eq											NA	NA	35%	–22%	5/31/98	NA	2.74	●
High expenses are simply too high a hurdle for even the fine team at Beutel Goodman. In this family, DSC is the better deal.																				
★½	**GWL Smaller Co (M) DSC**	Cdn Eq											NA	NA	39%	–26%	5/31/98	NA	2.57	●
There is a good mix of stocks in technology, energy, and some smaller financials but this has not been the recipe. A more growth oriented style and low emphasis on cyclical stocks has left this puppy behind more than 75% of its peers in 1999.																				
★½	**GWL Smaller Co (M) NL**	Cdn Eq											NA	NA	39%	–26%	5/31/98	NA	2.81	●
The no-load label here is more indicative of performance than of the fees. Investors are better off going DSC in this family and saving 0.25% of your investment each year.																				
★★½	**GWL US Equity (G) DSC**	US Eq											NA	NA	0%	–13%	8/31/98	3	2.53	●
Despite the continued big-cap leadership among US stocks, this fund has suffered with spotty performance overall, and a sub-par showing in 1999. The team at Great West Life is expecting some near-term weakness in the US market.																				
★★	**GWL US Equity Fund (G) NL**	US Eq											NA	NA	0%	–13%	8/31/98	3	2.77	●
Investors would do well to focus on the fees levied on an annually basis, rather than one-time sales charges that might be triggered. Going DSC and saving 25 basis points annually is better than buying this pricey offering.																				
★★	**Hansberger Asian Fund**	Fgn Eq											C	C	66%	–71%	1/31/94	NA	2.77	○
This fund has struggled since day one. Performance is poor with below-average marks in all market conditions. Korea accounts for 17% of this bank-laden fund.																				

Legend: ★ = overall past performance vs. similar funds (5 ★ max). Boxes show the quartile performance for a fund each calendar year vs. only similar funds (□ is the best score possible). ● = high; ● = average; and ● = a fund with low expenses.

Consistency: Overall Past Performance	Fund Name	Type	90	91	92	93	94	95	96	97	98	Aug. '99	Risk: Up	Down	% of Time Losing $	Biggest Drop	Date	No. of Mo's to Recover	Efficiency: MER
★½	**Hansberger European Fund**	Fgn Eq			□	□	□	□	□	□	□	□	D	C	29%	–22%	6/30/98	NA	2.48
Although the UK dominates this fund, lots of money is invested in areas of Europe that are not as familiar including the Netherlands, Spain and Austria. Performance has been relatively weak since Hansberger took over in '96.																			
★★	**Hemisphere Value Fund**	Bal						□	□	□	□	□	NA	NA	27%	–13%	5/31/98	NA	1.50
This is a tiny fund run out of Saskatoon that tries to make money for unitholders in all market conditions by being very active on the asset mix decisions. Unfortunately for unitholders, this fund has been outpaced by most of its peers every year.																			
★★★	**Hongkong Bank Asian Grth**	Fgn Eq					□	□	□	□	□	□	A	C	54%	–52%	8/31/97	NA	2.22
Healthy exposure to some smaller Asian markets – like Singapore and South Korea – added up to big profits for investors of this fund. This fund includes Japan – of which the manager has a neutral opinion.																			
★★★	**Hongkong Bank Balanced**	Bal	□	□	□	□	□	□	□	□	□	□	C	B	12%	–14%	5/31/98	8	1.79
Lower weighting in foreign stocks, coupled with heavier weightings in Canadian stocks, have added up to upper-quartile performance in 1999.																			
★★	**Hongkong Bank Emerg Mkts**	Fgn Eq						□	□	□	□	□	NA	NA	56%	–49%	12/31/94	NA	2.71
HSBC is bullish on Asia – and on South Korea in particular – which they feel has compelling economic fundamentals. This team also has a 12% weighting in South Africa – much more than most others in this category.																			
★★★	**Hongkong Bank Equity**	Cdn Eq	□	□	□	□	□	□	□	□	□	□	B	C	34%	–24%	5/31/98	NA	1.85
A 15% combined weighting in BCE and Nortel, in addition to good stocks in energy and high tech, have added up to consistently good results over the past few years. The top 15 holdings account for more than 50% of the fund's value.																			
★★★★	**Hongkong Bank Euro Growth**	Fgn Eq						□	□	□	□	□	NA	NA	0%	–17%	8/31/98	4	2.12
The managers have a positive outlook for the oil sector because of rising prices, but also because of a strong trend towards global consolidation. This type of global restructuring is a big theme for this fund, which has posted very strong performance.																			
★★½	**Hongkong Bank Sm Cap Grth**	Cdn Eq						□	□	□	□	□	NA	NA	30%	–31%	10/31/97	NA	2.15
The typically low resource content worked out well over the past few years, but it left this fund in the dust behind most other small cap funds in 1999. The Fairfax mess hasn't helped matters much either – the stock made up 3.5% as of July 31.																			
★★★	**Hongkong Bank U.S. Equity**	US Eq						□	□	□	□	□	NA	NA	0%	–14%	8/31/98	3	2.09
With a huge weighting in big high tech stocks, this fund has smoked most of its competitors over the last couple of years. This fund's mandate allows 10% to be invested in other countries, including Canada.																			
★★★	**Horizons Multi-Asset Fund**	Spec Eq								□	□	□	NA	NA	13%	–9%	8/31/94	13	2.60
This fund of hedge funds benefits from the fact that it's based in Barbados. The result is that unitholders only pay tax on the gains (in the form of capital gains and dividends) upon selling units. The fund MER plus that on underlying funds is very costly.																			
★★½	**Horizons RRSP Hedge Fund**	Spec Eq								□	□	□	NA	NA	39%	–21%	3/31/96	31	3.50
Proprietary computer models dictate when this hedge fund will long or short the market. It focuses on US stocks (primary focus) bonds and currency and reacts to market movements by trying to spot trends. It's aggressive and it hasn't worked well.																			
★★★	**ICM Equity Fund**	Cdn Eq	□	□	□	□	□	□	□	□	□	□	B	B	24%	–41%	6/30/91	55	0.09
Management fees are not included in these performance numbers since they're charged directly to investors. This fund uses a combination top down growth (Gryphon Inv Counsel) and bottom up value (Lincluden) to pick stocks.																			
★★★½	**ICM International Equity**	Fgn Eq					□	□	□	□	□	□	A	A	3%	–15%	8/31/98	3	0.40
Management fees are not included in these performance numbers since they're charged directly to investors. This fund, which excludes North America, also uses the blended top down growth/bottom up value styles to select securities.																			
★★★	**Imperial Growth Cdn Equ**	Cdn Eq	□	□	□	□	□	□	□	□	□	□	B	C	21%	–29%	5/31/98	NA	1.95
The top ten holdings of this old fund are filled with the country's largest companies. Its typical fully invested status exposes it to above average risk in down markets, but gives it a better shot at outperforming most in a bullish environment.																			

Legend: ★ = overall past performance vs. similar funds (5 ★ max). Boxes show the quartile performance for a fund each calendar year vs. only similar funds (☐ is the best score possible). ● = high; ○ = average; and ● = a fund with low expenses.

Consistency			Performance Trend										Risk						Efficiency	
Overall Past Performance	Fund Name	Type	90	91	92	93	94	95	96	97	98	Aug. '99	Up	Down	% of Time Losing $	Biggest Drop	Date	No. of Mo's to Recover	MER	
★★½	**Imperial Growth Divers**	Bal	2	3	3	4	2	3	3	2	3	2	D	C	14%	–16%	5/31/98	NA	2.00	○
Pension manager Canagex runs this balanced fund, which has about 13% in corporate bonds to boost yield on the fixed income side. Interestingly, foreign content sits at about 10% – all of which is sitting in SPDRs (S&P 500 index securities).																				
★★★	**Imperial Growth N.A. Equ**	US Eq	4	4	2	4	1	2	4	2	2	2	A	A	22%	–29%	7/31/81	19	1.70	●
Canagex doesn't even try to pick US stocks. Instead they go for S&P 500 index exposure by holding nearly 60% in SPDRs (Standard & Poors Depository Receipts). The 1.7% MER is high in light of that fact.																				
★★★	**Ind Alliance Diversified**	Bal	1	2	2	2	1	2	3	4	3	3	B	A	13%	–17%	5/31/98	NA	1.82	○
There is some active management of the asset mix in this fund and it's worked out well most of the time, judging by the top-quartile performance in down markets. Lead manager Luc Fournier is currently overweight Canadian and foreign stocks.																				
★½	**Ind Alliance Ecoflex A**	Cdn Eq					3	4	4	4	4	3	D	D	21%	–29%	5/31/98	NA	2.48	○
This seg fund has been kicked around for years with poor performance. So where did third-quartile performance come from? How about a substantial weighting in BCE and a variety of big resource stocks that have done very well so far in 1999.																				
★★½	**Ind Alliance Ecoflex D**	Bal					1	2	4	4	3	4	C	D	19%	–17%	5/31/98	NA	2.48	●
You can protect 80% of your capital by splitting your money between a Canadian equity fund and a mid-term gov't bond – at a MER under 1.5%. So why pay 2.48% for capital protection.																				
★★★	**Ind Alliance Ecoflex I**	Fgn Eq							1	2	4	2	NA	NA	25%	–18%	5/31/98	13	2.98	●
This seg fund is invested in the Templeton International Stock fund, and investors are charged 0.5% annually to have it in the form of a seg fund. A 20% Asian weighting has helped spike returns in 1999.																				
★★★½	**Ind Alliance Intl Fund**	Fgn Eq							1	1	4	2	NA	NA	25%	–18%	5/31/98	13	2.47	○
The difference between this and Ecoflex I is the mandate (this one includes the US) and the management – Industrial Alliance handles this one in-house. This $22 million fund is a well kept secret among this family's numerous offerings.																				
★★½	**Industrial American**	US Eq	3	4	3	1	3	4	3	4	4	1	C	B	12%	–29%	9/30/87	22	2.34	○
Veronica Onyskiw has failed to take advantage of the hot U.S. market since taking over the fund in 1996. This fund has been a sub-par performer, only producing one year of top quartile performance during the past decade.																				
★★★	**Industrial Balanced**	Bal			3	1	3	3	2	3	4	1	C	D	16%	–17%	10/31/97	18	2.32	○
Tim Gleeson is betting that Oil & Gas and Real Estate sectors will help the fund make a comeback in 1999 after last year's bottom-quartile return. On the foreign side, he feels Japan offers some compelling stories.																				
★★★	**Industrial Dividend Gro**	Div	4	4	4	1	2	4	1	1	2	4	B	A	24%	–33%	9/30/89	45	2.33	○
You won't find any preferred shares here as Bill Proctor's focus is on high-yielding growth stocks. The fund fell behind during the first quarter of 1999 due to the weakening of interest rate sensitive sectors like utilities and pipelines.																				
★★	**Industrial Equity**	Cdn Eq	4	4	1	1	3	4	4	4	4	3	D	D	31%	–52%	3/31/97	NA	2.43	●
This small cap value offering has failed to be revived even though new manager on the job Ian Osler has reduced positions in some poorly performing resource stocks while increasing exposure to the red hot communications stocks.																				
★★★	**Industrial Growth**	Cdn Eq	4	4	4	1	2	4	4	4	4	1	C	A	23%	–38%	10/31/97	NA	2.35	○
Alex Christ's continued emphasis on cyclical stocks has kept this fund at the back of the pack. After two straight years of negative returns, better days may have finally arrived as some resource sectors have finally staged a turnaround.																				
★★½	**Industrial Horizon**	Cdn Eq	3	4	4	1	1	4	4	2	3	2	D	B	27%	–22%	5/31/98	NA	2.33	○
Bill Proctor runs this mid to large-cap equity fund, which has failed to dazzle investors. Although Procter's anticipation of a rebound in oil & gas stocks has helped the fund this year.																				
★★★	**Industrial Income $1 Unit**	Bal	3	2	1	3	4	1	4	4	4	2	C	A	18%	–20%	7/31/79	37	1.82	○
Bill Proctor has been added to the management team of this $2.2 billion dollar fund to select some high yielding stocks. However, it won't likely be enough to cover the fixed annual distribution of $1 plus the fund's 1.82% MER.																				

Legend: ★= overall past performance vs. similar funds (5 ★ max). Boxes show the quartile performance for a fund each calendar year vs. only similar funds (☐ is the best score possible). ● = high; ● = average; and ● = a fund with low expenses.

Consistency: Overall Past Performance	Fund Name	Type	Risk: Up	Risk: Down	% of Time Losing $	Biggest Drop	Date	No. of Mo's to Recover	Efficiency: MER
★★★	**Industrial Pension**	Bal	B	A	27%	–34%	9/30/89	50	2.33
	This fund's respectable performance record has faced turbulence over the past year because of exposure to small cap names and value based stocks. Bill Procter is currently holding around 40 stocks and has 25% of the fund invested in bonds.								
★★★½	**Infinity Canadian Fund**	Cdn Eq	NA	NA	37%	–20%	7/31/98	NA	2.56
	Now managed by Goodman & Co., this fund's style is becoming more active, less comatose. Half of its Canadian stocks are in financial services.								
★★	**Infinity Income Fund**	Div	D	A	7%	–12%	10/31/97	NA	2.67
	This specialty income fund makes big use of royalty income trusts and REITs to juice the yield on this puppy. Fees are rich for this income product and will prove a high hurdle above which to leap.								
★★	**Infinity Wealth Mgmt**	Spec Eq	NA	NA	23%	–33%	12/31/80	26	2.67
	Dundee Investment Management now runs this fund, which has a mandate to invest in Canadian & US (up to 20%) financial services firms.								
★★½	**InvesNat Aggress Divers**	Bal	D	C	21%	–14%	5/31/98	14	1.91
	Exposure to BCE, Nortel, and some cyclicals have propelled this fund to top-quartile performance this year. Overall it's a poor performer and despite its name, it's not all that aggressive.								
★★★★	**InvesNat Amer Index Plus**	US Eq	NA	NA	0%	–11%	8/31/98	2	1.26
	Rather than buy this fund, investors would be better off to put 75% in SPDRs and 25% in a good small cap US fund. That will give you the same philosophy as this fund, with better diversification and much lower fees.								
★★½	**InvesNat Canadian Equity**	Cdn Eq	C	C	23%	–29%	8/31/97	NA	2.13
	The resource stocks that hurt lead manager Sylvain Belanger last year turned out to be big winners this year. That and a 15% combined weighting in Canadian heavyweights BCE and Nortel jumped started this fund to a top quartile showing in 1999.								
★★½	**InvesNat Dividend**	Div	D	C	7%	–8%	6/30/98	10	1.63
	National Bank's Jacques Chartrand has done a good job of protecting capital with an emphasis on preferred shares. However, that meant that he was left in the dust most years before 1998 – when times were better for this class.								
★★★	**InvesNat European Equity**	Fgn Eq	B	B	8%	–18%	8/31/98	NA	2.30
	The UK big caps that boosted performance last year have proved to be a thorn in the side of this fund. Improving economic fundamentals and industry consolidations should give this fund a shot in the arm.								
★★★½	**InvesNat Far East Equity**	Fgn Eq	NA	NA	40%	–48%	1/31/97	NA	2.64
	Despite being fully invested and having good exposure to some of the smaller markets in southeast Asia, this fund has struggled this year (in relative terms). This fund specifically excludes Japan.								
★★½	**InvesNat Japanese Equity**	Fgn Eq	NA	NA	75%	–48%	9/30/94	NA	2.52
	Large cap export-oriented stocks are the focus here (along with a small investment in Japanese Webs Index units). This portfolio has been recovering from a loss that started almost five years ago.								
★★½	**InvesNat Retire Balanced**	Bal	D	C	21%	–14%	5/31/98	14	2.11
	A conservative mandate, stocks focused on large caps, and a tendency to hold at least 10% in foreign stocks have added up to great returns for many balanced funds – but not this one! BCE, Nortel, and Japan have helped in 1999.								
★★★	**InvesNat Sml Capital**	Cdn Eq	B	B	30%	–28%	5/31/98	NA	2.18
	Natcan's Benoit Durand is a growth manager that certainly pays some attention to valuation. That blended style lead him to hold signicant positions in both tech and energy stocks, both of which have worked out very well so far this year.								
★★★½	**Investors Asset Allocat**	Bal	B	D	18%	–22%	4/30/98	NA	2.70
	Despite Eric Innes' active approach this fund costs a steep 2.71%, 0.31 percentage points higher than it was nearly five years ago. That same five-year period saw assets grow four-fold. Currently the fund is 40% in Canadian stocks and 34% foreign.								

Legend: ★= overall past performance vs. similar funds (5 ★ max). Boxes show the quartile performance for a fund each calendar year vs. only similar funds (□ is the best score possible). ● = high; ● = average; and ● = a fund with low expenses.

Consistency			Performance Trend										Risk						Efficiency	
Overall Past Performance	Fund Name	Type	90	91	92	93	94	95	96	97	98	Aug. '99	Up	Down	% of Time Losing $	Biggest Drop	Date	No. of Mo's to Recover	MER	
★★★	**Investors Cdn Equity**	Cdn Eq	1	2	1	2	2	3	3	3	4	2	B	B	21%	–31%	5/31/98	NA	2.47	●
Scott Penman's performance is lagging this year due in part to a 25% exposure to interest sensitive stocks, and lower (than most) exposure to energy stocks. It's been nearly five years since this fund has outpaced more than half of its peers.																				
★★★½	**Investors Dividend**	Div	2	1	3	3	3	4	3	1	2	2	A	B	18%	–30%	11/30/73	53	2.37	●
The MER on this fund was 2.04% – in 1994. Now that the fund is double its 1994 size (to almost $5 billion), fees have gone up to 2.37%! Unitholders deserve to share some of the benefits of that asset growth – namely a reduction in fees.																				
★★★	**Investors European Growth**	Fgn Eq	1	3	2	2	2	3	4	1	3	3	A	NA	8%	–15%	8/31/98	NA	2.43	●
Many in this group have already recovered from damage done during the summer of 1998. However, as we go to print, this fund is still struggling to get back up above water. Despite holding 1/3 in the UK, this fund has struggled this year.																				
★★★	**Investors Global**	Fgn Eq	2	3	4	4	2	2	2	2	2	4	C	A	13%	–23%	9/30/87	34	2.44	●
Ample academic research says stock performance is most influenced by country allocation. Although that's not how this team picks stocks, that thesis seems to have played out in this fund (for 1999), which has lagged its peers so far this year.																				
★★★½	**Investors Growth Plus Prt**	Bal	3	2	2	4	1	2	2	2	3	2	A	C	6%	–9%	1/31/90	13	2.45	●
This fund-of-funds has a global mandate and broad exposure to all major asset classes. Indirectly, this fund has less than 25% exposed to US stocks (just under half of equity exposure) and almost nothing in the hot Pacific Rim.																				
★★★	**Investors Growth Prtfl**	Fgn Eq	3	3	4	3	2	1	1	1	4	3	B	C	11%	–17%	1/31/90	18	2.60	●
This global portfolio has an unusually high proportion of Canadian stocks (25% of the fund), compared to about 3% for the average global equity fund. The country mix in this fund does not appear to have added much value (if any) in this fund.																				
★★½	**Investors Income Plus Prt**	Bal	1	2	3	4	2	4	4	2	3	2	D	B	8%	–8%	2/28/94	15	2.30	●
Indirect equity exposure adds up to about 20% of the portfolio, with the remainder exposed to income-oriented securities. Its conservative nature results in good marks in bear markets, but bottom quartile in bullish times.																				
★★	**Investors Japanese Growth**	Fgn Eq				1	2	2	3	3	2	4	D	A	38%	–45%	7/31/94	NA	2.44	●
Carlson Investment Management leads this fund with their conservative value-based approach. Big names are the focus in this portfolio and it's currently positioned in lots of cyclicals and consumer stocks.																				
★★★	**Investors Mutual of Cda**	Bal	4	3	3	1	1	4	2	2	4	1	A	A	21%	–28%	11/30/73	43	2.38	●
Investors Group's original flagship fund, this is a well-diversified portfolio with about 60% in equities. Performance has been slightly above average with great performance in up and down markets. Fees may prove to be a drag on the other 40%.																				
★★★	**Investors N.A. Growth**	US Eq	1	2	3	4	1	2	3	4	4	2	C	A	25%	–31%	11/30/73	54	2.37	●
Bill Chornous hasn't done well since taking charge of this fund four years ago. His higher than average Canadian equity component and value bias has hurt over the past few years.																				
★★★	**Investors Pacific Intl**	Fgn Eq		1	2	2	2	3	2	3	3	3	A	C	33%	–56%	8/31/97	NA	2.56	●
Jeremy Higgs' enthusiasm for Hong Kong has dwindled somewhat, evidenced by his reduced exposure to the region to less than 1/4 of this portfolio. This year, Higgs has missed much of the party in smaller southeast Asian markets.																				
★★★★½	**Investors Real Property**	Real						1	1	3	2	2	NA	NA	12%	–4%	10/31/92	34	2.43	●
Investors Group classifies this fund as "fixed income" – alongside their gov't bond fund. Credit the IG team for guiding this ship through the real estate storm with great relative performance.																				
★★½	**Investors Retire Grow Prt**	Cdn Eq	2	2	3	3	1	3	3	3	3	2	D	C	22%	–26%	5/31/98	NA	2.61	●
There isn't much to this fund of funds, which currently holds half in the Retirement Mutual, 30% in their Canadian equity, and 20% in the Global fund. For this, unitholders are paying a 0.17% premium for the structure. Overall, a poor performer.																				
★★½	**Investors Retire Plus Prt**	Bal	3	3	4	3	1	4	3	3	3	2	D	B	13%	–13%	5/31/98	NA	2.42	●
The only chance for this conservative fund-of-funds to outperform its peers is during bearish times – like 1994. At all other times, this puppy lags well behind most in its class.																				

Legend: ★= overall past performance vs. similar funds (5 ★ max). Boxes show the quartile performance for a fund each calendar year vs. only similar funds (□ is the best score possible). ● = high; ○ = average; and ● = a fund with low expenses.

Consistency			Performance Trend										Risk						Efficiency	
Overall Past Performance	Fund Name	Type	90	91	92	93	94	95	96	97	98	Aug. '99	Up	Down	% of Time Losing $	Biggest Drop	Date	No. of Mo's to Recover	MER	
★★½	**Investors Retirement**	Cdn Eq	□	□	□	□	□	□	□	□	□	□	C	A	28%	–31%	5/31/98	NA	2.42	○
Nearly 40% in cyclical stocks has been a plus in 1999 for this Canadian equity fund. Overall, performance is nothing to write home about and suffered hard during last summer's market meltdown.																				
★★½	**Investors Special**	US Eq	□	□	□	□	□	□	□	□	□	□	C	B	26%	–39%	11/30/73	57	2.38	○
No real difference between this and IG's North American Growth fund.																				
★★★½	**Investors Summa**	Cdn Eq	□	□	□	□	□	□	□	□	□	□	A	C	26%	–24%	5/31/98	13	2.52	●
Despite substantial exposure to interest sensitive stocks, this socially responsible fund has posted top quartile results so far this year (in addition to each of the last few years).																				
★★½	**Investors US Growth**	US Eq	□	□	□	□	□	□	□	□	□	□	B	A	17%	–49%	2/28/73	65	2.42	○
The notable absence of high technology in this portfolio is keeping this fund below its peers so far this year. But if you're emulating Warren Buffett, you'll likely not have anything invested in high tech stocks since it simply doesn't meet his criteria.																				
★★	**Investors World Grth Prt**	Fgn Eq					□	□	□	□	□	□	D	D	12%	–17%	8/31/97	20	2.64	○
The Japanese exposure that has hurt this fund for a couple of years looks good now, as Japan's economic picture brightens and confidence improves. Overall though, performance has been very weak.																				
★★★	**IRIS Balanced Fund**	Bal	□	□	□	□	□	□	□	□	□	□	C	A	16%	–17%	5/31/98	NA	1.95	○
This is an actively managed fund that holds roughly 14% in index securities (TIPs, SPDRs, and WEBs). Despite its overall top marks in down markets, this puppy lost a whopping 17% during the summer '98 meltdown.																				
★★½	**IRIS Canadian Equity Fund**	Cdn Eq	□	□	□	□	□	□	□	□	□	□	C	A	27%	–37%	4/30/81	21	1.91	○
Weak performance characterizes this fund, managed by Ubald Cloutier. It is only available in Ontario and Quebec, and typical of all large cap Canadian equity funds its biggest holdings are in TSE 35 stocks.																				
★★★½	**IRIS Dividend Fund**	Div						□	□	□	□	□	NA	NA	27%	–21%	6/30/98	NA	1.62	●
This offering has a slightly riskier make-up than its peers. Pierre Bernard of Laurvest has 20% of the fund in income trusts and also has a bias towards common shares rather than preferreds.																				
★★★	**IRIS Global Equity Fund**	Fgn Eq	□	□	□	□	□	□	□	□	□	□	B	A	12%	–31%	9/30/87	51	2.37	○
A solid history for this one, particularly when markets are declining. A generous exposure to U.S. equities by Andrew Offit of Wellington Capital Management has given this fund its edge.																				
★★½	**IRIS U.S. Equity Fund**	US Eq		□	□	□	□	□	□	□	□	□	D	A	15%	–43%	2/28/73	62	2.18	○
Returns have really soared on this one during the past three years. Matthew Megargel of Wellington Capital Management sticks with the blue-chip companies in this portfolio and has scored big with the likes of Microsoft, GE, & Citigroup..																				
★★★	**Ivy Canadian**	Cdn Eq				□	□	□	□	□	□	□	NA	NA	9%	–14%	6/30/98	NA	2.32	●
Jerry Javasky is still sitting on 38% cash – which represents a whopping $2 billion dollars of idle money for investors in this fund. This is presently holding back the performance of this large-cap offering.																				
★★½	**Ivy Enterprise**	Cdn Eq	□	□	□	□	□	□	□	□	□	□	D	A	30%	–32%	9/30/89	49	2.33	○
Chuck Roth, who took over the fund in late 1997, has been successful in reducing the fund's risk by focusing on high quality smaller firms trading at discount valuations. His relative lack of energy stocks has left him behind his peers so far in 1999.																				
★★★	**Ivy Foreign Equity**	Fgn Eq				□	□	□	□	□	□	□	B	C	0%	–9%	7/31/98	3	2.33	○
With Jerry Javasky once again being named lead manager after Bill Kanko's departure, investors in taxable accounts might want to take note of possible turnover in the fund, which could lead to a large capital gains distribution this year.																				
★★★½	**Ivy Growth & Income**	Bal				□	□	□	□	□	□	□	NA	NA	10%	–9%	6/30/98	NA	2.07	○
This fund's been a top contender in its class since inception, and has attracted a ton of new money. Javasky's cautious market outlook is reflected in the fund's asset mix, which has seen its equities position reduced to 40%.																				

Legend: ★ = overall past performance vs. similar funds (5 ★ max). Boxes show the quartile performance for a fund each calendar year vs. only similar funds (□ is the best score possible). ● = high; ● = average; and ● = a fund with low expenses.

Consistency			Performance Trend										Risk						Efficiency	
Overall Past Performance	Fund Name	Type	90	91	92	93	94	95	96	97	98	Aug. '99	Up	Down	% of Time Losing $	Biggest Drop	Date	No. of Mo's to Recover	MER	
★★½	**Jones Heward American**	US Eq	□	□	□	□	□	□	□	□	□	□	C	B	16%	–31%	9/30/87	22	2.50	●
Growth is the name of the game for this fund. It's full of tech stocks, including many Internet names like Charles Schwab, AOL and Yahoo. Performance has been great, but the volatility calls for a strong stomach.																				
★★½	**Jones Heward Cdn Balanced**	Bal	□	□	□	□	□	□	□	□	□	□	D	B	20%	–14%	9/30/87	21	2.40	●
Exposure to interest sensitives has hurt, but large positions in SPDRS and Japanese Webs have more than offset that. The bottom-up approach and large cap bias taken by the manager has allowed some of Canada's best companies to enter the portfolio.																				
★★★	**Jones Heward Fund Ltd.**	Cdn Eq	□	□	□	□	□	□	□	□	□	□	A	B	26%	–37%	5/31/81	23	2.50	●
One of Canada's oldest funds, this one follows a GARP approach to selecting stocks. Equities in this mainly large cap portfolio are selected through a bottom up analysis. Names like Nortel, BCE and Suncor helped performance so far this year.																				
★★½	**Lasalle Balanced**	Bal				□	□	□	□	□	□	□	C	D	18%	–13%	6/30/98	7	1.53	●
★★½	**Lasalle Equity Fund**	Cdn Eq								□	□	□	NA	NA	28%	–25%	4/30/98	NA	2.50	●
★★★½	**Leith Wheeler Balanced**	Bal	□	□	□	□	□	□	□	□	□	□	A	C	15%	–13%	5/31/98	NA	1.18	●
This fund may be worth your attention. Its MER is ridiculously low and performance has generally been good. Bill Dye has loaded up with lots of bank and energy stocks and all of them have been selected through bottom-up analyses.																				
★★★	**Leith Wheeler Cdn Equity**	Cdn Eq						□	□	□	□	□	A	D	24%	–26%	5/31/98	NA	1.50	●
David Jiles has been right on the money with his 20% allocation into resources. However, some of his other sector picks haven't panned out, namely financial services. Leith Wheeler is beginning to garner more attention; this fund should too.																				
★★	**Leith Wheeler US Equity**	US Eq						□	□	□	□	□	D	D	10%	–15%	4/30/98	7	1.34	●
This is a poor performer in an otherwise top-notch family. A more conservatively run fund with only a tiny weighting in tech stocks.																				
★★	**Lion Knowledge Industries**	Cdn Eq					□	□	□	□	□	□	D	D	55%	–46%	6/30/96	NA	2.90	●
A hot year or two and then a big setback. That's been the story for this unique, tiny small cap fund run by Graham Henderson of Pacific Capital. There are some very dynamic companies in the portfolio.																				
★★★	**London Life Cdn Equity(L)**	Cdn Eq	□	□	□	□	□	□	□	□	□	□	B	A	23%	–27%	5/31/98	NA	2.35	●
A stellar performer, this one's leading the pack this year due to its high weighting in interest sensitive sectors. The departure of star manager Rohit Sehgal was a tough loss for unitholders of this fund, who are doing better now.																				
★★★½	**London Life Divers (L)**	Bal	□	□	□	□	□	□	□	□	□	□	B	C	14%	–11%	6/30/98	7	2.35	●
The managers add some value to this balanced fund by dabbling in foreign stocks. The fund's been held back this year because of a large exposure in bonds.																				
★★	**London Life Intl Equ (JF)**	Fgn Eq							□	□	□	□	NA	NA	21%	–14%	8/31/98	4	2.50	●
The pros at Jardine Fleming have the reins on this fund, which has been given a boost this year due to its exposure to Japanese equities.																				
★★	**London Life US Equity (L)**	US Eq	□	□	□	□	□	□	□	□	□	□	D	B	16%	–29%	10/31/89	31	2.55	●
The managers keep this fairly diversified across all sectors. This has helped during choppy markets when the fund holds up well, but it has held it back from excelling in more bullish environments.																				
★★★½	**Lotus Balanced Fund**	Bal	□	□	□	□	□	□	□	□	□	□	B	B	18%	–18%	8/31/87	23	2.00	●
Good asset allocation in addition to maintaining a foreign equities position help keep this fund competitive. A lower than average weighting in bonds is benefiting the fund this year.																				

Legend: ★ = overall past performance vs. similar funds (5 ★ max). Boxes show the quartile performance for a fund each calendar year vs. only similar funds (☐ is the best score possible). ● = high; ● = average; and ● = a fund with low expenses.

Consistency			Performance Trend										Risk						Efficiency	
Overall Past Performance	Fund Name	Type	90	91	92	93	94	95	96	97	98	Aug. '99	Up	Down	% of Time Losing $	Biggest Drop	Date	No. of Mo's to Recover	MER	
★★½	**Lotus Cdn Equity**	Cdn Eq											C	C	43%	–31%	10/31/97	NA	2.00	●
Although small caps are roaring ahead this fund has been left in the dust. The managers have missed out on some hot plays in the resource sectors.																				
★★½	**Mackenzie Sent Cda Equity**	Cdn Eq											D	B	42%	–30%	8/31/87	70	1.91	●
Lots of smaller firms and resource companies are in this portfolio. It is reasonably priced but performance has been rather erratic.																				
★★	**Mackenzie Sent Global**	Fgn Eq											D	C	35%	–33%	10/31/87	75	0.47	●
This old fund is no longer available to new money but that doesn't matter – it wasn't that good anyway.																				
★★★★	**Manulife Cabot Blue Chip**	Cdn Eq											A	D	6%	–21%	6/30/98	10	2.50	●
This is the sister fund to the Manulife Cabot Canadian Equity fund, except that this one also invests in foreign stocks.																				
★★★★	**Manulife Cabot Cdn Equity**	Cdn Eq											A	D	11%	–27%	6/30/98	12	2.50	●
Good stock-picking has provided investors in this large-cap fund with some respectable returns.																				
★★	**Manulife Cabot Cdn Growth**	Cdn Eq											C	D	37%	–36%	10/31/97	NA	2.50	●
This small cap fund is still down in the dumps, even though its peers are racing ahead. The managers have been light on the hot sectors like forestry and base metals.																				
★★	**Manulife Cabot Emerg Grth**	Cdn Eq											D	D	37%	–31%	10/31/97	NA	2.50	●
This fund invests in the Manulife Cabot Canadian Growth Fund, and also maintains a foreign equity position. But this has not helped the performance.																				
★★★	**Manulife Cabot Glo Equity**	Fgn Eq											B	C	2%	–9%	8/31/98	3	2.50	●
A healthy weighting of almost 40% in U.S. equities has no doubt given this fund its edge. Richard Crook also has lots of money in Europe, particularly the U.K.																				
★★★	**Marathon Equity Fund**	Cdn Eq											B	B	38%	–49%	10/31/97	NA	2.51	●
Wayne Deans has suffered (along with most other small cap managers) since the small cap meltdown began over two years ago although performance is up recently. Expenses are high but performance has been good in all market conditions.																				
★★	**Maritime Life Am GIF (A&C)**	US Eq											NA	NA	0%	–8%	7/31/98	3	2.55	●
A well diversified portfolio, but that doesn't necessarily mean a good portfolio. Poor performance has only been enhanced by the 2.55% MER.																				
★★★	**Maritime Life Bal (A&C)**	Bal											D	A	15%	–11%	8/31/87	14	2.45	●
Middle of the road returns for this one, although the managers at Jarislowsky Fraser have been successful in keeping the fund afloat when the market turns ugly.																				
★★★	**Maritime Life Cdn Eq (A&C)**	Cdn Eq											NA	NA	28%	–27%	5/31/98	NA	2.55	●
Richard Crowe lets his view of the macro-economy guide his stock selection. Right now he likes many of the more economically sensitive stocks.																				
★★½	**Maritime Life Div Inc (A)**	Div											NA	NA	20%	–20%	6/30/98	NA	2.10	●
Genus Capital Management runs this fund, which currently has a very high cash weighting of almost 50%. Can't be producing a very high yield after management fees are deducted.																				
★★	**Maritime Life Div Inc (C)**	Div											NA	NA	21%	–20%	6/30/98	NA	2.25	●
Essentially the same fund as the previous one except that it has a deferred fee structure and sports a higher MER.																				

Legend: ★= overall past performance vs. similar funds (5 ★ max). Boxes show the quartile performance for a fund each calendar year vs. only similar funds (☐ is the best score possible). ● = high; ● = average; and ● = a fund with low expenses.

Consistency			Performance Trend										Risk							Efficiency
Overall Past Performance	Fund Name	Type	90	91	92	93	94	95	96	97	98	Aug. '99	Up	Down	% of Time Losing $	Biggest Drop	Date	No. of Mo's to Recover		MER
★★	**Maritime Life Glo Eq (A&C)**	Fgn Eq						☐	☐	☐	☐	☐	NA	NA	0%	–15%	8/31/98	4		2.75
A big exposure to U.S. equities suggests that this fund should have a better record, but overall, it's been a poor performer. High fees don't help.																				
★★★	**Maritime Life Growth (A&C)**	Cdn Eq	☐	☐	☐	☐	☐	☐	☐	☐	☐	☐	B	B	26%	–34%	12/31/80	26		2.55
This diversified Canadian equity fund plays it safe by keeping sector weightings close in line to the TSE 300 Index.																				
★★★	**Maritime Life Pac Ba (A&C)**	Fgn Eq						☐	☐	☐	☐	☐	NA	NA	58%	–50%	8/31/97	NA		2.75
The folks at John Hancock Advisors International have produced only average returns on this fund. But even average returns this year for the Pacific Rim funds look pretty good.																				
★★★	**Maritime Life S&P500 (A&C)**	US Eq						☐	☐	☐	☐	☐	NA	NA	0%	–17%	7/31/98	4		2.20
One of the older U.S. equity index funds. But its high MER makes it difficult for this fund to match the S&P 500 returns.																				
★★½	**Mawer Canadian Equity**	Cdn Eq			☐	☐	☐	☐	☐	☐	☐	☐	C	D	31%	–25%	5/31/98	NA		1.36
Run out of Mawer's offices in Calgary. Bill MacLachlan employs a disciplined value approach to seek out large-cap bargains. Returns have been mixed, but a low MER is always a benefit.																				
★★★½	**Mawer Cdn Bal Ret Savings**	Bal	☐	☐	☐	☐	☐	☐	☐	☐	☐	☐	B	B	11%	–11%	5/31/98	13		1.07
Donald Ferris adds some zest to this fund by utilizing the foreign content room. Solid performance and a really attractive MER are a couple of reasons to consider this one.																				
★★★	**Mawer Cdn Diversified**	Bal	☐	☐	☐	☐	☐	☐	☐	☐	☐	☐	C	B	11%	–12%	5/31/98	13		1.20
Active asset allocation by the Mawer team has churned out some decent returns for investors. You'll also find foreign equities, mostly U.S., at the 20% limit.																				
★★½	**Mawer US Equity**	US Eq				☐	☐	☐	☐	☐	☐	☐	C	D	0%	–15%	7/31/98	5		1.41
This offering has really stalled this year, as large-cap stocks in general have taken a back seat to their smaller counterparts. Overall, performance doesn't stand out, and it really suffers in down markets.																				
★★★½	**Mawer World Investment**	Fgn Eq	☐	☐	☐	☐	☐	☐	☐	☐	☐	☐	A	B	5%	–17%	8/31/98	10		1.50
Admirable results for this fund, which invests outside North America. Gerald Cooper-Key currently sees the most opportunity in Europe.																				
★★★½	**MAXXUM Cdn Balanced**	Bal	☐	☐	☐	☐	☐	☐	☐	☐	☐	☐	A	C	19%	–15%	5/31/98	11		2.15
The team approach style for this fund has certainly worked out well. Currently, the fund is fully invested with a slight tilt towards equities.																				
★★★	**MAXXUM Cdn Equity Growth**	Cdn Eq	☐	☐	☐	☐	☐	☐	☐	☐	☐	☐	B	A	29%	–56%	2/28/73	78		2.15
Suave stock-picking and investing the foreign content in U.S. equities has given this fund its edge. Jackie Pratt tilts towards large caps in this fund, which holds up well in weak markets.																				
★★★½	**MAXXUM Dividend**	Div	☐	☐	☐	☐	☐	☐	☐	☐	☐	☐	B	B	15%	–22%	8/31/89	35		1.75
Jackie Pratt relies on common shares rather than preferreds to provide yield to unitholders. Results have been good and a low MER always helps.																				
★★★½	**MAXXUM Prec Metals**	Nat Res	☐	☐	☐	☐	☐	☐	☐	☐	☐	☐	A	A	43%	–74%	6/30/96	NA		2.25
Precious metals have been tough to manage over the past few years, but Martin Anstee has improved the fund's performance this year by sticking with high-quality gold companies.																				
★★½	**McDonald Asia Plus Fund**	Fgn Eq							☐	☐	☐	☐	NA	NA	47%	–41%	8/31/97	NA		2.23
This tiny fund has a large portion of its money invested in Australia and New Zealand, unusual for an Asian fund. The MER is quite low for this group and performance, until very recently, has been quite good.																				

Legend: ★ = overall past performance vs. similar funds (5 ★ max). Boxes show the quartile performance for a fund each calendar year vs. only similar funds (☐ is the best score possible). ● = high; ● = average; and ● = a fund with low expenses.

Consistency			Performance Trend										Risk						Efficiency
Overall Past Performance	Fund Name	Type	90	91	92	93	94	95	96	97	98	Aug. '99	Up	Down	% of Time Losing $	Biggest Drop	Date	No. of Mo's to Recover	MER
★★½	**McDonald Canada Plus Fund**	Bal											C	D	23%	–25%	5/31/98	NA	2.28
Usually the equity portion of a balanced fund loads up on financial services. This one likes industrial and consumer products. This one also has an above average percentage in stocks – 65%. Both of these factors have helped performance. A good fund.																			
★★½	**McDonald Emerging Econ**	Fgn Eq											NA	NA	38%	–31%	7/31/97	23	2.87
John McDonald is active with every fund in this family, but then again, he's the founder of the company. This one is heavily weighted in the interest sensitives, the banks and the utilities, so this hasn't been a standout lately.																			
★½	**McDonald Euro Plus Fund**	Fgn Eq											NA	NA	19%	–25%	8/31/98	NA	2.47
The combination of top down and bottom up approaches used by McDonald hasn't worked for this fund. Performance has been terrible.																			
★★	**McDonald New America Fund**	US Eq											NA	NA	6%	–21%	5/31/98	6	2.20
There are a lot of tech and healthcare names in this portfolio, but many of them have been the wrong names. Performance has been consistently weak.																			
★★★	**McDonald New Japan Fund**	Fgn Eq											NA	NA	72%	–39%	5/31/96	38	2.45
This fund is only available in Ontario and New Brunswick but it's a good one. A heavy dose of manufacturing companies has given the portfolio a boost. With the re-emergence of Japan's economy, look for big things from this small fund.																			
★★★½	**McLean Budden Amer Growth**	US Eq											A	B	1%	–15%	7/31/98	4	1.50
An absolute top notch fund, which sports an enviable MER. Bill Giblin has loaded the fund with big cap stocks such as IBM and Procter & Gamble.																			
★★★½	**McLean Budden Balanced**	Bal											A	C	15%	–12%	5/31/98	8	1.15
Another gem in the McLean Budden family. You'll find a big-cap mix of low P/E stocks and a conservative stance on the fixed-income side in this portfolio.																			
★★★½	**McLean Budden Equity Gth**	Cdn Eq											A	C	25%	–27%	5/31/98	NA	1.50
Lewis Jackson focuses on large caps in this offering, and avoids making big sector bets. Performance has been a little weak recently, but history suggests that it won't last long.																			
★★★½	**MD Balanced**	Bal											A	D	15%	–12%	5/31/98	NA	1.28
Gord MacDougall of Connor, Clark & Lunn is in charge here. The fund's been an above average performer, although it shows a little weakness in down markets.																			
★★★	**MD Dividend**	Div											C	C	8%	–11%	6/30/98	NA	1.29
This is a classic dividend fund, as Stephen Gerring of T.A.L. Investment Council has loaded up on preferrred shares. It makes it tough to compete in hot markets, but you'll appreciate the strategy during choppy markets.																			
★★★	**MD Equity**	Cdn Eq											C	A	26%	–33%	11/30/73	56	1.27
A multi-manager approach here with McLean Budden and QVDG making large and small cap decisions respectively, while Templeton Global Advisors are in charge of foreign equities.																			
★★★	**MD Select**	Cdn Eq											B	D	33%	–22%	5/31/98	NA	1.29
John Priestmann of Guardian Capital has the reigns on this Canadian diversified fund. He made the right call by overweighting the oil & gas sector this year. A low MER also gives investors something to cheer about.																			
★★★★	**MD US Equity**	US Eq											A	C	1%	–14%	8/31/98	3	1.27
An excellent fund, which has really capitalized on the resilient bull market in the U.S.. Too bad it's only available to doctors.																			
★	**Merrill Lynch Cdn Equity**	Cdn Eq											NA	NA	45%	–36%	10/31/97	NA	2.82
This fund has been renamed the IG AGF Canadian Growth Fund. New manager Martin Hubbes should be able to give this fund a new outlook, as its history is not pretty. Hopefully, expenses will also come down.																			

Legend: ★ = overall past performance vs. similar funds (5 ★ max). Boxes show the quartile performance for a fund each calendar year vs. only similar funds (☐ is the best score possible). ● = high; ● = average; and ● = a fund with low expenses.

Consistency			Performance Trend										Risk						Efficiency
Overall Past Performance	Fund Name	Type	90	91	92	93	94	95	96	97	98	Aug. '99	Up	Down	% of Time Losing $	Biggest Drop	Date	No. of Mo's to Recover	MER
★★★	**Merrill Lynch Emerg Mkts**	Fgn Eq											NA	NA	58%	–47%	8/31/97	NA	3.31 ● (dark)
This one now goes by the name IG Scudder Emerging Markets Growth. A heavy cash weighting of almost one-third of the fund has held back its performance over the past year.																			
★★★½	**Merrill Lynch U.S. Alloc**	Bal											NA	NA	0%	–9%	7/31/98	5	2.74 ● (light)
The fund is now known as the IG Scudder U.S.Allocation. Decent results from this strategic asset allocation fund that is focused primarily on U.S. stocks and bonds, although the managers do have a small exposure in Europe.																			
★★★	**Merrill Lynch World Alloc**	Bal											NA	NA	10%	–10%	8/31/98	4	2.80 ● (dark)
This fund now goes by the name IG Templeton World Allocation. Let's hope the new management team at Templeton can work a little magic on this mediocre performer.																			
★★★★	**MetLife MVP Asi-Pac n-RSP**	Fgn Eq											NA	NA	25%	–25%	8/31/97	21	2.85 ● (light)
Great performance here but the MER is a tad high. This is a young fund but look out if MetLife can keep up this pace.																			
★★½	**Middlefield Growth**	Nat Res											D	D	36%	–31%	10/31/97	NA	2.59 ● (light)
This is a natural resource fund that is managed by Dennis Dunlop of the Middlefield Group. Choppy performance and a high MER characterize this fund.																			
★½	**Millennia Amer Equ Ser 1**	US Eq											NA	NA	0%	–13%	8/31/98	3	3.07 ● (dark)
This fund has really been mediocre at best. Canagex runs this family of segregated funds.																			
★½	**Millennia Amer Equ Ser 2**	US Eq											NA	NA	0%	–14%	8/31/98	3	3.25 ● (dark)
Same as the previous fund, except this one is the zero commission option.																			
★★	**Millennia Cdn Bal Ser 1**	Bal											NA	NA	27%	–14%	5/31/98	NA	3.01 ● (dark)
Canagex has really failed to failed to dazzle investors with this one.																			
★★	**Millennia Cdn Bal Ser 2**	Bal											NA	NA	27%	–14%	5/31/98	NA	3.19 ● (dark)
Same as the previous fund, except this one is the zero commission option.																			
★½	**Millennia Cdn Equ Ser 1**	Cdn Eq											NA	NA	39%	–29%	5/31/98	NA	3.02 ● (dark)
A mixture of both mid and large cap stocks in this fund, which really took it on the chin last August when the fund lost 28.8% if its value.																			
★½	**Millennia Cdn Equ Ser 2**	Cdn Eq											NA	NA	39%	–29%	5/31/98	NA	3.20 ● (dark)
Same as the previous fund, except this one is the zero commission option.																			
★½	**Millennia Intl Equ Ser 1**	Fgn Eq											NA	NA	9%	–17%	8/31/98	8	3.17 ● (dark)
This fund sticks to the more mature global markets. Surprisingly, only a 6% weighting in U.S. market, while exposure to Canadian equities is at 15%.																			
★½	**Millennia Intl Equ Ser 2**	Fgn Eq											NA	NA	9%	–17%	8/31/98	8	3.35 ● (dark)
Same as the previous fund, except this one is the zero commission option.																			
★★★★½	**Montrusco Select Bal +**	Bal											A	C	9%	–10%	5/31/98	7	0.00 ● (dark)
Here's an outstanding fund that holds a large chunk of its money in other Montusco funds, all fantastic in their own right. Manager Andre Marsan has been a believer in the KISS approch, Keep It Simple Stupid, and this has paid off big time.																			

Legend: ★= overall past performance vs. similar funds (5 ★ max). Boxes show the quartile performance for a fund each calendar year vs. only similar funds (▭ is the best score possible). ● = high; ● = average; and ● = a fund with low expenses.

Consistency			Performance Trend										Risk						Efficiency
Overall Past Performance	Fund Name	Type	90	91	92	93	94	95	96	97	98	Aug. '99	Up	Down	% of Time Losing $	Biggest Drop	Date	No. of Mo's to Recover	MER
★★★½	**Montrusco Select Balanced**	Bal											A	B	9%	−11%	6/30/98	7	0.00
This fund has not been as strong as the Balanced Plus fund, but performance in both up and down markets has been good. However, like the Balanced Plus fund, fees are separate so take performance with a grain of salt.																			
★★★½	**Montrusco Select Cdn Equ**	Cdn Eq											B	C	19%	−26%	5/31/98	NA	0.00
It'll cost you $150,000 to get into this fund but the TSE 35-like portfolio has been good to manager Peter Harrison. Fees are separate here so keep that in mind when making performance judgements.																			
★★★	**Montrusco Select E.A.F.E.**	Fgn Eq											B	D	18%	−22%	8/31/90	32	0.00
This fund is almost entirely invested in Hong Kong, Japan and the US so it's surprising that performance hasn't been better. Be leery of performance because fees are paid separately.																			
★★★	**Montrusco Select Growth**	Cdn Eq											B	C	27%	−41%	10/31/97	NA	0.00
This is mainly a small to mid cap type portfolio. Manager Mark Wait uses sophisticated software to filter stocks, then screens them further with a detailed qualitative analysis.																			
★★★	**Montrusco Select NT US Eq**	US Eq											A	B	7%	−19%	6/30/90	8	0.00
An important mantra at Montrusco is that "investing is a science and an art." That's why stock analysis is done by computers and people. That method helped sniff out lots of great picks, especially in the technology sector, for this fund.																			
★★½	**Montrusco Select St US Eq**	US Eq											NA	NA	4%	−20%	5/31/98	7	0.00
A top-down approach is utilized for this fund and manager Michel Bastien especially likes industrial and consumer products. Like all Montrusco funds, howver, fees are separate.																			
★★½	**Montrusco Select Tx US Eq**	US Eq											B	C	8%	−20%	5/31/98	7	0.00
There's a minimum investment of $150,00 for this fund plus fees are paid sepatately. Performance so far this year has been great.																			
★★½	**Mutual Amerifund**	US Eq											C	C	15%	−29%	9/30/89	20	1.96
This fund has been run by Bill Onslow of Altamira since its inception in 1986. Performance has been middle of the road but its MER is low.																			
★★★	**Mutual Diversifund 40**	Bal											B	B	16%	−12%	9/30/89	18	1.77
Managed by the team at Perigee, this fund is normally ahead of its peers, although a big weighting of almost 50% in bonds (in keeping with the fund's mandate) has put a damper on its returns in 1999.																			
★★½	**Mutual Equifund**	Cdn Eq											B	C	33%	−27%	9/30/89	49	1.79
This Canadian equity fund mainly sticks to mid and large cap stocks. An overweighting in the metal and mineral sector has helped out the fund recently.																			
★★½	**Mutual Premier American**	US Eq											D	D	5%	−15%	8/31/98	4	2.28
Bill Onslow of Altamira has the reins on this one. He's loaded up the fund with large-cap household names like WalMart and Microsoft. Overall, performance has been very weak.																			
★★½	**Mutual Premier Blue Chip**	Cdn Eq											D	D	20%	−24%	6/30/98	NA	2.27
As the name suggests, you'll find companies like BCE, Nortel, and the banks in this portfolio. Results have been decent.																			
★★★½	**Mutual Premier Divers**	Bal											NA	NA	14%	−13%	6/30/98	NA	2.28
Run by the team at Perigee, this tactical asset allocation fund has produced some good numbers. Currently, the fund is biased towards equities at 60% of the fund, which includes a 10% exposure to U.S. stocks.																			
★★½	**Mutual Premier Emerging**	Fgn Eq											NA	NA	57%	−49%	8/31/97	NA	3.31
The team Morgan at Grenfell Investment Management have been hot this year capitalizing on the resurgence of emerging markets. Watch out for the fund's high MER, though.																			

Legend: ★ = overall past performance vs. similar funds (5 ★ max). Boxes show the quartile performance for a fund each calendar year vs. only similar funds (☐ is the best score possible). ● = high; ● = average; and ● = a fund with low expenses.

Consistency			Performance Trend										Risk							Efficiency	
Overall Past Performance	Fund Name	Type	90	91	92	93	94	95	96	97	98	Aug. '99	Up	Down	% of Time Losing $	Biggest Drop	Date	No. of Mo's to Recover	MER	
★★★	**Mutual Premier Growth**	Cdn Eq				☐	☐	☐	☐	☐	☐	☐	B	C	26%	–37%	10/31/97	NA	2.28	average
This fund is managed by Nancy Collins and Wayne Provost of Perigee. Stocks like Le Groupe Forex and some picks in the oil & gas sector have provided the fund with some adrenaline this year.																				
★★★	**Mutual Premier Intl**	Fgn Eq					☐	☐	☐	☐	☐	☐	B	B	10%	–15%	8/31/98	11	2.31	average
Although a 20% weighting in Japan has been beneficial for the fund this year, a small exposure to other booming Southeast Asian markets has put this fund behind its peers.																				
★★½	**NAL-Investor Cdn Divers**	Bal	☐	☐	☐	☐	☐	☐	☐	☐	☐	☐	C	C	21%	–14%	5/31/98	NA	2.40	average
A sub-par history for this balanced offering. The management team at Elliott & Page currently have the fund evenly split between fixed-income & equity.																				
★★½	**NAL-Investor Cdn Equity**	Cdn Eq	☐	☐	☐	☐	☐	☐	☐	☐	☐	☐	D	C	34%	–26%	5/31/98	NA	2.50	low
There's really a mid-cap tilt to this fund. Not a great record, but Gordon Higgins' decision to overweight oil & gas stocks has been a plus this year.																				
★★★½	**NAL-Investor Equ Growth**	Cdn Eq						☐	☐	☐	☐	☐	NA	NA	23%	–24%	5/31/98	NA	2.50	low
Enviable record for this fund, which is run by McLean Budden. Large exposure to interest-sensitive stocks has hindered the fund's returns recently, though.																				
★★★	**NAL-Investor Glo Equity**	Fgn Eq			☐	☐	☐	☐	☐	☐	☐	☐	C	D	13%	–12%	8/31/98	3	2.75	low
This fund is managed by Richard Crook out of Manulife's offices in London. Performance has picked up this year, but this fund generally has a hard time during down markets.																				
★★★	**NAL-Investor US Equity**	US Eq					☐	☐	☐	☐	☐	☐	B	C	0%	–13%	8/31/98	3	2.70	low
Goldman Sachs holds a diversified portfolio of stocks in this offering, which has an above-average history. But this fund's high MER is going to stick out like a sore thumb if the U.S. market cools off.																				
★★★½	**National Balanced**	Bal				☐	☐	☐	☐	☐	☐	☐	A	D	17%	–16%	5/31/98	NA	2.25	average
This one outperforms during good times, but falters when markets are weak.																				
★★½	**National Equities**	Cdn Eq	☐	☐	☐	☐	☐	☐	☐	☐	☐	☐	B	B	28%	–34%	11/30/73	57	2.25	average
Mike Weir adds a mid-cap bias to this fund. A higher than average resource component, which hurt the fund last year, is now paying off.																				
★★★	**National Global Equities**	Fgn Eq	☐	☐	☐	☐	☐	☐	☐	☐	☐	☐	B	A	12%	–19%	8/31/90	17	2.65	average
This fund invests entirely into the Martin Currie International Growth Fund, which is managed by James Fairweather.																				
★★½	**Navigator American Growth**	US Eq							☐	☐	☐	☐	NA	NA	3%	–20%	5/31/98	7	2.99	low
This fund invests mainly in small and mid cap US companies. Manager Alfred Lockwood looks at companies in industries that he believes will outperform.																				
★★	**Navigator American Value**	US Eq							☐	☐	☐	☐	NA	NA	0%	–10%	8/31/98	3	2.99	low
Anthony Brown of Roxbury Captal Management has a bias towards technology stocks in this one.																				
★★★★	**Navigator Asia-Pacific**	Fgn Eq							☐	☐	☐	☐	NA	NA	38%	–46%	7/31/97	NA	3.01	low
While this fund's large bet on Hong Kong benefited the fund a few years back, it has missed out recently on some of the action in the smaller Southeast Asian markets.																				
★★½	**Navigator Cdn Focused Gth**	Cdn Eq				☐	☐	☐	☐	☐	☐	☐	B	D	36%	–47%	10/31/97	NA	2.99	low
This small cap portfolio, managed by Deans Knight Capital Management, really does well when resources are hot. The fund is one-third invested in oil & gas sector, which has given the fund a boost lately.																				

Legend: ★ = overall past performance vs. similar funds (5 ★ max). Boxes show the quartile performance for a fund each calendar year vs. only similar funds (□ is the best score possible). ● = high; ○ = average; and ● = a fund with low expenses.

Consistency			Performance Trend										Risk						Efficiency
Overall Past Performance	Fund Name	Type	90	91	92	93	94	95	96	97	98	Aug. '99	Up	Down	% of Time Losing $	Biggest Drop	Date	No. of Mo's to Recover	MER
★★★	**NN Asset Allocation**	Bal	□	□	□	□	□	□	□	□	□	□	B	B	15%	–11%	6/30/98	7	2.65 ●
	Ted Gibson of RT Capital Mangement actively manages the asset mix of this portfolio, with some good results. He provides a little extra zest to this segregated fund by utilizing the allowable foreign content.																		
★★½	**NN Can-Am**	US Eq				□	□	□	□	□	□	□	C	D	6%	–16%	7/31/98	4	2.65 ●
	Although its name doesn't suggest it, this is an index fund that tries to replicate the performance of the S&P 500 Index by investing in futures contracts.																		
★★★	**NN Can-Asian**	Fgn Eq					□	□	□	□	□	□	D	A	53%	–46%	8/31/97	NA	2.65 ○
	David Patterson of Newcastle Capital Management has a done a great job of beating his peers through a strategy of investing in Southeast Asia solely through index futures. Thus, the fund is fully RRSP eligible.																		
★★★½	**NN Can-Euro**	Fgn Eq							□	□	□	□	NA	NA	11%	–22%	8/31/98	NA	2.65 ●
	Country selection is the key decision for David Patterson in this RRSP-eligible fund. He's done a decent job of investing in the index futures of European markets.																		
★★½	**NN Canadian 35 Index**	Cdn Eq	□	□	□	□	□	□	□	□	□	□	C	D	31%	–28%	6/30/98	NA	2.00 ○
	The goal of this fund is to mimic the returns of TSE 35 Index. Its MER is very high even for a segregated index fund.																		
★★	**NN Canadian Growth**	Cdn Eq	□	□	□	□	□	□	□	□	□	□	D	A	24%	–27%	8/31/87	71	2.80 ●
	Performance has not been convincing for this diversified Canadian equity fund, although it holds up well in down markets.																		
★★★	**NN Dividend**	Div						□	□	□	□	□	B	D	22%	–14%	5/31/98	NA	2.60 ●
	Christian Langevin of ING Capital Management has this fund evenly split between common and perferred shares. It's been a below average performer and its high MER doesn't help.																		
★★	**NN Elite**	Spec Eq						□	□	□	□	□	NA	NA	26%	–17%	6/30/98	NA	2.30 ●
	This is a unique fund in Canada, managed by Newcastle. It's a fund of hedge funds, so you get some heavy expenses on this offering.																		
★★★	**Northwest Balanced Fund**	Bal							□	□	□	□	NA	NA	10%	–15%	5/31/98	11	2.85 ●
	This fund has managed to do okay despite its sky high MER. Richard Fogler of Kingwest & Co. presently has a bias towards equities, which has benefited the fund this year.																		
★★★½	**Northwest Dividend**	Div						□	□	□	□	□	NA	NA	27%	–23%	4/30/98	NA	2.54 ●
	This one's a mixed bag of common and preferred shares, income trusts and bonds. Returns have been weak the past few years.																		
★★★	**Northwest Growth Fund**	Cdn Eq				□	□	□	□	□	□	□	B	D	21%	–22%	5/31/98	14	2.85 ●
	Richard Folger manages this one with a mid-cap tilt. His decision to overweight the fund with oil and gas stocks has really worked out well.																		
★★★	**Northwest International**	Fgn Eq							□	□	□	□	NA	NA	0%	–14%	8/31/98	7	3.08 ●
	Good country selection by the U.S. investment management firm Oppenheimer has really given this fund a boost over the past few years. But beware of this fund's high MER.																		
★½	**O'Donnell Amer Sector Gro**	US Eq							□	□	□	□	NA	NA	19%	–14%	7/31/98	3	2.98 ●
	Elaine Garzarelli is a pretty big name around Wall Street these days but her performance with this fund has been lacking. High expenses don't help the case.																		
★★★★	**O'Donnell Canadian Fund**	Cdn Eq									□	□	NA	NA	82%	–26%	5/31/98	NA	2.81 ●
	Manager Glen Inamoto follows a "growth at a reasonable price" philosophy. He generally sticks to TSE 35-type companies and so far his tenure as manager has been quite successful.																		

Legend: ★ = overall past performance vs. similar funds (5 ★ max). Boxes show the quartile performance for a fund each calendar year vs. only similar funds (☐ is the best score possible). ● = high; ● = average; and ● = a fund with low expenses.

Consistency			Performance Trend										Risk							Efficiency
Overall Past Performance	Fund Name	Type	90	91	92	93	94	95	96	97	98	Aug. '99	Up	Down	% of Time Losing $	Biggest Drop	Date	No. of Mo's to Recover		MER
★½	**O'Donnell Cdn Emering Gro**	Cdn Eq							2	4	4	2	NA	NA	63%	–48%	10/31/97	NA		2.81
The management team takes a bottom up approach for this fund and tries to sift out smaller, lesser known companies with good growth rates. Like all O'Donnell funds, this one is bordering on very expensive.																				
★★★	**O'Donnell Growth Fund**	Cdn Eq							2	3	3	4	NA	NA	38%	–38%	10/31/97	NA		2.81
This fund can hold a maximum of 50 names so the impact of individual stocks can be quite significant. Holdings include non-bank financials, oil and gas companies and niche manufacturers.																				
★★★★	**O'Donnell Select Fund**	Cdn Eq									2	1	NA	NA	64%	–23%	5/31/98	NA		2.80
Mainly a big cap fund, there are a few small and mid cap names scattered throughout the portfolio. Performance has been excellent over the brief history of the fund but be aware of how much you're paying for this one.																				
★★	**O'Donnell U.S. Mid-Cap**	US Eq							4	1	4	2	NA	NA	0%	–14%	7/31/98	6		2.99
Performance of this fund has been very inconsistent but manager Marc Gabelli's father is a superstar in the US so unit holders can hope stock-picking is genetic. The MER on this one is quite high.																				
★★★½	**O.I.Q. FERIQUE American**	US Eq								1	1	4	NA	NA	3%	–16%	1/31/99	NA		0.47
This is a U.S. index fund, which aims to mimic the performance of the S&P 500 Index. A really competitive MER makes this fund a great choice for passive investors.																				
★★★½	**O.I.Q. FERIQUE Balanced**	Bal	1	1	4	2	1	2	2	1	1	4	A	A	11%	–15%	6/30/81	16		0.55
Guy Normandin of TAL Global Asset Management has the reins on this offering. It's achieved its banner history by outperforming in all market conditions.																				
★★★	**O.I.Q. FERIQUE Equity**	Cdn Eq	3	1	2	3	1	2	3	3	2	3	B	B	23%	–41%	6/30/81	22		0.56
The duo management team of PH&N and Natcan Investment Management have posted some pretty solid returns on this fund. The fund remains well diversified by sector, while some foreign investing, mainly in U.S. equities, adds a little pizzazz to the fund.																				
★★	**O.I.Q. FERIQUE Growth**	Cdn Eq								4	1	1	NA	NA	38%	–24%	6/30/98	10		0.69
This diversified Canadian equity fund has had some top-notch results under the direction of Denis Ouellet of TAL Global Asset Management. Its really low expenses warrants this one some consideration.																				
★★★	**O.I.Q. FERIQUE Intl**	Fgn Eq					3	4	3	1	1	4	B	A	23%	–15%	1/31/99	NA		0.76
This is a fully RSP eligible fund, which invests in the index futures of countries represented in the MSCI World Indicies. The managers don't attempt to match the performance of this index, but rather add value through strategic country weightings.																				
★★★	**Optima Strat Cdn Equity**	Cdn Eq	4	4	3	4	2	1	1	1	3	3	B	A	22%	–26%	8/31/87	23		0.40
Optima Strategy recently reduced its fees somewhat, but not enough to keep it from being the country's most expensive wrap program, in most cases.																				
★★★	**Optima Strat Intl Equity**	Fgn Eq						3	1	4	4	3	B	D	16%	–19%	8/31/98	NA		0.48
Despite the new fee structure, investors can still end up paying as much as 3.2% to 3.6% per year in this wrap program. In 1998, average fees charged to Optima clients totaled 3.4% of assets!																				
★★★★	**Optima Strat US Equity**	US Eq						1	1	1	1	4	A	C	0%	–11%	8/31/98	2		0.40
You cannot buy this fund on its own, only as a part of Optima Strategy's wrap program. Published returns are overstated due to the direct billing of management fees. The stated MER here only includes operating expenses.																				
★★★	**Optimum Balanced**	Bal	3	2	2	3	3	1	4	3	2	2	C	B	10%	–10%	2/28/94	14		1.46
This is a bond-heavy balanced fund which has had decent performance overall and it is relatively inexpensive. Exposure to the US market is attained through the use of derivatives.																				

Legend: ★ = overall past performance vs. similar funds (5 ★ max). Boxes show the quartile performance for a fund each calendar year vs. only similar funds (☐ is the best score possible). ● = high; ● = average; and ● = a fund with low expenses.

Consistency: Overall Past Performance	Fund Name	Type	Risk: Up	Risk: Down	% of Time Losing $	Biggest Drop	Date	No. of Mo's to Recover	Efficiency: MER	Comment
★★★	**Optimum Equity**	Cdn Eq	A	D	22%	–23%	5/31/98	NA	1.62	This fund is a great performer and has done well with its picks from the TSE 35. Up market performance has rocked while the fund has been rocked in down markets.
★★★	**Optimum International**	Fgn Eq	NA	NA	6%	–11%	8/31/98	3	1.96	Not really a tough formula for this fund – buy index futures for markets all over the globe and complement those with some quality stocks. This formula has reaped only modest performance, however.
★★★½	**Orbit North Amer Equity**	Fgn Eq	NA	NA	3%	–14%	6/30/98	6	2.65	This fund, only available in Ontario and Quebec, invests mainly in huge North American multinationals. Performance has dropped off a bit so far this year.
★★½	**Orbit World**	Fgn Eq	C	A	19%	–14%	11/30/94	29	2.65	David Marvin has amassed a well diversified portfolio that includes everything from American Internet stocks to Japanese electronics firms. The fund is an excellent performer in down markets.
★★★	**OTG Investment Balanced**	Bal	B	B	10%	–11%	6/30/98	10	1.00	For Ontario teachers, this is a decent-performing, low fee, one-decision fund which earns good grades for performance in bull and bear markets.
★★½	**OTG Investment Divers**	Cdn Eq	C	A	23%	–27%	4/30/81	20	1.00	This well established fund has had a pretty respectable run. It's cheap and it invests in Canada's biggest and best companies. Definitely a solid holding for any teacher who may own it.
★★	**OTG Investment Global Val**	Fgn Eq	D	C	3%	–8%	7/31/98	3	1.00	The majority of the names in theis portfolio are lesser known, but still large, companies from Asia and Europe. Performance has not been special even though fees are quite low.
★★★	**OTG Investment Growth**	Cdn Eq	C	A	26%	–29%	8/31/81	16	1.00	A solid big cap equity fund that has a good mix of financial services and technology companies. Susan Blanchard has done an excellent job with this one and a super low MER adds to the appeal.
★★★★	**PH&N Balanced**	Bal	A	D	4%	–13%	5/31/98	8	0.88	Three reasons to buy this fund: 1) It's been an awesome performer; 2) Fees are obscenely low for a balanced fund; 3) PH&N is a top-notch firm. The only catch is that you'll need at least $10,000 to get in (RRSP).
★★★	**PH&N Canadian Equity**	Cdn Eq	A	A	27%	–43%	11/30/73	52	1.07	Really a well diversified fund with industrial products and financial services taking up 45% of the mix. It has been a stellar performer in both up and down markets and the MER is dirt cheap.
★★★	**PH&N Canadian Equity Plus**	Cdn Eq	A	A	25%	–42%	11/30/73	56	1.16	This is the same fund as the Canadian Equity fund, except that its mandate allows it to include some foreign stocks (of course, only up to 20% of the portfolio).
★★★½	**PH&N Cdn Equ Plus Pens Tr**	Cdn Eq	A	A	21%	–37%	11/30/73	49	0.51	Virtually the same as the Canadian Equity Plus fund except this is the pooled version. It is hard to find a Canadian equity portfolio this inexpensive. Bear and bull market performance has been top notch.
★★★	**PH&N Dividend Income**	Div	C	A	13%	–22%	6/30/98	NA	1.13	Taking an edgier approach to dividend funds, PH&N had put significant dollars into oil companies and other non-typical "dividend" stocks. Performance has dropped off a bit this year but historical figures are awesome.
★★½	**PH&N Euro-Pacific Equity**	Fgn Eq	NA	NA	6%	–14%	8/31/98	4	1.39	Dominated by Japan and the UK, this fund has investments scattered mainly throughout Asia and western Europe. It's pretty cheap but performance has been stagnant.

Legend: ★ = overall past performance vs. similar funds (5 ★ max). Boxes show the quartile performance for a fund each calendar year vs. only similar funds (□ is the best score possible). ● = high; ○ = average; and ● = a fund with low expenses.

Consistency			Performance Trend										Risk						Efficiency
Overall Past Performance	Fund Name	Type	90	91	92	93	94	95	96	97	98	Aug. '99	Up	Down	% of Time Losing $	Biggest Drop	Date	No. of Mo's to Recover	MER
★★½	**PH&N N.A. Equity**	Fgn Eq				□	□	□	□	□	□	□	D	D	33%	–27%	5/31/98	NA	1.16 ●
This fund has an interesting mix of mid caps and mega-caps. Three quarters of the holdings are from the US with the rest being from Canada and Mexico. Performance hasn't impressed but it's cheap.																			
★★★½	**PH&N US Equity**	US Eq	□	□	□	□	□	□	□	□	□	□	A	A	16%	–43%	10/31/73	27	1.11 ●
This fund has been around for 35 years but it is still chugging along. Good picks in the technology and financial services sector have helped. Performance in both up and down markets has been stellar.																			
★★★½	**PH&N US Pooled Pension**	US Eq	□	□	□	□	□	□	□	□	□	□	A	A	17%	–49%	5/31/72	61	0.00 ●
This fund isn't free, but it's cheap. It's the pooled verion of the US equity fund. Performance numbers are quite good and they've been excellent in all market conditions.																			
★★★★	**PH&N Vintage Fund**	Cdn Eq	□	□	□	□	□	□	□	□	□	□	A	A	20%	–29%	8/31/87	23	1.73 ●
This fund was closed in 1993 so consider yourself lucky if you got in before that. Its investment mantra – select firms with above average growth prospects – has paid off well for unitholders.																			
★★★	**Principal International**	Fgn Eq	□	□	□	□	□	□	□	□	□	□	A	D	21%	–21%	5/31/98	NA	0.75 ●
A definite winner in up markets but its bear market performance is downright awful. However, a low MER makes a strong case for this little fund.																			
★★	**Pursuit Canadian Equity**	Cdn Eq	□	□	□	□	□	□	□	□	□	□	D	A	28%	–35%	9/30/87	69	1.50 ●
This fund is only available in Ontario. Over 40% of the money is in industrial products companies, a sector that includes technology. Up market performance has been poor while the fund has done well in down markets.																			
★★½	**Pursuit Global Equity**	Fgn Eq							□	□	□	□	NA	NA	19%	–17%	8/31/98	NA	1.75 ○
What initially appeared to be a great fund has really sputtered over the last two years. Many of the companies in the portfolio are large firms, mainly from Japan and Europe, but they are still unknown here in Canada.																			
★★½	**Pursuit Growth Fund**	Fgn Eq	□	□	□	□	□	□	□	□	□	□	D	A	17%	–18%	7/31/87	24	1.75 ●
Performance for this tiny offering has been all over the map. It's big into technology but right now a third of the fund is in cash. Of course, this can be a good or bad thing depending on market performance.																			
★★½	**Quebec Growth Fund Inc.**	Cdn Eq	□	□	□	□	□	□	□	□	□	□	B	B	33%	–74%	5/31/87	108	2.00 ●
This well established fund has had up and down performance. It's managed by Montrusco and offers a good mix of large and small companies.																			
★★½	**Quebec Prof Balanced**	Bal	□	□	□	□	□	□	□	□	□	□	D	A	2%	–7%	2/28/94	13	0.95 ●
This balanced fund has very conservative asset mix constraints. Up markets have not been kind to it but it has fared will in bear markets. The MER is quite low for this fund type.																			
★★★	**Quebec Prof Cdn Equity**	Cdn Eq	□	□	□	□	□	□	□	□	□	□	B	C	29%	–24%	5/31/98	NA	0.95 ●
Performance for this one has really picked up lately. Fees are way below those for the average Canadian equity fund, a quality that certainly adds to its appeal.																			
★★★	**Quebec Prof Growth & Inc.**	Bal						□	□	□	□	□	NA	NA	15%	–11%	5/31/98	NA	0.95 ●
Average overall performance is the result of this fund's flexible mandate to allow greater stock content. Low fees are a plus in this category.																			
★★½	**Quebec Prof Intl Equity**	Fgn Eq			□	□	□	□	□	□	□	□	C	C	1%	–11%	8/31/97	7	1.25 ○
Performance has been generally average over the life of this fund but it has picked up so far in 1999. The portfolio is very diversified with the biggest holding being Fonds Actions Asian Equity fund.																			
★★	**RCC Euro Fund**	Fgn Eq				□	□	□	□	□	□	□	D	B	13%	–25%	8/31/98	NA	9.79 ●
Stay away from this fund. Its MER of almost 10% should be against the law. Compound that with below average returns and you almost have the makings for a guaranteed money loser.																			

Legend: ★ = overall past performance vs. similar funds (5 ★ max). Boxes show the quartile performance for a fund each calendar year vs. only similar funds (□ is the best score possible). ● = high; ● = average; and ● = a fund with low expenses.

Consistency			Performance Trend										Risk						Efficiency
Overall Past Performance	Fund Name	Type	90	91	92	93	94	95	96	97	98	Aug. '99	Up	Down	% of Time Losing $	Biggest Drop	Date	No. of Mo's to Recover	MER
★★	**REA Inc Investiss IDEM**	Cdn Eq											D	C	32%	–19%	5/31/98	NA	2.28
This fund is concentrated in merchandising and consumer products companies. Performance in both up and down markets has been below average.																			
★★★½	**Resolute Growth**	Cdn Eq											B	B	45%	–30%	5/31/98	NA	2.00
Manager Tom Stanley has had some good numbers lately thanks to excellent small-cap selection. It's only available in B.C., Alberta, and Ontario.																			
★★★½	**Retrocom Growth LSVCC**	Spec Eq											NA	NA	5%	–1%	6/30/95	16	4.17
This fund is a rare bird in the LSIF community as it focuses on the construction industry. It gets into projects at the mezzanine level to mitigate some risk. Provincial tax credits are available in Ontario and Nova Scotia.																			
★★★	**Royal & SunAll Balanced**	Bal											B	D	15%	–12%	6/30/98	NA	2.30
This fund has shown middle of the road performance with above average results in bullish environments. Bonds make up about 55% of the portfolio and manager John Smolinski never puts more than 5% into one asset class.																			
★★½	**Royal & SunAll Cdn Growth**	Cdn Eq											NA	NA	28%	–38%	10/31/97	NA	2.35
This one invests in companies with market caps of under $350 million so there are some tiny firms in this fund. Things are finally starting to improve but time will tell whether this fund has really changed for the better.																			
★★★	**Royal & SunAll Equity**	Cdn Eq											A	B	16%	–23%	5/31/98	14	2.30
John Smolinski, manager of this well performing fund, takes a bottom-up approach to stock selection. He only buys companies that he feels will perform well over the next two or three years.																			
★★★	**Royal & SunAll Intl Equ**	Fgn Eq											NA	NA	2%	–14%	8/31/98	4	2.60
This fund is somewhat unique in that it invests heavily in warrants and income trusts. These holdings haven't made the fund into a star, but it is definitely good.																			
★★	**Royal Asian Growth**	Fgn Eq											A	D	63%	–58%	1/31/94	NA	2.97
This fund invests throughout Asia, excluding Japan, and focuses on emerging economies. Its six-year history has been shaky and a very high MER doesn't help much. Nearly a third is in financial services.																			
★★★	**Royal Balanced**	Bal											C	B	13%	–12%	5/31/98	NA	2.20
Lead Manager Mark Arthur has really diversified this conservative offering. It has not been a spectacular performer but with $7.4 billion in assets this fund is one of Canada's largest.																			
★★★	**Royal Canadian Equity**	Cdn Eq											A	A	28%	–43%	12/31/80	29	1.97
Really about as large cap of a fund as you can get with Canadian companies, this one has been a decent performer with top marks in up and down markets. John Embry has really gone all out on the diversification front.																			
★★	**Royal Canadian Growth**	Cdn Eq											D	C	33%	–32%	10/31/97	NA	2.27
The names are generally small to mid-cap for this fund and returns have also been generally small. There's a load of cash available and hopefully manager Eden Rahim can use it to pick some winners.																			
★★	**Royal Cdn Small Cap**	Cdn Eq											D	D	40%	–37%	10/31/97	NA	2.27
This has really been a rotten fund since inception. Manager Elizabeth Cheung was brought in during late 1997 and she has helped in the resucitation process. It performed better than half of its peers in 1998.																			
★★★★½	**Royal Dividend Fund**	Div											A	D	15%	–20%	6/30/98	NA	1.75
Financial services, utilities and pipelines make up nearly 60% of this offering but what do you expect from a dividend fund. It's certainly a great fund and even with a conservative mandate there have been some big winners.																			
★★★½	**Royal Energy**	Nat Res											A	B	46%	–52%	10/31/97	NA	2.34
Due to its narrow focus on the oil and gas industry, this fund's returns tend to be either hot or cold. Good candidate for a PAC plan. Lately, with the jump in oil and gas prices it's been red-hot.																			

Legend: ★ = overall past performance vs. similar funds (5 ★ max). Boxes show the quartile performance for a fund each calendar year vs. only similar funds (☐ is the best score possible). ● = high; ● = average; and ● = a fund with low expenses.

Consistency			Performance Trend										Risk						Efficiency
Overall Past Performance	Fund Name	Type	90	91	92	93	94	95	96	97	98	Aug. '99	Up	Down	% of Time Losing $	Biggest Drop	Date	No. of Mo's to Recover	MER
★★★½	**Royal European Growth**	Fgn Eq		☐	☐	☐	☐	☐	☐	☐	☐	☐	D	C	21%	–30%	9/30/87	71	2.48
Quality growth companies are the focus of this fund. It places emphasis on the larger markets of Europe and the mandate has paid off well as of late. Neglecting the smaller European markets held performance back previously.																			
★★½	**Royal Intl Equity**	Fgn Eq					☐	☐	☐	☐	☐	☐	C	B	9%	–15%	8/31/98	11	2.63
Having hardly any dough in Asia has put a dent into performance. Since inception, this fund has had only one good year so looking for a better international fund probably wouldn't be such a bad idea.																			
★★½	**Royal Japanese Stock**	Fgn Eq				☐	☐	☐	☐	☐	☐	☐	C	C	52%	–48%	5/31/88	73	2.63
This portfolio is mainly large cap corporations with a smattering of small caps. It's hard to consider a fund that has a ten-year compounded return of nearly zero but that's the story with most Japanese funds.																			
★★	**Royal Latin American**	Fgn Eq							☐	☐	☐	☐	NA	NA	38%	–31%	10/31/97	NA	2.99
A quarter of this fund is in foreign debt thus making it similar to a balanced fund. Most of the remainder is invested in Mexico and Brazil. Take a look at the calendar year returns – a model of inconsistency.																			
★★★	**Royal LePage Comm Real Es**	Real						☐	☐	☐	☐	☐	NA	NA	40%	–13%	6/30/98	NA	3.40
This is one of the few real estate funds remaining that actually has direct ownership of commercial properties so really it's an open-ended REIT.																			
★★½	**Royal Life Science & Tech**	Spec Eq							☐	☐	☐	☐	NA	NA	5%	–19%	10/31/97	13	2.74
Jim Young has no problem holding tons of cash, like when he had 30% this summer. Time will tell if that was a good idea but history shows that this has been an average performer.																			
★★★½	**Royal Precious Metals**	Nat Res	☐	☐	☐	☐	☐	☐	☐	☐	☐	☐	A	B	49%	–64%	6/30/96	NA	2.53
If you had invested $1000 in this fund three years ago, you'd have just under $700 today. Ouch! Don't blame John Embry for gold's decline. He's a super manager and when gold heats up, watch out.																			
★★★	**Royal Trust Adv Balanced**	Bal	☐	☐	☐	☐	☐	☐	☐	☐	☐	☐	C	A	16%	–12%	5/31/98	14	1.97
John Kellet makes the asset mix decisions on this fund of funds. Currently, the portfolio contains slightly more equities than bonds.																			
★★★	**Royal Trust Adv Growth**	Bal	☐	☐	☐	☐	☐	☐	☐	☐	☐	☐	C	B	19%	–17%	9/30/87	20	2.18
There's about a 65/35 split between equities and bonds for this fund that holds Royal Bank funds exclusively.																			
★★★	**Royal Trust Adv Income**	Bal	☐	☐	☐	☐	☐	☐	☐	☐	☐	☐	D	A	4%	–7%	2/28/94	15	1.81
The Royal Bank bond fund dominates this one with a 40% chunk. The mortgage fund gets 21% and so does the Canadian equity fund. Manager John Kellet is obviously playing the markets conservatively.																			
★★½	**Royal U.S. Equity Fund C$**	US Eq	☐	☐	☐	☐	☐	☐	☐	☐	☐	☐	C	A	17%	–54%	2/28/73	65	2.11
Big holder of American multinationals, with consumer goods making up a third of the portfolio. This is the type of fund that you would expect to grow as the US economy grows.																			
★★★	**Royal U.S. RSP Index**	US Eq										☐	NA	NA		–3%	2/28/99	1	0.50
50bps gets you into this State Street-managed RRSP-eligible US equity index fund. The index in this case is the S&P 500.																			
★★½	**Saxon Balanced Fund**	Bal	☐	☐	☐	☐	☐	☐	☐	☐	☐	☐	C	C	28%	–26%	4/30/87	70	1.75
It appears as though Rick Howson has finally started to turn around this well diversified fund. A low MER helps make an impressive case for this one.																			
★★½	**Saxon Small Cap**	Cdn Eq	☐	☐	☐	☐	☐	☐	☐	☐	☐	☐	C	B	29%	–28%	9/30/89	42	1.75
Bob Tattersall selects smaller small caps than most in this category and this increased risk can enhance returns. Performance rocked in 1997, 1998 and has been excellent so far in 1999.																			

Legend: ★ = overall past performance vs. similar funds (5 ★ max). Boxes show the quartile performance for a fund each calendar year vs. only similar funds (☐ is the best score possible). ● = high; ● = average; and ● = a fund with low expenses.

Consistency			Performance Trend										Risk						Efficiency
Overall Past Performance	Fund Name	Type	90	91	92	93	94	95	96	97	98	Aug. '99	Up	Down	% of Time Losing $	Biggest Drop	Date	No. of Mo's to Recover	MER
★★½	**Saxon Stock Fund**	Cdn Eq											C	C	32%	–29%	4/30/87	71	1.75
Not your typical Canadian equity fund. There are lots of resource stocks and plenty of smaller names. Performance has been nothing to write home about until very recently but the MER has always been relatively low.																			
★★★½	**Saxon World Growth**	Fgn Eq											A	C	26%	–32%	6/30/89	31	1.75
Bob Tattersall is famous for his fundamental value approach and apparently he has found some great buys in the US, a component that makes up half of the fund. Note his rotation into Japan this year.																			
★★★½	**Sceptre Balanced Growth**	Bal											A	B	14%	–14%	5/31/98	NA	1.46
Lyle Stein is a star but this fund has lagged way behind the competition – even with its super low MER. That's probably because his value approach hasn't been in vogue lately.																			
★★★½	**Sceptre Equity Growth**	Cdn Eq											A	B	27%	–35%	10/31/97	NA	1.44
The fund is cheap, holds up well in tough markets, recovers fast from drops, and offers big long term gains. Performance recently has been slow but Allan Jacobs is a winner and it's a good idea to stick with him.																			
★★★½	**Sceptre International**	Fgn Eq											A	A	20%	–26%	9/30/87	19	2.09
We keep saying he will, but manager Lennox McNeely has not yet been able to pull this fund from out of the doldrums. Hopefully a doubled up focus on stock selection will give performance a shot in the arm.																			
★★	**Scotia Amer Growth**	US Eq											D	B	19%	–36%	9/30/87	68	2.07
This fund has had ho-hum performance historically. It is currently heavy in technology stocks and two of the top ten names are oil companies. Even though this one's no-load, I'd look elsewhere for an American fund.																			
★★★★	**Scotia Canadian Balanced**	Bal											NA	NA	0%	–11%	7/31/98	6	1.65
The management team at Scotia Cassels has done a spectacular job with this one. It is virtual 50/50 split between stocks and bonds and the latter asset class has added tons of value.																			
★★★	**Scotia CanAm Stk Index**	US Eq											B	D	2%	–16%	7/31/98	4	1.34
This index fund holds a combination of S&P futures contracts and Canadian T-bills in order to make it RRSP eligible. Buy it if you're a skeptic of active management but never expect to exceed the S&P's returns.																			
★★	**Scotia Cdn Bluechip**	Cdn Eq											D	C	29%	–28%	8/31/87	50	1.91
The stock holdings of this fund are very, very similar to those of the balanced fund and many of them have been big winners so far this year. Dismal historical performance has hurt the rating but this one's turning around.																			
★★★	**Scotia Cdn Growth**	Cdn Eq											B	A	29%	–31%	11/30/73	53	2.09
This fund has been in existence for nearly forty years and it's been a decent performer. Down market performance has been excellent and plans to further concentrate the portfolio should increase the importance of stock selection.																			
★★½	**Scotia Intl Growth Fund**	Fgn Eq											C	B	12%	–27%	9/30/87	44	2.23
Manager Montrusco has put 50% of this fund's money into a diversified US portfolio. Having only 15% in Asia, however, has held performance numbers back so far this year.																			
★★★★	**Scotia Latin Amer**	Fgn Eq											NA	NA	35%	–42%	8/31/97	NA	2.39
This well performing fund is managed in-house and the team has invested almost half of the assets into Mexico. A relatively large chunk of cash is available for use when good buys are found.																			
★★★½	**Scotia Pacific Rim**	Fgn Eq											NA	NA	41%	–41%	8/31/97	NA	2.43
55% of this fund is in Japan, a big winner this year, and the rest is spread all over Asia. Despite the rally in that part of the world, however, this one has lagged its peers lately.																			
★★	**Scotia Prec Metals**	Nat Res											C	D	67%	–68%	6/30/96	NA	2.19
Everyone knows about the recent decline in gold and this fund has fared just as poorly as any similar fund, if not worse. The portfolio is highly concentrated with the top five holdings making up almost 40% of the fund.																			

Legend: ★ = overall past performance vs. similar funds (5 ★ max). Boxes show the quartile performance for a fund each calendar year vs. only similar funds (▀ is the best score possible). ● = high; ● = average; and ● = a fund with low expenses.

Consistency			Performance Trend										Risk						Efficiency	
Overall Past Performance	Fund Name	Type	90	91	92	93	94	95	96	97	98	Aug. '99	Up	Down	% of Time Losing $	Biggest Drop	Date	No. of Mo's to Recover	MER	
★★★½	**Scotia Total Return**	Bal	1	1	1	1	4	3	3	2	2	4	A	B	14%	–13%	5/31/98	14	2.27	●
This more actively managed balanced fund has had good success over the years, with above average marks in bull markets. The bond portfolio's duration is quite high so look for enhanced gains or losses.																				
★★★★	**Scudder Greater Europe**	Fgn Eq							1	2	1	2	NA	NA	9%	–20%	8/31/98	NA	2.00	●
The managers of this low-cost fund have decided to stick to high-quality growth companies, mainly from western Europe. This should make for good returns in the future without too much undue risk.																				
★★★★	**Scudder Pacific**	Fgn Eq							4	1	1	4	NA	NA	47%	–39%	8/31/97	22	2.00	●
Here's a fund that blows the competition away. Maybe because it's well diversified all over Asia or maybe the bottom-up approach taken by the management team simply kicks butt, but whatever the reason, it's cheap and has performed well.																				
★★½	**Spec United Amer Equity**	US Eq	3	3	3	4	4	1	1	4	2	3	C	A	22%	–40%	2/28/73	73	2.31	●
The team at MFS Institutional Advisors from Boston has managed to pick up the performance since taking over the fund in 1995. A portion of the fund is devoted to smaller names, but the big focus is on large-cap stocks.																				
★★★	**Spec United Amer Gro C$**	US Eq	4	1	1	1	1	1	3	3	1	3	A	A	15%	–59%	2/28/73	78	2.41	●
John Ballen and Toni Shimura of MFS Institutional Advisors put this fund back on track in 1998 after trailing its peers for a few years. This fund's managed to outperform in choppy markets by diversified the portfolio with 299 holdings.																				
★★½	**Spec United Asian Dynasty**	Fgn Eq					2	2	3	3	4	1	A	D	68%	–54%	5/31/96	NA	2.67	●
Overall, this one's been a poor performer, faring terribly in down markets. Managers Chris Burn and Barry Dugan of MFS Institutional Advisors employ a bottom-up stock picking approach, with country allocation a by-product of the process.																				
★★½	**Spec United Asset Alloc**	Bal	3	4	3	3	3	3	4	2	2	3	D	C	15%	–13%	6/30/98	NA	2.26	●
This fund's dismal performance record has experienced a turnaround since David DeGase of AMI Partners took the reins in late 1996. The portfolio is presently positioned with 38% in both Canadian equities and bonds, with foreign content at 20%.																				
★★★½	**Spec United Cdn Bal Port**	Bal	2	2	2	1	3	1	3	3	3	3	A	C	17%	–14%	5/31/98	NA	2.20	●
This is a fund of funds which has done well from good positioning in Spectrum's Canadian bond and equity offerings.																				
★★★½	**Spec United Cdn Equity**	Cdn Eq	2	1	1	1	2	3	2	3	3	3	A	A	27%	–36%	11/30/73	57	2.41	●
While Kiki Delaney's departure is a blow to the fund, newly appointed managers Brian Dawson and Susan Shuter of McLean Budden are no slouches. They use both a growth and value approach, in addition to a concentrating on large-cap equities.																				
★★★	**Spec United Cdn Growth**	Cdn Eq	4	2	3	2	1	1	4	3	4	3	A	A	29%	–45%	2/28/73	65	2.36	●
Let's hope sunnier days lie ahead for this fund, which is now run using a multi-manager approach. Bob Tattersall looks after value stocks, while John Mulvihill searches for growth stocks and Mercury Asset Management is responsible for the foreign position.																				
★★	**Spec United Cdn Invest**	Cdn Eq				3	4	2	1	1	2	2	D	A	27%	–28%	11/30/73	52	2.39	●
What a great move by Spectrum by rehiring Kim Shannon recently, after she left AMI Partners for rival Merrill Lynch Asset Management earlier this year. She's really added some adrenaline to the fund since taking over in 1996.																				
★★	**Spec United Cdn Stock**	Cdn Eq	3	3	4	4	1	3	3	2	2	3	D	B	31%	–23%	5/31/98	NA	2.39	●
New managers assigned to the fund are MFS Institutional Advisors, who are have taken the place of McLean Budden. The pros at MFS manage several of Spectrum's foreign equity offerings, but this is their first shot at a Canadian equity fund.																				
★★½	**Spec United Diversified**	Bal	3	3	4	3	4	3	2	1	2	3	C	C	18%	–12%	5/31/98	NA	2.19	●
This balanced fund's long-term record was mediocre at best until the team at McLean Budden was handed responsibility in 1997. You'll find a big-cap mix of low P/E stocks, a conservative stance on the bond portfolio and a low MER.																				

Legend: ★= overall past performance vs. similar funds (5 ★ max). Boxes show the quartile performance for a fund each calendar year vs. only similar funds (☐ is the best score possible). ● = high; ● = average; and ● = a fund with low expenses.

Consistency			Performance Trend										Risk						Efficiency
Overall Past Performance	Fund Name	Type	90	91	92	93	94	95	96	97	98	Aug. '99	Up	Down	% of Time Losing $	Biggest Drop	Date	No. of Mo's to Recover	MER
★★★	**Spec United Dividend Fund**	Div											C	B	10%	–11%	2/28/94	18	1.66
Stuart Pomphrey of McLean Budden ensures that this fund stays true to its name by sticking with preferred shares, which offer decent yield and lower risk. This is an excellent choice for investors looking for a real dividend fund.																			
★★★★	**Spec United Emerg Markets**	Fgn Eq											A	C	53%	–49%	8/31/97	NA	2.77
Ewen Cameron Watt of Mercury Asset Management combines a top-down country with a bottom-up stock approach, which has produced competitive returns. However, the fund has yet to regain the 50% that it lost during the Asian crisis in 1997.																			
★★★★	**Spec United Euro Growth**	Fgn Eq											NA	NA	10%	–17%	8/31/98	NA	2.65
Mercury Asset Management focuses on smaller European stocks in this offering. To combat some of the risk inherent in this mandate, the managers try to focus on the mature markets like the U.K. and France.																			
★★★	**Spec United Glo Divers**	Bal											B	D	9%	–10%	2/28/94	16	2.41
The Mercury Asset Management team use active management for portfolio decisions in this global asset allocation fund with excellent results thus far. The fund currently has 58% in equities, and 35% in bonds, with a bias towards U.S. and Europe.																			
★★½	**Spec United Glo Telecomm**	Fgn Eq											C	NA	8%	–18%	8/31/98	4	2.60
Maura O'Shaunessy of MFS Institutional Advisors has done well by concentrating in the U.S. market, including the Internet favorites like America Online Inc. and communications giant MCI World Com Inc.																			
★★½	**Spec United Global Equity**	Fgn Eq											D	D	13%	–24%	8/31/98	3	2.43
This large-cap global fund has consistently delivered bad results to investors. But the history of this fund really isn't relevant since the fund was handed over to David Mannheim and the forty-member team at MFS Institutional Advisors in 1996.																			
★★	**Spec United Global Growth**	Fgn Eq											C	C	31%	–56%	2/28/73	76	2.41
Chip Skinner of Mercury Asset Management has this fund invested in 255 stocks. The fund is heavily weighted in U.S. equities, which account for just over half of the portfolio.																			
★★½	**Spec United Optimax USA**	US Eq											C	C	2%	–11%	8/31/98	2	2.46
Here's an unusual fund run by the team at Chicago-based Weiss, Peck & Greer. They use a sophisticated computer model to optimize risk/return tradeoff, in order to deliver superior performance compared to the S&P 500, but with lower risk.																			
★★	**Special Opportunities**	Fgn Eq											C	C	41%	–65%	10/31/87	NA	2.15
Buckland Channing has been around forever but his experience has not helped the performance of this fund much. Holdings are divided almost evenly between stocks and fixed income securities. Average performance in all markets.																			
★★	**Sportfund LSVCC**	Spec Eq											NA	NA	33%	–33%	12/31/97	NA	NA
This fund is currently closed to new investors and is only available to people in Ontario. Manager Joel Albin focuses on investing in the sports and fitness industry but right now he has less than half of the fund's money in stocks.																			
★★★½	**Standard Life Balanced**	Bal											A	D	17%	–12%	6/30/98	12	2.00
Overall performance has been good for this fund, but it has seriously lagged in tough times. The team that manages the portfolio has been reducing equity holdings lately.																			
★★★½	**Standard Life Growth Equ**	Cdn Eq											NA	NA	24%	–28%	4/30/98	NA	2.00
The top holding of this fund is JDS Uniphase, a big winner. Performance has also been boosted by the recent run-up in oil and gas, a 25% holding in the fund.																			
★★★½	**Standard Life Nt Resource**	Nat Res											NA	NA	48%	–46%	10/31/97	NA	2.00
The value approach used by Standard Life has paid off lately. Bottom-up analysis performed by team members has led to a 45% allocation in oil and gas, a sector that has been a big winner.																			
★★½	**Standard Life U.S. Equity**	US Eq											NA	NA	0%	–13%	7/31/98	5	2.00
This fund, like all funds from this family, is not segregated. Performance this year so far has been lacklustre. Consumer and industrial products combine to make up over 65% of total holdings.																			

Legend: ★= overall past performance vs. similar funds (5 ★ max). Boxes show the quartile performance for a fund each calendar year vs. only similar funds (☐ is the best score possible). ● = high; ● = average; and ● = a fund with low expenses.

Consistency			Performance Trend										Risk						Efficiency
Overall Past Performance	Fund Name	Type	90	91	92	93	94	95	96	97	98	Aug. '99	Up	Down	% of Time Losing $	Biggest Drop	Date	No. of Mo's to Recover	MER
★★★	**STAR Cdn Bal Gro & Inc**	Bal											NA	NA	16%	–8%	6/30/98	NA	2.15
This fund of funds is for the conservative investor looking to capitalize on the good performers within the Mackenzie Canadian line-up.																			
★★★★	**STAR Cdn Max Equ Growth**	Bal											NA	NA	26%	–19%	5/31/98	NA	2.31
Good returns for this mixed bag of Canadian Mackenzie Funds.																			
★★★½	**STAR For Max Long-Trm Gro**	Bal											NA	NA	5%	–10%	8/31/97	7	2.27 ●
This one's largely a mix of their global funds, with lots of exposure in the U.S. and Europe.																			
★★★	**STAR Forgn Bal Gro & Inc**	Bal											NA	NA	0%	–4%	8/31/98	3	2.24 ●
Mixed performance for this portfolio. It's suffering this year because of its international bond exposure.																			
★★★★	**STAR Forgn Max Equ Growth**	Bal											NA	NA	11%	–17%	5/31/98	11	2.37
You'll find an aggressive mix of regional and global foreign funds here. A good strategy for investors over the past few years.																			
★★★	**STAR Inv Bal Gro & Income**	Bal											NA	NA	0%	–7%	6/30/98	6	2.20
High global bond component has held back this portolfio in 1999.																			
★★★½	**STAR Inv Cons Inc & Gro**	Bal											NA	NA	2%	–6%	6/30/98	6	2.12
Lots of Ivy funds in this conservative portfolio.																			
★★★	**STAR Inv Long-Term Growth**	Bal											NA	NA	16%	–10%	5/31/98	NA	2.20
This global balanced fund has a lot of its money invested in Mackenzie's Canadian funds. Performance has lagged recently.																			
★★★	**STAR Inv Max L-Term Gro**	Bal											NA	NA	7%	–10%	7/31/98	5	2.28
Primarily Universal funds in this one, which has produced average returns.																			
★★½	**STAR Reg Bal Gro & Inc**	Bal											NA	NA	7%	–8%	5/31/98	7	2.17
Extra foreign exposure achieved through their Universal RRSP funds.																			
★★½	**STAR Reg Cons Inc & Gro**	Bal											NA	NA	5%	–6%	5/31/98	7	2.09
A big focus on fixed income in this portfolio, which has produced mixed results.																			
★★★	**STAR Reg Long-Term Gro**	Bal											NA	NA	9%	–9%	5/31/98	11	2.21
Middle of the road performance for this slightly aggressive portfolio.																			
★★★★	**STAR Reg Max Equity Gro**	Bal											NA	NA	20%	–17%	5/31/98	13	2.31
This portfolio maintains its RRSP eligibility through the use of Mackenzie's quality derivative foreign funds. Universal funds make up most of the portfolio and overall fund selection has helped performance.																			
★★★½	**STAR Reg Max L-Term Gro**	Bal											NA	NA	5%	–11%	5/31/98	7	2,27
If you want diversification you'll get it here. Universal holds about three quarters of this quality fund's money.																			

Legend: ★ = overall past performance vs. similar funds (5 ★ max). Boxes show the quartile performance for a fund each calendar year vs. only similar funds (□ is the best score possible). ● = high; ○ = average; and ● = a fund with low expenses.

Consistency			Performance Trend										Risk						Efficiency	
Overall Past Performance	Fund Name	Type	90	91	92	93	94	95	96	97	98	Aug. '99	Up	Down	% of Time Losing $	Biggest Drop	Date	No. of Mo's to Recover	MER	
★★★½	**Stone & Co Flagship Stock**	Cdn Eq							□	□	□	□	NA	NA	29%	–25%	5/31/98	NA	2.88	●
This McLean Budden managed fund invests in the big names of Canadian business. The value approach used by the firm has been good for performance very recently. We would really love the fund if its ridiculously high MER were reduced.																				
★★½	**Strat Val Amer Equity**	US Eq	□	□	□	□	□	□	□	□	□	□	D	B	20%	–44%	1/31/73	47	2.70	●
Andrew Couch has the reins for this mid- to large cap fund, which has failed to dazzle investors. But most of this fund's history isn't relevant since Strategic Value took over these ailing funds from Laurentian Bank in 1997.																				
★★½	**Strat Val Asia Pacific**	Fgn Eq						□	□	□	□	□	NA	NA	59%	–46%	5/31/96	NA	2.70	○
This fund's trailed its peers in the recovery of Southeat Asian markets this year. The pros at the international investment firm of Investec Guiness Flight have been off on their top-down process.																				
★★	**Strat Val Cdn Balanced**	Bal	□	□	□	□	□	□	□	□	□	□	D	C	16%	–14%	5/31/98	NA	2.70	●
Mark Bonham hasn't been able to revive this middle of the road performer. Its hefty MER doesn't help the cause.																				
★★½	**Strat Val Cdn Equity**	Cdn Eq	□	□	□	□	□	□	□	□	□	□	D	B	27%	–34%	11/30/73	56	2.70	●
This one's heavy into Canadian technology and financial services companies. That hasn't helped performance though. It appears that many of the holdings are not in line with SVC's value philosophy and the MER is a bit inflated.																				
★★★	**Strat Val Cdn Small Co**	Cdn Eq	□	□	□	□	□	□	□	□	□	□	C	B	20%	–25%	10/31/97	20	2.70	●
This fund's really benefiting this year from the renewed interest in small caps, particularly in the resource sector. Ian Nakamoto took over the fund this year from Christine Hughes.																				
★★½	**Strat Val Commonwealth**	Bal	□	□	□	□	□	□	□	□	□	□	D	B	15%	–29%	1/31/73	43	2.70	●
This fund has been around since 1933 but performance has been shabby for the past several years. Most of the names in the portfolio are huge multi nationals like General Electric and Colgate Palmolive.																				
★★★	**Strat Val Dividend**	Div	□	□	□	□	□	□	□	□	□	□	B	B	18%	–16%	4/30/81	18	2.70	●
For this portfolio, manager Mark Bonham has emphasised the common equity of quality companies that pay a decent dividend. Performance hasn't been great but the fund has been pretty good in both up and down markets.																				
★★	**Strat Val Emerging Mkts**	Fgn Eq						□	□	□	□	□	NA	NA	50%	–48%	8/31/97	NA	2.95	○
Utilities and consumer products dominate the holdings of this portfolio. Manager and Oxford University graduate James Hancocks sniffs out cheap companies and hopes to win big. Unfortunately, performance has been quite poor.																				
★★★	**Strat Val Europe**	Fgn Eq						□	□	□	□	□	NA	NA	7%	–17%	8/31/98	4	2.70	●
Performance has been decent for this mid to large cap fund. Nearly 70% of the holdings are divided between industrial products, consumer products and real estate and construction.																				
★★½	**Strat Val Glo Balanced**	Bal	□	□	□	□	□	□	□	□	□	□	C	A	7%	–11%	8/31/90	16	2.70	○
Not a great performer but has been excellent in down markets. Huge multi national corporations are the main holdings of this balance fund.																				
★★½	**Strat Val International**	Fgn Eq	□	□	□	□	□	□	□	□	□	□	D	B	18%	–48%	1/31/73	47	2.70	●
This fund holds many of the same names as some of Strategic Value's other international funds. Maybe that's why performance has been so poor.																				
★★½	**Strategic Value Fund**	Fgn Eq								□	□	□	NA	NA	43%	–60%	11/30/97	NA	3.50	●
Technically, this isn't a mutual fund. It can use leverage, buy options and short sell. Performance so far this year has been awesome but only risk-tolerant investors with real dough (minimum investment is $150,000) should think about buying in.																				
★★★	**Talvest Asian**	Fgn Eq	□	□	□	□	□	□	□	□	□	□	B	A	40%	–46%	1/31/94	NA	3.26	●
Here's a good pick if you want to benefit from the recovery in the Asian markets. Duncan Mount's been right on the money with country allocation this year. This fund offers excellent downside risk but beware of its high MER.																				

Legend: ★ = overall past performance vs. similar funds (5 ★ max). Boxes show the quartile performance for a fund each calendar year vs. only similar funds (▀ is the best score possible). ● = high; ○ = average; and ● = a fund with low expenses.

Consistency: Overall Past Performance	Fund Name	Type	90	91	92	93	94	95	96	97	98	Aug. '99	Risk: Up	Down	% of Time Losing $	Biggest Drop	Date	No. of Mo's to Recover	Efficiency: MER	
★★★	**Talvest Cdn Asset Alloc**	Bal	1	2	4	3	1	4	3	2	1	1	D	A	9%	–13%	6/30/98	10	2.42	●
This fund offers extra foreign exposure by investing in foreign bond and index futures, which presently favour Europe. Jean-Guy Desjardins uses an active asset allocation strategy, which has been very rewarding to investors.																				
★★★	**Talvest Cdn Equity Value**	Cdn Eq	1	1	4	4	2	3	4	3	3	2	B	A	26%	–30%	7/31/81	21	2.40	○
Good stock-picking in the oil and gas and forestry sectors have given this fund a lift. Monique Malo focuses on mid to large sized companies and limits the number of holdings in the fund to around 50.																				
★★★★	**Talvest CdnEquGrowth**	Cdn Eq									1	1	NA	NA	47%	–27%	6/30/98	NA	2.10	●
This fund has done remarkably well by sticking with some of the larger growth companies such as Nortel Networks and BCE. Denis Ouelett has produced some solid performance in this fund's short history.																				
★★½	**Talvest Dividend**	Div							3	4	1	2	NA	NA	6%	–13%	6/30/98	10	1.99	○
Denis Ouelett's conservative approach has produced mixed results for this fund. He's currently reducing the fund's position in interest rate sensitive stocks in favour of high-yielding securities in consumer and merchandising sectors.																				
★★★½	**Talvest European**	Fgn Eq		2	2	2	3	3	3	1	3	2	A	A	7%	–19%	8/31/90	21	3.03	●
Sarah Caygill has a knack for delivering top-notch performance in all market conditions. The fund is currently positioned in the more mature markets of Europe with particular attention to the electronics and media sector.																				
★★★	**Talvest Glo Asset Alloc**	Bal	4	3	4	1	1	4	4	4	2	2	B	B	12%	–11%	8/31/90	16	2.75	○
This one-decision fund has produced decent results for investors.																				
★★★★★	**Talvest Glo Sml Cap**	Fgn Eq										1	NA	NA	0%	–14%	8/31/98	4	2.90	●
The recovery in small cap stocks has helped this fund produce some eye-popping returns in its first year. The pros at Nicholas-Applgate Capital Management have done well with their picks in healthcare and E-commerce.																				
★★½	**Talvest Global RRSP**	Fgn Eq				3	4	3	2	2	2	2	D	D	16%	–12%	8/31/98	3	2.50	○
This fund remains fully RRSP eligible from its strategy of investing in foreign index bond futures. Positions in the U.S. and U.K. currently make up over one-half of the portfolio.																				
★★★½	**Talvest Mill Next Gen**	Cdn Eq					2	1	2	1	2	2	A	D	28%	–27%	10/31/97	NA	0.00	●
This fund invests in North American equities but retains full RRSP eligibility by using derivatives. You'll find a concentrated portfolio of 30 to 40 small and mid-cap stocks.																				
★★★½	**Talvest Value LineC$**	US Eq			2	2	3	1	2	4	3	1	A	D	8%	–16%	8/31/98	4	3.01	●
Hot picks in the retail sector such as Costco and WalMart have helped this fund's returns this year. Criteria for stock selection are based on Value Line ranking system, which aims to find the best U.S. growth stocks.																				
★★★	**Templeton Balanced**	Bal	4	4	4	1	3	3	2	1	3	4	B	C	29%	–27%	8/31/87	72	1.91	○
Peter Moeschter is responsible for the equity portfolio in the fund, which presently makes up 65% of the fund, while Jeffery Sutcliffe is in charge of fixed-income decisions.																				
★★	**Templeton Canadian Stock**	Cdn Eq	3	4	4	2	2	4	3	2	3	4	D	C	36%	–19%	5/31/98	NA	2.44	○
Although Templeton's value style has produced excellent results for their foreign funds, it has yet to provide investors in this Canadian offerring with any eye-catching returns.																				
★★	**Templeton Cdn Asset All**	Bal						4	3	3	3	4	NA	NA	13%	–12%	5/31/98	13	2.15	○
George Morgan tries to give this fund an edge by maxing out the foreign content. Results have been pretty mediocre so far.																				
★★★½	**Templeton Emerging Market**	Fgn Eq				1	2	2	1	2	1	2	B	B	41%	–48%	8/31/97	NA	3.33	●
Dr. Mark Mobuis has managed to stay one step ahead of his peers with some suave stock-picking using Templeton's classic value philosophy. These days he's finding lots of bargains in Mexico and South Africa.																				

Legend: ★ = overall past performance vs. similar funds (5 ★ max). Boxes show the quartile performance for a fund each calendar year vs. only similar funds (▔ is the best score possible). ● = high; ● = average; and ● = a fund with low expenses.

Consistency			Performance Trend										Risk						Efficiency
Overall Past Performance	Fund Name	Type	90	91	92	93	94	95	96	97	98	Aug. '99	Up	Down	% of Time Losing $	Biggest Drop	Date	No. of Mo's to Recover	MER
★★★	**Templeton Glo Smaller Co**	Fgn Eq	4	1	1	3	3	1	1	3	4	4	B	C	17%	–22%	10/31/89	19	2.58 ●
Due to lofty valuations, the fund's U.S. equity exposure has been reduced to 16% over the past year. Norm Boersma is finding better buys in Europe and Southeast Asia.																			
★★★	**Templeton Global Balanced**	Bal						2	1	2	4	2	NA	NA	9%	–9%	5/31/98	11	2.55 ●
Decent results so far for this one-decision fund. Heather Arnold is in charge of equity selection, while Thomas Dickson is the fixed-income specialist.																			
★★½	**Templeton Intl Balanced**	Bal						4	1	3	4	4	NA	NA	20%	–12%	5/31/98	14	2.55 ●
You may want to consider this one if you're looking for exposure outside North America. Geographically, the managers currently favor Europe, which makes up 60% of the fund.																			
★★★½	**Tradex Equity**	Cdn Eq	2	4	2	3	1	1	1	1	2	2	A	A	21%	–35%	2/28/73	52	1.27 ●
This PH & N-managed fund invests in many of Canada's largest companies and performance has been spectacular all around. A low MER strengthens the case for this fund; however, it's only available to public sector employees and their families.																			
★★★	**Tradex Global Equity Fund**	Fgn Eq							4	2	1	2	NA	NA	40%	–40%	8/31/97	NA	2.50 ●
Essentially, the money that Barry Olliff receives from his unit holders is invested into mutual funds from all over the world. He then simply selects the countries that he believes will do best. Recent performance has been good.																			
★★	**Trans-Canada Dividend**	Div	1	4	3	4	2	2	3	3	4	4	D	A	21%	–35%	11/30/73	39	4.60 ●
This Sagit-managed fund has a very high MER that is not justified by performance. I'd definitely skip this one.																			
★★	**Trans-Canada Pension**	Bal	4	4	4	1	4	4	1	1	4	1	D	C	31%	–26%	4/30/98	11	4.56 ●
Here's another snoozer from Sagit. Performance has been poor all around and it is certainly not helped by the sky-high MER.																			
★★	**Trans-Canada Value**	Cdn Eq	4	4	4	1	4	4	4	4	4	1	D	A	32%	–39%	10/31/97	17	4.60 ●
This tiny fund is loaded with names you don't hear often. That's because it's a value fund – it tries to stay away from the markets' "stock de jour." Frankly, their approach hasn't worked. And look at that MER – OUCH!																			
★★★	**Transamerica BIG**	Bal	1	3	1	4	1	3	3	4	2	1	D	A	6%	–14%	5/31/98	8	1.80 ●
This fund is 65% equities and that portion is littered with many excellent growth companies like JDS Uniphase and Celestica. The MER is quite reasonable as well.																			
★★½	**Transamerica Grow Cdn Bal**	Bal					2	4	3	4	2	1	D	D	12%	–13%	5/31/98	8	2.46 ●
A good mix of technology names along with conventional companies has really boosted the performance for this one. Strangely, the fund has performed poorly in both up and down markets.																			
★★★½	**Triax Growth Fund LSVCC**	Spec Eq								3	3	1	NA	NA	32%	–20%	5/31/98	14	3.60 ●
Altamira Management is in charge of this fund, which has attracted assets quickly because of its focus on investing in publicly traded companies. The fund has also invested in some high profile private ventures including Indigo Books and Music Inc.																			
★★½	**Trimark Discovery Fund**	Fgn Eq								4	4	3	NA	NA	11%	–22%	5/31/98	6	2.70 ●
The focus here is on smaller names, particularly in the technology sector, although Rick Serafini also finds some promising buys in the pharmaceutical industry. Portfolio heavily biased to U.S. equities.																			
★★★½	**Trimark Indo-Pacific**	Fgn Eq						1	1	2	3	2	NA	NA	38%	–50%	8/31/97	NA	2.95 ●
Excellent country selection from the pros at Lloyd George Management has helped the performance of this fund. Good diversification in this fund, which should help this fund during volatile times.																			
★★½	**Trimark RSP Equity (DSC)**	Cdn Eq	3	2	2	2	1	4	4	4	3	1	C	C	18%	–25%	4/30/98	NA	2.00 ●
New managers Keith Graham and Geoff MacDonald are certainly seeing sunnier days than was the case last year. The revival of this fund is due to its resource picks.																			

Legend: ★= overall past performance vs. similar funds (5 ★ max). Boxes show the quartile performance for a fund each calendar year vs. only similar funds (□ is the best score possible). ● = high; ○ = average; and ● = a fund with low expenses.

Consistency			Performance Trend										Risk						Efficiency	
Overall Past Performance	Fund Name	Type	90	91	92	93	94	95	96	97	98	Aug. '99	Up	Down	% of Time Losing $	Biggest Drop	Date	No. of Mo's to Recover	MER	
★★★½	**Trimark Select Balanced**	Bal	□	□	□	□	□	□	□	□	□	□	A	C	12%	–13%	4/30/98	12	2.25	○
The managers currently have the fund positioned aggressively with 60% in equities. Bond whiz Patrick Farmer is weary about any further increases in bond yields due to an overactive economy.																				
★★½	**Trimark Select Cdn Growth**	Cdn Eq				□	□	□	□	□	□	□	D	C	17%	–20%	4/30/98	NA	2.35	○
Are performance numbers finally on the mend? Only time will tell but the re-emergence of value stocks and increased interest in the resource sector should help put this large fund over the hump.																				
★★★	**Trimark Select Growth**	Fgn Eq	□	□	□	□	□	□	□	□	□	□	A	C	10%	–24%	6/30/90	11	2.36	○
Bill Kanko has returned as lead manager for this fund after a five-year stint with Mackenzie. Bet on Japan is paying off this year for these value investors.																				
★★★½	**Trimark The Americas**	Fgn Eq										N/A	NA	NA	39%	–31%	10/31/97	NA	2.70	●
The managers have a dual focus in this unique fund; they search for smaller companies in North America and larger names in Latin America. The fund is currently evenly positioned in both places.																				
★★★½	**Universal Americas**	Fgn Eq										N/A	NA	NA	20%	–27%	9/30/87	22	2.47	●
An unusual fund that invests in North America, primarily the U.S. and Latin American equities. The fund's performance has been held back by its position in Brazil, which has suffered from a devalued currency.																				
★★★★½	**Universal Cdn Balanced**	Bal								□	□	□	NA	NA	19%	–10%	6/30/98	7	2.32	○
Dennis Starritt and Dina DeGeer have done a great job of not only stock selection, but also in the asset allocation decision, which presently has one-third of the fund in cash, signaling their uneasiness about the market's valuations.																				
★★½	**Universal Cdn Growth**	Cdn Eq	□	□	□	□	□	□	□	□	□	□	D	B	30%	–29%	9/30/89	45	2.34	○
This fund has become a popular choice for as a core Canadian Equity fund since Dina DeGeer and Dennis Starritt took over in 1995. There are currently 30 companies in the fund with minimal exposure to cyclicals.																				
★★½	**Universal Cdn Resource**	Nat Res	□	□	□	□	□	□	□	□	□	□	B	C	46%	–54%	10/31/97	NA	2.35	○
Resource stocks are finally rebounding after languishing in the wilderness over the past few years. Fred Sturm deserves particular credit for being able to keep this fund competitive by diversifying into foreign resource stocks.																				
★★	**Universal Far East**	Fgn Eq					□	□	□	□	□	□	C	C	63%	–56%	8/31/97	NA	2.57	●
This fund has come on strong recently, although Diahann Brown's decision to underweight Hong Kong and overweight Taiwanese electronic stocks has been a definite drag on the fund over the past few years.																				
★★★½	**Universal Future Fund**	Cdn Eq	□	□	□	□	□	□	□	□	□	□	B	C	25%	–24%	5/31/98	11	2.33	○
John Rohr emphasizes technology stocks in this Canadian specialty fund, with a smaller portion being allocated to resource based stocks. He's currently avoiding the e-commerce stocks because of nutty valuations.																				
★★½	**Universal Intl Stock**	Fgn Eq	□	□	□	□	□	□	□	□	□	□	C	C	25%	–19%	8/31/90	32	2.37	○
Iain Clark presently has the bulk of the fund invested in Europe, including the U.K. Japan has the next largest weighting at 13%, while exposure to Asia remains low.																				
★★★★	**Universal Japan**	Fgn Eq						□	□	□	□	□	B	D	65%	–40%	7/31/94	60	2.50	○
Japan's market has been on a tear this year. This fund's kept ahead of the game as Campbell Gunn of Thornton Management Ltd has correctly predicted a rise in software and telecommunications stocks.																				
★★★	**Universal Prec Metals**	Nat Res						□	□	□	□	□	C	C	58%	–66%	6/30/96	NA	2.40	○
Reports of gold selling by central banks are holding back the price of gold. Fred Sturm is branching out into other precious metals like Palladium and platinum, and also into diamonds for diversification of the portfolio.																				
★★★	**Universal US Emerg Growth**	US Eq				□	□	□	□	□	□	□	B	D	10%	–29%	6/30/96	15	2.35	○
Despite compelling valuations, lack of liquidity is holding back investors' enthusiasm for small caps. This fund has proven to be particularly volatile. When the markets are hot, this fund outperforms; the opposite is true when the market retreats.																				

Legend: ★= overall past performance vs. similar funds (5 ★ max). Boxes show the quartile performance for a fund each calendar year vs. only similar funds (□ is the best score possible). ● = high; ● = average; and ● = a fund with low expenses.

Consistency			Performance Trend										Risk						Efficiency
Overall Past Performance	Fund Name	Type	90	91	92	93	94	95	96	97	98	Aug. '99	Up	Down	% of Time Losing $	Biggest Drop	Date	No. of Mo's to Recover	MER
★★★½	**Universal Wld Bal RRSP**	Bal						□	□	□	□	□	B	NA	7%	–8%	9/30/94	10	2.36 ●
Barbara Trebbi and Michael Landry run this fund, which achieves exposure to global equities and bond through a conservative index futures strategy. Equities are currently favoured in the fund, making up 60% of the portfolio, with the remainder in bonds.																			
★★★½	**Universal Wld Emrg Gth**	Fgn Eq					□	□	□	□	□	□	C	A	51%	–41%	8/31/97	NA	2.50 ●
The crises in Southeast Asia and Brazil have given emerging market investors little to cheer about the past few years. This fund has an excellent rating in down markets as Peter Basset of Henderson International mainly sticks to larger companies.																			
★★★½	**Universal World Asset All**	Fgn Eq					□	□	□	□	□	□	C	NA	23%	–13%	2/29/96	16	2.41 ●
The managers focus on mature markets and use proprietary economic research to make asset allocation decisions. Strong performance in 1998 was a result of the fund's heavy exposure to U.S. equities.																			
★★½	**Universal World Grth RRSP**	Fgn Eq						□	□	□	□	□	NA	NA	11%	–15%	8/31/97	16	2.38 ●
This fund, which invests in equity indexes, has been a real hit with investors because of its full RRSP eligibility status. Returns slipped a bit last year because of the manager's decision to decrease exposure to the U.S. market.																			
★★★★★	**Universal World Real Est**	Real										N/A	NA	NA	60%	–7%	6/30/98	13	2.50 ●
Here's a specialty global fund that will provide excellent diversification benefits to a portfolio. Although a single sector fund carries more risk, its global mandate allows the manager to seek for the best real estate value worldwide.																			
★★	**University Ave Canadian**	Cdn Eq		□	□	□	□	□	□	□	□	□	D	D	34%	–33%	6/30/96	NA	2.40 ●
Management changes have been a regular event. Hopefully new manager Robert Boaz can finally turn things around and return performance to the levels of the early '90's.																			
★★	**University Ave U.S. Gro**	US Eq	□	□	□	□	□	□	□	□	□	□	D	B	36%	–33%	9/30/87	101	2.40 ●
Almost 20% of this fund is in cash and the top ten stocks make up about 60% of the holdings. For such a concentrated portfolio, stock-picking needs to be good but it hasn't been.																			
★★★½	**VenGrowth LSVCC**	Spec Eq							□	□	□	□	NA	NA	0%	–3%	6/30/98	5	4.00 ●
A proven performer in the LSIF category. The fund has received so much money that the managers have recently decided to close off this one and start a clone.																			
★★★	**Vision Europe**	Fgn Eq			□	□	□	□	□	□	□	□	B	A	6%	–17%	8/31/98	4	2.95 ●
This fund is filled with lots of European telecom and consumer products plays. This is the only mutual fund managed by this firm and the focus has paid off for unitholders. Performance has been good until just recently.																			
★★	**Vista Cap Gains 2**	Cdn Eq	□	□	□	□	□	□	□	□	□	□	D	C	30%	–40%	10/31/97	NA	2.38 ●
The numeral 2 in the name means they whack you with higher fees. Just get the number 1. Or better yet, go straight to Sceptre and get Lyle Stein directly.																			
★★★	**VistaFund Am Stock 2**	US Eq						□	□	□	□	□	NA	NA	0%	–12%	5/31/98	5	2.38 ●
This one focuses or growth companies. Performance has picked up lately but it has higher fees than its front-end sister.																			
★★★	**VistaFund Amer Stock 1**	US Eq						□	□	□	□	□	NA	NA	0%	–12%	5/31/98	5	1.63 ●
Low fees and US stock exposure are attractive. But the fund needed a new manager to pick up performance. Peter Marshall from Seamark has been tapped for the job.																			
★★	**VistaFund Cap Gains 1**	Cdn Eq	□	□	□	□	□	□	□	□	□	□	D	B	29%	–40%	10/31/97	NA	1.63 ●
After a string of bad news results, Lyle Stein of Sceptre was just brought in to pick up the big cap equity offering.																			
★★★	**VistaFund Diversified 1**	Bal	□	□	□	□	□	□	□	□	□	□	B	A	17%	–15%	5/31/98	11	1.63 ●
Peter Marshall of Seamark Asset Management took over in March '98. The fund really is well diversified and holds many mid cap names. The low MER strengthens the case for this one.																			

Legend: ★= overall past performance vs. similar funds (5 ★ max). Boxes show the quartile performance for a fund each calendar year vs. only similar funds (▭ is the best score possible). ● = high; ● = average; and ● = a fund with low expenses.

Consistency			Performance Trend										Risk						Efficiency
Overall Past Performance	Fund Name	Type	90	91	92	93	94	95	96	97	98	Aug. '99	Up	Down	% of Time Losing $	Biggest Drop	Date	No. of Mo's to Recover	MER
★★½	**VistaFund Diversified 2**	Bal											D	A	21%	–15%	5/31/98	13	2.38
A carbon copy of the Diversified 1 fund but with higher fees. But don't blame Peter Marshall for that. He's new and his services have been great for Manulife so far.																			
★★½	**VistaFund Equity 1**	Cdn Eq											D	B	24%	–29%	10/31/87	51	1.63
Gord Higgins of Elliott & Page was just tapped to run the account in early 1998. The MER here is quite low and there are some solid names in the portfolio but this is not a stand-out fund.																			
★★	**VistaFund Equity 2**	Cdn Eq											D	B	25%	–26%	8/31/87	23	2.38
This is the deferred sales charge version of the Vistafund Equity 1. Higher fees make this version less attractive.																			
★★★	**VistaFund Global Equ 1**	Fgn Eq											NA	NA	2%	–13%	8/31/98	4	1.63
The mandate of this fund says nothing in North American stocks. Interestingly there's 3% in the US. Most of the money is in Japan, the UK and western Europe. The MER is quite low for this well performing fund.																			
★★½	**VistaFund Global Equity 2**	Fgn Eq											NA	NA	2%	–13%	8/31/98	4	2.38
Again, the number 2 in the title means it's got higher fees than the surprisingly cheap number 1 version.																			
★★½	**Westbury Cdn Life Balance**	Bal											D	D	14%	–19%	5/31/98	NA	2.41
30% of this fund is in TIPS 35 units. Another 30% is in bond futures. The rest is diversified but this is a pretty easy way to manage money. It should, but doesn't, result in a lower MER.																			
★★½	**Westbury Cdn Life Equity**	Cdn Eq											B	C	38%	–26%	5/31/98	NA	2.40
There's a pretty significant focus on financial services with this fund so performance has lagged this year. Then again, performance has lagged multiple times over the past few years.																			
★★★	**Working Opportunity EVCC**	Spec Eq											NA	NA	7%	–6%	7/31/98	NA	2.80
This LSIF received a big payoff of $100 million from their investment in software company HotHaus Technologies Inc last year. It's only available in BC but this is really a quality fund.																			
★★★★½	**Working Ventures Cd LSVCC**	Spec Eq											NA	NA	11%	–6%	4/30/99	NA	2.96
Fees are low and performance has been quite good but do investors really want a quarter of their fund sitting in cash like this one? Probably not, but still, this is a super labour sponsored fund managed by Jim Hall.																			
★★★	**YMG Balanced Fund**	Bal											C	A	15%	–29%	11/30/73	39	1.79
This fund benefited in 1999 from its conservative asset mix, especially on the fixed income side, where the mid-term bonds performed well despite rising rates.																			
★★½	**YMG Growth Fund**	Cdn Eq											C	C	37%	–38%	10/31/97	20	2.75
Since he took over a few years ago, Mal Spooner has had explosive performance in this tiny fund. Credit takeovers in the tree sector for some of those gains, along with some exposure to technology.																			
★★	**YMG International Fund**	Fgn Eq											D	C	22%	–19%	8/31/98	NA	2.30
Bill Chinery's got a yawner on his hands here. The fund's super big cap exposure has been a positive, as have holdings in the Japanese market this year. But he's missed the US market by being light – a sin that's not easily forgiven these days.																			
★★★½	**Zweig Global Balanced**	Bal											NA	NA	0%	–5%	8/31/98	3	2.75
High cash weighting has helped this fund this year as international bonds tumble. On the equities side, Carlton Neel likes Japan, but is leery about U.S. stock market levels.																			
★★½	**Zweig Strategic Growth**	US Eq											C	D	13%	–18%	7/31/98	NA	2.49
The focus here is on U.S. small cap names, although David Katzen also keeps an eye out for large cap companies that offer exceptional growth. The manager is very cautious in his outlook for equities as the fund's cash is at 44%.																			

Top 100 Websites

With so many new websites appearing daily, adding to the millions already out there, it's tough to find out those that are right for you. To simplify the process for you, we have gone through all the best (and worst) investing websites out there, and ranked the top 100 based on various criteria. Each site is also categorized into one of eight listings, ranging from Mega Site to personal finance. Before you start surfing, take a peek at this listing here and figure out what's best for your needs. If you're into Mega Sites, see how we've ranked them compared to their peers. If a friend told you about a site, see what we think of it. What we're hoping is that you'll use this guide to help you with your investing needs, and also save you countless hours surfing unessesarily on the net. As with our mutual fund ultimate tables, these sites are ranked comparatively to their peers. A top quartile ranking means that the site is in the top 25% of all similar sites (Mega Sites are only ranked against other mega-sites, and so on).

Here is an explanation of the various categories of sites:

Mega Sites — these sites combine both personal finance (retirement savings, planners, insurance, etc.) and investment research (eg. detailed stock quotes, research, charting, etc). They are usually one-stop shop sites.

Research — These sites are characterized by their vast resources when it comes to researching a stock or mutual fund. This could include news, detailed quotes, or analysts recommendations.

Personal Finance — These sites deal strictly with personal finance matters, including investment planning, savings, and tax planning.

Portal Sites — These sites act as portals to other financial sites. Usually from these sites are links to literally hundreds of other websites on the net.

Exchange Sites — These are the sites put out by the exchanges themselves. They have much in common — most of them are great learning tools for investors.

IPO Related Sites — IPO's are always in the headlines today, and that's why there's now an abundance of sites dedicated to them on the net.

Annual Reports and Regulatory Filings — These sites include those that provide corporate annual reports, and those that deal with regulatory filings.

Others — These sites couldn't be easily categorized, but they're still very useful for investors

Sites were ranked on six overall criteria. These are explained here:

Ease — How easy is it to navigate through the site? Is everything easy to understand, or are you lost from the start?

Content — How much information is available to access on the site?

Quality — How useful and timely is the information on the site?

Uniqueness — How unique is the information? Do all sites have it, or is this one-of-a-kind?

Look — Is the site easy to comprehend? Is it visually appealing?

Overall — What's the overall ranking of this site?

🍁 — This signifies that a majority of the site is Canadian content

Site	Category	Address	Cost	Ease of Use	Content	Quality	Uniqueness	Look	Overall	Description
411 Stocks	Research	www.411stocks.com	free	A	B	B	C	B	B	This site gives you the 411 on stocks, but who really wants the 411? There's other sites that offer more for the same price. If you're in a hurry, though, and want to do a quick check, then this site is worth a try. It doesn't get any easier.
ABC News	Mega Site	www.abcnews.com/sections/business	free	B	C	C	D	B	C	Here's a big media player who fails to deliver. There is an abundance of articles regarding investing, but you'd really expect more from this big name. Unless you own stock in Disney and want to support them, avoid this site.
AltaVista	Research	http://finance.altavista.com	free	B	C	B	D	B	C	This is AltaVista's offering in the financial world. It's one of the more basic sites out there — you can do better
Annual Report Gallery	Reports	www.reportgallery.com	free	C	C	B	B	C	C	This site differs from other annual report sites in that it also offers links to other investing areas. Unfortunately it's weaker than the other sites in their ability to get annual reports. Try the other sites for annual reports.
Barchart.com	Research	www.barchart.com	free to $240	C	C	B	A	B	B	Here you get free charts, quotes, and indicators for US listed securities. The same for futures and commodities will cost you. The technical and fundamental indicators are interesting. Don't bother subscribing.
Bay-Street.com	Research	www.bay-street.com	free	B	B	C	C	C	C	What's most disappointing about this site is that it you'd think it was Canadian, right? Well, it does have some Canadian content, but it's mostly another American site. It's not even a good American site, really.
Big Charts	Research	www.bigcharts.com	free	A	B	B	A	A	A	It doesn't take a genius to figure out what you'll find at this site. But that's not all, they're also detailed info on companies. You can check Canadian stocks on this site, but there is a site dedicated to Canada at www.canada26.bigcharts.com.

Site	Category	Address	Cost	Ease of Use	Content	Quality	Uniqueness	Look	Overall
Big Tipper	Other	www.bigtipper.com	free	A	A	B	A	B	A

With so many pro analysts out there, it's hard to keep track of who's saying what. This site takes care of that. It keeps track of who's recommending what, and when. It then follows their picks, so you'll know who to listen to.

Site	Category	Address	Cost	Ease of Use	Content	Quality	Uniqueness	Look	Overall
Bloomberg	Mega Site	www.bloomberg.com	free	B	B	A	A	A	A

Quality site that has it all — articles, personal finance, stocks, mutual funds, portfolios and more. The detail isn't the best, but it's probably more than you need. Market monitor is amazing — if your computer can handle it.

Site	Category	Address	Cost	Ease of Use	Content	Quality	Uniqueness	Look	Overall
Briefing.com	Research	www.briefing.com	free to US$300	A	B	A	A	A	A

This site's access can be broken into three — free, $70/yr, and $300/yr. The free stuff's great — be sure to check it out. Jury's still out on whether or not pay services are useful — there's always a 30 day free trial, so see for yourself if you like it.

Site	Category	Address	Cost	Ease of Use	Content	Quality	Uniqueness	Look	Overall
Canstock	Research	www.canstock.com	free to Cdn.$300	B	C	C	B	B	B

One of a few of the indepth Canadian sites available. Detailed information on stocks, mutual funds, and bonds, but really, you can get all this and more for free at other sites.

Site	Category	Address	Cost	Ease of Use	Content	Quality	Uniqueness	Look	Overall
Canada Stockwatch	Research	www.canada-stockwatch.com	free to Cdn.$600	D	A	B	B	B	B

This Canadian based site seems like it has a lot to offer, but awkward navigation makes this tough. One highlight is the live ticker that you can customize on your PC.

Site	Category	Address	Cost	Ease of Use	Content	Quality	Uniqueness	Look	Overall
Carlson Online	Research	www.carlsononline.com	free to Cdn.$120	B	C	B	C	C	C

Although this once was a completely free site, most of what you'll want from this site is still free. Nothing really stands out, though.

Site	Category	Address	Cost	Ease of Use	Content	Quality	Uniqueness	Look	Overall
CBOE	Exchange	www.cboe.com	free	A	A	B	B	A	A

Great site from Chicago Board of Options Exchange. Like other exchange based sites, the best part of this site is the educational section. If you want to learn about options, make sure you check them out. Good options chains, too.

Site	Category	Address	Cost	Ease of Use	Content	Quality	Uniqueness	Look	Overall
CBS Marketwatch	Mega Site	www.cbsmarketwatch.com	free	A	B	A	A	A	A

This site has it all. Personal finance is great, as is investing resources. Tons of articles only make it that much better. It's hard to find something wrong. If you must, it's stock research could be a little more indepth.

Site	Category	Address	Cost	Ease of Use	Content	Quality	Uniqueness	Look	Overall
Chicago Board of Trade	Exchange	www.cbot.com	free	C	B	B	A	B	B

If you're interested in futures, or want to learn more about them, this is probably one of the few sites on the net for you. It's apparent that futures aren't popular by the lack of sites devoted to them.

Site	Category	Address	Cost	Ease of Use	Content	Quality	Uniqueness	Look	Overall
Chicago Mercantile Exchange	Exchange	www.cme.com	free	B	B	D	A	C	C

If anything, this is an interesting site to play around with. It will give you more info on the exchange and what it does. It's not the type of site that an investor would enjoy for long, though.

Site	Category	Address	Cost	Ease of Use	Content	Quality	Uniqueness	Look	Overall
CNBC	Research	www.cnbc.com	free	C	A	A	A	A	A

You had to know this site, from those guys at the 24 hour cable super-channel, was going to be good. Great stock info, articles, interviews, and more. They could add some personal finance info in, but nonetheless, a great site.

Site	Category	Address	Cost	Ease of Use	Content	Quality	Uniqueness	Look	Overall
CNCurrency.com	Mega Site	www.cncurrency.com	free	C	A	C	B	B	B

This site is geared more towards personal finance, and it shows. There's an abundance of learning tools for you to use for any type of finance need you may have. Neat calculators, too. Surprisingly, nothing about currencies.

Site	Category	Address	Cost	Ease of Use	Content	Quality	Uniqueness	Look	Overall
CNNfn	Mega Site	www.cnnfn.com	free	A	A	A	C	A	A

Another top notch site. It has a great ability to brings things together in one place. Good economic and world stats, too. One complaint — their company stock info (which is great) isn't their's — it's from Quicken.com

Site	Category	Address	Cost	Ease of Use	Content	Quality	Uniqueness	Look	Overall
Companies Online	Other	www.companiesonline.com	free	A	C	B	A	B	B

If you need to know a company's web site, look it up here, and they'll let you know the URL address. It's helpful for that, but not much else. It's the brainchild of Lycos and Dun & Bradstreet.

Site	Category	Address	Cost	Ease of Use	Content	Quality	Uniqueness	Look	Overall
Daily Rocket	Research	www.dailyrocket.com	free	B	C	B	C	C	C
This average site has some decent investing areas. Most of what you find here is available elsewhere, though. There are some good articles, but really, it's nothing special.									
Daily Stocks	Portal	www.dailystocks.com	free	A	A	C	D	B	B
You get tons of links from this portal, but some of them can be completely useless. If you have nothing better to do, then give it a shot. But if you're in a hurry, I wouldn't bother wasting time.									
Directions	Portal	www.ndir.com	free	B	A	A	A	B	A
This is a very unique site on investing in Canada. The real quality is all the educational tidbits — it's truly a joy to read. The site also acts as a portal for stock info. There's really too much there to describe here — you'll have to see for yourself.									
Finance Wise	Portal	www.financewise.com	free	C	B	B	A	B	B
This is a search engine that specifically focuses on finance orientated sites. Some bugs still. After registering, you must bookmark the site, otherwise you have to register again. Plus, it's pretty slow, and its searches stink.									
Financial Post	Research	www.nationalpost.com/financialpost	free	B	C	D	B	B	C
This site is basically the newspaper online. While other publications take advantage of the internet to give more to readers, the National Post has missed that boat. The only reason to check this site out is if you want to read the paper.									
Financial Web	Research	www.financialweb.com	free	C	A	A	A	B	A
This site acts as an umbrella site for it's numerous offerings. For stock information, Rapid Research, has great data on stocks. There's also sites dedicated to mutual funds, IPO's, Options, and more. You can get lost, though.									
Fortune Investor	Research	www.fortuneinvestor.com	free to US $420	A	A	A	B	A	A
The free area of this site is one of the better ones around. Combining great stock info, a good stock screener, and business news all in one site put it ahead of most of the others. There are four subscription options to try if you need more.									

Site	Category	Address	Cost	Ease of Use	Content	Quality	Uniqueness	Look	Overall
Fox Market Wire	Research	www.foxmarketwire.com	free to US$35	B	B	C	B	C	B

It's disappointing to see them ask you to pay for something you can get elsewhere for free. Their free services are alright, but really, is alright good enough for you?

Site	Category	Address	Cost	Ease of Use	Content	Quality	Uniqueness	Look	Overall
Free Edgar	Reports	www.freeedgar.com	free	C	A	A	A	C	B

If you want SEC filings (US company's only), then this is your site. You can have access to free SEC filings in real time. There is some basic information on the company's. Basically, come here if you want filings, and that's it.

Site	Category	Address	Cost	Ease of Use	Content	Quality	Uniqueness	Look	Overall
Futures Online	Other	www.futuresmag.com	free	B	D	C	A	C	C

This is a site for commodity traders. Its content is pretty weak. There is an educational area to learn more about futures, but it links to the Chicago Board of Trade. Just go there instead.

Site	Category	Address	Cost	Ease of Use	Content	Quality	Uniqueness	Look	Overall
GlobeFund	Research	www.globefund.com	free	B	B	A	B	B	B

One of the few sites dedicated to Canadian mutual funds, and it's a dandy. There's a bunch of tools for investors to use to analyze their funds. Another well put-together site by the Globe and Mail.

Site	Category	Address	Cost	Ease of Use	Content	Quality	Uniqueness	Look	Overall
GlobeInvestor	Research	www.globeinvestor.com	free	B	B	A	A	A	A

This site is one of a few investing sites put together by the Globe and Mail. Here you get quality research on stocks, markets, and investing in general. It's a great site.

Site	Category	Address	Cost	Ease of Use	Content	Quality	Uniqueness	Look	Overall
Gomez	Other	www.gomez.com	free	B	B	A	A	B	B

This site offers you scorecards on different internet retailers, including booksellers and travel agents. Why should you care? Well, it also offers ratings on online brokers, and should you decide to try one, this is a good start.

Site	Category	Address	Cost	Ease of Use	Content	Quality	Uniqueness	Look	Overall
Hollywood Stock Exchange	Other	www.hsx.com	free	A	B	B	A	B	B

Every now and then you need to take a break from trading in stocks and bonds. That's when you start trading in movie stars and singers. Okay, so this site is different, but it's fun, too. The HSX works like a real exchange, only the securities are different.

Site	Category	Address	Cost	Ease of Use	Content	Quality	Uniqueness	Look	Overall
Hoover's Online	Research	www.hoovers.com	free to US$110	A	B	B	A	B	B

For the full price, you have access to their company reports which have some interesting, but not necessarily useful, information. For free, you can check out company capsules, which are brief info bits on companies — it's not bad.

Site	Category	Address	Cost	Ease of Use	Content	Quality	Uniqueness	Look	Overall
imoney	Mega Site	www.imoney.com	free	B	B	B	A	A	A

This is the only real Canadian indepth mega-site available (the others listed here are simple Canadian version of US sites). Personal finance on the site is great; unfortunately investing resources is somewhat lackluster.

Site	Category	Address	Cost	Ease of Use	Content	Quality	Uniqueness	Look	Overall
Individual Investor Online	Research	www.iionline.com	free	B	A	C	A	B	B

This site is filled with articles, commentaries, and analysts picks. It's a good site, offering unique items like their Magic 25 (top stock picks) and Investor University (education area).

Site	Category	Address	Cost	Ease of Use	Content	Quality	Uniqueness	Look	Overall
Insider Trader	Research	www.insidertrader.com	free to US$215	A	C	B	B	B	B

This site prides itself on the insider trading reports it delivers. These reports are free on this site, but they're also free on a number of other sites. It's presented nicely here, though. The fee services aren't what you really need.

Site	Category	Address	Cost	Ease of Use	Content	Quality	Uniqueness	Look	Overall
Inter@ctive Investor	Research	www.zdii.com	free	D	B	A	B	C	B

This site, from Ziff Davis, has tons of information for you to browse through. Know what you want before checking the site out, though, because you might get lost.

Site	Category	Address	Cost	Ease of Use	Content	Quality	Uniqueness	Look	Overall
Investing for Kids	Personal Finance	http://tqd.advanced.org/3096/	free	A	B	C	B	B	B

If you have kids and want them to learn about investing, this site's a good place to start. It was designed by kids to make it easier for other young ones to understand. It's a nice starting point.

Site	Category	Address	Cost	Ease of Use	Content	Quality	Uniqueness	Look	Overall
Investools	Research	www.investools.com	free to varies	B	C	B	B	B	B

Overall, a decent site, but its abundance of reports and newsletters from advisors makes this site above average. Keep in mind, though, that for most reports there is a fee to pay.

Site	Category	Address	Cost	Ease of Use	Content	Quality	Uniqueness	Look	Overall
Investor Commun. Business	Reports	www.icbinc.com	free	B	A	A	A	A	A

Over 3500 annual reports are available at this site, including Canadian. Find your company, click on it, then wait for the report in the mail. Service usually a week, some take longer. Great site and service.

Site	Category	Address	Cost	Ease of Use	Content	Quality	Uniqueness	Look	Overall
Investor Guide	Portal	www.investorguide.com	free	A	A	A	D	B	A

While this isn't a Mega Site, it acts like one by bringing everything together for you. There are great links to check out (including personal finance) — Investor Guide even gives a brief description of the sites themselves.

Site	Category	Address	Cost	Ease of Use	Content	Quality	Uniqueness	Look	Overall
Investor's Business Daily	Research	www.investors.com	free to US$720	C	C	A	A	B	B

Most of the site is free, including daily articles from the paper. When you subscribe, though, you get amazing technical charts on over 10,000 stocks. These charts are what Mr. O'Neil is known for, but they are expensive. Maybe too expensive.

Site	Category	Address	Cost	Ease of Use	Content	Quality	Uniqueness	Look	Overall
Invest-O-Rama	Portal	www.investorama.com	free	A	A	A	B	B	A

This site has what you'd expect a portal to have, but what sets it apart is the multitude of articles, research, and investing resources. A notch above the others.

Site	Category	Address	Cost	Ease of Use	Content	Quality	Uniqueness	Look	Overall
IPO.com	IPO	www.ipo.com	free	C	C	B	B	C	C

If you have any interests in recent or upcoming IPO's, check this site out. Not as useful as IPO Central, but it does offer some advantages — you can get in on some IPOs here, although it won't be companies like Yahoo.

Site	Category	Address	Cost	Ease of Use	Content	Quality	Uniqueness	Look	Overall
IPO Central	IPO	www.ipocentral.com	free	C	B	A	B	B	B

Here, you get good indepth info and financials on recent or upcoming IPOs. Also some historical data on past IPOs (best/worst performers, etc.). To learn more about IPOs, check out some of their great learning tools.

Site	Category	Address	Cost	Ease of Use	Content	Quality	Uniqueness	Look	Overall
IPO Intelligence Online	IPO	www.ipo-fund.com	free	D	D	C	B	C	C

This site gives good info on past IPOs, and has good listings of best/worst, biggest/smallest, etc. Other than that, there's not much here. Try one of the other IPO sites.

Site	Category	Address	Cost	Ease of Use	Content	Quality	Uniqueness	Look	Overall
Just Quote Me	Portal	www.justquoteme.com	free	A	B	C	C	C	C
Kiplinger Online	Personal Finance	www.kiplinger.com	free to US $149	B	A	A	B	B	A
Market Guide	Research	www.marketguide.com	free	A	C	B	B	C	C
Market Player	Research	www.marketplayer.com	free	C	B	C	C	B	C
Money.com	Mega Site	www.money.com	free	A	B	B	B	A	B
Microsoft Investor	Mega Site	www.moneycentral.com	free	C	A	A	A	A	A
Multex Investor	Research	www.multexinvestor.com	free to US $150	B	C	B	A	B	B

Just Quote Me
Not much proprietary research here. It basically just serves as a portal for investment sites. I'd try one of the other portal sites that actually offer some of their own stuff.

Kiplinger Online
This is a great site when it comes to investing help — things like retirement, taxes, and insurance. It's one of the better ones out there in those areas. Individual stock research is below average, though.

Market Guide
There's really nothing special here. Most of what you get is available at better sites. One exception — this site has free insider trading and institutional holdings of equities. If you like that, go nuts, otherwise, swing somewhere else.

Market Player
Not much useful offered at this site other than stock screening and charting. They're big on imaginary games, and they continually have a free stock contest with prizes going on. If that's your thing, try it out — otherwise don't bother.

Money.com
Good articles and investing information highlight this site. Check out their readings on retirement and taxes, too. Individual stock information is basic.

Microsoft Investor
They are in the process of developing a new site, and well, it'll be tough to make it any better. This site has it all for you. The personal finance stands on its own, and the investing research is also great. Be sure to check the new site out when it's ready.

Multex Investor
No quotes or personal finance here. Instead, look for great reports on US listed companies (200,000 in all). Most reports do have a fee, but the free ones from Multex offer you insight into companies that is really helpful.

Site	Category	Address	Cost	Ease of Use	Content	Quality	Uniqueness	Look	Overall
NASDAQ	Exchange	www.nasdaq.com	free	A	A	A	B	A	A

All exchange based sites have one thing in common — they're all great. On top detailed info on Nasdaq, NYSE, and AMEX stocks, there's portfolios, options, and stock screens. Educationally, it's one of the best.

Site	Category	Address	Cost	Ease of Use	Content	Quality	Uniqueness	Look	Overall
New York Stock Exchange	Exchange	www.nyse.com	free	A	C	B	A	A	B

Again, a great site when it comes to learning about investing and the New York Stock Exchange. Unfortunately, not much info on stocks and companies. But the educational center more than makes up for it.

Site	Category	Address	Cost	Ease of Use	Content	Quality	Uniqueness	Look	Overall
Nordby	Research	www.nordby.com	free	A	B	B	A	B	B

This is a more basic site, but it still has some powerful punches to it. Today's Broker Reports is one such section that gives a listing of reports from the largest brokerages in the US. And it's free. Nowhere else on the net is something like that available.

Site	Category	Address	Cost	Ease of Use	Content	Quality	Uniqueness	Look	Overall
North American Quotations	Research	www.naq.com	free	B	D	D	D	C	D

Why waste time going to a site like this, when there are so many others out there.

Site	Category	Address	Cost	Ease of Use	Content	Quality	Uniqueness	Look	Overall
OANDA	Other	www.oanda.com	free	B	B	A	A	B	B

Not many sites are dedicated to exchange rates, but here's one that has what you'll need. It also has nice little converters and tools that are beneficial. It's not flashy, but we are talking about currencies here.

Site	Category	Address	Cost	Ease of Use	Content	Quality	Uniqueness	Look	Overall
Ont. Securities Commission	Other	www.osc.gov.on.ca	free	C	B	C	A	B	B

This site is set up to help prevent you from getting fleeced investing in Ontario companies. It's an interesting read, but the only time you'll really need to go here is if something's gone wrong, and you want to take action.

Site	Category	Address	Cost	Ease of Use	Content	Quality	Uniqueness	Look	Overall
Option Source	Other	www.optionsource.com	free	B	B	A	B	A	B

Here's a site heavy on teaching investors not only the basics in options, but also advanced techniques. It's a great site in that respect, but it doesn't offer much else. Option chains are average.

Site	Category	Address	Cost	Ease of Use	Content	Quality	Uniqueness	Look	Overall
PRARS	Reports	www.prars.com	free	C	A	B	A	B	B

The Public Register's Annual Report Service has access to annual reports of over 2000 US listed companies. As such, Canadian content is weak. Both online and hardcopy versions available.

Site	Category	Address	Cost	Ease of Use	Content	Quality	Uniqueness	Look	Overall
Quicken	Mega Site	www.quicken.ca	free	A	A	A	A	B	A

Great site. You can take care of all your needs here — from taxes and insurance to stocks and mutual funds. On top of having great resources, there's also great learning tools for investors. It's all here.

Site	Category	Address	Cost	Ease of Use	Content	Quality	Uniqueness	Look	Overall
Quote.com	Research	www.quote.com	free to US$1200	A	B	B	B	B	B

You get what you'd expect for free. For the pay service — well, $1200 is a lot of money, and unless money flows like water with you, I'd consider not subscribing (although there are cheaper plans). Basically, an average site.

Site	Category	Address	Cost	Ease of Use	Content	Quality	Uniqueness	Look	Overall
QuotesCanada.com	Research	www.quotescanada.com	free	D	D	D	C	B	D

Avoid this site like the plague. Okay, so that's being a bit harsh, but the only reason it's listed here is because it's Canadian, and there aren't many of them out there.

Site	Category	Address	Cost	Ease of Use	Content	Quality	Uniqueness	Look	Overall
Raging Bull	Research	www.ragingbull.com	free	B	B	C	B	B	C

An abundance of message boards, particularly on tech stocks, can make for an interesting read. Not much else here, though.

Site	Category	Address	Cost	Ease of Use	Content	Quality	Uniqueness	Look	Overall
Reuters Money Net	Research	www.moneynet.com	free	D	B	C	B	B	C

What happened here? This used to be a top quality site, but what's left looks like, well, you know. I wouldn't even bother visiting here unless they really overhaul the site. It really doesn't say much about Reuters.

Site	Category	Address	Cost	Ease of Use	Content	Quality	Uniqueness	Look	Overall
ROB Top 1000 Companies	Other	www.robmagazine.com/top1000/	free	B	A	C	A	B	B

If you're interested in learning about the largest, most profitable, or fastest growing Canadian companies, then check this site out. There's no investing research, but it still gives you an idea about the companies of size in Canada.

Site	Category	Address	Cost	Ease of Use	Content	Quality	Uniqueness	Look	Overall
S&P's Personal Wealth	Mega Site	www.personalwealth.com	free to US$120	A	A	A	B	A	A
Here's a great site from Standard and Poor's that combines the best elements of personal finance with investing resources. The free area doesn't really give you much — you have to subscribe to get the goods, and they don't fail to deliver.									
SEDAR	Reports	www.sedar.com	free	C	B	B	A	B	B
If you are interested in any corporate filings from Canadian companies, then this site is for you. Annual Reports, Notice of filings, and Press Releases are all available for your perusal.									
Silicon Investor	Research	www.techstocks.com	free to US$200	B	B	C	A	B	B
Don't bother coming to this site unless you're interested in what others have to say about your favourite tech stocks. Its posting boards are really popular and fun to read (be careful, though). Other than that, this site just doesn't do it.									
Smart Money	Mega Site	www.smartmoney.com	free	A	A	B	B	A	A
From Dow Jones and Co. comes this awesome site. Great investing and personal finance information. Plus, its research on stocks is also first class. Best yet, it's completely free — a definite top 10 investing site.									
StockFever	Portal	www.stockfever.com	free	A	B	B	D	B	C
Another site that pulls everything together for you. What's different is that it also offers stock recommendations from other investors like you. But do you really care if Sandman recommends Yahoo at $178?									
Stockpoint	Research	www.stockpoint.com	free	B	A	B	B	B	B
This is an above average site that has what you'd expect, and then a little more. Neat features include its stock and mutual fund screeners, and it's interactive charts. The charts take quite some time to load, though.									
Stocks.com	Portal	www.stocks.com	free	D	B	C	C	C	D
With such a great domain name like stocks.com, you'd think they'd come up with something nice here. Well, they haven't, and the best advice for you is to stay away. The best advice for them is to sell their domain name and get out of this business.									

Site	Category	Address	Cost	Ease of Use	Content	Quality	Uniqueness	Look	Overall
Stockscape	Research	www.stockscape.com	free	C	B	C	D	B	C

There's not much on this site you can't find elsewhere. One thing you can't find free anywhere else, though, is VSE short positions, which Stockscape offers to you. Don't be fooled by that, though, there's not much here.

Site	Category	Address	Cost	Ease of Use	Content	Quality	Uniqueness	Look	Overall
StockSmart	Research	www.stocksmart.com	US$140	A	B	B	B	B	B

Unfortunately, none of this site is free. When you pay, most of what you get is available elsewhere for free. There is a free trial available — I'd try that before even considering subscribing to see if you really do need what it has.

Site	Category	Address	Cost	Ease of Use	Content	Quality	Uniqueness	Look	Overall
StockWarrants.com	Other	www.stockwarrants.com	US$150	B	B	C	A	B	B

If warrants is your type of thing, then this is one of a few sites on the net for you. If you don't know or care about warrants, don't bother, you have to pay just to access the site.

Site	Category	Address	Cost	Ease of Use	Content	Quality	Uniqueness	Look	Overall
StockWiz	Portal	www.stockwiz.com	free	A	B	B	D	C	C

Type in a stock symbol, and presto — links to hundreds of other sites with info about that stock. Quotes, charts, news, and much more. This brings everything together for you. Try Investorama first, though — they have more for you.

Site	Category	Address	Cost	Ease of Use	Content	Quality	Uniqueness	Look	Overall
The Financial Center	Mega Site	www.tfc.com	free	C	B	C	B	A	C

This site has some interesting articles, on top of the essential stock details. Personal finance is new, and it's not too bad. There are other sites out there, but this one's decent.

Site	Category	Address	Cost	Ease of Use	Content	Quality	Uniqueness	Look	Overall
The Motley Fool	Research	www.fool.com	free to US$50	C	B	B	A	A	A

Okay, so it doesn't have the most indepth research around. But that's not why you visit this site. You do so because of the thousands of messages posted on basically every stock around. Articles are fun to read, too. You really have to check it out.

Site	Category	Address	Cost	Ease of Use	Content	Quality	Uniqueness	Look	Overall
The Street.com	Research	www.thestreet.com	free to US$100	C	B	A	B	B	B

What a difference a year makes. Before, it was a small investment site with a loyal crowd following. Now, it's a behemoth worth more than half a billion US. Its services — they're okay, but it's the articles you want — and you must pay for them.

Site	Category	Address	Cost	Ease of Use	Content	Quality	Uniqueness	Look	Overall
Thomson Investors Network	Research	www.thomsoninvest.net	free to US$360	B	B	B	B	A	B
Although its name comes from Canada's richest man, Kenneth Thomson, this is a gathering of Thomson's American companies, including First Call. There are some nice features here.									
Toronto Stock Exchange	Exchange	www.tse.com	free	C	B	B	A	A	B
This classy site has only gotten better in the past year. Still completely free, more indepth information (like options) has been added to an already full site. A great learning resource, too.									
USA Today	Mega Site	www.usatoday.com/money	free	C	B	C	C	B	C
You'd expect more from this leading US daily paper. It does have some decent calculators, but other than that, its personal finance section is sub-par. Investing info is also below that of many other sites.									
Value Line	Research	www.valueline.com	free	B	C	C	C	B	C
There are some nice interesting stories and articles at this site. While the site is free, to access just about anything, you need to subscribe, which means giving some personal info, including an e-mail address. I wouldn't bother based on that.									
Vancouver Stock Exchange	Exchange	www.vse.com	free	B	C	B	A	A	B
Another well done site by the folks in BC. You get the goods on Vancouver listed stocks, but also helpful investing information that beginners would find really useful.									
Vanguard	Personal Finance	www.vanguard.com	free	A	B	B	B	A	B
Great site for your financial planning needs. As Vanguard is a US mutual fund company, there's also indepth info on mutual funds (including their own). Educationally, it's a good site, and the planning can be a benefit to you.									
Vector Vest	Research	www.vectorvest.com	up to US$545	C	B	C	A	B	B
This site is home of a unique stock analysis program that combines technical and fundamental data to provide you with lots of stock picks. It's a bit pricey, but there is a 5 week trial version for only $29.95 if you're really interested. I'm not.									

Site	Category	Address	Cost	Ease of Use	Content	Quality	Uniqueness	Look	Overall
ViWes InvestInfo	Other	www.viwes.com	free	C	C	B	C	B	C

This site is dedicated to short positions on Nasdaq traded stocks. It gives a number of lists, including the top short positions monthly. Other sites have individual stock short positions, but this is one of a few to group them all together.

Site	Category	Address	Cost	Ease of Use	Content	Quality	Uniqueness	Look	Overall
Wall Street City	Mega Site	www.wallstreetcity.com	free to US$420	B	A	B	A	A	B

There's tons of nice research available here, best of all, most of what you need is free. Premium services are okay, but probably not worth the cost.

Site	Category	Address	Cost	Ease of Use	Content	Quality	Uniqueness	Look	Overall
Wall Street Journal	Mega Site	www.wsj.com	US $49	B	B	A	A	B	B

Based on who this site is from, you can guess what kind of information you will get. Good company research, but an emphasis on business news and articles. A good site, but to access it you must subscribe.

Site	Category	Address	Cost	Ease of Use	Content	Quality	Uniqueness	Look	Overall
Wall Street Research Net	Research	www.wrsn.com	free to varies	C	C	B	B	B	B

Not much distinguishes this site from others. A neat feature is the WRSN Technical Indicators which tells you to buy, sell, or hold a security based on a number of technical indications. It has what you'd expect an average site to have.

Site	Category	Address	Cost	Ease of Use	Content	Quality	Uniqueness	Look	Overall
Wall Street Voice	Research	www.wsvoice.com	varies	A	B	B	B	B	B

This site is a warehouse of over 200,000 research reports by the big Wall Street firms. Unfortunately, it's not free. Prices vary, but I've seen reports for US$200. That's pretty expensive — don't bother unless you're a serious investor.

Site	Category	Address	Cost	Ease of Use	Content	Quality	Uniqueness	Look	Overall
Wit Capital	IPO	www.witcapital.com	free	C	B	A	A	B	B

What sets this site apart from other IPO sites is the ability to get in on some quality IPOs. Luck has to be on your side, though, because with popular IPOs, a random number generator picks who's in and who's watching.

Site	Category	Address	Cost	Ease of Use	Content	Quality	Uniqueness	Look	Overall
Wright's Investor Services	Research	www.wisi.com	free	C	B	C	B	B	C

As a free site, it's not bad. It gives good info on US companies. Best yet, it gives info dating back all the way to 1988 (if applicable). If you need old data for free, this is your place.

Site	Category	Address	Cost	Ease of Use	Content	Quality	Uniqueness	Look	Overall
Yahoo! Finance	Mega Site	http://ca.quote.yahoo.com	free	A	A	A	A	A	A

Probably the best free site around — it really has everything you need. This site is so good that a lot of other investing sites on the net will use Yahoo! Finance as their souce. The US version is even better — www/quote.yahoo.com.

Site	Category	Address	Cost	Ease of Use	Content	Quality	Uniqueness	Look	Overall
Zacks Investment Research	Research	www.zacks.com	free to US$600	B	A	A	A	A	A

Great stock info on things like profiles, earnings estimates, analysts ratings and more. For free, you can get a company report, which is a scaled down version of their "Whole Enchilada" report. Try the free stuff — otherwise it gets costly.

Glossary

AMR (Average Monthly Rankings) A rating system based on a fund's monthly performance relative to other funds just like it. Monthly performance scores are averaged to provide a fund's ranking within its group.

Asset allocation The relative weights of equities, bonds, cash, real estate, and other asset types held in a portfolio at a given time. In a tactical asset allocation mutual fund, the portfolio manager weights each type to maximize total return when economic conditions change.

Automatic Reinvestment An option available to investors in a mutual fund or other investment whereby income (dividends, interest, or capital gains) distributions are used to purchase additional units of the fund.

Balanced portfolio The distribution of investments into several asset categories to help increase returns and reduce risk. The basic components of a balanced portfolio are cash, bonds, and equities. The weighting of the different components varies depending on the age and risk tolerance of the investor.

Bear market A stock market which is declining in value over an extended period (this is measured by an index of representative stocks, like the TSE300). A "bearish" investor believes share prices will fall.

Blue-chip stocks Stocks with good investment qualities. They are usually common shares of well-established companies with good earning records and regular dividend payments that are known nationally for the quality and wide acceptance of their products and services. (Think "IBM.")

Bond A debt instrument issued by governments and corporations. A bond is a promise by the issuer to pay the full amount of the debt on maturity, plus interest payments at regular intervals.

Bottom-up A style of investing that places a priority on examining companies that may be appropriate for investment. Less emphasis is placed on macroeconomic considerations. A "bottom-up" investor makes buy and sell decisions based on close scrutiny of the financials of a company. See also Top-down.

Bull market A stock market whose index has been rising in value. A "bullish" investor believes share prices will rise.

Canada Deposit Insurance Corporation (CDIC) An agency of the Government of Canada that insures the deposits of Canadians in banks and trust companies up to $60,000.

Capital Cost Allowance (CCA) A tax deduction available to reflect the depreciation of various types of assets. Applied to buildings (either commercial or residential), CCA can be used to shelter rental income from real estate investment trusts (REITs).

Capital gain/loss A profit (or loss) made on the sale of an asset when the market price rises (or falls) above the purchase price — usually in real estate, stocks, bonds, or other capital assets.

Closed-end fund A mutual fund in which the total number of units is limited. If units are not purchased when the fund is initially offered, they can only be purchased from another owner. They often trade on stock exchanges.

Common share A class of stock that represents ownership, or equity, in a company. Common shares entitle the holder to a share in the company's profits, usually as a dividend. They may also carry a voting privilege.

Consumer Price Index (CPI) A statistical measure of the increase in the cost of living for consumers. Often used to demonstrate general increases in the level of inflation over a period of time.

Current yield A term applied to money market funds, which refers to the actual rate of return over the past seven days, annualized.

Cyclical stock A stock within a specific industry sector that is particularly sensitive to changes in economic conditions. The natural resources sector tends to be cyclical, as do particular stocks in the sector.

Deferred Sales Charge (DSC) An increasingly popular alternative for mutual funds that charge front-end acquisition fees. Here, a fee is paid when the investor sells units in the fund. This usually begins at 4.5 percent of the unit's value in the first year and declines by 0.5 to one percent per year, eventually reaching zero percent several years into the future. Sometimes called an "exit fee."

Distribution fees Fees levied by some mutual fund companies on the value of units purchased with a back-end load or deferred sales charge. While most funds have stopped charging these fees, a few hold-outs remain.

Distributions The payments made by a mutual fund to its unitholders of the interest, dividends, and/or capital gains earned during the year. Shareholders may either take distributions in cash or reinvest them in additional shares of the fund.

Diversification Spreading investment risk by investing in a variety of asset categories (stocks, bonds, gold) in different industries and/or countries.

Dividend tax credit A special tax credit applied to reduce the effective rate of tax paid on Canadian dividend income.

Dividend A portion of a company's profit paid out to common and preferred shareholders, the amount having been decided on by the company's board of directors. A dividend may be in the form of cash or additional stock. A preferred dividend is usually a fixed amount, while a common dividend may fluctuate with the earnings of the company.

Dollar-cost averaging An investment program in which contributions are made at regular intervals with specific and equal dollar amounts. This often results in a lower average cost per unit because more units are purchased when the prices are depressed than when they are high.

Equity funds Mutual funds that invest in common and preferred shares.

Ex-dividend The date on which distributions that have been declared by a mutual fund are deducted from total net assets. The price of the fund's shares or units will be reduced by the amount of the distribution.

Fixed asset mix For balanced funds, an approach that fixes the asset mix to be maintained in the fund: often 50 to 60 percent equity and 40 to 50 percent fixed income. Compare to an asset allocation fund, where there is no pre-set fixed asset mix.

Fixed-income funds Mutual funds that invest in mortgages, bonds, or a combination of both. Mortgages and bonds are issued at a fixed rate of interest and are known as fixed-income securities.

Front-end commission charge An acquisition fee based on the total value of mutual fund units purchased. The fees can range from two to nine percent, but average four to five percent on most purchases.

GIC (Guaranteed Investment Certificate) A deposit certificate usually issued by a bank or trust company. An interest-bearing investment that matures after a specified term, usually anywhere from 30 days to five years. The interest remains fixed during this period.

Growth investing An approach to investing that places greater emphasis on a stock's future growth potential than on its current price. A growth manager may therefore be prepared to pay a higher price for a stock than a value manager would if he or she believes it has attractive future growth potential. It is viewed as a more aggressive style of management than value investing.

Growth stock Shares of a company whose earnings are expected to grow faster than average.

Hedging The strategy of taking positions in more than one commodity, security, or asset category in an attempt to reduce investment risk. An investment in gold or oil/natural gas, for example, is often seen as a hedge or protection against inflation.

Income splitting The process of diverting taxable income from an individual in a high tax bracket to one in a lower tax bracket.

Index fund A mutual fund designed to match the performance of a recognized group of publicly traded stocks, such as those represented by the TSE 300 Index or the Standard & Poor's 500 Index in the United States.

Index For stocks, an indicator of broad market performance. The Dow Jones Industrial Average includes the shares of 30 large companies; the Toronto Stock Exchange's Composite Index includes 300 companies; the Standard & Poor's index contains 500 companies. These indices are developed from statistics that measure the state of the economy, based on the performance of stocks or other key indicators such as the Consumer Price Index.

Investment fund See Mutual fund.

Leverage Using borrowed funds to maximize the rate of return on investment. A potentially dangerous strategy if the investment declines in value.

Limited partnership See Tax shelter.

Liquidity The ease with which an asset can be sold and converted into cash at its full value.

Management Expense Ratio (MER) The total of all management and other fees charged to the fund, shown as a percentage of the fund's total assets.

Management fee The amount paid annually by a mutual fund to its managers. The average annual fee in Canada is between one and two percent of the value of the fund's assets.

Marginal tax rate The rate at which tax is calculated on the next dollar of income earned. This rate steps up progressively as your income rises.

Market timing The process of shifting from one type of investment to another with the intention of maximizing the return as market conditions change.

Money market fund Fixed-income mutual funds that invest in short-term securities (maturing within one year).

Mortgage A legal instrument given by a borrower to the lender entitling the lender to take over pledged property if conditions of the loan are not met.

Mortgage-Backed Securities (MBS) These invest in first mortgages on residential properties, and provide higher yields than many other savings options.

Mutual fund A professionally managed pool of assets, representing the contributions of many investors, which is used to purchase a portfolio of securities that meets specific investment objectives. See also Open-end fund and Closed-end fund.

Net Asset Value (NAV) The value of a fund's assets, less its liabilities. The NAV is used to calculate the buying or selling price of shares or units in a fund, usually expressed as the Net Asset Value Per Share (NAVPS).

Net Asset Value Per Share (NAVPS) The total market value of all securities owned by a mutual fund, less its liabilities, divided by the number of units outstanding.

No-load fund A mutual fund that does not charge a fee for buying or selling its units.

Open-end fund A mutual fund whose units are offered for sale on a continuous basis; the fund will also buy back units at their current price (net asset value per share). Sometimes called an investment fund. The most common type of mutual fund.

Portfolio A group of securities held or owned for investment purposes by an individual or institution. An investor's portfolio may contain common and preferred shares, bonds, options, and other types of securities.

Prospectus A thorough description of an investment vehicle offered to the public. A prospectus will describe the investment objective and style, and must also identify any investment restrictions, as well as the officers of the company.

Real Estate Investment Trust (REIT) A form of real estate mutual fund with the difference that the REIT trades on a stock exchange. As a result, it provides greater liquidity than is usually available through a traditional real estate mutual fund. The units generally trade at a discount from Net Asset Value.

Real rate of return The stated rate of return, less inflation and taxes.

Registered investment A security held in a tax-sheltered plan — most often an RRSP or RRIF — that has been approved by Revenue Canada.

Risk tolerance The ability of an individual investor to tolerate risk. Risk tolerance is a function of the individual's personality and other factors, and is an important element in determining investment strategy.

Risk-free return The return available from securities that have no risk of loss. Short-term securities issued by the government (such as treasury bills) normally provide a risk-free return.

Risk The possibility that some or all of the money put into an investment will be lost.

RRIF (Registered Retirement Income Fund) A non-annuity investment vehicle for maturing RRSPs. One of the options available to RRSP holders upon cashing in their retirement funds at age 69 or sooner. RRIFs generally provide for a series of payments that increase each year.

RRSP (Registered Retirement Savings Plan) A savings program approved by Revenue Canada that permits tax-deferred saving for retirement purposes. Contributions to an RRSP are tax-deductible. Earnings on contributions are sheltered from tax while they remain in the plan.

Sector rotation A style of investing that identifies prospective investments (or the weighting of an investment portfolio) according to which sectors of the economy are poised to do well. Often associated with the "top-down" approach to investing.

Segregated funds Funds sold and administered by life insurance companies.

Self-directed RRSP RRSP whose investments are controlled by the plan holder. A self-directed RRSP may include stocks, bonds, residential mortgages, or other types of investments approved by Revenue Canada.

Systematic Withdrawal Plan (SWP) A plan for withdrawing money from a mutual fund on a regular basis — monthly, quarterly, semi-annually, or annually. Used mostly by investors who require a steady stream of income from their investments.

Tax shelter An investment that, by government regulation, can be made with untaxed or partly taxed dollars. The creation of tax losses in order to offset an individual's taxable income from other sources thereby reduces tax liability.

Taxable income The amount of annual income that is used to calculate how much income tax must be paid: total earnings for the year, minus deductions.

Term deposit Similar to a guaranteed investment certificate. An interest-bearing investment to which an investor commits funds for a specified term and rate of interest.

Top-down A style of investing that considers the economic "big picture" to identify sectors of the economy that are expected to outperform. Less importance is attached to identifying individual companies that may do well. See also Bottom-up.

Total return The amount of income earned from an investment, together with its capital appreciation, expressed as a percentage of the original amount invested. It indicates an investment's performance over a stated period.

Treasury bills Short-term debt securities sold by governments, usually with maturities of three months to one year. They carry no stated interest rate, but trade at a discount to their face value. The discount represents the market's valuation of the future return at maturity.

Unit In mutual funds, a unit represents a portion, or share, of the total value of the fund. Units are purchased by investors, and rise or fall proportionately with the net asset value of the fund.

Value investing An approach to investing that attempts, through the use of various analytical models, to identify companies that are fundamentally strong but that may be out of favour in the marketplace and trading at prices that represent a good buy. This conservative approach is often associated with Sir John Templeton and is one that many investment managers claim to use.

Volatility A measure of a mutual fund's tendency to fluctuate in value. More volatile funds are traditionally considered to have a greater degree of risk, although the fluctuation in value may, in fact, be either up or down.

Index

Z